BEWARE THE BRITISH SERPENT

Beware the British Serpent

The Role of Writers in British Propaganda in the United States, 1939–1945

Robert Calder

McGill-Queen's University Press
Montreal & Kingston · London · Ithaca

© McGill-Queen's University Press 2004
ISBN 0-7735-2688-9

Legal deposit second quarter 2004
Bibliothèque nationale du Québec

Printed in Canada on acid-free paper that is 100%
ancient forest free (100% post-consumer recycled),
processed chlorine free.

This book has been published with the help of a grant
from the Canadian Federation for the Humanities and
Social Sciences, through the Aid to Scholarly
Publications Programme, using funds provided by
the Social Sciences and Humanities Research Council
of Canada. Funding has also been received from the
University of Saskatchewan Publications Fund and the
College of Arts and Science, University of Saskatchewan.

McGill-Queen's University Press acknowledges the
support of the Canada Council for the Arts for our
publishing program. We also acknowledge the financial
support of the Government of Canada through the Book
Publishing Industry Development Program (BPIDP) for
our publishing activities

**National Library of Canada Cataloguing
in Publication**

Calder, Robert Lorin, 1941–
    Beware the British serpent: the role of writers in British
    propaganda in the United States, 1939–1945 /
    Robert Calder.
    Includes bibliographical references and index.
    ISBN 0-7735-2688-9
    1. World War, 1939–1945 – Propaganda. 2. Propaganda,
    British – United States – History – 20th century. I. Title.
    D810.P7G7234 2004   940.54′88641′0973   C2003-905555-8

Typeset in Palatino 10.5/13
by Caractéra inc., Quebec City

For Holly

Contents

Contents

Preface

In 1963 H.G. Nicholas, Fellow of New College, Oxford, who had been an official in the American Division of the British Ministry of Information during the Second World War, wrote: "The awareness, after the fall of France, that victory depended on the U.S.A., sank deep into the consciousness of every Briton and lay behind every major decision that the Government took from that time onwards. To secure the closest possible cooperation of the U.S.A. in our war effort became, next to the defeat of Hitler himself, the main objective of British policy."[1]

The shock of facing Nazi Germany alone in the summer of 1940 may have intensified British efforts to solicit the aid and perhaps the intervention of the United States, but the truth is that even before the outbreak of war the British government knew that some sort of American participation was essential to victory. On its own, Britain might have been able to defend the island, but it would have taken the military and industry strength of the United States to wrest control of the European continent from Hitler. In order to bring America into the conflict, the British government conducted a secret intelligence and propaganda campaign so extensive that the American writer Gore Vidal has called it "the largest, most intricate and finally most successful" conspiracy directed at the United States in the twentieth century.[2]

The part played by British intelligence in this campaign – which included the use of agents, front groups, and collaborators, the manipulation of polling data, and the covert influencing of American election campaigns – has been described by historian Thomas E. Mahl in his *Desperate Deception: British Covert Operations in the United States, 1939–44*. The work of the propagandists in the early years of the war has been admirably documented in historian Nicholas John Cull's

1995 monograph, *Selling War: The British Propaganda Campaign against American "Neutrality" in World War II*. Cull traces the policies and practices of the British propaganda effort from the end of the First World War to Pearl Harbor, from the formation of the Ministry of Information's American Division to the development of an aggressive and effective publicity machine in the United States. Among the many propaganda instruments he identifies – including radio, press, and film – he briefly mentions the work of British authors, particularly novelists, essayists, journalists, and correspondents.

In the First World War, as Peter Buitenhuis demonstrated in *The Great War of Words*, British authors had played an extensive and significant role in the propaganda campaign aimed at the United States. In the competition with Germany for American support, Britain had the enormous advantage of a common language, and it employed a number of writers to remind Americans of the culture and tradition they shared with Britons. "Language conditions response," argued Buitenhuis, "and ... culture controls perceptions."[3]

The novelist John Buchan served as director of intelligence at the Ministry of Information, and other prominent writers who participated in propaganda included H.G. Wells, Ford Madox Ford, Hugh Walpole, Rudyard Kipling, Arnold Bennett, James M. Barrie, John Galsworthy, and John Masefield. When Buchan finished his work at the ministry in December 1918, he wrote: "It would have been almost impossible to essay the great task of enlightening foreign countries as to the justice of the Allied cause and the magnitude of the British effort without the co-operation of our leading writers."[4]

When Buitenhuis turned his attention to the Second World War, he determined that British authors were not nearly so involved in propaganda work. Examining the Ministry of Information's failure to create an authors' advisory committee or to appoint well-known writers to important positions, he concluded: "It was the end of an era of influential participation by British writers in official propaganda. Thereafter, with a few notable exceptions, writers took a back seat and found their way only into minor roles in various departments."[5]

It seems to me to be a mistake, however, to assume that because only a small number of authors were employed doing "official" propaganda, writers in general were not contributing significantly to the British propaganda campaign. In the United States, where much of the population was isolationist, anglophobic, and deeply suspicious of anything that looked like foreign propaganda, official propaganda was unworkable. Writers, because they could operate seemingly independent of the government – living on royalties in the United States and writing for the American market as many had always done – could generally escape the accusation of being foreign agents. Moreover, since their "propaganda" usually involved reminding Americans of their shared heritage of British traditions, culture, and values, authors avoided the censure directed at those visitors who lectured Americans on their failure to accept their international responsibilities.

Throughout the war British writers – notably W. Somerset Maugham, Noel Coward, Sir Norman Angell, Charles Morgan, Phyllis Bentley, Eric Ambler, Cecil Roberts, Sir Philip Gibbs, Harley Granville-Barker, and C.S. Forester – made lecture tours of the United States at the urging of the Ministry of Information. The American visits of others such as H.G. Wells and Vera Brittain, though not initiated by the ministry, were supported because of their potential propaganda value.

A great many British authors – among whom were Maugham, Rebecca West, Graham Greene, J.B. Priestley, Helen MacInnes, Storm Jameson, Arthur Koestler, Margaret Kennedy, F. Tennyson Jesse, Mollie Panter-Downes, John Strachey, Margery Allingham, and Phyllis Bottome – contributed essays, articles, short stories, poems, novels, and non-fiction books. In the case of some writers, such as Maugham, Priestley, Jameson, and Bottome, their pens were clearly commissioned by the Ministry of Information. Many others were encouraged to write by the ministry, some felt it was their duty to help, and others undoubtedly simply saw a professional opportunity.

From 1940 to 1945 the words of many British writers reached Americans over the British Broadcasting Corporation's North American Service. Priestley, whose Home Service broadcasts were immensely popular in Britain, became a familiar and trusted voice in the United States, and Walpole, Louis MacNeice, John Brophy, Clemence Dane, S.P.B. Mais, and J.L. Hodson spoke regularly to America about Britain under the Blitz, the survival of its traditions, culture, and institutions, and its increasing egalitarianism.

Life in wartime Britain and the nature of the struggle against Nazism was brought dramatically to many more Americans by feature films such as *Mrs Miniver*, *Random Harvest*, *The Mortal Storm*, *Foreign Correspondent*, *Eagle Squadron*, and *This Above All*. Many of these films were adaptations of works by authors such as Maugham, Greene, MacInnes, Jan Struther, James Hilton, Eric Knight, Geoffrey Household, and Phyllis Bottome. Many were also the products of scripts by British screenwriters: Hilton, Forester, R.C. Sherriff, Keith Winter, Arthur Wimperis, Christopher Isherwood, Frederick Lonsdale, and Claudine West.

Despite the presence of Maugham, Masefield, Priestley, MacNeice, and Walpole, few of the British authors who did propaganda work in the Second World War were of the stature of the writers Buitenhuis identified as significant participants in First World War publicity: Bennett, Kipling, Wells, Galsworthy, and Ford. For the most part, they were middle-brow writers of popular literature, and generally politically moderate or right of centre, and little of what they produced as part of the propaganda campaign has literary merit today. This should surprise no one since, as Graham Greene observed in 1941, the conditions of a nation at war elevates the popular author to an importance beyond aesthetics: "The popular writer in war-time – or any period of social convulsion – comes into his own. He knows how to speak to people who are not interested in aesthetic problems; nobody will waste his time analysing the literary qualities of *Uncle Tom's Cabin* – the book belongs to history and not to literature."[6]

The following is a study of the history of the literature that was produced in all its forms by British authors as part of the campaign to influence American attitudes toward Britain throughout the Second World War. It goes beyond Cull and Buitenhuis to show that writers played a significant role, not just in Vidal's "vast conspiracy to manœuvre an essentially isolationist country into war,"[7] but also in the continuing struggle to keep it focused on Europe rather than the Pacific, to break down the enduring anglophobia, and to situate Britain favourably in a postwar world inevitably dominated by the United States.

Acknowledgments

~

I am grateful to the following people who kindly responded to my inquiries and gave me their perspectives on the work of British authors during the Second World War: Alistair Cooke, the late Sir Isaiah Berlin, Sir Michael Levey, the late Sir James Joll, David Daiches, Lady Lancaster, Paul Berry, the late Herb Caen, the late Ralph Gustafson, Alan Bishop, and the late Jerome Weidman. Michael Coren generously offered his encouragement and support at a particularly critical time; and throughout the writing my colleague Len Findlay provided many challenging and useful responses to my ideas. In the early stages, Warren Cariou cast his shrewd critical eye over the manuscript, and at the end Carlotta Lemieux edited it meticulously. The book is so much the better for their careful readings.

The research for this book could not have been done without the assistance of the staff of the following institutions: the Public Record Office, Kew; the British Broadcasting Corporation Written Archives Centre, Reading; the House of Lords Record Office; the Churchill Archives Centre, Churchill College, Cambridge; the British Library; the Newspaper Library, Colindale; the National Archives of Canada; the William Ready Division of Archives and Research Collections, McMaster University; the Society of Authors; the Department of Special Collections, Stanford University; the Harry Ransom Humanities Research Center, University of Texas at Austin; the Berg Collection of English and American Literature, New York Public Library; the National Register of Archives; and the Murray Library, University of Saskatchewan.

I wish to thank the Controller of H.M. Stationery Office for permission to quote from Crown copyright records. "Let Us Be Friends" and

"Don't Let's Be Beastly to the Germans" are Copyright © The Estate of Noel Coward, and Cecil Roberts's "A Man Arose" is reprinted with the permission of the Society of Authors.

Much of the research and writing of this book was done during two sabbatical leaves granted me by the University of Saskatchewan, during which I was generously funded by a Social Sciences and Humanities Council of Canada research grant. I am grateful also for the support of the University of Saskatchewan Publications Fund.

Finally, I am indebted to my wife Holly for her unwavering support and encouragement for a project that so often took me abroad or to my study.

Margaret Storm Jameson, president of PEN, worked for the British cause as both a writer and editor (Hulton/Archive by Getty Images [HAGI])

Creator of Mr Chips and Shangri-la, James Hilton worked tirelessly for Britain in Hollywood (HAGI)

Author of the Horatio Hornblower novels,
C.S. Forester wrote articles and screenplays
to support Britain (HAGI)

The BBC's most effective broadcaster, J.B. Priestley rehearses a talk (HAGI)

Discreet and effective, W. Somerset Maugham spent most of the war working for Britain in the United States (HAGI)

H.G. Wells, a political gadfly who did more harm than good for the British cause in the United States (HAGI)

The always debonair Noel Coward returns to London from one of his American tours (HAGI)

A popular speaker in the United States, Vera Brittain found that her pacifism prevented her from leaving Britain for most of the war (William Ready Division of Archives and Research Collections, McMaster University Library, Hamilton, Ontario)

BEWARE THE BRITISH SERPENT

The Yanks Aren't Coming
American Isolationism

The sources of the powerful non-interventionist belief that gripped the United States in the 1930s were varied but, in at least one respect, fundamental. The country had, after all, been founded so that a democratic, free, and liberal society could flourish independent of the political convolutions, class restrictions, and economic hardships of Europe. America went to war with a European power to win its independence, a fact thereafter taught to every schoolchild and celebrated every Fourth of July. The millions of immigrants over the next two centuries crossed the Atlantic either because of disenchantment with their lives in Europe or in response to the American dream of freedom, material well-being, and the worth of the individual. Though they might retain a sentimental attachment to their home country, few were prepared to jeopardize the dream by becoming embroiled in the seemingly endless European conflicts. As novelist John Dos Passos observed, "Repudiation of Europe is, after all, America's main reason for being."[1]

American isolationism was given clear political expression as early as 1775, when John Adams, political theorist of the American independence movement, wrote: "We ought to lay it down, as a first principle and maxim never to be forgotten, to maintain an entire neutrality in all future European wars."[2] In 1793, when Britain went to war against France, with whom the United States had a treaty, the American president, George Washington, adopted a policy of strict neutrality. Convinced of the need to establish a strong national identity independent of Europe, he wrote that the country should be "free from political connections with *every* other country, independent of *all*, and under the influence of *none*. In a word, I want an *American* character that the powers of Europe may be convinced that we act for *ourselves* and not for *others*."[3] "'Tis our true policy," he stated three years later in his Farewell Address – a document published in the newspapers and destined to take its place beside the Declaration of Independence and the Constitution in the national psyche – "to steer clear of permanent Alliances with any portion of the foreign world."[4]

Neutrality, however, did not guarantee that the United States would be free from European entanglements. As the war between Britain and France continued, the British interfered with American shipping, seizing American sailors on the high seas and impressing them into service in the Royal Navy; and they supplied American native people with arms so that they might impede the settlement of the American West. The end of the War of 1812, fought between Britain and the United States along the Canadian border, resolved these issues, and the peace accord between Britain and France in 1815 removed one major foreign impediment to American freedom to develop as it wished.

Within a decade, however, the threat of Russian expansion southward from Alaska and fear of the restoration of Spanish control of Central and South America led to the Monroe Doctrine, whose principles became a fundamental part of American foreign policy for more than a century. In a message to Congress on 2 December 1823, President James Monroe re-emphasized American isolationism in three dicta: no more European colonization of the New World; no more European intervention in the governments of the western hemisphere; and no involvement of the United States in European affairs. At the heart of this cornerstone of American foreign policy was a belief that a beneficent geography separated the Old and New Worlds, and that the Atlantic could insulate the United States from European aggression and European contamination.

The isolationist position was reiterated in President Grover Cleveland's 1885 inaugural address when he announced his foreign policy of "neutrality, rejecting any share in foreign broils and ambitions upon other continents ... the policy of Monroe and of Washington and Jefferson."[5] Cleveland's statement came in that remarkable century of relative peace and equilibrium in Europe from 1815 to 1914, when the United States was able to expand and develop in freedom from foreign entanglements. By the end of the nineteenth century, Americans had come to believe that this was the normal and permanent state of international relations.

When the First World War broke out in August 1914 there had not been a war in Western Europe since 1871 – that is, in the memory of most people – and Americans were both surprised by its happening and bewildered about its causes. Though the majority wanted an Allied victory, there was no general call for American intervention into what President Woodrow Wilson as late as 1916 called "a drunken brawl in a public house."[6] Wilson made a formal proclamation of neutrality and urged his compatriots to remain neutral in thought as well as deed, but ironically it was to defend its rights as a neutral nation that the United States eventually declared war on Germany in April 1917. When the American demand that its citizens and ships have the right to travel freely on the high seas was met by the sinking of three American ships by German submarines on 18 March, Wilson led the United States into its first European war, though it is doubtful that many Americans then understood the extent to which their country would become involved.

Behind this immediate cause of American intervention lay the intellectual Wilson's idealistic belief that the United States could lead the European powers to a just and lasting peace, a "peace without victory." His Fourteen Points, which in January 1918 outlined the basis of his program for peace and called for a league of nations to guarantee political independence and territorial integrity, were enthusiastically received by many Americans. He took a leading role in the peace conference in Paris, and although the Treaty of Versailles, signed on 28 June 1919, failed to reflect Wilson's principles in several essential ways, it did provide for the League of Nations.

Wilson was awarded the 1919 Nobel Peace Prize for his efforts, but when conservative politicians in the United States proposed to blunt the article providing for collective security, the vote to ratify the Treaty of Versailles failed in the Senate. Ironically, at a time when the American public was prepared to adopt a more interventionist role in European affairs, its politicians ensured that it would have no place in the League of Nations, an absence which arguably contributed to the failure to create equilibrium in Europe over the next twenty years.

When Winston Churchill began his six-volume history of the Second World War, he wrote that he regarded it as a continuation of his account of the First World War and that together his books would describe another Thirty Years' War. More recently, novelist Mordecai Richler reiterated a common view when he called the Second World

War "no more than a second act. Some second act."[7] If the wars were indeed a tragedy in two acts, Americans used the intermission – called by some "the Long Armistice" – to conduct a number of critical examinations of their part in the drama and their willingness to play any continuing role. Few things came to fuel Americans' reluctance to intervene in the Second World War more than their perception of their involvement in the First World War. As playwright Robert Sherwood, an adviser to Franklin Roosevelt, observed: "Americans in 1939 were fortified with the experience that the previous generation had conspicuously lacked, the experience of involvement in European war, and they wanted no more of it."[8]

The first of many historical interpretations of American intervention in the First World War came as early as July 1920, when Sidney B. Fay published a series of articles in the *American Historical Review* disputing the commonly held view that Germany had been the prime belligerent. Arguing against the popular view that the United States had fought for good and against evil, he suggested that the country had in fact been duped into joining the conflict. In 1928 Fay followed this with *The Origins of the World War*, which used archival material to show that the causes and purposes of the war were not what Americans had been led to believe.

The argument that the United States had been the victim of Allied deception was repeated in Frederick Bausman's *Let France Explain* (1922), which traced the cause of the war to France. In the same year, John Kenneth Turner attacked Woodrow Wilson and Wall Street financiers in his *Shall It Be Again?* And in a series of articles in the *Freeman*, reprinted in pamphlet form as *The Myth of a Guilty Nation*, Albert Jay Nock found Germany blameless and American intervention ill considered. According to historian Manfred Jonas, these articles "were widely distributed and enormously effective in shaping public opinion."[9]

In two book reviews in the *New Republic*, as well as in articles in *Current History* and *Christian Century*, and ultimately in his book *The Genesis of the World War*, published in 1926, Harry Elmer Barnes expanded the argument that rather than going to war to fight German militarism, the United States had been deluded by Allied propaganda and ensnared by ill-advised economic dealings. At the same time, Bausman's second book, *Facing Europe* (1926), used the First World War to prove that all European nations were unscrupulous and were driven only by their own selfish interests: "The Allies beguiled us into this war by false propaganda, concealing both the origins of their war and their secret profits, while we did everything we could to aid them and got nothing by way of compensation."[10] In *Why We Fought* (1929), C. Hartley Grattan found three sources of blame: American ignorance of the real Allied goals; pro-British Wall Street bankers; and the manipulation of American public opinion by clever propagandists.

As late as 1934, Walter Millis, an editorial writer for the *New York Herald Tribune*, repeated the argument that the United States had been tricked into war, in his book *Road to War: America, 1914–1917*. The tone of his study was reflected in the dust jacket reference to "the Frenzied Years of 1914–1917 when … a peace-loving democracy, muddled but excited, misinformed and whipped to a frenzy, embarked on its greatest foreign war." "Read it and blush!" urged the jacket copy. "Read it and beware!"[11] Read it Americans did, in such numbers that it became a Book-of-the-Month Club selection and a considerable influence on public opinion. A year later, the journalist and pacifist Oswald Garrison Villard attacked the idea that the First World War had been a moral struggle. "The excuse made by many pro-Ally Americans," he wrote in his weekly column in the *Nation*, "was that there was a higher law; that conscience and moral indignation overruled patriotism and loyalty to the policy of their government. The world was on fire; they must take sides. It was Evil against Good; who could hesitate?"[12] In reality, said Villard, the Allies and the Central Powers were morally indistinguishable.

By the 1930s many Americans had come to believe that the argument of moral cause as the reason for their country's participation in the First World War had simply disguised the real motive: the protection of American financial investments. The failure of the peace talks, moreover, were seen to be the result of the undermining influence of the arms industry, called "the Merchants of Death" by liberal journalist Helmuth C. Engelbrecht in his 1934 book of the same name. With George Seldes's *Iron, Blood and Profits* (1934) and especially the publication of an article called "Arms and the Men" in the March 1934 issue of *Fortune* magazine, the cumulative pressure of opinion impelled the United States Senate to establish a committee under the chairmanship of Gerald P. Nye to investigate the manufacture and sale of armaments and munitions. Even before the committee's 1400-word report was made public in 1935, its findings (as reported outside the hearing room by Senator Nye, an ardent isolationist from North Dakota) were widely publicized in bold headlines. They corroborated the

accusations of Seldes, Engelbrecht, and others that munitions manufacturers had profited very much from the war, that they had strong
links with the War and Navy Departments, and that they had helped
rearm Germany in violation of the Treaty of Versailles. The arms deal-
ers, concluded the committee, should not be free to incite the country
to enter future wars.

Responding to the concern about the arms trade, and in an attempt
to remove the economic and political elements that seemed to have
taken the United States into the First World War, Congress passed a
series of acts in the 1930s. The first Neutrality Act, signed by President
Franklin Roosevelt on 3 August 1935, required the president to
impose a partial arms embargo on the outbreak or during the progress
of war between two or more foreign countries. As well, he could at
his discretion proclaim that Americans travelling on ships of belligerent countries did so at their own risk, and there would be created
a National Munitions Control Board to license and supervise the
American export of arms.

The Neutrality Act of 1936 extended these provisions to 1 May 1937
and added a mandatory ban on loans by American citizens to belligerent governments. The Neutrality Act of 1937 retained these articles
while cleverly ensuring that the American export trade would continue during a European war. Based on a "cash-and-carry" scheme
devised by financier Bernard Baruch, the provision permitted the sale
of any goods except armaments to belligerents, who would then
assume immediate title and be required to have them transported on
non-American ships. In this way, it was hoped, American trade could
be conducted without the participation on the high seas of American
citizens, goods, or ships, thus dissociating Americans from any future
European conflict.

By the late 1930s the belief in non-interventionism was as strong in
the United States as it had ever been, and it attracted adherents from
an extraordinarily wide and diverse cross-section of American life.
According to Manfred Jonas, "isolationism owed whatever unity it
had during the thirties not to geography, nor politics, nor class structure, but to faith in unilateralism and fear of war."[13] Some members
of the movement were pure isolationists who believed in an inward-
looking, self-sustaining society; others were internationalists who
were nevertheless opposed to joining a foreign war. Some were capitalists who feared the destruction of the American free enterprise
system; others were socialists who foresaw the loss of New Deal social

gains in another major war. Some were motivated by narrow, partisan interests, while others were moved by a deeply felt pacifism. Although non-interventionism was the dominant credo of the time, it was far from a homogeneous movement.

The purely isolationist faction – that which believed that the United States should make no attempt to influence events anywhere else in the world in order to concentrate on an independent course – was led by Senators Hiram W. Johnson of California and William E. Borah of Idaho. Other prominent Progressive senators, who were opposed to the use of force and who saw the Great Depression of the 1930s as a result of the First World War, were Robert La Follette Jr of Wisconsin, George Norris of Nebraska, and Gerald P. Nye. All three came from the American Midwest, which was the most intensely isolationist region of the country and remained so throughout the Second World War. In part this resulted from the fact that many of the region's people had ethnic ties to Germany and Scandinavia, though the latter group's faith in neutrality diminished with Hitler's invasion of Denmark and Norway in 1940. As well, the largely agrarian base of the middle western states meant that rather than profiting from any industrial trade, its economy would suffer in wartime. Finally, and perhaps most fundamental to the average person's outlook, was the insulation that came from being located in the centre of a large continent. As the English author Cecil Roberts noted on a visit to Illinois early in the war, "A thousand miles from the Atlantic, two from the Pacific, what should Chicago fear from any god-damn foreign nation?"[14] Several years later, when John Wheeler-Bennett asked the executive committee of the America First organization at what point it would consider it necessary to resist the Germans with force, he was told: "When they cross the Rio Grande."[15] Similarly, the English writer and journalist Sir Philip Gibbs concluded that for, say, a Texan on a 300-acre ranch, "it needed an intellectual struggle not to be an isolationist."[16]

The impregnability to attack of the United States as a whole became an argument increasingly repeated by isolationists as another war approached in Europe. Major General Hagood's *We Can Defend America* (1937) stated that the country would be impervious to attack provided appropriate defensive measures were adopted. In *The Ramparts We Watch* (1938), Major George Fielding Eliot concluded: "We have been given a geographical position far removed from dangerous neighbors. The genius of man has not yet created instruments of aggressive warfare which can span the oceans which protect us on either hand."[17] This impregnability argument was given wide circulation in three books published in 1939: Boake Carter's *Why Meddle in Europe?*, Stuart Chase's *The New Western Front*, and Oswald Garrison Villard's *Our Military Chaos*. Villard stated the thesis succinctly: "It is not humanly possible for Germany with a navy one-fourth the size of ours to conquer our fleet, or produce transports enough to bring a sizable force to the United States."[18]

People in the American Midwest felt distanced from Europe in ways that went much deeper than mere military security. As the English writer and pacifist Vera Brittain learned from a Wisconsin friend in 1940, Europe was intellectually and politically remote from the middle of the United States:

The lessons of the last war – the futility of it, have sunk deep out here. And there is no sense of European history; all our history here really dates from 1917. And what people remember are the secret treaties, the vindictiveness of Versailles, the defaulted war debts and the post-war blindness of France and England. There is also a deep-seated suspicion of British and French motives, based partly on these recent memories, and partly due to the suspiciousness which people feel when they are up against something they don't understand – the European system. In the East people feel more at home in discussing Europe – not so here.[19]

This suspicion of European political intrigue led people in the American Midwest to view intervention in a European war as much more perilous than one in the Pacific. Fighting a single enemy, Japan, the United States could operate relatively independently of others, whereas a European conflict would mean becoming enmeshed in complex political alignments and yielding some control of events to a variety of allies. Even after Hitler declared war on the United States on 11 December 1941, the war against Japan remained the primary focus of many midwesterners, just as, for security reasons, it was for those in the Far West. In Marcia Davenport's words, "The European was the East Coast's war, and the Pacific was that of the West Coast and the middle west."[20]

Across the United States as a whole, non-interventionists came from a wide spectrum of political and social faiths. Liberals such as Robert Maynard Hutchins, president of the University of Chicago, cynically viewed the reactionary leadership of Britain and France as having capitulated at Munich, and feared that participation in war would necessarily lead to a rescinding of civil liberties. This argument had its strongest impact on the young and led to many "Keep us out of the war" demonstrations on university campuses. Attractive, too, was the purely pacifist stance, vigorously enunciated from the 1930s on by a number of organizations: the American Peace Society, the World Peace Foundation, the Carnegie Endowment for International Peace, the National Society for the Prevention of War, the Women's International League for Peace and Freedom, and the Keep America Out of the War Congress. So strong was the movement that in 1932 a peace petition was taken by a mile-long procession of automobiles to President Herbert Hoover in Washington.

Socialists such as Norman Thomas were convinced that intervention in a war would interrupt and might even reverse the social and economic gains made under the New Deal. "It is preposterous to think," Thomas wrote in the *Nation* in 1937, "that the workers in the United States, in the supreme emergency of war, can maneuver the capitalist state and its military organization to gain their own ends."[21] The distinguished historian Charles A. Beard argued for neutrality on the grounds that the United States could perfect an economic system only so long as it avoided becoming inextricably caught in international economic and political structures. In 1939 C. Hartley Grattan's *The Deadly Parallel* warned that participation in another war would mean the end of American social control of economics.

On the far left, the American communists went through a number of chameleon changes worthy of the controlling oligarchy in George Orwell's *1984*. In the 1920s they had opposed the League of Nations as an impediment to the future economic unity of all people, but a decade later they were repeatedly calling for American participation in stopping Hitler. Barely three weeks after the signing of the German-Russian non-aggression pact in August 1939, however, they became vociferous supporters of strict American neutrality. This was their unequivocal position until Hitler invaded Russia on 22 June 1941, when they were forced to make yet another about-face, adapting their slogan from "The Yanks Are Not Coming" to "The Yanks Are Not Coming – Too Late."[22]

Ironically, while the German invasion of Russia brought American communists back into the interventionist camp, it provided considerable ammunition for the isolationists. Hitler, they claimed, was turning his attention away from Britain and the Atlantic to the east and Russia, thus eliminating America's need to support the Allies. Furthermore, since such a repressive, totalitarian regime as Stalinist Russia was now an ally of Britain, how could the war be seen as a fight for democracy and freedom? As former president Herbert Hoover said in a radio broadcast on 29 June, Russian participation "makes the whole argument of our joining the war to bring the four freedoms to mankind a gargantuan jest." Senator Bennett Champ Clark asked more colourfully if anyone could "conceive of American boys being sent to their deaths singing 'Onward Christian Soldiers' under the bloody emblem of the Hammer and Sickle."[23] For many, the slogan became "Let the dictators fight it out among themselves."

On the right wing, conservative Americans feared that another war might destroy the country's free enterprise system and open the door to fascism, socialism, or communism. Some businessmen – notably, Robert E. Wood, chairman of the board of Sears Roebuck, Jay C. Hormel, and James D. Mooney – were convinced that Hitler would win and that the country should be ready to do business with him. German technology, they believed, was not only invincible but was the foundation for future economic success.

There were, of course, segments of the American public whose ties to Europe, ethnic or political, dictated that they be non-interventionist. Irish Americans had always been anti-British; but when war broke out, organizations such as the Irish Foundation and the Ancient Order of Hibernians frequently pointed to Eire, which since 1921 had been an independent state within the British Commonwealth yet had refused to take up arms. If a small country in the British Isles and within range of German bombers could remain neutral, why could not a powerful country an ocean away also do so? The large Italian American community admired Mussolini's achievements and his restoration of Italy to a respectable European power, and though not on the whole wishing to offer material support, was not prepared to help bring him to heel.

German American organizations, with much closer ties to the government of the home country, were far more active. No one in the German Foreign Office believed that the majority of Americans would ever support the enemies of France and England, but a neutral United States would do much to ensure a freer hand for Germany. Therefore it gave financial support to several groups: the German-American Bund, the American Fellowship Forum, and the American Nationalist Confederation. Established in 1939, the American Fellowship Forum called itself a cultural organization, but its purpose was to propagate

Nazi theories of racism and to slow down American military prepa-
rations. More visible was the Bund, led by a German immigrant, Fritz
Kuhn, until his conviction for embezzlement in 1939. Created to
"awaken the slumbering racial consciousness of German-Americans,"[24]
its propaganda and other activities were so heavy handed that it was
shunned by many German Americans and was kept at arm's length
even by other isolationist organizations.

If the Bund failed publicly, it achieved a measure of success behind
the scenes. Having links to some members of Congress who were
staunch isolationists, it was able to use the offices of at least twenty
politicians to send propaganda written by Nazi agents through the
mail on congressional franking privileges. In one case, material orig-
inating from the offices of a German "cultural" organization called
the Steuben Society was posted in a senator's envelopes; and in
another, pro-German isolationist literature was disseminated from the
office of Representative Hamilton Fish.[25] Behind much of this activity
was George Sylvester Viereck, a poet and novelist who had written
pro-German propaganda in the United States in the First World War.
Registered officially as a German agent with the German Library of
Information in the 1930s, Viereck was a skilful propagandist who
argued in a variety of publications that "the complete abstention from
the quarrels of Europe and Asia is the only policy that can prevent a
world conflagration."[26]

According to one estimate, there were between 400 and 700 isolationist groups operating in the United States in the early years of the
Second World War, and though most had no official connection with
any Axis power, they were frequently anti-Semitic and usually fascist
in nature. Among them were William Dudley Pelly's Silver Shirt
Legion, the Knights of the White Camellia, the No Foreign Wars Committee, the Christian Mobilizers, the Crusaders for Americanism, the
Paul Reveres, the American Patriots, and the Ku Klux Klan.

The most influential of these extreme groups was that led by Father
Charles E. Coughlin, a Michigan Catholic priest, whose radio programs
reached nearly 4 million listeners and to whose weekly magazine,
Social Justice, Viereck was a frequent contributor. Especially popular
among Irish Americans, he preached fervent non-intervention, rabid
anglophobia, and an anti-Semitism not much less blatant than that
coming out of Nazi Germany. Coughlin may have appealed only to a
narrow-minded and bigoted section of the public, but he wielded considerable power, as when, for example, in 1935 he elicited thousands

of letters and telegrams which helped defeat the passage of the World
Court protocol in the United States Senate. Only when Attorney
General Francis Biddle persuaded Coughlin's archbishop during the
war to order the priest to cease political and propaganda activities was
he silenced.

While each of these diverse groups, holding disparate political
views, had its adherents and its impact on American public opinion,
it was not until a year into the war that the most formidable and
influential non-interventionist organization emerged. As German
domination of all Europe came closer and the Roosevelt administration began to move to offer more assistance to the Allies, many of the
extreme elements joined with a much larger number of moderate,
reputable, middle-of-the-road Americans to form the America First
Committee.

In the first months of the war Americans were strongly sympathetic
to the Allies and wanted to see Hitler defeated, but they did not wish
to go to war. In an American Institute of Public opinion poll conducted on 24 October 1939, 96.5 per cent of respondents said that the
United States should not declare war and send an army abroad;[27]
82 per cent believed that the Allies would win,[28] and during the
phony war of the winter of 1939–40 most Americans hoped that some
measure of support could be given the Allies from a position of neutrality. President Roosevelt had always been more interventionist than
the country he led, but the crafty politician in him recognized the
danger in taking steps for which the public was unprepared.

Two days after Britain and France declared war on Germany,
Roosevelt invoked the provisions of the Neutrality Act of 1937, but
on 21 September he called on Congress to repeal the arms embargo.
By then a vigorous and vocal opposition had begun to form, led by
Senators Nye, La Follette, and Borah. They were soon joined by
Charles A. Lindbergh, the famous aviator, and by Norman Thomas
and Herbert Hoover, all of whom spoke to large radio audiences. The
response was the arrival in Washington of a million pieces of mail in
a three-day period, nearly all of them supporting the retention of the
arms embargo. Through some skilful management, however,
Roosevelt won the vote in Congress, and on 4 November he signed
a new Neutrality Act which permitted Americans to sell arms and
munitions to European belligerents on a cash-and-carry basis. On the
surface, this appeared to treat all combatants equally; in reality, since

the Atlantic was largely controlled by the British navy, the greatest benefit was to Britain and France.

With the end of the phony war, and the German invasion of Denmark, Norway, Holland, and Belgium, followed by the fall of France in June 1940, the majority of Americans came to believe that Hitler would win. According to polls taken in June, 80 per cent of people in the United States favoured increasing aid to the Allies, but only 14 per cent were yet prepared to enter the war.[29] As the Battle of Britain raged in the summer and autumn and the German invasion of the British Isles appeared imminent, Roosevelt responded to Churchill's plea for help by agreeing on 2 September to provide fifty aged destroyers in exchange for bases in Bermuda, the West Indies, and other British colonies in the American hemisphere, and a guarantee that the Royal Navy would never be surrendered to Germany.

On the day after Roosevelt informed Congress of the destroyers-for-bases deal, the America First Committee was formed under the leadership of R. Douglas Stuart, a Yale law student and son of the first vice-president of the Quaker Oats Company, and Robert E. Wood of Sears Roebuck and Company. Members of its national committee included Alice Roosevelt Longworth, the daughter of Teddy Roosevelt; Edward Rickenbacker, the most celebrated American air ace of the First World War; the actress Lillian Gish; and Charles Lindbergh. Among its supporters were Oswald Garrison Villard, Robert Maynard Hutchins, Henry Ford, General Hugh S. Johnson, writers Kathleen Norris and Irvin S. Cobb, and Laura Ingalls, who was later convicted of being a paid German agent. In the Senate, the America First Committee was most prominently endorsed by Burton Wheeler, Gerald Nye, and Rush Holt.

From its headquarters in Chicago, the America First Committee hired one of the leading New York advertising agencies, Batton, Barton, Durstin, and Osborn, to design its campaign against intervention. Its position was based on three principles: that the United States should build an impregnable defence; that democracy at home could be preserved only by staying out of the European war; and that Roosevelt's "aid short of war" stance was certain to enmesh the United States in the war. At the core of the campaign was the old argument that the European war was just another in a series of battles between Britain and Germany – what Villard had called "this ungodly, revolting mess in Europe, in which one can have respect for neither side in the power politics struggle for the control of Europe."[30]

From September 1940 until the Japanese attack on Pearl Harbor, the America First Committee was a powerful voice for non-intervention. It did not prevent Roosevelt from signing the Lend-Lease Act in March 1941, nor did it stop the repeal of the article of the Neutrality Act which forbade the arming of merchant ships. Moreover, in retrospect it seems unlikely that it could have prevented the entry of the United States into the war. There can be no doubt, though, that the America First campaign significantly slowed American aid to the Allies, and arguably it delayed American military involvement. Had the Japanese not forced the issue so dramatically, Roosevelt might well have been unable to take the country into war for some time, or, if he had done so, it would have been without a strong mandate from the country.

Historian Thomas A. Bailey has written that "the torpedoes that sank the American battleships in Pearl Harbor also sank 'American Firstism.'"[31] It would be more accurate to say that it was the America First organization, not its beliefs, that was blown out of the water on that December morning. The committee immediately ceased holding rallies and distributing literature, and within a week the national executive committee had voted to disband. By April 1942 it was legally dissolved, and over the next three years a number of its most prominent members vigorously joined the American war effort.

It was the Japanese who had made America First untenable, however, and although Hitler declared war on the United States on 11 December, it did not necessarily follow that opposition to intervention in Europe was dead. The initial statement from the headquarters of the America First Committee on the evening of 7 December had clearly signalled its orientation toward the Pacific: "The America First Committee urges all those who have subscribed to its principles to give their support to the war effort of this country until the conflict with Japan is brought to a successful conclusion."[32] That the statement was intentionally worded to allow for the possible continued opposition to American involvement in the European war was revealed in a teletype from Douglas Stuart to John T. Flynn dated 8 December.[33]

The America First Committee was nonetheless dismantled, largely because it had so strongly opposed participation in the war that it would have been unable to function in the angry wartime atmosphere following Pearl Harbor. But many of its leading figures – for example, Nye, Wheeler, and Fish – and non-interventionist newspapers such as Robert McCormick's *Chicago Tribune*, Joseph Patterson's *New York*

Daily News, and Eleanor Patterson's *Washington Times-Herald* continued to oppose any efforts to aid the European Allies. As indicated by Isaiah Berlin's wartime political report, sent weekly from Washington to the Foreign Office in London,[34] the continued influence of the isolationists was the cause of considerable concern. Historian Selig Adler has stated that "in the flames that covered Pearl Harbor on that Sunday in December, the old isolationism was consumed and a new variety was fashioned."[35]

With the United States now irreversibly involved in a war that had been thrust upon it by the Japanese attack, much of the old isolationist energy was devoted to a policy of "Pacific First." That this orientation was to some extent shared by the American government is indicated by the War Office order, made within days of the United States' entry into the war, to stop all lend-lease shipments then loaded in American ports. This resulted in shipments of vital matériel destined for the Middle East being halted, probably for use in the Pacific. "The British," commented Robert Sherwood, "were afraid that there might now be a drastic reorientation of American strategic thinking – that the formerly accepted strategy of 'Germany first' might be abandoned and the whole weight of American power concentrated on Japan."[36]

The impulse behind this position was explained in a memorandum from Harold Butler, head of the British Information Service in Washington, to Brendan Bracken, the British minister of information, on 10 August 1943:

The Japanese war has always been felt to be America's war more keenly than the war against Germany. The Japanese threat to the U.S. is still regarded as more real and imminent than the German threat. The Japanese are genuinely hated, whereas there are still latent sympathies for Germany due to the success of German propaganda in attributing the present war to the Treaty of Versailles and to the existence of millions of Americans of German blood … The *Chicago Tribune* and its allies never cease to complain of the lack of support given to General MacArthur, whom, incidentally, they are trying to groom as a Presidential candidate … There is then a real danger that American enthusiasm for the European war may wane and a certainty that the Germans will make every possible effort to encourage that tendency.[37]

In the face of this Pacific pull, said Butler, there was a need for the British government to stress such things as the impossibility of defeating Japan until Germany had been beaten, the potential threat of

Germany to the United States, the danger of an inconclusive peace in the European war, and the British determination to fight Japan as soon as Germany was defeated.

In addition to the deep and widespread anger over Pearl Harbor, the apparently greater Japanese military threat to the American mainland, and the inevitable antipathy born of racial difference, the Pacific First movement had its political basis and its political supporters. The Chinese had a strong lobby in the United States among sinophiles and, according to Isaiah Berlin, among "isolationists who see in it a useful foil to preoccupation with European issues, Anglophobes and other anti-imperialists, a combination opposed both to involvement in Europe, and to the foreign and to some extent domestic policies of the Administration."[38] When the Chinese recalled their military mission in January 1943 to protest inadequate American aid, Pacific Firsters accused the Roosevelt administration of favouring Britain over China, which was seemingly in danger of collapsing. On 18 February, Madame Chiang Kai-shek addressed both houses of Congress, and her argument that Japan was a more formidable opponent than Germany and should therefore be given priority by the United States "was greeted with loudest applause of any passage in her speech, the whole House standing."[39] A month later, Berlin reported that the Pacific First movement was gaining support as a result of Madame Chiang's activities, particularly a tumultuous reception at a mass meeting in New York.[40] When in April Americans were given gruesome reports of Japanese executions of several of James Doolittle's pilots, the national anger, observed Berlin, made the "Pacific front permanently a more burning issue than [the] European front is ever likely to be."[41]

The Pacific First arguments were most vigorously made in May 1943 when Senator Albert Benjamin ("Happy") Chandler, who had assumed the leadership of the movement, delivered an impassioned speech warning that Russia might well remain out of the Pacific war, preferring to control much of Europe. Britain would have to watch Russia, and the United States would be left to fight a strengthened Japan alone. Other senators charged that Britain had failed to use the large number of Indian troops against the Japanese in Burma. Outside the Senate, sympathetic members of the press argued that if Britain would use the two million soldiers stationed on its soil to open a second front, the United States would be free to take care of the

Japanese. Yet other Pacific Firsters believed that Germany should be left relatively intact in order to deter Russia from becoming interested in the Pacific and even in Alaska.

The comments of Chandler and other Pacific Firsters caused real concern to the British mission in the United States. Robert Bruce Lockhart's diary records a visit in June 1943 from John Wheeler-Bennett, who was on leave in Britain from his position in the British Embassy in Washington:

Jack is not happy about feeling in the U.S. The country is united against Japan, and there is real determination to defeat Japan. There is not the same determination about defeating Germany. The war in Europe is remote; even the soldier has little idea what he is fighting for in North Africa. There is always the danger that the American armed services will rebel against the policy of "Germany first, then Japan." The Navy is Pacific-minded, ... and Jack says "watch Somerville." Latter is the Supply Chief. He does not like us. Altogether China [under Chiang Kai-shek] is the most popular of the Allies; Britain and Russia dispute the bottom place.[42]

From Pearl Harbor to Hiroshima, the British government was aware of the need to combat Pacific Firstism, and as early as 1942 it recognized that the stability of the postwar world would depend upon an American focus on European affairs. Shortly after the entry of the United States into the war, Frank Darvall, deputy director of the American Division of the Ministry of Information, reminded Ronald Tree, the parliamentary private secretary to the minister, that American isolationism would always remain a threat:

It should ... be remembered that to secure American collaboration in the defeat of the Axis was only one of our objects. Unless we can also secure maximum American collaboration in the conclusion of a satisfactory peace and in the establishment and maintenance of an international political and social order which will prevent a recurrence of aggression, and secure a satisfactory system of international relationships and standard of living throughout the world, our victory will be largely worthless. There is no guarantee as things are that the United States will not revert at the end of this war, as it did at the end of the last one, to an attitude of annoyance with its former Allies and desire to limit its overseas commitments. Unless we can during the war period, when our opportunity for doing so is greatest, produce

a real rapprochement between the British and American peoples and a genuine appreciation in both countries that they must pull together through the
next decades, we shall have fought the war in vain.[43]

A year later, David Bowes-Lyon, in charge of Political Warfare Executive activities in Washington, stated the problem more succinctly.
"He feels," Bruce Lockhart noted in his diary, "that we can do more
in Washington. If ever the Americans got an efficient political warfare
team, they would run away with the war and with the peace."[44]

The Strangling Old School Tie
Anglophobia in the United States

In its campaign to secure American aid during the Second World War, Britain was doubly damned. As a European power, it was a target for American isolationists and non-interventionists of all stripes who sought to keep the United States out of what they saw as yet another in an endless line of Old World power struggles. As the country that had originally colonized most of the United States and against which the emerging nation had fought for its independence, it was the object of both respect and distrust. Britain had given birth to the United States, albeit unwillingly, and for more than a century the strains in their relationship had been not unlike those in a family when a maturing adolescent asserts its rights as an independent adult. By 1939, other forces – political, historical, economic, cultural, and ethnic – had combined to create a strong anglophobia against which the British government and its advocates had to fight vigorously throughout the war.

In his book *Less than Kin: A Study of Anglo-American Relations*, William Clark, a British press attaché in Washington during the war, wrote: "The American nation came into being as a result of the war with Britain. Anglo-American relations began in conflict and that conflict has never been far beneath the surface in the past 175 years."[1] Clark's observation was corroborated by a poll taken in June 1942, six months after the United States had entered the war, which revealed that 11 per cent of Americans believed that their compatriots still harboured a bitterness against Britain because of the Revolutionary War.[2]

The American Revolutionary War left Britain and the United States in a relationship which by the twentieth century was unique in the world: two major powers sharing a common language, common origin, common culture, and similar judicial systems but fundamentally different political and social structures. The American democratic, republican experiment was a challenge to British institutions, and throughout the nineteenth century many Britons had not only derided American society but had publicly voiced the hope that the experiment would fail. For their part, says H.C. Allen, "Americans reacted even more strongly. All their hatred of arbitrary government, all their dislike of aristocratic inequalities, all their animosity towards the ways of the Old World, became centred in their reaction to everything British. Anti-British sentiments became almost a *sine qua non* of American political success."[3] Great Britain, in the view of many Americans, was dominated by a rigid class system and was dedicated to seeing its empire on every part of the earth. In the words of Ronald Tree, parliamentary private secretary with special responsibility for American affairs in the Ministry of Information during the war, Americans thought that Britain was "a country of picturesque and servile peasantry ruled over by a land-owning class with affected and effeminate voices."[4]

Convinced of the integrity of their own democracy and the egalitarianism of their society, Americans continued in the twentieth century to see Britain as a country divided between two classes: what the American journalist Samuel Grafton called "cap-in-hand England" and "old-school-tie England."[5] Because the working class and the lower-middle class were rarely able to travel to the United States, Americans were little exposed to Britons other than the affluent and privileged, and many did not like what they perceived to be their snobbery and superciliousness. In 1931, for example, G.H. Payne's *England: Her Treatment of America* identified six things which made the British offensive to Americans: an apparently instinctive and unconscious assumption of superiority, an inability to cooperate on an equal basis, an assumption of propriety of British interests, an obviously highly organized and widespread propaganda, a refusal to permit trade rivalry, and an unethical and at times immoral diplomacy.[6] Payne's conclusion, though meant to be conciliatory, clearly traced the source of this antagonism to the English class system: "America and Britain ... must dominate the world for the benefit of the world and not for the benefit of the English ruling class ... The peace of the world may be insured by England and America, but only if England is rid of the carbuncles of two hundred and fifty years of selfishness ... Give the British people the opportunity to govern their own country and the prospect of war between America and England will forever vanish."[7]

The likelihood that the United States would have gone to war with Britain at any time in the twentieth century was virtually nonexistent; at the same time, few Americans were ready to go to war *for* Britain if it meant safeguarding the interests of the upper classes.

In September 1940 the British writer J.B. Priestley argued that Britain needed to demonstrate that this perception of its social structure was outdated: "The Americans, though very much on our side as anti-Nazis, still need convincing that all our talk is not so much 'hokum.' Now can we honestly say that when we choose our persons to represent us in America we are doing so on a fine new democratic basis? The answer is that we cannot. We have done little to remove their deep-rooted suspicions of our 'old school tie' methods."[8] Few such suspicions were removed when a few months later Lord Halifax was appointed British ambassador to the United States. A titled and hereditary landowner, as well as a reserved and haughty introvert, he seemed to epitomize the British ruling class, a view soon confirmed when he rode to hounds on a fox hunt in Virginia at a time when many of his countrymen were dying in battle.

Of course, not all Americans were opposed to the idea of a ruling elite; some looked apprehensively at the influence of the British left in general and the Labour Party in particular. Britain was thus simultaneously seen as a feudal society and a breeding ground for socialism, a paradox summarized sarcastically by David Cohen in the *Atlantic Monthly* in 1942:

When Britain is defeated ... it is because of her stupidity, smugness, and the strangling Old School tie. So much for the fighting. What of the aftermath? If we struggle through to victory with the inert British strangling our whipcord Yankee necks, we shall have struggled merely to save England's repulsive, undemocratic caste system, while at the same time there is no doubt that the ingrates will abandon the caste system for socialism and so imperil our political and economic system here in America. They're clever, those British; They'll fool you every time.[9]

In 1943 Samuel Grafton wrote of American anxiety about growing socialism in Britain: "A ripple of fear runs through a segment of American life: 'Is England going socialist?' It is like a horrible parody of 1938. The original Clivedeners used to tell each other through long ... weekends that Herr Hitler must be allowed to have his own way, else Europe would 'go Communist.' Now it is no longer Communism in Czechoslovakia, it is socialism in England. The same old damaged goods still stand on the same old bargain counter, and are still finding buyers."[10]

As disturbing as the British class system might be, William Clark claimed that "imperialism remains for Americans the greatest blot on the British copy-book,"[11] the very label "British Empire" igniting anger and distrust in widely diverse segments of the American populace. When British author Louis MacNeice taught poetry at Cornell University for a spring semester in 1940, his students were "nearly all of them isolationist or indeed anti-British, thought of the British as crooks and of the war as an imperialist war." He explained: "When Harriet Cohen, who was giving a piano recital, stayed in the house and, having told all the boys to call her Harriet, went on to talk British propaganda, the boys were wonderfully polite but I could see them writing her off as a phoney; they remarked afterwards that she could not play the piano."[12]

In the early years of the war, Colonel McCormick's isolationist *Chicago Tribune* played on this antagonism by referring to England and France as the "empires" in any headline or news story. In 1944 Sir Norman Angell was told by an American liberal: "You must expect criticism, even bitter and unjust criticism, so long as the Empire exists at all. Until you dissolve it and give those parts of it that want it complete freedom and independence, we shall regard you as something in the nature of, if not Public Enemy No. 1, then at least as a great public criminal."[13]

Because the United States had once been part of it, the British Empire was resented far more intensely than the colonial holdings of France, Portugal, or Holland. It was easy for Americans to see their own war of independence reflected in the struggles for autonomy of various British possessions, so that, for example, when the question of Indian self-government became critical in 1943, some placards in the United States read: "It is 1776 for India."[14]

The British Empire provided strong ammunition for American noninterventionists. In 1939 Benjamin C. Marsh, executive secretary of the People's Lobby, called Britain "the mother of aggression" whose imperial interests should not be protected by American money.[15] In October of that year Senator D. Worth Clark challenged interventionists: "Paint me a picture of the six years of persecution of the Jews, the Catholics, and the Protestants in Germany, paint it as gory and bloody as you please, and I will paint you one ten times as brutal, ten times as savage, ten times as bloody in the 500 years of British destruction, pillage, rape and bloodshed in Ireland."[16] Two years later, Senator Nye, in an attack on Britain which stretched over ten pages of the *Congressional Record*, argued that it was "the most aggressive aggressor the world has ever known ... the very acme of reaction, imperialism and exploitation."[17]

General Hugh S. Johnson claimed that Britain was fighting the war only "to maintain her dominant Empire position with her own kinsmen and also over black, brown and yellow peoples in three continents."[18] "The British Empire is not a democracy and never has been," wrote the American novelist Theodore Dreiser in *America Is Worth Saving*, and it "now holds 500,000,000 of its world-scattered colonials as well as 29,000,000 of its natives in educationless, moneyless and privilegeless bondage." The European war, therefore, had "no more to do with the problem of democracy or civilization in Europe or the world" than it had "to do with the state of the inhabitants of Mars, if any."[19]

According to historian Wayne Cole, the America First Committee drew much of its strength from the chronic dislike and suspicion of Britain in many Americans.[20] Nowhere was this more evident than in the words of its most distinguished and popular speaker, Charles Lindbergh, whose speech to 20,000 people in Chicago in the summer of 1940 drew boos at every mention of England. At a rally in Des Moines, Iowa, on 11 September 1941, he notoriously claimed: "The three most important groups which have been pressing this country toward war are the British, the Jewish and the Roosevelt Administration. Behind these groups, but of lesser importance, are a number of capitalists, Anglophiles, and intellectuals who believe that their future, and the future of mankind, depends upon the domination of the British Empire."[21] Lindbergh's speech ignited a firestorm of criticism, from the nearly unanimous censure of newspapers and magazines to the repudiations of Wendell Willkie and Thomas Dewey. But all the denunciations were of its anti-Semitism; its anti-British elements elicited no opposition.

The entry of the United States into the war did little to quiet American suspicions of British imperialism. Six weeks after Pearl Harbor, Harold Nicolson recorded in his diary that Sibyl Colefax had urged him to write a book about "How we got our Empire": "She has been got at by [U.S. Ambassador John G.] Winant, who foresees a strain

on Anglo-American relations and some difficulty owing to the fact
that America has no idea at all of our imperial mission. I do not think
that I have the necessary afflatus to write such a book. There is India,
for instance, about which I know nothing and regarding which I have
the feeling we are wrong."[22]

India, with its 400 million inhabitants and its continuing struggle
for independence, became a particularly sensitive issue with Americans in 1942. The failure in April of Sir Stafford Cripps's mission to
secure the agreement of the various Indian factions to a plan for the
eventual British withdrawal and Indian self-government was interpreted in the United States as another sign of Britain's unwillingness
to surrender any part of her empire. On 12 April, Roosevelt reported
to Churchill his grave concern about the adverse effect on American
public opinion:

The feeling is held almost universally that the deadlock has been due to the
British Government's unwillingness to concede the right of self-government
to the Indians notwithstanding the willingness of the Indians to entrust to the
competent British authorities technical military and naval defence control. It
is impossible for American public opinion to understand why if there is willingness on the part of the British Government to permit the component parts
of India to secede after the war from the British Empire it is unwilling to
permit them to enjoy during the war what is tantamount to self-government
... Should the current negotiations be allowed to collapse because of the issues
as presented to the people of America ... it would be hard to overestimate
the prejudicial reaction on American public opinion.[23]

Against Roosevelt's urging was Churchill's conviction that constitutional change in India in wartime would lead to anarchy and to
eventual subjugation by Japan. When in August 1942 the All-India
Congress Committee began a campaign of civil disobedience to force
the British to leave, its leaders, Mohandas Gandhi and Jawaharlal
Nehru, were jailed.

As Roosevelt had predicted, the American reaction was strongly
negative, and it became a very public issue in two of the country's
most influential publications. On 28 September the New York Times
ran a full-page advertisement entitled "INDIA: The Time for Media-
tion Is Now," which called for Roosevelt and Chiang Kai-shek to ask
the British to hold new conferences to develop a plan for Indian
independence. Among the endorsers were such prominent Americans

as Clare Booth, Pearl S. Buck, John Gunther, Lillian Hellman, William L. Shirer, Norman Thomas, and Upton Sinclair.[24]

Of much more concern to the British was an article entitled "An Open Letter from the Editors of *Life* to the People of England," published in *Life* magazine on 12 October. Written by Russell Davenport, who was chairman of the Board of Editors of *Fortune* magazine but was purporting to speak for the majority of Americans, it claimed that the United States was fighting the war for principles but could see no principles in the British policy in India:

How do you expect us to talk about "principles" and look our soldiers in the eye? We Americans may have some disagreement among ourselves as to what we are fighting for but one thing we sure are not fighting for is to hold the British Empire together ... If your strategists are planning the war to hold the British Empire together, they will sooner or later find themselves strategizing all alone ... Quit fighting a war to hold the Empire together ... After victory has been won, then the British people can decide what to do about the Empire ... But if you cling to the Empire at the expense of a United Nations victory, you will lose the war. Because you will lose us.[25]

Because of *Life*'s wide circulation, this attack on British imperialism caused considerable anxiety in London when cabled to the Ministry of Information by its New York office. The ministry immediately forwarded the article to the Foreign Office, where the head of the American Department, Neville Butler, thought it so "highly damaging" that it should be brought to the attention of the secretary of state for foreign affairs, Anthony Eden.[26]

After considering the advisability of an official government response, the Foreign Office proposed that Sir Norman Angell, who was in the United States, should reply, and then that the journalist and member of parliament Vernon Bartlett should draft a response, which would be signed by J.B. Priestley and other prominent Britons who were respected in the United States for their progressive views. In the end, Bartlett's article was published[27] under his name only, since it seemed unlikely that a group of signatories could agree on a suitable text. Although he had been commissioned by the American Division of the Ministry of Information, his cable was sent to *Life* from him personally, and the bill for its transmission was sent to him at the House of Commons to avoid any hint of official inspiration or participation.[28]

Although the Indian problem became less prominent in the American media as the political situation in the subcontinent reached a stalemate, neither India nor the British Empire in general ever stopped being a concern for many Americans. Churchill's famous comment, "I did not become the King's First Minister in order to preside over the liquidation of the British Empire,"[29] may have impressed British listeners at the lord mayor's luncheon in London in November 1942, but it exacerbated anti-imperial sentiments in the United States. Within a week Wendell Willkie had told a *New York Herald Tribune* forum on current affairs that Churchill had "in the last few days seemingly defended the old imperialistic order and declared to a shocked world 'We mean to keep our own.'"[30]

According to Clark, "without consciously realizing it, most Americans had presumed that the war would result in the dissolution of the British Empire, and they deeply resented [Churchill's] statement to the contrary."[31] In August 1943 Harold Nicolson noted in his diary that Angell, having returned from three years in the United States, found Americans "deeply Anglophobe" and quick to oversimplify moral issues: "'Imperialism' is evil; so they must condemn British imperialism as sin," never remembering their own imperialism or that they came into existence through British imperialism.[32] As late as September 1944, Isaiah Berlin's Washington dispatch referred to "the thought long embedded in the background of American consciousness that while our intention to fight in the Pacific may be genuine, the fruits of it will not be considerable and the primary purpose of it is reconquest of our Far Eastern Empire, to which our title is in any case dubious."[33] Even in March 1945, with peace in sight and the San Francisco Conference imminent, Berlin reported: "If there is one subject upon which the bulk of United States opinion is united, it is the undesirability of colonial possessions as such. When Americans think of colonies they think of British colonies first."[34]

Britain's class system and its empire did much to undermine its claim to Americans that it was fighting a moral war against Hitler. Added to this were deeply rooted suspicions of British diplomacy, arising from the First World War and its aftermath and fostered in part by the question of war debts. As the main agent of finance for the Allied war effort, Britain had borrowed approximately $4 billion from the United States, which it then lent to other countries, so that by the end of the First World War Britain was owed more than it owed the United States. In the postwar period, no debtor nation except

Finland made more than token repayments, and when the U.S. Congress passed the Johnson Act in 1934 prohibiting loans to any government in default of a debt to the United States, Britain ceased repayments completely.

The debt question was complicated by such matters as German reparation payments and the belief that wartime expenditures should be adjusted according to a country's ability to pay. For many Americans, however, the issue was simply a moral one: Britain was welshing on a debt. Resentment increased further when, in response to American calls for repayment, Britons began to mutter that Uncle Sam had become Uncle Shylock.

The British default of debt repayment remained a source of irritation in the United States throughout the 1930s and into the Second World War. William Empson reported in June 1940 that the old war debts were "much the most prominent feature of the war situation in the minds of nearly all Americans, including many intelligent and well-informed persons."[35] For more partisan non-interventionists, they offered strong ammunition. When lend-lease was enacted, an America First bulletin commented that the British theme song was "There'll always be a dollar,"[36] and a year later *Life*'s "Open Letter" to England was quick to remind the British that lend-lease was created despite the history of their unpaid debts.[37]

For many Americans, the Second World War was largely the result of crafty and cynical British diplomacy. Arriving in New York in October 1939, Alfred Duff Cooper found the common belief that the war had been caused by the harsh conditions imposed on Germany by Britain and France in the Treaty of Versailles.[38] Indeed, a poll in March of that year had revealed that 40 per cent of Americans believed that Germany had been treated unfairly.[39]

Even more widespread was the conviction that the British policy of appeasement had encouraged Hitler's territorial ambitions. The main target of this criticism was naturally the Chamberlain government, but many Americans blamed the upper-class pro-Hitler Tories behind it. As early as 1938, the group of staunch appeasement advocates who met at the country home of Lord Astor – among whom were Chamberlain, Sir John Simon, Sir Samuel Hoare, Geoffrey Dawson (editor of the *Times*), and Philip Kerr (later, as Lord Lothian, ambassador to the United States) – became known on both sides of the Atlantic as the "Cliveden set." The term took on a special notoriety in the United States, so much so that Lady Astor felt compelled to refute the allegations of pro-Hitlerism in the *Saturday Evening Post*. It remained nonetheless a strong symbol of the cynical self-interest of the British upper class until Chamberlain resigned as prime minister in May 1940.

The British and French abandonment of Czechoslovakia at Munich severely damaged Britain's standing in the eyes of many Americans. In the first winter of the war, Duff Cooper suggested to a prominent American journalist that he should give some publicity to Hitler's treatment of the Jews. "But we have known all that for a long time," the reporter replied. "We withdrew our ambassador from Berlin in protest. What did you do?" When Duff Cooper conceded that Britain had done nothing, he was told: "Yes you did; your Prime Minister signed an agreement with Hitler."[40]

The impact of Munich on American attitudes is evident in Elmer Davis's carefully argued article, "Is England Worth Fighting For?", which was published in the *New Republic* in February 1939. Chamberlain's call for "the democracies" to resist any attempt to dominate the world by force rang hollow, said Davis, considering that four months earlier Chamberlain had been unwilling to fight for Czechoslovakia. It was true that the United States shared with Britain "the much advertised community of ideals, democracy and civil liberties … a faith that many people feel is worth fighting for," but Czechoslovakia shared that faith and Britain had concluded that it was not worth fighting for. "In the next crisis," Davis noted pointedly, "Britain will stand in much the same relation to America as Czechoslovakia stood to England in the last crisis."[41]

Davis's analysis of Chamberlain's capitulation at Munich led him inevitably to conclude that Britain would fight only when there was a direct and immediate threat to its interests, and that the war would be fought in defence of those interests and not because of any common ideals. Moreover, no matter on what grounds the United States joined the struggle, the effect would be to preserve the Chamberlain government and the British Empire: "If we save the decent civilized England that many of us love … we save and strengthen the ruling oligarchy, which would sell us out at the next peace conference, if it saw any advantage in doing so, as readily as it sold out the Czechs at the Peace-till-February Conference at Munich."[42]

Similar to the charge against the appeasers was the belief in many parts of the United States that Hitler had been allowed to take Europe into war because of British complacency. When Sir Philip Gibbs toured the United States in the autumn of 1941, he was repeatedly asked, "Why was England so unprepared?"[43] This scepticism about Britain's conviction was encouraged by its long months of relative military inactivity in the winter of 1939–40. Americans had expected the most powerful belligerents to clash quickly and decisively, and as William Empson explained, they wanted some "tough" action to cheer forward.[44] When little seemed to be happening, American sympathy for Britain waned, and the phrase "phony war," a more pejorative phrase than the British "bore war," was coined in the United States.

Although the Battle of Britain persuaded many Americans that Britain could fight with courage and determination, it did not dispel all doubts. America First speakers were fond of saying that the British would fight to the last drop of American blood, a claim seemingly given credence by affluent Britons sitting out the war in the United States. In a memorandum to the Foreign Office in 1940, the British author Pamela Frankau reported hearing many references in New York to "the British who drown their sorrows at the Stork Club."[45] It did not help that the first three years of the war saw no significant British military successes, a record that suggested to some Americans that Britons could not, or would not, fight.

After Dunkirk, a joke went around the United States that the initials of the British Expeditionary Force stood for Back Every Fortnight. In April 1942 Harold Nicolson and other British politicians heard Roosevelt's personal adviser, Harry Hopkins, state: "There are many people in the U.S.A. who say that [the British] are yellow and can't fight." "It is true," admitted Nicolson, "that we have been beaten in everything we do."[46] In May the American journalist Edward R. Murrow returned from the United States to repeat the message. "The anti-British feeling is intense," he told Nicolson, partly because of the frustration inevitably felt by a lack of early victory and partly because of the British failure to hold Singapore.[47]

For some Americans, particularly Pacific Firsters, the surrender of the British at Hong Kong, Singapore, and elsewhere in the Far East proved that they were not committed to the defeat of Japan, that they had somehow encouraged Japanese aggression in order to manipulate the United States into a global war. On the afternoon of 7 December, Senator Nye had told an America First meeting in Pittsburgh that the Japanese assault on Pearl Harbor was "just what Britain had planned for us."[48] When Churchill, broadcasting on radio after the fall of

Singapore, referred to the United States' entry into the war as what he had "dreamed of, aimed at and worked for, and now it has come to pass,"[49] he seemed to confirm the anglophobes' darkest suspicions. In part, this explains the comment of Elmer Davis, made on CBS radio shortly after Pearl Harbor, that there were Americans who hoped that the United States would win the war but that Britain would lose it.[50]

Until the end of the war, Pacific Firsters continued to accuse Britain of lacking real commitment in the Pacific and the Far East. In June 1943 Isaiah Berlin reported: "Incorrigible 'Pacific Firsters' have taken refuge in the aside that irresistible Mr. Churchill and his adroit British advisers have as so often bamboozled innocent Americans into forgetting their true Pacific interests and continuing with American plans."[51] In August 1943 when, at the Quebec Conference, Lord Louis Mountbatten was appointed supreme Allied commander of the Southeast Asia Command, some American newspapers charged that his selection over Douglas MacArthur demonstrated that reactionary British interests were winning over American ones. This lobby was powerful enough that a month later Isaiah Berlin suggested that if the Roosevelt administration sent supplies to a European theatre, it would do so in apprehension of "resultant fire to which they would be exposed from powerful 'Pacific Firsters.'"[52]

One of the best analyses of American wartime attitudes to Britain can be found in Andre Visson's article "Suspicions Old and New," published in the *Atlantic Monthly* in June 1943. A European who was Washington correspondent for *Time* magazine, Visson wrote with greater objectivity than most journalists of the time, and his article is particularly interesting since it looks forward to postwar relations as well as back to traditional friction. About 25 per cent of Americans were anti-British, he said, for a number of reasons. Some were familiar: Britain's colonial empire, which it intended to preserve after the war; the domination of the British aristocracy, perceived as being superior, condescending, and Machiavellian; the $6 billion given Britain through lend-lease, in spite of its non-payment of earlier debts; and the failure of Britain to pull its own weight in the war.

According to Visson, none of these complaints about the past was as serious as the American apprehension about the future, especially about British sincerity in the postwar world. Britain could not be trusted to cooperate: "Its aims are said to be 'selfish and imperialistic.' Its bankers and industrialists are expected to resume their fight against their American competitors on the world markets. British diplomats are supposed to outsmart their American cousins."[53] He added that the American public would feel happier about the British if they would abandon their bases in the Far East, but they had been slow to make concessions in India and the Near East.

Visson's article neatly summarizes most of the political and economic grounds for anglophobia in the United States before and during the war. Some were complex arguments made by politicians and academics, and some were simpler – and in many cases uninformed – judgments made by ordinary people. Many of the criticisms of Britain had arisen years earlier and many were deeply felt; all presented problems for those arguing the case for Britain.

In addition, there were various less intellectual elements of anglophobia in the United States. In the melting pot of America was an array of national groups, each with its own reason to wish for Britain's defeat and all influential enough that in 1943 Sir Norman Angell told Harold Nicolson: "Already ... in left wing circles it is a disability to possess an Anglo-Saxon name."[54] In addition to the Germans and Indians, there were the Italians, who, even before the entry of Italy into the war, were angered by the League of Nations' economic sanctions against Italy over Abyssinia which had been put into effect at the urging of Britain. There were also the Czechs, for whom Munich remained a bitter betrayal, and the Poles, who also had felt ultimately abandoned.

The national groups in the United States were naturally fertile ground for anti-interventionists, especially extremists such as Father Coughlin. In February 1940 his *Social Justice* magazine published a manifesto entitled *Beware the British Serpent*, which was divided into sections for each of the groups supposedly maltreated by the British: the Italian Americans, Polish Americans, and Irish Americans.

Of all the groups, none was as large or influential as the Irish Americans, who had brought to the United States bitter memories of centuries of domination by England. To the argument that Britain was fighting for freedom and democracy, one official of the New York division of the Ancient Order of Hibernians retorted: "The Irish have always been credited with a keen sense of humour, and they fully realize the joke of referring to England as a democracy." Even if the Axis won, he continued, Ireland could not be worse off than it had been under centuries of British tyranny.[55]

At the outbreak of the Second World War, this historical animosity was intensified by a new campaign of violence against England by the Irish Republican Army, culminating in a bombing in Coventry on 25 August 1939, which killed five people and outraged the British public. When two IRA men were later executed for the crime, Irish Americans were incensed. English journalist S.K. Ratcliffe had the misfortune to lecture in Boston several days later and needed police protection from Irish American demonstrators. Similarly, Duff Cooper was picketed by Irish protesters in Boston and New York, and Cecil Roberts was harassed by them while speaking in Miami.

Irish hostility frequently manifested itself in less formal circumstances, as William Empson discovered in the winter of 1939–40: "The immense number of Irishmen, usually not very rich, prominent in bars, who hate the British very actively, ought also to be mentioned. What they seem to hate most is the British voice ... To them one of the most insanely and obviously repulsive forms of the British voice is the B.B.C. voice."[56]

As Empson's experience implies, a substantial amount of American anglophobia was more visceral than cerebral. Through books and magazines, radio, films (many of them products of Hollywood), and contact with the occasional visiting lecturer or dignitary, Americans developed a perception of the character and personality of the average Briton, and many did not like it. This view may have been based on a lack of understanding of British manners and customs and on popular stereotypes, but its currency among ordinary Americans, whose opinions ultimately influenced government policy, caused concern among those presenting the British case. As a result, more than one eminent Briton felt compelled to address the issue in the American popular press.

In April 1942 the author Somerset Maugham, who had been in the United States at the request of the Ministry of Information since October 1940, was asked by the ministry to write an article for the *Saturday Evening Post* entitled "Why D'You Dislike Us?" "I do not think I exaggerate," he began, "when I say that among the rich people who have apartments in Park Avenue and country houses on Long Island or in Connecticut, among the businessmen and manufacturers of the Middle West, among the politicians and civil servants in Washington, and even among the men of letters spread up and down the country, the general attitude toward the English is one of dislike."[57] The principal charges against the English, he said, were complacency, superciliousness, stinginess, bad manners, inhospitableness, snobbery, and lack of a sense of humour.

Maugham attempted to refute these accusations by pointing out that the British stinginess and inhospitableness resulted from the large difference in incomes between Britain and the United States; that class distinctions and snobbery were not exclusive to the British, Americans having their own class structures; and that the apparent bad manners of the British were only a manifestation of their innate shyness. The British seemed to Americans to have no sense of humour only because British humour depended upon irony whereas American humour was built on exaggeration.

Maugham identified superciliousness and complacency as the supposed British traits which most irritated Americans, and because they could be observed in the conduct of political business as well as individual behaviour, they were the most troublesome to the British cause. René MacColl, who ran the press office of the British Information Services in New York during the war, encountered a typical reaction while on a tour of the southwestern states in November 1943. He described Richard Lloyd Jones, the publisher of the Tulsa *Tribune*, "lashing himself into a swift tropical rage. He thundered on about British superiority and smartness. 'We want to be good friends with you, but you're too snooty and smart. From Charles Dickens, through to Rudyard Kipling, and on down to modern times, we have had your goddam lecturers making fun of us. Why the hell don't they stay away?'"[58]

Always a shrewd observer, Maugham was well aware of a number of his compatriots whose condescending attitude was damaging Britain in American eyes. In March 1942 he wrote to Lady Juliet Duff that the distinguished conductor Sir Thomas Beecham had "put up the back of everyone he has had to do with. We all shudder when he is going to make a speech," said Maugham. "It is really tragic how so many English people over here seem to go out of their way to make themselves offensive. I don't suppose any of you in England have a notion how much we are disliked over here."[59]

In Beecham's case, the British government was well aware of how much bad publicity he had created in the United States. One California woman had been so provoked by his behaviour that she wrote directly to Churchill to complain that he was insulting the American people and in doing so was like many Britons who were "biting the hand that feeds them."[60] Her complaint was repeated in a Foreign Office survey of opinion in the United States in April 1941, which concluded: "It is fortunate that the supercilious musings aloud of this pampered virtuoso have not attracted much notice."[61]

In his *Saturday Evening Post* article, Maugham suggested that such abrasive British visitors should be issued a document instructing them about what they should and should not do in the United States. Privately, he believed that the instructions should be more stringent, that they should "explain how he should behave and what he *should not say*" (emphasis mine).[62] Such instructions were routinely given to British airmen training in North America, but it would have been a brave official who offered them to independent and formidable people such as Beecham.

Maugham's response to the charge of complacency was to argue that the current changing political and economic power made the United States the most influential country in the world, a fact acknowledged even by Winston Churchill. Although the British certainly had acted in an insufferably superior manner for a century or more, he said, there was no longer any inclination to patronize the United States. The reality was that American culture, habits, and customs were now being copied across the Atlantic.

Like many such wartime writings, Maugham's article ended with the hope that Americans might regard British faults with more indulgence, that misunderstandings between the two countries could "be mitigated by good sense and good will."[63] In fact, in the succeeding weeks, the *Saturday Evening Post* was inundated with correspondence, and Maugham himself received more than three hundred letters corroborating his points and adding other grievances. Writing to the English novelist G.B. Stern, he summed up the response and added several more sources of anglophobia that he had not thought suitable for publication. He acknowledged that the Americans hated the British then more than ever. Oh yes, he said, they hate us all right and the worst of it was that about half of it was the fault of the British themselves, and that made him angry. As for the other half, Britons could do nothing about their nineteenth-century imperialism, nor could they do anything about the inferiority complex of the Americans.[64]

The question of American hostility to the British character was taken up again in June 1944 by the eminent philosopher Bertrand Russell in an article in the *Saturday Evening Post* entitled "Can Americans and Britons Be Friends?" The mere pretence of good relations between the two peoples, he said, was dangerous: "It would be better to drag the lingering dislike and suspicion out into the open, to analyse them, and to deal with their causes. This would be the subject for a book."[65] Although there was antipathy to the other country on each side of the Atlantic, there was a much stronger dislike of Britain in the United States than a dislike of the United States in Britain.

Like Maugham, Russell identified arrogance and conceit as the British traits that most alienated Americans, and he too argued that they were now much less evident than in years past. The contemporary Briton was suffering from an inherited resentment in the United States, which had been passed down from father to son, a legacy that was hard to eradicate. Russell echoed Maugham's argument that innate British shyness and reticence often created the false impression of coldness and rudeness. Even in love, the average Englishman was unlikely to open his heart, so it was hardly surprising that he would appear restrained and uninterested in more ordinary social interaction.

Much of Russell's article was a conventional defence of the British character, but he went further in offering the surprising argument that "it is a misfortune for Anglo-American friendship that the two countries are supposed to have a common language."[66] Because Britain and the United States shared English, there was a greater expectation of similarity of customs and manners than applied, for example, to Italians or Chinese. Trivial differences therefore became magnified, leading to misunderstanding and disproportionate irritation. The common language, combined with geographical separation, resulted in "a much larger fund of misrepresentation about each other than about any other nation."[67]

While Britons and Americans may have shared the same language, they spoke it differently, and here, said Russell, was another source of tension. Because the British tended to speak more precisely and of course without the many colloquialisms native to the United States, they appeared patronizing: "A Frenchman in America is not expected to talk like an American, but an Englishman speaking his mother tongue is thought to be affected and giving himself airs."[68]

Despite the efforts of Maugham, Russell, and many others to soften American attitudes to them, anglophobia remained a concern for the British until the end of the war. Indeed, as the tide began to turn against the Axis and Japan, and as the Allied victory became inevitable, the British became increasingly concerned with a postwar world that would be dominated by America, particularly an America that might be hostile to Britain. In a December 1943 paper entitled "Publicity and Policy in the United States," Robin Cruikshank, director of the American Division at the Ministry of Information, warned his colleagues that the approach of peace would make public relations with America more, not less, difficult. "As victory draws nearer," he wrote, "a good many U.S. inhibitions will disappear. Critics who were scared, or shamed, by adversity will consider success a license to become vocal." Up to a quarter of the American population, he estimated, were anti-British."[69] Cruikshank's assessment was corroborated a month later by Sir Gerald Campbell, director general of the British Information Services and at the time based in Washington, who cited author James Hilton's comment that the United States "is bored with us."[70]

In March 1944 David Bowes-Lyon reported to Robert Bruce Lockhart "a gloomy view of Anglo-American relations which he said had now reached their lowest level":

The reasons for this were not caused by election tactics. The reason was fundamental; the Americans now realised their immense power in production and on land, air and sea. They were becoming intensely national and were determined to use their power. The British had pushed the world around for the last hundred years and now the Americans were going to do it. Effects of this change of attitude were visible everywhere, particularly in India, where [General Joseph W.] Stilwell refused point-blank to co-operate with Mountbatten and took the line, popular in U.S., that Americans wanted to help China, were not interested in helping Britain reconquer jungle colonies like Burma or Malaya.[71]

As late as November 1944, J.L. Hodson was told by a fellow journalist just back from the United States that he had never felt so despondent over Anglo-American relations. "We have lost ground steadily for months," said Hodson. "The majority of Americans still don't feel this German war is their war, or that they've any business to be in it ... I think America will make it very difficult for us in the Pacific War – they'll either try to keep us out or deprive us of any credit for what we do when in it."[72]

3

The Magic of the Word
Mobilizing Authors for War

From the middle of the 1930s until the end of the Second World War, British attempts to combat anglophobia in the United States were confronted by an enormous problem: the Americans had seen it all before. If this war was indeed no more than the second act of a bloody modern tragedy, many Americans had learned from the first act. Writing in 1940, Harold Lavine and James Wechsler observed: "The greatest obstacle to Allied propagandists in World War II was the propaganda that preceded American entry into World War I."[1]

Although propaganda had been a relatively new technique of warfare in 1914, it had not taken the British long to use it effectively. A month after war broke out, C.F.G. Masterman, a member of the cabinet, was secretly appointed director of propaganda, and for three years he guided operations covertly from the offices of the Insurance Commission at Wellington House. Only in 1917, when Lloyd George's government created the Department of Information, was the public made aware of British propaganda activities; and a year later the department was elevated to the Ministry of Information under Lord Beaverbrook.

Much of the propaganda generated by Masterman's agency was directed toward neutral countries, the most important of which was the United States. In Peter Buitenhuis's words, "The most complex and important role of Wellington House was to persuade the people of the United States that the Allied cause was just and necessary, that they should support the Allied war effort and, ultimately, that they should join the war on the allied side."[2]

Wellington House influenced American public opinion in a number of ways. It encouraged the flow of favourable news and comments by providing American correspondents with interviews, tours, and visits to the front. It provided a newsletter to American papers, many of which were grateful for the free copy, and it sent out millions of pamphlets on various wartime subjects, some written by private people on their own initiative and many commissioned from well-known public figures.[3] Even American authors were encouraged to write for the Allied cause.

Until the United States entered the war in 1917, the American activities of Wellington House were disguised. These operations were controlled by Sir Gilbert Parker, an author well known on both sides of the Atlantic for his historical romance novels. Supposedly merely a concerned private citizen, he operated from his home in London, sending thousands of letters and pamphlets to influential Americans. When the entry of the United States into the war removed the need for secrecy, Parker retired, and the British Bureau of Information was set up in New York.

In the years following the First World War, the full propaganda activities of Wellington House were gradually revealed through memoirs and historical research, and many Americans became convinced that the primary cause of American intervention had been British propaganda. As early as 1920, H.L. Mencken wrote: "When he recalls the amazing feats of the British war propagandists between 1914 and 1917 – and then even more amazing confessions of method since – [the American] is apt to ask himself quite gravely if he belongs to a free nation or a crown colony."[4] When the 1930s became increasingly politically unstable, this anger over the past became mixed with apprehension for the future. In April 1936, Representative William T. Schulte warned against "the same propagandists that lit the torch that led the way for the god of war into America in 1917."[5] Similarly, in July 1937, M.J. Hillenbrand of Dayton University predicted that England would "again hamstring American public opinion with its propaganda machine."[6]

Such suspicions were given credence by a number of scholarly studies published in the 1930s, in particular two books written to warn Americans about the danger of being manipulated into another war. In 1935 James D. Squires, a professor at Colby College, published *British Propaganda at Home and in the United States from 1914 to 1917*, in which he argued that British propaganda had been instrumental in leading the United States into the conflict. Four years later, when a European war had become inevitable, this thesis was presented more directly and emphatically by H.C. Peterson in his *Propaganda for War: The Campaign against American Neutrality, 1914–17*. The United States, he said, had been forced to declare war on Germany in 1917 because, in response to British propaganda, it had already abandoned strict neutrality and given the Allies material and diplomatic and moral support. The lesson for Americans, he concluded, was that "it is impossible to be unneutral and keep out of war."[7]

If these revelations of the past alerted some Americans, one prediction of the future alarmed others. In 1938 British publicist Sidney Rogerson brought out a book entitled *Propaganda in the Next War* in Basil Liddell Hart's series "The Next War." In any future war, as in the last, he declared, the result would depend "upon the way in which the United States acts, and her attitude will reflect the reaction of her public to propaganda properly applied."[8] Britain would have to do "much propaganda" to keep the United States even benevolently neutral, he averred: "It will need a definite threat to America, a threat, moreover, which will have to be brought home by propaganda to every citizen, before the republic will again take arms in an external quarrel."[9]

Germany wasted little time in referring to Rogerson's book in its overseas radio broadcasts, and it was the main source of Dr Wilhelm von Kries's *Strategy and Tactics of the British War Propaganda*, published in 1941 by the German Information Service in its "Britain Unmasked" series directed toward American readers. Rogerson also became a favourite bogeyman of American isolationists, being cited, for example, by John T. Flynn in a speech at an America First rally in Chicago in December 1940. As well, excerpts from his book were read into the *Congressional Record* by Gerald Nye in May 1939. Even on the day that Pearl Harbor was bombed, Senator Nye reminded an America First rally in Pittsburgh that Rogerson had suggested that the threat which might bring the United States into the next war was Japan.[10]

The cumulative effect of the work of Squires, Peterson, Rogerson, and others was to instill in many Americans a supersensitivity to British propaganda which verged on paranoia. Writing in the *American Mercury* in December 1937, for example, Albert Jay Nock complained that the United States was "infested and itchy with foreign propagandists, especially those of the British persuasion." Whenever international affairs took a turn unfavourable to British interests, he suggested, people should study the lists of passengers arriving in New York by ship. There, they would be "astonished to see the volume of infiltration by first-string British panhandlers" – politicians, dignitaries, lecturers, writers, and many others over to push the British cause."[11] Nock's point seemed proven one October day in 1939 when British politician Duff Cooper, writers Cecil Roberts, S.K. Ratcliffe, Phyllis Bottome, critic Ellis Roberts, and scholar I.A. Richards all arrived on the ss *Manhattan*. On the following day, one newspaper headline proclaimed: "The British Are Here to Get Us In."[12] Lecturing in the United States a few months later, Roberts saw a sign on an auditorium marquee calling him "the foremost British propagandist," and he won his audience over only by playing along with the claim.

The English literary critic William Empson, returning to Britain by way of the United States in the winter of 1939–40, also found himself the object of American suspicions. "There were times," he wrote, "when I felt quite sure that if I had stood on my head and sung 'Three Blind Mice' [my American hosts] would have wondered placidly why the British Government had paid me to do *that*."[13] Journalist and lecturer Jay Allen, alluding to some of the more lurid propaganda stories of the First World War, commented after a tour: "In the Midwest one gets the feeling that men are waiting with shotguns to shoot down the first propagandist who mentions Belgian babies."[14] In June 1940 British correspondent Alistair Cooke reported that "for an active variety of reasons, fears and memories, which probably no living neurologist could hope to classify," Americans had not been reassured by the British government's announcement that it was not conducting propaganda in the United States.[15]

Cooke's conclusion that there was no evidence of any organized British propaganda in the United States did not persuade isolationist Americans. In an article in *Scribner's Commentator* in November 1940, for example, Kenneth Monroe cited Minnesota Senator Ernest Lundeen's comment that there had "been in recent years appropriated for [British] propaganda in this country the sum of ONE HUNDRED SIXTY-FIVE MILLION DOLLARS." So effective was the British propaganda, said Monroe, that anyone who spoke in favour of isolationism was at once "smeared by the press as a 'Fifth Columnist,' 'Nazi,' 'Fascist,' 'traitor.'"[16] Porter Sargent, an education specialist whose letterhead proclaimed him an "adviser to parents and schools," published a weekly bulletin monitoring anything that remotely smacked of British propaganda. Sent to faculty members of private schools, colleges, and universities, as well as to selected members of the general population, a hundred or so of these appeared in book form as *Getting Us Into War* in 1941.

Perhaps nowhere was the fear of British war propaganda more luridly expressed than in the isolationist posters demanding "absolute neutrality – now and forever!":

BEWARE THE BRITISH SERPENT!! Once more a boa constrictor – "Perfidious Albion" – is crawling across the American landscape, spewing forth its unctuous lies. Its purpose is to lure this nation into the lair of war to make the world safe for international plunder. More than ever we Americans must now evaluate this intruder into our garden of Eden, appraising Britain down to the last pennyweight of truth.[17]

In the face of such acute sensitivity to foreign propaganda in the United States, the British Foreign Office and the Ministry of Information approached the problem of influencing American public opinion in the late 1930s and early war years with extreme caution. Inactive since the end of the First World War, the ministry was brought to life again in September 1936 to "present the national case to the public at home and abroad in time of war."[18] In reality, as Ian McLaine has demonstrated in *Ministry of Morale: Home Front Morale and the Ministry of Information in World War II*, a much greater emphasis was placed on shaping opinion within Britain than in other countries.

Although in the early years of the war the Ministry of Information was much ridiculed as an elephantine bureaucracy, the American Division was small. Its first director was Sir Frederick Whyte, who had variously been the president of the Legislative Assembly of India, political adviser to Chiang Kai-shek, and director general of the English Speaking Union. Having also travelled widely throughout the United States, he had some familiarity with the American view of foreign affairs.

In a paper prepared even before his appointment on 26 August 1939, Whyte outlined his position on British attempts to shape public opinion in the United States. "The less the British Government attempts by direct propaganda to justify themselves," he argued, "the better."[19] To the American public, through an interview published in the *New York Sun* in October 1939, he was unequivocal: "We are not competing [with the Axis powers] with visiting lecturers, paid propagandists or professional partisans this time. Some people tell us in fact that we are leaning over backward in our efforts to lose this war of propaganda."[20] By late January 1940 this position had not changed. "All evidence available," he wrote to the director general of the Ministry of Information, "confirms the wisdom of continuing the policy of no overt propaganda in the United States of America."[21]

Whyte's strategy of "no propaganda" reflected the position of the Chamberlain government and Foreign Office officials in the early years of the war, but it would be a mistake to conclude that "no propaganda" meant no effort to shape American public opinion. Whyte's warning, after all, was against "*direct* propaganda" and "*overt* propaganda" (emphases mine), not against propaganda itself. In fact, from the beginning of the war, and especially after Churchill became prime minister, the Ministry of Information and the Foreign Office maintained a program of indirect and covert propaganda, though they preferred to use the less pejorative term, "publicity." Whyte's original mandate thus was to work through cultural groups such as the English Speaking Union, an Anglo-American organization which sponsored visiting speakers and published material, and to encourage the making of films and pamphlets directed toward the United States.

Shortly after the outbreak of war, the British ambassador in Washington, Lord Lothian, urged his government to expand the cultural initiative to include the use of established British authors. Writing to the Foreign Office on 28 September, he argued that there was no need for fundamental explanations of the Allied cause because Americans were already familiar with it. "But," he added, "articles about what British war aims are or ought to be by well-known authors like H.G. Wells, Hugh Walpole or about the ideological conflict, eg. like Rauschning's book, are extremely valuable. What we most need is to induce the Americans to think deeply about the war, its causes and its cure."[22]

Lothian's call for greater use of British writers clearly had its effect on British policy. In April 1940 the Foreign Office proposed to transfer F.R. Cowell to the American Division of the Ministry of Information. Commenting on the move, Cowell noted that his Foreign Office background gave him a prestige which could help in dealing with people who were suspicious of the ministry. "This," he said, "applies particularly to authors (who were outraged at the beginning of the war by a 'warning' to hold themselves in readiness to help the M. of I. – H.G. Wells for instance) ... The M. of I. is predominantly *political*. For the

U.S.A. culture is quite as strong a card as politics especially in books and films. It would be fatal to have a *merely* M. of I. approach."[23]

Whyte's response to the Foreign Office was to welcome the addition of Cowell. It would, he observed, "help us perform even more effectively in the future the two tasks to which you refer as being regarded by the Ambassador as of special importance: of stimulating articles in the British Press suitable for reproduction in America [and] of inspiring articles by British authors for publication, through commercial channels, in the United States."[24]

Although British authors came to be employed extensively during the Second World War, early attempts to involve them administratively nearly sank under the weight of bureaucratic procedure. It was, in fact, the authors themselves who first suggested their usefulness in a wartime propaganda campaign through their professional organization, the Society of Authors, Playwrights and Composers. Seven months before the war, its secretary, Denys Kilham Roberts, wrote to Humbert Wolfe – a minor poet and man of letters who was at the time a civil servant in the Ministry of Labour – regarding a central bureau that was being established by the ministry to coordinate the participation of members of learned societies and creative bodies in a National Service scheme. Kilham Roberts pointed out that the society was the official representative of roughly four thousand authors in the country and had close contacts with other writers' societies throughout the world. "In my capacity as Secretary," he added, "I have at the Society's headquarters an efficient and well-trained staff of ten whose experience would render them, in the event of a national emergency, invaluable to the Government in the spheres of Propaganda or Censorship, and I imagine that it is in one or both of these spheres that the Society and its organisation would be likely to be most of service to the country."[25]

In late February 1939 the National Service Department of the Ministry of Labour informed Kilham Roberts that the Central Registry Advisory Council, which was set up to advise the government on the use of people with scientific, technical, professional, and higher administrative qualifications, had established committees to deal with the individual professions. He would be contacted soon. At a meeting with Wolfe, Kilham Roberts was told that the Ministry of Labour would have problems in creating a register of authors, and the Society was invited to set up its own committee to do two things. First, it could consider the most appropriate employment in non-combatant

duties of authors over thirty years of age; and, second, it could prepare a list of names of authors and their particular qualifications for
wartime service. "I should add," Wolfe concluded somewhat dismiss-
ively, "that in any circumstances all authors of 30 or over, like other
citizens, might well consider undertaking part-time duties in connection with the A.R.P. [air raid precautions]."[26]

Following this meeting, Wolfe joined the society and was elected to
its council so that he could work more closely with it. Kilham Roberts
wrote to a dozen prominent authors asking whether they would be
prepared to speak in a National Service scheme. He received replies
from Ernest Raymond, Ashley Dukes, J.B. Priestley, Philip Guedalla,
R.C. Sherriff, Rex Mottram, Compton Mackenzie, Owen Rutter, and
St John Ervine. Most were prepared to help, but Mackenzie offered
only a "provisional promise," and Ervine wanted to know more specifically what was expected of him. "Priestley," reported Kilham
Roberts, "has refused to take any part, partly on the ground of over-
tiredness and partly, as he says, because 'I need to know more than
I do now about the policy of the present Government before I am
prepared to go touting them!'"[27] Despite this early reluctance, Priestley
went on to become one of the most important literary figures in the
British war effort, though he remained one of the government's most
outspoken critics.

By the middle of April 1939 a committee made up of Wolfe, Kilham
Roberts, and L.A.G. Strong had been struck to collect and classify
information about writers in a form that would be useful in time of
war. When Wolfe was too busy to participate, the other two sent out
a questionnaire of their own devising and, to their surprise, found
it to be the subject of a question in the House of Commons. At one
point in the questionnaire, authors were invited to describe their
political views and their attitude to conscription and military service.
Mr Mander, MP for Wolverhampton, concerned apparently that the
Ministry of Labour was collaborating in an attempt to weed out
writers because of their political beliefs, rose to challenge the legality
of the questionnaire. In an effort to defuse the situation, Wolfe promised to raise the matter with the society, and when Kilham Roberts
sent its members a letter of explanation, Mander agreed to withdraw
his question.

According to Kilham Roberts, he received only about six complaints
from the more than three thousand authors who had received the

questionnaire. Those few complaints and Mr Mander's concern, however, touch on a fundamental problem which British officials faced throughout the war whenever they utilized authors. Like the population as a whole, the writing community covered the political spectrum, from extreme left to extreme right, but unlike the general population, the writers expected to have the freedom to express their views. Many, in fact, would have argued that their role was to remain outside the political establishment and retain their freedom to function as critics of society and of the war.

The difficulty for the government lay in co-opting authors for the cultural impact of their pens without either giving them a blank cheque to perhaps voice damaging criticism or being seen to stifle them. As the war progressed, Priestley became one of the co-opted whose political opinions disturbed those in power, while H.G. Wells, having declined an early invitation to do war work, embarrassed the government with frequent and outspoken public statements. George Bernard Shaw was deliberately excluded from radio broadcasts, and Vera Brittain was repeatedly denied permission to leave the country. Michael Arlen was forced to resign his position as civil defence public relations officer for the East Midlands when questions were raised in the House of Commons about his Bulgarian background and whether "the general tone of his writing made him a fit individual to hold the important position."[28]

Such questions about the political beliefs of writers became more directly the concern of the Ministry of Information in July 1939, when the Society of Authors' initiative became subsumed by the ministry's Authors' Planning Committee, chaired by Raymond Needham. A.D. Peters, the prominent literary agent, was the committee secretary, and Strong and Kilham Roberts joined R.H.S. Crossman, Dorothy Sayers, A.P. Herbert, and Professor John Hilton as members. Another list of potentially useful authors was devised, but as Kilham Roberts warned Cecil Day Lewis on 31 August, no official employment of authors could take place until the outbreak of war: "Until the Ministry becomes a thing of substance instead of a shadow, which it is unlikely to do until War actually breaks out, anything definite in the way of officially reserving services of authors is apparently impossible. All I can do is to say, quite unofficially, that it is likely the Ministry will in fact have use for your services and I suggest that you not at present attach yourself to any other branch of National Service."[29]

On 5 September, only two days after the declaration of war, the ministry spoke officially when Peters sent the following letter – which Kilham Roberts had obviously paraphrased – to about seventy writers:

I am directed by the Minister of Information to inform you that your name has been entered on a list of authors whose services are likely to be valuable to the Ministry of Information in time of war.

The Minister will be grateful, therefore, if you refrain from engaging yourself in any other form of national service without previously communicating with the Ministry of Information. He would also be glad to have any particulars that you may care to supply about your specialized knowledge in any field likely to be of interest to the Ministry and of your acquaintance with foreign countries and languages.

Please send particulars of any change of address, and all communications to me at Room 133, at the above address.

Yours faithfully,
A.D. Peters[30]

Some writers found Peters' letter high-handed and patronizing. To the request for a list of qualifications, the well-known writer and former diplomat Robert Bruce Lockhart snorted: "If this is the way the Ministry works in regard to British authors, what on earth will its knowledge be of foreign countries?"[31] On the same day, Sir Hugh Walpole had written directly to the minister of information, Lord Macmillan, to offer his services, grandly pointing out that he had been in charge of propaganda in Russia in the Great War and later had worked under Beaverbrook in the earlier incarnation of the ministry. Furthermore, he knew all the British writers and their works as well as anyone. However, he added: "I suggest that I would be of especial use with regard to America. I was there as a child and have been on lecture tours there constantly and my name is widely known there."[32] Having thus displayed his credentials, Walpole was indignant at having to answer to Peters, but he was nonetheless eager to accept the ministry's invitation.

Other writers responded differently. Vera Brittain, who had been an ardent pacifist for twenty years, replied that she would cooperate only if her work contributed to peace and not to national hatreds. H.G. Wells, a prominent figure in the propaganda campaign in the Great War, reacted angrily. Writing in the *New Statesman and Nation* two months later, he confessed: "I have been approached, and I suppose quite a number of us have been approached, more or less officially, to do propaganda in Europe and America. [But] I am not going to be a stalking horse for the Foreign Office again."[33]

Many writers, however, were anxious to join the war effort – some for patriotic reasons and some for financial ones – but were ignored or rejected. Ernest Raymond, having received a dismissive reply from the Ministry of Labour in April, waited in vain to hear from the Ministry of Information. In the end, he served, in his words, only as "a hopelessly confused lance-corporal in the Home Guard."[34] Evelyn Waugh personally telephoned Peters in an attempt to join the Ministry of Information, but after several months of frustration he eventually joined the Royal Marines. Francis Brett Young, who believed that his reputation in the United States would make him a valuable propagandist, was not taken on by the ministry, though in 1941 it asked him to write a pamphlet on the British Empire. "It appears to me ridiculous," he complained to Charles Evans, "that men like myself and Priestley, among the leaders of our profession, should be excluded from performing the work which we are best qualified to do."[35] Similarly, William Gerhardie approached the Ministry of Information and a number of other government offices but ended up becoming a fire guard before joining the BBC's European Productions department.

Although a number of writers took their lack of employment by the Ministry of Information as a personal slight, the truth is that beyond asking the writers to be prepared to serve, the ministry still had not formulated a clear and comprehensive scheme for their use. Even as the Peters letter was in the post, Raymond Needham was proposing that the Authors' Planning Committee be replaced by an Authors' Advisory Panel, a representative group of writers who would be individually called upon for advice or suggestions. In addition to three members of the original committee – Sayers, Strong, and Herbert – he suggested Helen Simpson, Lord Elton, Sir Hugh Walpole, J.B. Priestley, Charles Morgan, Sir Edward Grigg, Osbert Sitwell, J.M. Keynes, Noel Coward, E.M. Delafield, R.C. Sherriff, Harold Nicolson, P.G. Wodehouse, Rebecca West, and Mary Agnes Hamilton.[36]

The proposal for an Authors' Advisory Panel was postponed while the deputy director general, A.P. Waterfield, tried to appoint a director of literary publicity, who would be in charge of a Literary Division with Peters as assistant director and Kilham Roberts as consultant. Then, Waterfield suggested, when the American, Home, or European division wanted the services of an author, the Literary Division would provide an appropriate one. "The author," he said, "will be then told what we want and asked if he will be willing to undertake the job with – in nine cases out of ten – a pretty free hand to express his views on the subject in his own words and along his own lines of thought." The director would need to be able to "persuade the reluctant and placate the indignant if necessary."[37]

Anxious to find a female director in order to place a woman on the ministry's council, Waterfield considered Dorothy Sayers, Mary Agnes Hamilton, Helen Simpson, and Margaret Storm Jameson. When Sayers sensibly responded, "Why should a good writer be turned into a bad administrator?" he offered the position to Jameson, the current president of PEN (Poets, Playwrights, Essayists, Novelists). In doing so, he was following the advice of Humbert Wolfe, who had written: "I have found her very clear-minded, sensible and unemotional. She stands deservedly high in the literary world and does not belong to any particular faction."[38]

Jameson responded favourably to the invitation, but within a week Waterfield had changed his mind and recommended the appointment of Surrey Dane, who was in charge of publicity material in the form of pamphlets and periodicals. In gracefully accepting the change of plans, Jameson offered to help in any way, pointing out that PEN had close relations with writers in the United States and South America: "It is possible that our relations with these countries, and our special knowledge and experience, can be useful to you in some way. It is freely at your disposal."[39]

Amid these visions and revisions, A.D. Peters resigned from the ministry, writing to Waterfield on 29 September: "Work has not developed in the way I had anticipated."[40] Two weeks later his criticisms were more specific:

Existing here in the void as I do, with no means of contact with my superiors except memos whose ultimate fate is unknown to me, it is obviously impossible for me to be of any service, even in matters of which I have some knowledge and experience. But I should like to put on record my opinion that the whole method of dealing with the printed word in the Ministry is wrong. The work at present is spread all over the departments, in some cases in the hands of people whose qualifications for it are by no means apparent.[41]

Peters' disenchantment with his role at the ministry appears to have been aggravated by the intrusion of Sir Hugh Walpole into the process.

At the suggestion of Lord Macmillan, Walpole had contacted John Hilton, director of home publicity, and by early October was offering his own suggestion for an authors' committee, including the addition to the membership of Sir Ronald Storrs, Alan Bott, Mrs Robert Lynd, J.B. Priestley, and C.S. Forester ("a novelist immensely popular in America as well as in this country"). The unsalaried committee, he said, should be independent and advisory, attached to the ministry but not on staff, and its purpose would be "to bring the whole force of British culture to the aid of the British Government."[42]

When Waterfield suggested to Walpole that Peters should join their discussions, Walpole "was *much* averse to that!"[43] For his part, Peters saw the Walpole scheme as a backward step. "We are back where we started," he wrote Waterfield, "but with this difference: that authors and publishers are criticising the whole conduct of literary affairs inside the Ministry with a bitterness which I consider wholly justified."[44]

Peters' criticisms of the Walpole plan was echoed even more strongly by Humbert Wolfe, whose advice Waterfield sought. Wolfe agreed with Peters that authors believed that they were not being used effectively and that they had a very real contribution to make if properly organized. But, he added, "I cannot feel that the appointment of a Committee of Authors would not lead to anything but continuous bickering and would not be of real help to the Department. After many years' experience in working on committees with authors, I have found them, apart from their special gifts, extraordinarily ignorant and ill-informed people on most topics. The reason for this is the obvious one: that their contacts with the outside world are often limited and that they tend to live in a small and separate universe."

Wolfe went on to complain about Walpole's revised list of authors, noting the exclusion of Compton Mackenzie, Michael Arlen, Sylvia Townsend-Warner, Daphne du Maurier, and Rosamond Lehmann. These omissions, he argued, indicated how difficult it was to compile a list that was truly representative, and a truly representative committee would be so large and controversial that it would be nearly impossible to get any guidance from it. A better alternative, he went on, would be to appoint a publisher – A.S. Frere, of William Heinemann Ltd, for example – to solicit the appropriate work from writers.[45]

Waterfield remained committed to the idea of an authors' committee, and early in November Walpole confided to his diary that there was a "great meeting at M. of I. about my committee. Had things all my way. Everybody charming."[46] In late November, however, W.H. Stevenson, the head of the Literary and Editorial Unit, voiced his opposition. "So many diverse views will be represented," he argued, "that there will be endless discussions and, I fear, minor results. If, on the other hand, they are only called together at lengthy intervals, they will grumble about having nothing to do." The best results, he concluded, could be obtained by ministry contact with individual authors according to a general policy: "To ask every author to use every opportunity of addressing his public – whether by the written or spoken word – through all the many channels which are available to him. It is believed that their influence will be greater if their words reach the public in this way as the expression of their own personality, than would be the case if they were merely a mouthpiece for the Ministry. Each author is asked to keep in touch with the Ministry."

To bolster his argument, Stevenson pointed to a number of authors – for example, E.M. Delafield, F. Tennyson Jesse, Naomi Jacob, Helen Simpson, and Sacheverell Sitwell – who had already indicated what they might be able to write for the war effort. Ann Bridge was writing a book on England before and after the outbreak of war for publication in the United States. A.A. Milne was considering a booklet treating the moral problems of those who were uncomfortable supporting the war effort. On the other hand, warned Stevenson, "My pre-war contact with Jack Priestley does not lead me to think that he will be amenable to outside suggestion of any kind."[47]

Unconvinced by Stevenson's arguments, Waterfield suggested that the problem of unwieldy size could be countered by creating a number of subcommittees – for example, Fiction, General, Political, Home Morale, with an American list to be devised by Sir Frederick Whyte. Waterfield, however, accepted Wolfe's suggestion of consulting a publisher and brought in Geoffrey Faber, who was told that most of the books sought by the ministry would be for circulation in other countries – especially France and the United States. Faber was even more skeptical about the effectiveness of authors in committee. "Authors are," he said, "with rare exceptions, egocentric persons. They are not cohesive; they are not good at collectively tackling an impersonal problem." Publishers, on the other hand, are skilled at knowing the subjects on which books should be written and at finding the authors to write them. They are, concluded Faber modestly, "better able to give informed advice than any other class of persons."[48]

Faber's commentary finally convinced Waterfield that an authors' committee was unworkable and he so advised the director general and the minister on 21 December. A week later, Waterfield informed all parties that Macmillan had abandoned the idea of an authors' committee, though he was "anxious that more direct and immediate action should be taken to enlist the help of certain of the leading writers of the day in the production of pamphlets and other propaganda material of the more ephemeral type."[49]

Despite Macmillan's decision, the Society of Authors continued to pursue the idea of an authors' planning committee. Its president, John Masefield, wrote to the ministry to object, and in the spring of 1940 the society's periodical, the *Author*, published the comments of a number of writers in a symposium on the role of authors in the war. Although some agreed with Margaret Kennedy that wars are won through physical violence, not pens, the predominant view was that expressed by Ernest Raymond. Despite his several rebuffs, Raymond argued that the Ministry of Information was the most important ministry and that authors were the most important members of the community. He referred his readers to Kipling's story "The Man with the Magic of the Word," in which a tribe under attack immediately elevated a wordsmith to a great position because he could stir and stiffen the hearts of the people to perform great fighting deeds.[50]

In the summer of 1940 the Society of Authors' campaign to be officially involved in the war effort was taken over by J.B. Priestley, who although considered difficult by the Ministry of Information, was by then a very popular radio broadcaster both in Britain and abroad. Priestley chaired a new body called the Authors' National Committee, with Denys Kilham Roberts as secretary and Margaret Storm Jameson and John MacMurray on the editorial board. George Bernard Shaw was invited to join the group, but his opinion of writers in committee echoed those of Wolfe and Faber. "Evidently," he wrote Priestley, "you have never been on a Committee of Authors. I had ten years of it in the Society of Authors. In their books they are more or less delightful creatures according to taste. In committee, to call them hogs would be an insult to a comparatively co-operative animal."[51]

Storm Jameson participated in the formation of the Authors' National Committee, along with the ubiquitous Hugh Walpole, but she had little more confidence in its success did than Shaw. Priestley was overbearing ("Does he want to be our first Minister of Culture?" she wrote in her journal) and was dismissive of her suggestions. "Nothing will come of it," she noted. "Furious with myself for wasting time on a discussion of no interest to me. Shall I ever have the courage to say No to these music-hall turns?"[52]

More eager to do a music-hall turn was Hugh Walpole, who helped Kilham Roberts devise yet another list of "eminent" suitable authors at the end of August 1940. By the following February, Kilham Roberts was able to canvass nearly a hundred well-known writers, most of whom responded positively. Priestley wanted the new minister of information, Walter Monckton, to attach writers to the various armed services, much as artists were accompanying many units in battle. When Monckton rejected this suggestion, William Collins, the publisher, was asked to produce a series of books about the problems of reconstruction after the war, and the result was Priestley's own *Out of the People*, which appeared in February 1942.

Out of the People was the only book published in the proposed series. The wartime paper shortage and Priestley's insistence that reconstruction of British society could be done only along socialist lines – a view not shared by his editorial board or the publisher – ended the project. At the same time, the Authors' National Committee, deprived of Priestley's energy while he was heavily involved in broadcasting, lecturing, and writing, faded away.

The quiet death of the committee ended any attempt to give writers a formal, structured role in the war effort. It did not, however, stop the employment of authors as individuals, either within government agencies or as loosely attached freelance writers. The Society of Authors continued to encourage its members to write articles and books that would further the British cause. The spring 1942 issue of the *Author* contained an anonymous article describing the kind of literature wanted in the United States and outlining how to get it published. Such writing, concluded the author, is "of great value politically. This nation can only be reached and swung through its emotions."[53] In the autumn of 1943 Phyllis Bentley, having recently returned from a three-month tour of the United States, wrote in the *Author*: "It is clearly important that British ideas and ways of life should be known to the Americans … If one really believes in the value (and I use this word in the moral not the mercenary sense) of one's ideas, the opportunity of presenting them to two or three million American readers is worth some preliminary labour of explanation."[54]

According to Peter Buitenhuis, the Ministry of Information's decision to abandon the idea of a writers' committee signalled the end of influential participation by British writers in official propaganda. Thereafter, Buitenhuis concluded, authors were generally used only in minor roles in various government departments. However, while it is true that fewer writers of the stature of Rudyard Kipling, John Galsworthy, Arnold Bennett, Ford Madox Ford, and James M. Barrie – who all wrote propaganda in the First World War – were officially employed in the Second World War, it is untrue that authors were not used extensively in the war of words. Many were employed in government departments – Malcolm Muggeridge, Graham Greene, V.S. Pritchett, John Betjeman, Cecil Day Lewis, Laurie Lee, and Phyllis Bentley in the Ministry of Information – and many more were supported, encouraged, and directed in propaganda work in semi-official ways. The Wolfe/Stevenson proposal to employ a publisher who would have an overview of the British writing community led to the appointment of Hamish Hamilton to the American Division in 1941. Moreover, their suggestion that the ministry solicit propaganda material from individual authors became the practice of the Ministry of Information and the Foreign Office for the duration of the war. Selected lecturers were sent to the United States, books, pamphlets, and newspaper and magazine articles were suggested, broadcasts to North America were developed, and film scriptwriters and producers were encouraged. The result was a considerable army of British writers whose words became weapons in the battle for American commitment to the war.

4

Making the War Seem Personal
British Authors in the United States

We shall as before send over our leading literary lights and other men with names well known in the United States to put our point of view over the dinner table. Our trouble will be to find men with equally commanding reputations to step into the shoes of such as Kipling, Barrie, Shaw, Galsworthy, and Wells.

Sidney Rogerson, *Propaganda in the Next War*, 1938[1]

Of all the instruments of propaganda employed by the British government to influence American public opinion during the Second World War, none was as problematic as that of lecturers and visitors to the United States. American paranoia about propagandists, and the Foreign Agents Act (which required the registration of anyone who was in the pay of a foreign government or who spoke or wrote in the United States with its assistance) precluded sending official government agents. Indeed, any lecture by a foreigner on the political questions of the war invited suspicion and criticism. Even Duff Cooper's tour in 1939, when he was out of office, was considered harmful by Lord Lothian "not because of anything he has said in public but because nobody believes that an ex-Sea Lord can come over here now with the consent of the British Government except with the object of influencing America's attitude to the war."[2] George Catlin, husband of Vera Brittain and an experienced lecturer in the United States, summed up Cooper's tour more sharply by commenting that "no Englishman should visit America for the first time."

Confronted with the need to conduct any propaganda campaign in the United States with great sensitivity, the British faced the additional problem that, of all propaganda activities, lecturers and visitors were the least manageable. BBC radio broadcasts could be very closely monitored and censored, but any British subject, once let loose in America, might say almost anything out of private political conviction or naiveté. Controlling the damage by silencing or recalling the visitor to Britain was very difficult in a country whose democratic sentiments put it on guard against any apparent suppression of free speech.

The files of the Foreign Office, which carefully monitored the activities of British subjects in the United States, reveal that a number of visitor/lecturers damaged the British cause in the early months of the war. In the autumn of 1939 the film director Alexander Korda horrified British authorities by proudly announcing that *The Lion Has Wings* was an official British government film made for propaganda purposes. In July 1940 Sir George Paish, an eminent septuagenarian economist, arrived in the United States to prepare for a six-month lecture tour to begin in November. In an interview with the isolationist Senator Burton Wheeler, he declared: "I am responsible for getting the United States into the last war ... and I am going to get this country into this war."[3] When Wheeler reported Paish's remark to the Senate, he was interrupted by Minnesota's Ernest Lundeen, who grumbled: "I think the gentleman referred to ... should be deported from the United States." Virginia Senator Carter Glass added: "If there is not a law to deport him, he should be deported anyway."[4] Paish's comments gave isolationist senators a pretext to demand an investigation of all British propagandists in the United States, and the indiscreet economist was promptly advised by Lord Lothian to return to the United Kingdom as soon as possible. Interviewed by the *Washington Post*, a member of the British Embassy in Washington remarked: "We wish someone would drop Sir George Paish over Germany as a pamphlet."[5]

Muriel Lester, lecturing in the United States for the first eighteen months of the war, told a Chicago audience that Hitler and God actually wanted the same thing – healthy, happy, and good people – but they had different methods of achieving an ideal world. God had failed and now Hitler was trying his hand, and she encouraged the United States to maintain a strict neutrality and to supply food to the occupied territories. Considering Lester's speeches and articles for the American press "extremely damaging" to the British cause, the Foreign Office had her detained in Trinidad in the autumn of 1941, to be returned to the United Kingdom for making "seditious utterances thoroughly reactionary."[6]

Less serious, but nonetheless considered damaging by the Foreign Office, were British visitors to the United States who reinforced the already strong anglophobic prejudices. Sir Thomas Beecham's supercilious behaviour and insulting remarks about Americans in his 1941 tour caused the Foreign Office to comment: "In normal times this type of man helps to perpetuate the dislike many people have for Englishmen. With things as they are he is a positive menace."[7] Similarly, the visit in July 1941 of two Mechanised Transport Corps women, who behaved like prima donnas, led Sir Angus Fletcher of the British Library of Information in New York to write: "Again and again I have had to listen to friendly Americans ... exposing the insufferable condescension, self-complacency, pretentiousness, neglect of elementary courtesies, which far too many 'representative' English visitors are prone to."[8]

Harley Granville-Barker, coordinator of English speakers and lecturers in the United States for the British Library of Information, summed up the danger of the uninformed dilettante lecturer: "I have yet to meet the Englishman who, whether in peace or war, when he can think of nothing else to do, doesn't fancy that it might be an awfully good idea to go over to America and 'talk.' He is received with a seemingly innocent blend of politeness and curiosity which flatters him much, and he returns little guessing the mischief he may have done."[9] Alfred North Whitehead, professor emeritus of philosophy at Harvard, made the point more succinctly to his son, T. North Whitehead, at the Foreign Office in February 1940: "No Englishman ought to be allowed to make public speeches over here."[10]

Faced with the various problems presented by British lecturer/visitors in the United States, the Foreign Office and Ministry of Information, with the advice of Lord Lothian, adopted a cautious approach. No lecturer/visitors in the pay of the British government were sent over, and those who might speak on political issues were discouraged or prevented from travelling. On the other hand, as B.E.T. Gage suggested in a Foreign Office memorandum, "There is no reason why we should not indulge in [activities] bordering on *propaganda* provided they are subtle enough to avoid suspicion. Amongst those I would include the arrangement of private visits to the United States by British approved personalities."[11]

The appropriate "personalities" were those with established American contacts, especially those who had been invited to write or speak by American institutions, universities, service clubs, women's groups, and other organizations. They were also to have a thorough knowledge of the contemporary United States and a sensitivity to American opinion. In general, said Sir Frederick Whyte in February 1940, "The Ministry [of Information] has felt that the type of British visitor who could be of most service is not the lecturer or publicist, but the business man or scholar, whose reason for visiting the United States in time of war was *bona fide*. For such, efforts have been made to ensure that their visit should result in favourable publicity for the British cause."[12] This position was endorsed by Lothian, who, though opposed to lecturers speaking about politics, believed that "lecturers on scientific, literary or artistic subjects who stick to their lasts in public but who represent the British view sensibly and calmly and not aggressively in private, on the whole do ... a lot of good."[13]

The kind of lecturer/visitor who more than any other fitted the requirements of the British propaganda campaign was the author, a fact recognized by the Ministry of Information at the beginning of the war. Its weekly report for late October 1939 noted: "The American Division continues to interview writers with American connections and lecturers proposing to proceed to America, encouraging the former along certain lines but usually suggesting to the latter that they should not in the immediate future carry out any project to visit the United States."[14]

Writers were always prominent among what Alistair Cooke called "the British migratory lecturers – in the early Autumn they are as familiar a sight as the warbler winging south, and after six or seven decades their habits are almost as well known."[15] From Dickens and Wilde to Hugh Walpole, Vera Brittain, and Cecil Roberts, a procession of British men and women of letters had travelled the length and breadth of North America bringing a touch of the literary Old Country to universities, service clubs, and literary societies. Ironically, while Americans resented British speakers who patronized them on matters of politics and social organization, a great many of them nevertheless looked with awe at British art and literature as having a greatness not yet achieved by that of the New World. Moreover, in 1939 authors had not yet lost their authority with the public, and the pronouncements of Shaw, Wells, Maugham, and many others were given a deference that no longer exists in the twenty-first century. Those who could write so skilfully and apparently knowledgeably of man and superman, of wars in the air, or of human bondage, were assumed to possess the vision or wisdom to provide guidance in a

time of upheaval and political chaos. At the very least, they seemed
to provide a more objective view than their political counterparts. In
Chicago in November 1941 the author Sir Philip Gibbs was introduced by a priest who said that Gibbs "had not come as a propagandist but as a literary man, a journalist, and war correspondent, and
therefore a recorder of events."[16]

While Americans resented being lectured about their political
responsibilities, they were eager to hear first-hand accounts of life in
wartime Britain; and the testimonies of writers, like other visitors, had
an impact beyond that of radio and newspaper reports. The American
author Paul Horgan remembers being taken to luncheon with Somerset
Maugham in the early summer of 1941, the year after the eminent
author had fled his Riviera villa as France was being overrun. "It
would be interesting now," he thought, "to meet not only Maugham
the celebrated writer but also Maugham the survivor, who could be
the emblem of what the Hitler war could portend for us in the United
States if we should be drawn into it ... Through the prospect of meeting Mr. Maugham, the war suddenly seemed personal."[17]

If many British authors fell short of the vision and wisdom attributed to them by the public, they at least had some familiarity with
the United States and the complexity of its social and political life.
Catlin had warned of the Englishman visiting the United States for
the first time, but by 1939 there was an experienced contingent of
British writers which had regularly toured the country during the
interwar years. The New York lecture agencies – notably Colston
Leigh and W.B. Feakins – always boasted of a lengthy list of authors.

Writers were also attractive to the British propaganda effort because
they could earn their own way in the United States and thus not be
on the government payroll. In 1939 there were over 100,000 American
organizations that brought in paid lecturers. These included fraternities and sororities and other university student clubs, church groups,
service clubs such as the Lions, Rotary, and Kiwanis, women's groups
and book societies, college alumni organizations, and various insti-
tutes dealing with international relations. The women's groups, so
cruelly satirized by Dylan Thomas in "A Visit to America," were
numerous, frequently large, and pervasive. The English writer Bernard
Newman noted: "The women's clubs of America are as much a feature of the national life as the men's Rotary, Kiwanis, Lions, Elks and
the like. More than once I had an audience of a thousand women at
a tea club. Every town will support dozens of lecture courses, and the
world is combed for speakers who can talk with authority on an

amazing variety of subjects. No lecturer will ever have a more atten-
tive audience."[18] These groups, which had always paid well to hear
a visiting British author, were now eager to learn how Britons were
coping in the crisis. On the other hand, the English Speaking Union,
which had branches throughout the United States, rarely paid a fee,
but it provided very useful connections to local groups and at least
covered travel expenses.

Because British authors had toured the United States regularly for
decades, they had the added advantage of being less liable than other
lecturers to excite the suspicions of propaganda-sensitive Americans.
Moreover, audiences accustomed to seeing the book promotion tour
as part of the writer's professional life were unlikely to consider such
wartime travels in America in a sinister light. Writers were simply
doing what they had always done.

As the war went on, the British authorities developed a proactive
approach to sending authors to the United States, but in the early
months of the phony war they were content to work with those who
had long-standing engagements there. Such was the case with Cecil
Roberts and S.K. Ratcliffe, who sailed from Southampton to New York
in October 1939, along with such other public figures as the author
and journalist R. Ellis Roberts, the Cambridge professor and author
of *The Meaning of Meaning*, I.A. Richards, and the novelist Phyllis
Bottome. A fellow passenger was Duff Cooper, who in October 1938
had resigned in disgust from the Chamberlain cabinet over the
Munich pact. According to Cecil Roberts, however, he was going
"more as a successful author than as a statesman, for he had gained
some *reclamé* with his admirable *Talleyrand*."[19]

Cecil Roberts, who had been going to the United States for twenty
years and had for months been booked to tour in the winter of 1939–
40, was interviewed three times by the director of the American
Division of the Ministry of Information. Sir Frederick Whyte emphasized that nothing should be done to antagonize Americans and that,
because of the Neutrality Act, there would be no financial assistance
from the British government. For similar reasons, the ministry could
not secure his passage to the United States. Roberts replied that as a
well-known author on an American tour, he would be self-supporting,
and that he was already booked to sail on the ss *Manhattan*. Three days
after their final meeting, Whyte summarized his position in a letter:

In continuation of our discussion and correspondence may I say that if you
can arrange to proceed to the United States as you suggest, on business

connected with your books, etc., you will certainly be doing a useful service. The decision has been made here not only not to engage in covert propaganda, but to send no agents or lecturers of our own to the United States at present. I suggest you carry out your programme, and if we can be of any assistance to you, please let me know.[20]

In conversation, Whyte had indicated that the "assistance" might come from the British Library of Information in New York, to which he would give Roberts a letter of introduction, but he told Roberts to be sure to contact the library director in private and not in his office. Ratcliffe, who had also been briefed by Whyte, and Duff Cooper, whose political status meant a visit from the prime minister's parliamentary private secretary, were issued the same warning. Similarly, when the American lawyer Fanny Holtzmann made a proposal for a propaganda scheme for America, Whyte did not discourage her but "explained fully to her our policy toward the United States and made it clear that she must not quote American Division or any Government Department or official personage as recognising or approving her scheme."[21]

When Roberts presented his letter of introduction to Angus Fletcher, the director of the British Library, in his office at the Rockefeller Plaza Centre on an October afternoon, Fletcher "was very scared and confessed the fact," noted Roberts: "If such obvious publicists as myself were seen coming into his office the conclusion would be drawn that they were organising propaganda. I should have telephoned him for a private meeting."[22]

In 1939 S.K. Ratcliffe was seventy-one and embarking on his twenty-seventh successive season on the American lecture platform. His incisive style made him a popular speaker, and as a former editor of the *Statesman* in India, he was especially well equipped to counter American accusations of British imperial exploitation of that country. On this tour, Ratcliffe moved through the isolationist Midwest, giving lectures with such titles as "Why Britain Went to War," "Britain in Wartime," and "What Next in Europe?", which dealt with the aims of the Allies and the future of Europe.

At the end of his tour, in May 1940, Ratcliffe sent the Foreign Office a thorough report of his activities, as well as those of other visiting Britons.[23] His work was considered enough of a success for Frank Darvall to pressure the Foreign Office to continue the Ministry of Information's policy regarding lecturers: "On the question of lecturers to the United States we ought not, I think, allow ourselves to be misled by the volume of criticism which has, in fact, been largely inspired by Mr. Duff Cooper and Lord Marley. S.K. Ratcliffe, and his type of lecturer, continues to do good rather than harm. We should, therefore, I think, not so much discourage lecturers in general as continue our present practice of discouraging only those who have no intimate experience of the American lecture platform."[24]

I.A. Richards is an example of another, less obvious, means of influencing American public opinion. Returning to teach at Harvard University on a Rockefeller grant, he did not do any public lecturing of Ratcliffe's and Roberts's sort, but became one of many distinguished British visitors involved in what Lavine and Wechsler called "the propaganda of the social lobby, the personal conversation, the casual brush."[25] A 1941 report on the demand and supply of British lecturers in the United States submitted by the British Library of Information to the Ministry of Information outlined the value of academic visitors: "British professors as a rule get no publicity in the larger papers. They do a great deal of extra curricular speaking at Rotary Clubs, Kiwanis, War Relief rallies, etc. and according to their personalities and social qualities, exercise varying, but important, influence in their communities. The risk of being labelled propagandists is a serious matter to them but they can and should be cultivated as important factors in the attempt to interpret British life and thought to American people."[26]

In February 1941, Sir Stephen Gaselee of the Foreign Office urged Martin Charlesworth to go to the United States on the same basis. "The Ministry of Information and the British Council," he said, "are still very anxious not to do anything in the United States which could be construed as sending British propagandists there, and we are accordingly confined to the visits of those who go to lecture on general subjects and only incidentally and in private conversation put the British case. Such [is] my colleague I.A. Richards, who is still there."[27] In 1942 Richards changed from a quiet influencer to an overt propagandist when he became involved with American, not British, opinion making. The brilliant founder of a cult of literary criticism became a scriptwriter for the Disney studio, which had been commissioned to produce a series of short propaganda films.

Louis MacNeice played a similar role, holding a special lectureship in poetry at Cornell University from 12 February to 31 May 1940. While there he stayed in Telluride House, a residence for young men of exceptional promise, and according to his biographer Jon Stallworthy, its intense intellectual life was broadened by the presence of such outsiders as MacNeice: "They were Good Americans, isolationist, suspicious of Europe in general and England in particular. They regarded the war as an imperialist war. Few had been to Europe, so their interactions with their European fellow residents was educationally important."[28] As well as teaching at Cornell, MacNeice lectured or read his poetry at Vassar, Skidmore College, Northwestern, and Syracuse, and in the cities of Buffalo and Montreal. "In July," he later recalled, "I received orders to return to the U.K.,"[29] and for the remainder of the war he wrote scripts for BBC radio programs, many of which were aimed at American listeners of the overseas service.

Another British writer who lectured at American universities during the war was the actor, director, and playwright Harley Granville-Barker, author of *The Voysey Inheritance* (1905), *Waste* (1907), and *The Madras House* (1910). Sixty-three years of age when the war broke out, he nonetheless wanted to be part of the fight. After fleeing Paris with his wife in June 1940, he went to Lisbon, where he received a telegram from the British Consul in New York which said: "Could you come New York official employment or Canada similar object. Important." His inquiries in England had been answered with a recommendation to do what he could in North America, so he travelled to the United States in August on a visa describing him as a "government official."[30] According to his biographer, Eric Salmon, "his real work in North America was to consist of lecturing and writing,"[31] and during the winter of 1940–41 he lectured at both Harvard and Yale. "I'm told this is of use," he confided to John Gielgud, "and other jobs of the sort and other work is in prospect, as much, I expect, as I can tackle."[32]

When Granville-Barker wrote to his friend Gilbert Murray about his wish to be back in a more front-line job in Britain, Murray replied that he was not surprised that the ministry wanted Granville-Barker to stay in America: "They seem to attach great value to having the right kind of people there, not extremists of the Left or Right, who could give some intelligible account of things. They asked me to go, but partly I felt I was a little elderly for so much travel."[33]

In the spring of 1941 Granville-Barker was appointed to an official position, coordinator of English speakers and lecturers, in the British Library of Information. In May he sent two lengthy reports on the use of British lecturers – one to the Foreign Office and the other to Harold Nicolson – but before long he was eased out of the position for not being "the right kind of person" for the job. According to Aubrey Morgan, head of the British Information Services at the time, Granville-Barker lacked judgment and could neither cope with the temperaments of the visiting lecturers nor produce large audiences for them. Morgan appointed Barbara Hayes, a niece of Sir Norman Angell, as head of the Speakers' Section.[34] Granville-Barker remained in the United States until May 1945, speaking again at Yale and Harvard, and giving a series of lectures at the University of Toronto and at Princeton University.

Phyllis Bottome, who was the biographer of the psychologist Alfred Adler as well as being a novelist, ostensibly went to the United States to work on the screenplay of her novel *The Mortal Storm*, which was about Germany during the Nazis' rise to power. During her seven months there she lectured frequently, and on her return home she gave the Ministry of Information a report on her tour and on the current American attitudes to Britain.[35] Occasionally, she later recalled, her talks had led to her getting "rapped over the knuckles by columnists for being an insidious propagandist who, by inheritance half-American, could get under the skin of [her] audience and lead them to their doom."[36] One such columnist was the pro-isolationist Boake Carter, who noted that Bottome was accompanied by her husband, Captain A.E. Forbes-Dennis of the British army, and that in a November 1939 speech in Evansville, Indiana, "Cousin Phyllis unfolded her technique, which consists chiefly in hoping that we heathen souls will do away with the Nazis for her."[37]

Despite drawing some fire from isolationist commentators, Bottome seems to have pleased the Foreign Office. At the end of her American visit, the British Library of Information reported that she had "established a reputation for being an outspoken critic of Mr. Chamberlain and his policy as well as of Hitler. She advocated a change of leadership in England and with younger, more competent and more realistic men. Said G[reat] B[ritain] did not desire any force from U.S., but needed U.S. to act as an 'arsenal' to prevent loss of war."[38]

In arguing for the United States to act as an arsenal rather than a participant in the war, Bottome was following the British government's strategy of the time, which was to accustom Americans to the seriousness of the Nazi threat so that when the appropriate provocation occurred, they would be militarily and psychologically ready to enter the war. On the other hand, in criticizing the prime minister and calling for a change in leadership, Bottome may have discomfited some British officials. It was nonetheless a message with great appeal to Americans in the winter of 1939–40, and there was value in being seen to allow her to express it freely. Chamberlain and his government looked too much like the appeasers who had allowed Hitler to grow in strength, and they were doing little on their own to resolve their difficulty. Although Churchill hardly fitted Bottome's call for "younger" leaders, he was certainly more competent and realistic, and on assuming the prime ministership he instantly became one of Britain's most effective propaganda weapons in the United States.

Bottome was not alone in having her criticism of the government tolerated by British officials. Surveying visiting lecturers for the Institute of Propaganda Analysis in May 1940, Lavine and Wechsler noted a change of British policy in the winter of 1939–40, when "the green light was flashed, especially to those lecturers who had heretofore been most critical of Mr. Chamberlain and therefore least suspect ... It is noteworthy, moreover, that the British Government offered only encouragement to those of its critics who volunteered to espouse the Allied position in the United States without abandoning their misgivings about the Prime Minister."[39]

To have sent to the United States, or to have permitted to go there, only those speakers who mouthed the official government line would undoubtedly have aroused suspicion. On the other hand, the willingness of the British government to allow British subjects some criticism of itself when addressing an American audience did not go unnoticed in a country that saw itself as founded on the democratic right of individual free speech. When in the autumn of 1940 H.G. Wells repeatedly attacked the appointment of Lord Halifax as ambassador to the United States, causing questions to be raised in the House of Commons, the *San Francisco Chronicle* argued that "there could be no better evidence of sincerity offered to American opinion ... than the fact of Mr. Wells being at liberty – in fact given some expedition by government – to speak freely."[40]

This apparent official tolerance of free-speaking lecturers was severely tested by the case of Vera Brittain, well known in the United States for *Testament of Youth* (1933), her moving account of the waste of human life in the First World War. Following two highly successful tours of North America, she was contracted in November 1938 for another visit in January 1940. By September 1939, however, the lecture agency Colston Leigh was urging her to go immediately and lecture throughout the autumn and winter. "Think important," it cabled, "for Anglo-American friendship."[41]

According to Brittain's biographers Paul Berry and Mark Bostridge, the Ministry of Information also was eager to have her tour the United States: "Americans wanted British lecturers, but were also deeply suspicious of unfamiliar visitors from Britain who might be war propagandists in disguise ... A lecturer like Vera, with her longstanding American connections and, more critically, her pacifism, was viewed as being above suspicion, and was therefore in a position to maintain friendly Anglo-American relations while reporting back to Britain on the reactions to the war which she had encountered."[42]

More generally, Brittain could respond to the demand cited by Colston Leigh, for British lecturers who provided first-hand accounts of life in wartime Britain, especially from the female perspective – and, indeed, in the tour she was often advertised as "A Nurse of the Great War." To an apprehensive America, women lecturers presented less of a threat than men. "Women," commented a British Press Service report in 1940, "are likely to be received with less suspicion than men, and in speaking on subjects dealing with the part played by British women in the war, women are usually well received and create a favourable impression."[43]

Brittain herself had ambivalent feelings about touring the United States. In 1937 she had joined Canon Dick Sheppard's Peace Pledge Union, whose roughly 136,000 members made it the most vigorous antiwar voice in Britain, and she was a member of its governing council. In October 1939 she created her own "Letter to Peace Lovers," which reached 2,000 subscribers every fortnight throughout the war. When, in September 1939, Brittain received A.D. Peters' invitation to serve, she replied: "I shall be happy to co-operate with the Ministry of Information in any way which does not conflict with my beliefs as a pacifist. Though I could not undertake any form of military propaganda, I would gladly assist in the study, discussion and exposition of peace aims, preliminary peace terms and peace negotiations."[44]

Having thus declared her pacifism, Brittain was understandably disconcerted to learn of the interest of the Ministry of Information in her going to the United States (it had also, apparently, wanted her husband, George Catlin, to teach there for the duration of the war). "Whole aspect of going u.s.a.," she wrote in her diary, "would certainly differ if one was officially sent. Life unbearably full of complications and upheavals."[45]

Brittain seems to have resolved the issue by concluding that she could tour America with the support of the Ministry of Information, and report back to it, without muting her own pacifist voice. Edward

R. Murrow, who was in Britain broadcasting for CBS, persuaded her
that someone needed to speak there to counteract the more militant
position of Duff Cooper and others, and he offered to try to arrange
for her to broadcast on American radio. In the end, Brittain arrived
in New York on 16 January 1940, having been preceded by Catlin,
who had been lecturing across Canada since October for the Canadian
Institute of International Relations.

Brittain clearly left for America with the support of the Ministry of
Information. When, several hours before her departure from Britain
for Lisbon, she was refused permission to take some of her documents
with her, she sought the help of the ministry. Having learned at the
air terminal that no written material or photographs could be carried
through France, she telephoned Frank Darvall, who arranged for her
to be rushed to the Censorship Department of the General Post Office.
There her lecture notes were censored and sealed, and she was allowed
to proceed.[46]

If the Ministry of Information was satisfied that Brittain would be
an appropriate British representative to the United States, the Foreign
Office emphatically was not. On 2 January it had been informed that
Brittain was carrying a resolution of the Peace Pledge Union stating
that the women of Britain were determined on peace and that they
were appealing to Mrs Roosevelt to do her utmost to bring about a
negotiated end to the war. The Ministry of Information, concluded the
Foreign Office, was not only wrong to have assisted "a crank and a
self-opinionated one at that" to gain an exit permit, but it had helped
Brittain retain the Peace Pledge Union material. Fearing the undesir-
able publicity that would have resulted from preventing her departure,
the Foreign Office decided not to intervene but to ask Lord Lothian to
warn her against injudicious comments and to monitor her activities.[47]

On her arrival in New York, Brittain told reporters that she intended
to lecture on the place of autobiography in literature, the effect of
totalitarian governments on the status of women, and other related
subjects. A suggestion of her ambiguous relationship with the British
government was revealed in her assurance that she would give "a
purely objective description of wartime England."[48] To the question
of how she, an avowed pacifist, was being treated in England, she
responded: "Well, the fact that I am here is proof enough that we have
a democracy."[49]

Over the next twelve weeks, Brittain talked in thirty-eight cities on
such subjects as "Peace – When and How," "Women in Transition,"

"Youth and War," "Wartime England," and "A Personal Confession of Faith: Why I Wrote *Testament of Youth*." In doing so, she seems to have been able both to express her own views and to voice various positions of the British government. In Minneapolis in February, she offered herself as a refutation of the isolationists' charge that British lecturers in the United States were paid propagandists. As proof she pointed to the frequent variance between her comments and official government pronouncements, most notably her repeated insistence on a negotiated peace. While her statements did not bring her government censure, she added, it certainly did not bring her government money.

Examples of her independent commentary can be found in her talk "War-Time England," given in Oneonta, New York, in March. First, she spoke of the "mental blackout" in Britain – the veil of propaganda that was making it increasingly difficult to distinguish truth from falsehood. Reading the comparatively uncensored American press made her feel that she was reading the truth for the first time, she said, adding that America's natural sympathy for Britain would continue if it was not poisoned by British propaganda. She expressed the hope that the United States would "act the part of the great neutral, a part which was lacking in the peace negotiations after the last war," and she told Americans: "I do not want to see your nation go into this war, but to take the place of a detached and powerful neutral at the peace table."[50] In stating that she did not want America's entry into the war, Brittain was echoing the official British public position at the time. A neutral participant in a peace process, however, was far from the role envisaged for the United States by the British government.

On the other hand, Brittain frequently articulated themes encouraged by the British opinion makers, when they did not clash with her own beliefs. Her lecture "Peace – When and How" reiterated the argument that the Allies were at war with Nazism, not with the German people themselves – an important point in the United States, where there were many German immigrants. At a time when British spokesmen were trying to counter the American belief that Britain was a rigid class-controlled society by arguing that the war was a great social leveller, Brittain talked of the sociological impact of the evacuation of children from London to the country. She told an audience in Ann Arbor, Michigan, that upper-class people who had previously had no opportunity to know the working class were now brought into daily contact with children and mothers from the slums.

"It is my sincere desire," she declared, "that this 'first-hand glance' into the lives of the lower classes will lead to a nation-wide movement for social reform."[51] In Toronto, she argued that after the war "there will be a new scheme of things. After all, that was Chamberlain's chief desire. He wanted to be a great social reformer prime minister. That was the reason he wanted to keep out of the war. After the war is over, if we have any money, it will come."[52]

Brittain had not been long in the United States before she reported back to the Ministry of Information. Writing to Frank Darvall from Chicago on 23 January, she described the angry reaction of ordinary Americans to the British practice of stopping and censoring American mail. She also discussed the anglophobia of the Midwest, whose citizens saw Stalin as a greater threat than Hitler, and she enclosed a cutting from the *Chicago Tribune*.

Darvall replied to Brittain on 7 February in a three-page letter, whose length and detailed analysis suggests that special care was being taken with her. His explanation of the government's policy of censoring neutral mail and his comments on anti-British feeling in the United States and Soviet aggression against Finland were not only a response to her concerns but were, in effect, a briefing paper for what she might say when these issues were raised by her audiences.

When the Foreign Office was given a copy of Brittain's 23 January letter to Darvall, someone noted on her file: "Miss Vera Brittain is quite sensible in this letter – may she remain so!"[53] Two weeks later, however, her American tour came under public scrutiny – not in the United States but in her own country. During question period in the House of Commons on 21 February, Sir Henry Page Croft, the right-wing Conservative MP for Bournemouth, asked whether Brittain had had "any connection with the Ministry of Information." Responding "blandly," as Brittain later characterized it, Sir John Reith, who had replaced Macmillan as minister of information in January, replied, "No, Sir, none whatever ... Miss Brittain is not employed by the Ministry of Information and has no connection with it."[54] The ministry's policy of sending no paid lecturers meant, of course, that Brittain was not "employed," but in saying that she had no connection with it Reith was being disingenuous.

The real target of Croft's question was not Brittain herself but the Peace Pledge Union, which was under public attack at the time. Nonetheless, British officials in the United States felt it necessary to warn

Brittain, through her husband, to deny any official connection with the Ministry of Information. On 4 April they wrote to Catlin:

The Ministry of Information has been disturbed at hearing from this side that Vera Brittain was unofficially connected with them. The precise terms of the report are not available, but they hope that any such impression will not be given because it is, of course, contrary to the facts. No doubt your wife would herself not wish her independence to be thus compromised in this way. Unfortunately, Americans so often give an exaggerated interpretation of such facts as permission to leave England so as to give it the stamp of official approval and hence, by a short step, to imply an official relationship. In any case, if the opportunity arises I am sure she will wish to squash any story of the kind.[55]

On her return to London in April, Brittain personally delivered her impressions of the American situation to Basil Mathews, deputy director of the American Division of the Ministry of Information. In early June she met again with Mathews, this time with Catlin present, to "talk over the general Anglo-American situation."[56] With the ministry, she had not blotted her copybook; Darvall was able to report that Lord Lothian was not disturbed by her presence in the United States and that "most of the reports that we have received about her indicated that she has not done any real harm by what she has said and done there."[57] Croft's question, however, had done its damage.

In July, Colston Leigh offered to arrange another autumn lecture tour for Brittain, and Catlin was invited to lecture for a term at Kansas State University. His application for an exit permit was endorsed by the Ministry of Information, but Brittain was surprised to be told by Frank Darvall that it was unlikely that she would be allowed to visit the United States again for the duration of the war.

Berry and Bostridge imply that it was the Ministry of Information that blocked Brittain's exit permit, but documents in the Foreign Office files reveal that the opposition to her travel came not from the ministry but from the Home Office. In August Brittain asked the ministry to support her application for a permit, and the minister, Duff Cooper, agreed that she should be allowed to travel. When, despite this ministerial approval, the Home Office advised the Passport Office to turn Brittain down, Frank Darvall sought the support of T. North Whitehead of the Foreign Office, pointing out that both the American and Secretarial Divisions of the ministry believed that there was a case for an appeal. North Whitehead replied that the Foreign Office was in agreement that to refuse Brittain's exit permit was likely to create publicity more damaging than anything she might say in the United States.[58]

On 15 November 1940, E. St J. Bamford of the Ministry of Information wrote a letter of appeal to F.A. Newsam, pointing out that "the practice of the Passport Office was to refuse applications for exit permits by lecturers unless the Ministry of Information certified that they were travelling on business of national importance." In this case, said Bamford, the ministry had not been consulted by either the Passport Office or the Home Office, and "no mention was made of the fact that the application had received the support of the Ministry of Information." He hoped that the Home Office would reconsider the case. If the permit was still to be denied, he said, "We must leave it to you to justify the decision and to explain the position to Miss Brittain."[59] When the Passport Office had first informed Brittain on 25 September that her exit permit had been refused, it had offered no reason. Nor was an official explanation ever given to her by any other branch of government. Yet for the remainder of the war she was not allowed out of the country.

At almost the same time as Brittain was being prevented from travelling to the United States, Sir Norman Angell, a somewhat unusual candidate for government support, was being encouraged to go. A journalist and author, Angell was known throughout the world for his antiwar book *The Great Illusion*, which had been published in 1910 and revised in 1933. During the First World War, he had been one of the founders of the Union of Democratic Control, an organization that insisted on a workable peace and open diplomacy – which made him *persona non grata* with the Foreign Office. After a brief career as a Labour member of parliament, he was knighted, and in 1933 he was awarded the Nobel Peace Prize.

In spite of these strong pacifist credentials and although he was sixty-seven, Angell was approached one day in 1940 at the Ministry of Information by John Hilton: "Why don't you do a lecture tour in America? The F.O. would welcome it and I'm sure we at the M.O.I." When Angell pointed out that the Foreign Office had discouraged his trips to the United States in the last war, Hilton laughed: "You don't know how much the F.O. has learned since then."

Angell consulted Harold Nicolson, who was parliamentary secretary to the Minister of Information, Duff Cooper, and he was soon told by Hilton: "Get off immediately. Duff Cooper feels more strongly even than I do that you can be of most use in the United States. We can get you a berth on a ship to Halifax in two days." "All so very different," mused Angell, "from my position at the beginning of the first war, when my passport was refused, my writings put on the index, and I was listed as an ideologically dangerous and subversive person."[60]

Following Ministry of Information policy, Angell went to America as if he were an entirely private visitor. Other than the securing of passage, he received no government assistance and, he later claimed, no instructions. His reputation as a Nobel Prize–winning pacifist gave him both a credibility with the American public and an ability to support himself with American dollars on the lecture tour. As it happened, he gave his first lecture within twelve hours of docking in New York, and within a month he was writing a book, *America's Dilemma: Alone or Allied?*, which advocated American entry into the war. When another book, *Let the People Know*, an analysis of what would be needed in the postwar world, was critically acclaimed and made a Book-of-the-Month Club selection, he was flooded with invitations to speak.

Angell spent the rest of the war in the United States, returning home for several weeks each year to renew his credentials as someone who could report personally on the state of wartime Britain. His countless lectures generally focused on two main themes. First, as he told Columbia University students in August 1940, it was an error to see the British Empire as "an estate owned by the British for their private enrichment," since the "undoing of imperialism" had been the outstanding trend in British politics during the previous fifty years.[61] Second, it was dangerous continually to present Russia as an instrument of progress that needed to be strengthened in any peace settlement and Britain as an instrument of reaction whose power should be diminished. These arguments, according to Angell's biographer J.D.B. Miller,[62] had a wide-ranging effect on moderate Americans, and it made him anything but "ideologically dangerous and subversive" in the eyes of the Foreign Office.

Many other writers were judged to meet the criterion of the Ministry of Information that they were "travelling on business of national

importance," and they were persuaded, or at least permitted, to go
to America. In the autumn of 1939 the biographer and historian Philip
Guedalla was passing through the United States on his way back to
Britain from a British Council tour of South America. After consulting
with Lord Lothian, he lectured on the subject "Can the Allies Defeat
Hitlerism?"[63] A year later, Guedalla's agent urged Lothian to persuade him to undertake a lecture tour, since a number of anglophiles
had sent invitations. Lothian telegraphed the ministry, and Duff
Cooper personally wrote to Guedalla to point out that lecturing in
the United States was "a field in which your activities can be most
usefully exerted."[64] Convinced that his special knowledge of South
American culture made him more useful to the ministry's Latin American section, Guedalla declined. Ironically, he soon resigned from his
position there because of the running of the section, and until his
death in 1944 he wrote books supporting the war effort: *Mr Churchill:
A Portrait* (1941), *The Liberators* (1942), *The Two Marshalls* (1943), and
Middle East: A Study in Air Power (1944).

The lyrical poet Alfred Noyes – best known for his epic trilogy *The
Torch-Bearers*, as well as for his patriotism and his love of the sea –
was fifty-nine when the war broke out and was too old to serve. In
December 1939 he wrote to the London *Times* to suggest that the
Ministry of Information be abolished for six months because its
employees were "highly salaried amateur inspectors of the Press."[65]
This attitude did not, however, prevent him from taking his family to
Canada a year later or from having his name added to the British
Library of Information's list of speakers; he lectured extensively in
the United States throughout the war.

Strongly Catholic since his conversion in 1925, Noyes told American
audiences that a decline in morality had led to the European crisis
and that the only solution was a return from neopaganism to Chris-
tianity. He demonized Nazi Germany, telling 1400 members of the
Catholic Carroll Club in New York in 1941 that the American gesture
of welcoming British children "is a perfect illustration of what the
Christian side stands for, while the sinking of the *Benares* in mid-
Atlantic graphically represents what the other side stands for."[66] The
only practising Christian statesman in Europe, he added, was Lord
Halifax, the new British ambassador to the United States.

In his Carroll Club speech and others, Noyes blamed the decline in
morality on the undermining of moral and ethical principles by writers and artists in the previous twenty-five years. The moral decay that

led to the fall of France, he claimed, could be traced to Proust's *Remembrance of Things Past*, whose characters showed marked signs of perversion.[67] The British counterparts were D.H. Lawrence and James Joyce, whose *Ulysses* was "wretched, chaotic and a disgrace to literature and a disgrace to our civilization because of the acceptance it has received by a large body of half-baked intellectuals."[68] Appearing in April 1942 on a platform at Columbia University with its President Nicholas Murray Butler and Herman Rauschning, Noyes concluded that "the whole trend of our intellectual life and of the world today was 'destructive.'"[69]

While Noyes's demonizing of Hitler's Germany was consistent with the British propaganda campaign, his attributing the European war to the influence of artists and intellectuals was uncommon. But it was a message that would have appealed to the segment of the American population that was looking for scapegoats. A *New York Times* editorial in April 1942 suggested that Noyes's attack would attract a number of people: "His words about some of the demigods of as late as a decade ago will meet with far less indignant protest, and even with a good deal of quiet support, than would have been the case only a few years ago."[70]

According to Eric Ambler, who applied to travel to the United States in 1940, "plenty of authors were doing lecture tours abroad for the MOI ... but I had one thing in my favour: I was becoming a substantial dollar earner and could prove it."[71] Interviewed at the Ministry of Information by Denis Brogan, an Oxford specialist in American history and politics, he was queried about the American groups he might address. "How would you," asked Brogan, "answer a bloody-minded American Rotarian who wants to know when Britain is going to repay her debt to America incurred during the Great War?"[72] Ambler's response, gleaned from newspaper editorials, satisfied Brogan, and he proceeded to the eastern United States, where he gave a number of lectures.

In July 1940 Jan Struther (the pen name of Joyce Maxtone Graham) moved to New York with two of her children. A writer of poems and short pieces for *Punch*, the *Spectator*, and the *New Statesman* in the 1930s, she became very well known in the United States when her collection of essays, *Mrs Miniver*, became a best-seller and a Book-of-the-Month Club selection. On the strength of this popularity, she was invited to give a series of lectures. Explaining that she could neither do anything useful on the land in Britain nor carry stretchers, and was merely another mouth to feed, she told a reporter that she had arrived "not as a visitor but as an immigrant."[73] With this explanation, she instantly gained a credibility with Americans that she would not have had as an apparent deserter of Britain in time of trouble.

Struther did in fact remain in the United States for the rest of her life, and during the war her lectures on behalf of the British war effort in New York, Toledo, Rochester, Cleveland, Flint, Boston, Los Angeles, and many other cities were identified as especially useful in a British Press Service survey:

In presenting an optimistic picture of the ultimate outcome of the war, in which she does not attempt to minimize the hardships but is full of hope for the future, she is given a good press and is obviously popular. Her lectures usually centre around the "Mrs Minivers" of Britain and the part they play in the England of today. Miss Struther, in asking for all aid short of partici-pation, shows a Britain fighting for a democracy which "will be worth its weight in gold to the whole world," and she tells of the changes in the British social structure "which are so great that in every country with the exception of Britain and the United States they could not have come about except through revolution."[74]

In March 1942 Struther's speech to six hundred women at a gath-ering of the International Federation of Business and Professional Women in New York described the early days of the war in Britain, when women were faced with a kind of "sitzkrieg." At a time when there was no real deprivation, only the prospect of shortages, and no spectacular sacrifices, only a slow erosion of the way of life they were used to, woman had to fight "the insidious invaders such as doubt, fear, anxiety and the very human desire to gossip and exchange infor-mation."[75] In September 1942 she was the guest speaker at the opening of a fundraising campaign by the New York and Brooklyn Federations of Jewish Charities, stressing that in Britain some wartime social ser-vices such as communal feeding centres would be maintained after the war and would help break down regional differences.

Pamela Frankau, daughter of the novelist Gilbert Frankau and her-self a journalist, novelist, and short story writer, went to the United States in March 1940. For nine months, she worked in Hollywood and travelled extensively, lecturing and discussing war issues with the American families with whom she stayed. Wherever she went, she cast a practised novelist's eye on both Americans and fellow Britons, and on her return to London in November she submitted a lengthy report of her observations to the Ministry of Information and the Foreign Office.

According to Frankau, the accounts sent back by the American war correspondents were ineffective because readers had quickly become accustomed to a steady diet of stories told in the same American voice. Moreover, letters from England were discounted because Americans assumed that they were always heavily censored. On the other hand, argued Frankau, "nothing impresses the American mind with such authority as the human voice saying 'I was. I saw. I did.' They repeat the first-hand stories again and again." Thus, "private persons arriving in the States to fulfil lecture contracts have the real opportunity for propaganda," and they are more effective if they return to Britain periodically to renew their knowledge of the "civilian front line."[76]

This analysis – and other comments about the effectiveness of films, the behaviour of British refugees in the United States, and the American political situation – impressed the Foreign Office, causing T. North Whitehead to note: "Miss Frankau is evidently a brilliant observer and states her impressions concisely. Well worth reading with care."[77] Within weeks, the Foreign Office was encouraging her to return to the United States after a few months. "We should certainly be ready to support your application for an exit permit when the time came," wrote Sir David Scott. "With your understanding of the American psychology, you are unusually well equipped for the job."[78] Frankau decided against returning to the United States, however, preferring to join the Auxiliary Territorial Service, where she worked herself up to captain. Her knowledge of the United States nonetheless continued to be used in a number of BBC broadcasts to North America.

Phyllis Bentley, a novelist from Halifax, best known for *Inheritance*, a saga of the Yorkshire textile industry, had been a secretary in the Ministry of Munitions in the First World War. On the outbreak of the Second World War, she put her name forward to the Ministry of Information and the Women's Voluntary Service. When by late 1940 she had not been employed, she undertook a three-month tour of the United States because, as she said, "It seemed to me that I should be more useful to my country lecturing on *In England Now* to the still-isolationist Americans, than simply sitting all day twiddling my thumbs."[79] Initially refused an exit permit by the Passport Office, she later secured one with the help of the American Division of the

Ministry of Information, "which wished me to make my tour."[80] Her
lecture notes were approved by the Censorship Bureau and sealed in
a package with seven official seals, and after a delay of several months,
the ministry secured passage for her from Liverpool to New York.

Bentley arrived in the United States in mid-January 1941 and in the
following five months gave over fifty lectures and wrote articles and
reviews for the American press. According to Harold Latham, editor-
in-chief of the Macmillan Company in New York, she was a "brilliant
lecturer" who "held large audiences at close attention."[81] Her wartime
audiences were "curious, eager, excited, enthusiastic," said Bentley,
adding: "I honestly felt that in my small way I did a good job for my
country."[82] Part of that job was influencing American opinion over
the dinner table at the White House, where Bentley was impressed
by Eleanor Roosevelt's skill at eliciting the views of the guests on
certain political questions. By the end of the meal, she recalled, the
matters would be settled in the president's mind.

On Bentley's return to Britain in July, the Ministry of Information
awarded her an "A" priority for ship's passage. When her departure
was delayed for some weeks, Pamela Frankau wrote to the Foreign
Office on her behalf, arguing: "She has done a good job lecturing and
you already know my views on the desirability of English lecturers
coming and going, particularly going."[83] Bentley had impressed the
Ministry of Information as well, and on her return Frank Darvall
recommended that she be hired to work in the publications section
of the British Library of Information, particularly in supplying material about the parts played by British women in the war effort.

Bentley was eventually appointed to the American Division in
March 1942, with responsibility for providing information to the
British Information Services in the United States. This included up-
to-date reference books, feature articles about the British war effort
for publication in American magazines, and a monthly bulletin called
Britain, to be issued in New York. As well, she wrote a booklet entitled
Here Is America and numerous articles about American issues, and
gave thirty-one lectures about the United States to various military
units stationed in Yorkshire.

Bentley remained with the Ministry of Information until December
1944, continuing to work in the American Division. In the autumn of
1943 she was assigned to the British Information Services in New York
for a few months, and during her stay she attended the giant Writers'
Congress held in Hollywood. In the midst of lengthy, platitudinous

speeches, Bentley won over the twelve hundred delegates by bringing greetings from the Yorkshire Bookmen and her little Halifax Author's Circle, thereby reminding them that the literary culture which they shared still flourished in such societies in beleaguered Britain. Her more serious article on the cultural changes in Britain during the war was published in book form in the United States in *Writers' Congress, 1943*.

Another British literary visitor to the United States in 1941 was the novelist Mary Dolling O'Malley, whose marriage to the diplomat Owen O'Malley required that she adopt the pen name Ann Bridge. At the outbreak of the war, she was a well-established author, best known for the novels *Peking Picnic* and *Enchanted Nightshade*, and within a month she was employed by the Ministry of Information "in rather a vague" capacity: "I was to use such contacts as I had in the United States to place articles on England's war effort over there, to ascertain the right type and length of article and then to coax English writers to produce them."[84] This involved devising sketches for the desired articles and then corresponding with prospective authors and appropriate newspapers and journals. As well, Bridge was to write a book on England before and just after the outbreak of war, specifically for publication in the United States,[85] but this project was never completed.

Bridge left the ministry in the spring of 1940 to join her husband, who was then serving in the diplomatic service in Hungary, and a year later they had to flee to the United States by way of Russia and Japan. Arriving in San Francisco on 1 June, she spent the first few weeks in Hollywood, where she was offered the job of writing an English girl's dialogue for a screenplay about the flight from Paris in 1940. Finding the film colony too artificial, Bridge travelled to the eastern seaboard and arranged with Colston Leigh for a lecture tour in the winter of 1941–42. On the way, she lectured to the Red Cross in New Orleans, accepting no fee. In Boston, in early December, she was scheduled to address a women's discussion group on the topic "Should America Enter the War?" but the Japanese attack on Pearl Harbor rendered the question superfluous.

Although her marriage to a British diplomat meant that Bridge had to be cautious in her public utterances, it gave her an entry into the circle of international diplomats who were familiar to each other through years of foreign service. Her *modus operandi* there was described in an interview with Robert Van Gelder in the *New York Times*: "By the simple strategy of declaring that she is half-American – which is true – and failing to add that her father is English and that she was brought up in England, Miss Bridge has lured a number of Germans whom she has met in various parts of the world since the war began into comparatively free and easy conversation. The discomfiture of those who cannot understand Hitler's dervishy policies is pretty to watch, says Miss Bridge."[86]

One occasion when Bridge's diplomacy failed her shows how carefully Britons had to tread in the United States. At a meeting at the Yale Club with John Farrar of Farrar and Rinehart, Stephen Vincent Benét, Walter Millis, and other journalists, it was decided that she should reverse her role and interpret to her fellow Britons the American reaction to being at war. Her article "America Goes to War," published in the *Times*, was well received at home and the Foreign Office was pleased, but when copies reached Boston there was an outcry of indignation. Her comment that Americans had come to see war as "a disfiguring and rather shameful disease, like ringworm or impetigo, which nice clean nations simply don't get"[87] led thirty-two people to telephone the British consulate to demand that she be deported. Bridge returned to Britain on 2 June 1942, but it was at her own choosing.

In September 1941 the novelist Charles Morgan arrived in the United States, where he was well known for his Hawthornden Prize–winning *The Fountain* (1932) and for *Sparkenbroke* (1936). He had offered his services in the event of war to the Admiralty as early as February 1939, and by September he was editing a weekly intelligence report for the Royal Navy. This lecture tour, ostensibly at the invitation of the Institute of International Education, based in New York, was strongly supported by the Ministry of Information.[88]

On 19 September, as a guest of the New York Drama Critics Circle at the Harvard Club, Morgan argued that the state-controlled wartime economy in Britain provided a basis for a democracy that was not subject to the boom and slump fluctuations of the past. Thus, he implied, the average Briton would come out of the war with a greater sense of security than before. Two days later he was a guest of honour, along with a former RAF pilot, at a luncheon of the Common Interests Committee of the English Speaking Union, which was attended by Sir Gerald Campbell, director general of the British Information Services, and Alice Duerr Miller, the American author of the immensely popular poem "The White Cliffs."

In an interview in October with Robert Van Gelder in the *New York Times*, Morgan attempted to counter the view of many Americans that

Britain was at war only to preserve its empire. "One gathered from his talk," reported Van Gelder, "that one purpose he had in coming here … was to give such assurance as one individual can that the English are not as interested in hanging on to property as they formerly were. 'One thing we know' [Morgan said] 'is that there is to be no reward for us of ease or gain or comfort. Perhaps for our grandsons. But we do not seek in victory vengeance, profit or even the preservation of what we possess. All victory can mean is an opportunity to replant, to safeguard the early growth, to leave the maturity to others. We're dedicated to the future, the only sensible thing to do. What possible use is care for your possessions with bombs smashing them, and flaming bombers dropping into your street?'"[89]

Morgan had always had an affinity for France, a relationship that had been strengthened by his award of the Legion of Honour in 1936 in recognition of his writing. This gave him an authority with the French Resistance, which smuggled his articles into occupied France, and in the United States it made him a useful advocate for France. The French, since their capitulation to Hitler in June 1940, had been viewed contemptuously by many Americans as a decadent, corrupt nation that had sold out to the Germans.

In 1942, however, the United States had entered the war, and since France was now an important ally, it was necessary to rehabilitate her in American eyes. Thus Morgan, like Somerset Maugham – another English writer with long and close ties with France – could speak authoritatively on the essential civilized France that could arise out of the ashes of the humiliation of 1940. At a luncheon sponsored by the Coordinating Council of French Relief Societies at the Plaza Hotel in New York, on 9 January 1942, Morgan argued that the alleged political corruption that had led to the French disaster had destroyed, not France but its "decaying Third Republic." "In the grand strategy of civilization," he declared, "France is inevitably included. Without her, we English and you Americans shall be in danger of turning what should be the University of the World into a vocational training college."[90]

Morgan's message to his American listeners may have been what the Ministry of Information wanted, but whether his delivery of it was effective is another matter. In July 1940 Sir Thomas Bazley of the War Office had recommended that a Morgan article entitled "Armour for Civilians" be broadcast on radio because "its value in the U.S.A. might be considerable." But the BBC officials had rejected Morgan as the reader because he was "a hopeless broadcaster" who sounded "timid & prim & precious."[91] Years later, Harold Latham described Morgan as having a "forbidding personality. Severe in manner, rarely smiling, speaking in low tones with carefully chosen words" "He seemed cold, unresponsive," noted Latham. "I felt that he was looking down his nose at me all the time."[92] Alistair Cooke, who was a correspondent in the United States during the Second World War, corroborated this assessment, describing Morgan as being in accent and manner "just what every isolationist American thought of as arch or snobby upper-middle-class Brits."[93]

Of course, there were other ways of influencing American public opinion than merely from the lecture platform, and Morgan was likely more successful at the dinner table and in the reception hall. In Rochester, New York, for example, he stayed in the house of the president of the university, who had been at Balliol College, Oxford, shortly after Morgan and whose wife had been brought up in France. In his travels, Morgan said, he met the poor scholars and the very rich merchants. Back in London in July 1942, he discussed with the Foreign Office the idea of setting up an interdepartmental body to encourage cultural links between Britain and America through universities and colleges.[94] In the final year of the war, he travelled to France and Holland, writing about his experiences for both British and American readers.

Another of Colston Leigh's British lecturers who travelled to the United States in 1941 was Major General Ian Hay Beith, more popularly known as the author and playwright Ian Hay. During the First World War, he had twice been sent across the Atlantic by the Foreign Office to speak for the British cause. Early in the Second World War, he served in the War Office as director of information, but he resigned from this position early in 1941. At the end of April he wrote to the foreign secretary, Anthony Eden, requesting permission to go to the United States on the same basis as in the last war, carefully pointing out that he met the requirements of British policy in that the invitation had been "direct and unsolicited." In fact, the invitation had been "direct" only in that Colston Leigh had directly approached the British Embassy in Washington, which then forwarded the invitation to London with its support.[95]

Agreeing to Beith's request, Eden advised him to consult the Ministry of Information, which would make the application for an exit permit. When Beith docked in New York on 20 September, he described himself as being on "detached duty," a phrase that perfectly captures the ambiguous nature of the role of so many of the touring British writers. In any case, his first public statement in America – a confident assertion that Britain was "one hundred times better prepared than it was a year ago"[96] – echoed the current position of the British government. Unfortunately, Beith's name was not widely known in the United States, and, disappointed by a lack of engagements, he soon returned to Britain.

"Detached duty" describes the American visit of another figure with First World War experience – the distinguished journalist and author Sir Philip Gibbs. During the first winter of the war, he worked as a war correspondent in France, but in October 1941 he went to the United States for a lecture tour that lasted nine months. He had been preceded there by his son Anthony, who was working as a journalist but was also speaking on behalf of Britain and the British relief effort and generally presenting the British point of view.

In New York, Gibbs gave two lectures at Columbia University, the first of which was presided over by its pro-interventionist president, Nicholas Murray Butler. Butler then, as he customarily did with visiting Britons, entertained Gibbs at dinner with professors and their wives who were sympathetic to Britain. In Youngstown, Ohio, Gibbs addressed the directors of steel corporations, bankers, and other executives associated with the steel industry who had come from Detroit, Cleveland, and Pittsburgh. In Boston, he spoke at the Tavern Club to judges, lawyers, doctors, professors, architects, scientists, and other leaders in civic life. Other lectures took him across the United States: to Columbus, Ohio; Tulsa, Oklahoma; San Francisco; Baltimore; Lexington, Kentucky; Lansing, Michigan; Cleveland; Washington; Worcester, Massachusetts; and other places.

In Anadarko, Oklahoma, Gibbs addressed a very different sort of audience – native Americans – and he was surprised to discover that the common literary and cultural heritage of Britain and the United States had become part of their heritage: "They were [reading] the books upon which I had been brought up and which I had devoured as a boy. *Little Men* and *Little Women*, *Robinson Crusoe*, *David Copperfield*, *A Tale of Two Cities*, *Treasure Island*, *Sherlock Holmes*, and all the old favourites. It seemed to me astonishing, or at least remarkable, that these children of the tribes should have as their mental background the works of Dickens and Scott and stories like *The Scarlet Pimpernel*, which I saw on their shelves."[97]

In general, Gibbs learned that while Americans would not tolerate obvious propaganda, they were eager to hear about life in wartime Britain, the British war effort, and the chances of an Allied success.

"I have no natural gifts of eloquence or oratory," he claimed, with perhaps a touch of false modesty, "but just can tell a plain straight tale of things seen. I told them about England under bombardment, and what happened in towns and villages, and in the air-raid shelters, and in the minds of our folk. Something reached out to them."[98]

Because of his reputation in the United States, Gibbs was much interviewed and photographed, and broadcast on radio. Even if he arrived in a city at six-thirty in the morning, reporters would be searching the train for him or stationed at his hotel to go up to his room to get his views on the latest developments in the war. He had constantly to respond tactfully to the tricky questions about Britain's attitude to Indian independence, its blockade of food sent by relief organizations to Belgium and Holland, and its failure to strike at the Continent while Hitler was preoccupied with the invasion of Russia.

Gibbs returned to Britain in the summer of 1942, and the following year he edited a collection of seventeen essays entitled *Bridging the Atlantic*. Its tone was set by the Liberal Party's Sir Archibald Sinclair in his essay "The Common Ideal": "The two nations are bound together by a common language and literature, and by common religious and political beliefs. Both peoples have the same faith in individualism, both have what Lincoln called 'a patient confidence in the ultimate justice of the people.'"[99]

Much of the impetus for Gibbs and the other author/lecturers who toured the United States in 1940 and 1941 came from Duff Cooper, the current minister of information. In the first year of the war, he had strongly disagreed with the British government's policy of discouraging overt propaganda, and as minister he was determined to send any lecturer or visitor who could be useful without arousing excessive suspicion. His successor Brendan Bracken did not share this conviction, and in August 1941 he announced to the House of Commons that the Ministry of Information would send no more lecturers because they did more harm than good. In response to this statement, Frank W. Richardson of the New York Society of Colonial Wars' committee on speakers wrote to the *Times* to point out that many British speakers had performed admirably in America and only a few had failed. Among those he singled out for praise were Sir Philip Gibbs, Charles Morgan, Jan Struther, Ian Hay Beith, and Phyllis Bentley. Moreover, S.K. Ratcliffe and Cecil Roberts, he reported, had been "highly popular on American platforms for a quarter of a century" and were especially effective for their oratory, tact, and knowledge of such issues as independence for India. "Anglo-American friendship,"

Richardson concluded, "is firmer than ever before, and it owes much to these British lecturers."[100]

The visits of British authors to the United States do seem to have been reduced following Bracken's announcement, but they did not cease entirely. In fact, after Pearl Harbor, there was less need to disguise government support for lecturers. Thus, Mary Agnes Hamilton was officially sent by the Ministry of Information in the autumn of 1942, and Phyllis Bentley's second visit, in 1943, was as a paid employee of the British Information Services. Bernard Newman, who was already in the United States when Bracken made his statement, had his travel expenses paid by the Ministry of Information.

Newman was a prolific writer of novels and non-fiction books about espionage, travel, and European affairs. A grand-nephew of George Eliot, he had served in the First World War and later gained a reputation as a student of military strategy when his novel *The Cavalry Went Through* (1930) was quoted with praise by the military historian Basil Liddell Hart. During the interwar period, Newman had been a professional lecturer, travelling in more than sixty countries.

Shortly after Dunkirk, Newman joined the Ministry of Information as a staff lecturer, giving, he later estimated, about five hundred talks on twenty-eight subjects during the first year. As well, he produced a number of books to promote the British cause: *The Story of Poland* (1940), *Siegfried Spy* (1940), *Savoy! Corsica! Tunis!* (1940), *Death to the Fifth Column* (1941), *One Man's View* (1941), *Secret Weapon* (1942), and *The New Europe* (1942). The novel *Secret Weapon* had Churchill as a character, complete with a fictional speech in the House of Commons – a Churchillian rhetoric which Newman then used as a peroration for his own lectures. In a wonderful confusion of life and art, Newman's invention began to be quoted in newspapers throughout Britain as if the words were those of the prime minister himself.

According to Newman, a director of the Ministry of Information asked him in the summer of 1942 to tour the United States to help dispel some of the American ignorance of the British. After consulting the British high commissioner in Ottawa, Malcolm MacDonald, and being invited to speak across Canada, he began his American visit in Washington. There he met with President Roosevelt and lectured at a forum for senators, members of Congress, senior officials, and civil servants on such matters as India, the Second Front, Churchill, censorship, sabotage, British communism, air power, and Europe after the war. As well, a radio program he did with Henry Baukhage reached an audience estimated at eleven million and led to many more invitations to broadcast over more local networks throughout the country.

From Washington, Newman travelled across the United States to Alabama, Kansas City, Santa Fe, Albuquerque, Hollywood, San Francisco, and other points. In Chicago he spoke to an audience of four thousand, and at one army camp there were a thousand soldiers present and many more thousands listening around loudspeakers. Just as J.B. Priestley's Yorkshire accent was more appealing to North American radio listeners than the usual Oxbridge/BBC sound, so too was Newman's Lancashire voice. "Not even my worst enemy," he said, "would call me 'high hat' or a 'stuffed shirt' ... Had I the cleverest speaker in the world at my disposal, I would not send him to the U.S.A. if he had what is commonly called an 'Oxford accent.' Nobody would listen to him – particularly if he carried with it evidence of belief in his superior mind and tradition. The best ambassador ... is the ordinary man; politicians may wrangle, but I will back the British plumber to get on terms with his American colleague within five minutes."[101]

When Newman heard of Bracken's announcement that no more lecturers would be sent across the Atlantic, he countered: "I see no reason why cultural lecturers should be held back; if they are propagandists at all, they proclaim ideals which should be sacred to us all."[102] For his own part, Newman's talks went far beyond the common cultural heritage, and every audience contained several isolationists who were ready to ask an awkward question and members of the Hearst press who were ready to quote an injudicious reply. Like many other lecturers, however, his ideas filtered into the American public discourse. Noting that a speaker's message is not restricted to his visible audience, he later wrote that he found some of his arguments being quoted across America: "Especially replies to questions which often lend themselves to columnist use; they were seldom acknowledged, but that did not trouble me a whit."[103]

Newman flew back to Britain in late 1942 and turned to lecturing British audiences about their American allies. As well, he wrote an account of his months in the United States, *American Journey* (1943), and he wrote three more war books over the next two years.

Mary Agnes Hamilton, another employee of the Ministry of Information, was a novelist, historian, and author of the political biographies *J. Ramsay MacDonald* (1929) and *Sidney and Beatrice Webb* (1933). Her novel *Dead Yesterday* (1916) had provoked a controversy because of its description of the dilemma faced by the British intellectual on the outbreak of war in August 1914. She joined the ministry in February 1940 and then in 1941 moved to the Ministry of Reconstruction, where she served on the committee that developed the Beveridge Report on Social Insurance and Allied Services, the blueprint for Britain's postwar social legislation. The latter work led to her being sent by the American Division of the Ministry of Information to speak in the United States in November 1942. Since the Beveridge Report was strong evidence of the British government's intention to create a new, more democratic, and more egalitarian society, the ministry was anxious to have it advertised in America.

Shortly after her arrival in New York, Hamilton spoke for Britain at the *New York Herald Tribune* forum at which Wendell Willkie denounced Churchill for declining to liquidate the British Empire. Although the Beveridge Report was generally well received, it inevitably drew fire from those concerned about British socialism, in particular the medical faculty in Seattle, which refused to sanction Hamilton's talk because Beveridge referred to a National Health Service.[104]

Back in Britain, Hamilton rejoined the Ministry of Information in May 1944 and was assigned to the American Division to assist with the provision of material to the British Information Services in New York, especially that which would help dispel American suspicion of British imperialism. "I had learned from direct inspection," she recalled, "how necessary that was."[105]

James Lansdale Hodson, a novelist and playwright who had served in the First World War and then worked as a journalist, toured the United States in the winter of 1943–44. Like Gibbs, he was a war correspondent at the beginning of the war, and over the next few years he published a series of diaries which captured the feel of daily life in Britain and on the various battlefields: *Through the Dark Night* (1941), *Towards the Morning* (1941), *Before Daybreak* (1942), *War in the Sun* (1942), and *Home Front* (1944). As well, he worked on the official films *Desert Victory* and *Tunisian Victory* and broadcast to North America.

In the United States, Hodson was more of a visitor influencing opinion across the dinner table, but he also lectured at Reed College and other universities, gave press conferences, and "addressed some remarks to the American people."[106] On his return to England, he wrote another diary, *And Yet I Like America*, a plea for mutual understanding and respect intended for both British and American readers.

From Cecil Roberts and S.K. Ratcliffe in 1939 to J.L. Hodson in 1944, there was a stream of British authors who were sent to the United States by the Ministry of Information; and if they were not sent, they were encouraged and assisted by the ministry because they would be of use. As well, there were the British writers already in America in some professional capacity, who lectured and influenced public opinion through social channels. James Hilton, author of *Goodbye, Mr Chips* and *Shangri-La* (filmed as *Lost Horizon*), was writing screenplays in Hollywood and speaking for Britain up and down the West Coast. C.S. Forester, well known to Americans because of the success of his three Horatio Hornblower novels, published in the late 1930s, was also a screenwriter who had lived in California for some years, and he worked for the British Information Services and was a popular lecturer. Roald Dahl, who had seen combat in the RAF in the Middle East, joined the British Embassy in Washington in January 1942 and became a familiar figure in Washington's political and social milieu.

Few of the authors discussed in this chapter could be considered major figures of the British literary world – either in critical reputation or in popularity with the general reading public. They were useful because they were familiar with the United States, could speak to particular issues, and had plausible reasons to be in the country. In 1940, however, three British writers whose names would be familiar to the vast majority of Americans – H.G. Wells, Noel Coward, and Somerset Maugham – toured America with the encouragement of the Ministry of Information. Two of these excursions became public relations disasters, while the third was a measured success.

5

Uncoordinated Observations
Noel Coward and H.G. Wells

In the summer of 1940 Henry Ludwig Mond, the second Lord Melchett, whose company Imperial Chemicals Industries was heavily involved in the manufacture of special weapons and munitions, spent four months in the United States discussing war strategy with American officials and the British Embassy in Washington. On his return to Britain in October, he sent a nineteen-page report on Anglo-American relations to the Oxford physicist Frederick Lindemann (later Viscount Cherwell), Churchill's most influential scientific adviser. When this document was forwarded to the Foreign Office, it was of particular interest because of Melchett's recommendation that there be greater coordination of the visits of prominent Britons to America:

During the past weeks several British authors with an intimate knowledge of the United States and a wide appeal to their reading and theatrical public – in some cases equal to the most popular American literary and dramatic authors – have been in, or passed through the United States. I have in mind Mr Wells, Sir Norman Angell, Mr Coward, Mr Somerset Maugham. One of the great advantages which we have in dealing with America is common language and, therefore, common knowledge of each other's current literature, but there does not seem to have been any concerted effort to bring these individuals into any plan or scheme for the assistance of our war effort, and in certain cases their uncoordinated observations have been the cause of controversy at home which has by no means assisted the idea of British national unity in the present emergency upon which America so much relies and so much hopes for after the painful object lessons of the disintegration of France and other European countries as a result, in popular opinion, of internal disaffection.

This is not necessarily a question of severe regimentation but I am convinced that the patriotism of these and other prominent men of letters whose affairs might bring them to the United States at the present time is such that they would be only too willing to help in any general scheme under the coordinating influence of a prominent and responsible individual resident in the United States specifically for that purpose and under the guidance and influence of the Ambassador in person.[1]

On one level, Lord Melchett's comments are a reiteration of the argument that propaganda points could be effectively scored by the presence of famous British authors to remind Americans of the common linguistic and literary traditions shared by Britain and the United States. However, his reference to the "uncoordinated observations" that had led to controversy at home and the appearance of British disunity was made as a result of the disastrously negative publicity surrounding the visits of two of the four authors he mentioned. Except for a Boston lecture in which Sir Norman Angell annoyed Americans by suggesting that the RAF was fighting not for Britain but for the United States, he had spoken judiciously, and Somerset Maugham had only just arrived in New York when Melchett made his report. But the visits of Noel Coward and H.G. Wells, the other two very well known writers who visited the United States in 1940, were public relations fiascos.

In 1940 Noel Coward was well known in America as a multitalented everyman of the theatre: playwright, actor, singer, dancer, director, producer, and composer. Almost a dramatic chameleon, he had been acclaimed for writing such highly polished comedies of manners as *Hay Fever* (1925), but was also known for more serious studies of the brittle, disillusioned post–First-World War generation, such as *The Vortex* (1924), a play about a drug addict with a fixation for his mother. As well, he had written musicals (*Bitter Sweet*, 1929) and operettas (*Conversation Piece*, 1934), and a highly successful collection of one-act plays performed in groups of three under the title *Tonight at 8.30* (1936). Although it interested Americans far less than the British, *Cavalcade* – his jingoistic saga of an English family and life above and below stairs from the Boer War to the end of the First World War – enjoyed a great success in 1931.

Of course, Coward's greatest creation was "Noel Coward," his own public persona. From the time in 1925 when he had been photographed in bed wearing a Chinese dressing gown and an expression of drugged stupor (a result of his having blinked at the photographer's flash), he had come to epitomize sophistication and even decadence. He became, according to his biographer Philip Hoare, a symbol of the jazz age[2] (in Cecil Beaton's words, "sleek and satiny, clipped and well groomed, with a cigarette, a telephone, or a cocktail at hand.")[3] "For the first time since Oscar Wilde," says Hoare, "a writer's appearance seemed as important as what he wrote."[4]

What Coward wrote – and said – was nonetheless an essential part of his public persona, and here too he resembled Wilde. Like the author of *The Importance of Being Earnest*, he believed that the function of the theatre was to amuse rather than educate or reform, and he too became famous for a quick and flippant wit delivered with an air of cool detachment. As a result, reviewers and critics frequently called him frivolous, arch, trivial, thin, brittle, superior, or insolent, a judgment epitomized by Hannen Swaffer's describing him as "an expert in putting on the boards flippancy, froth and inconsequence, so expertly shimmered that, trifling as it is, it looks like genius."[5] However ungenerous Swaffer's characterization may have been, it represented the popular view of Coward, which was no impediment to success in the theatre but which prevented him from playing the part he envisaged for himself in the Second World War.

During the last year of the First World War, the eighteen-year-old Coward had been turned down for active service on medical grounds, having induced the symptoms of fever by drinking a potion. After being attached to the Artists' Rifles OTC and suffering a nervous breakdown, he was discharged from the army with a small pension. Perhaps haunted by a sense of having thus shirked his responsibilities, he was eager to serve his country in some meaningful capacity when war broke out again twenty-one years later.

Coward got his opportunity in the summer of 1939 when Sir Campbell Stuart – a veteran of the First World War propaganda campaign who was organizing covert propaganda for the coming war – invited him to set up a bureau of propaganda in Paris to liaise with the Commissariat d'information under another playwright, Jean Giradoux. However, when Coward sought the advice of Winston Churchill, he was told that he would be no good in the intelligence service. "Get into a warship and see some action," Churchill told him. "Go and sing to them when the guns are firing – that's your job!"[6] A disappointed Coward wanted to do more than merely sing "Mad Dogs and Englishmen" to sailors. "I knew in my innermost heart," he wrote later, "that if I was intelligently used by the government, preferably in the field of propaganda, where my creative ability, experience of broadcasting and knowledge of people could be employed, I could probably do something really constructive."[7]

Coward took up his position in Paris in early September 1939 and remained there until the middle of April. His phony war in the City of Light seems to have confirmed the suspicions of his critics. As if to prove Lady Mendl's wish that this should be a "gay war," he moved first into the Ritz and then into a newly decorated apartment across the Place Vendome near Van Cleef & Arpels. Together with his companion, Cole Lesley, Coward lunched at Maxim's, dined with the Duke and Duchess of Windsor, and partied at Lady Mendl's Villa Trianon in Versailles.

Inevitably, Coward's Paris life came to the attention of the British press, which demanded to know what this theatrical sophisticate was doing there. The *Daily Telegraph* reported that he had been seen "sauntering along the Rue Royale in naval uniform,"[8] and the *Sunday Pictorial* continued the attack by featuring him in a two-page article entitled "The Civilians in Uniform." As Philip Hoare has pointed out, Coward had simply been wearing a stylish navy-blue blazer, which could be mistaken for naval dress, but the damage had been done. On his next visit to England, Churchill questioned him about the allegations and became convinced that Coward's public reputation was such that it would preclude his working in sensitive positions, particularly in intelligence work.

By March 1940 Coward had grown bored with his Paris routine, which had become repetitive and unproductive, and Sir Campbell Stuart suggested that he should take a six-week leave in the United States. While there, said Stuart, he could "travel about a bit, listen to what was being said, talk to leading newspaper owners and editors, etc., and obtain a certain amount of first-hand information on the general attitude of mind."[9] The Foreign Office recognized that Coward knew America well, and it was reassured by his promise not to attempt any overt propaganda there:

On arrival he will refuse to discuss the war and will say that he is on holiday, but if requested, he will consent to sing a few songs in broadcast, and perhaps speak a little in a flippant vein. But he intends to take great care to do nothing that might be described as propaganda. During his visit he might fly over to Hollywood in order to tell some of the English film stars what he thinks about them for tootling off from Europe as soon as war was declared and for making disparaging remarks about this country.[10]

Coward arrived in New York on 20 April and, as promised, told the press awaiting at dockside that he was on leave from his position in Paris to attend to theatre and film interests in the United States. As well, he "sang a few songs" at the huge Allied Relief Ball held at the Hotel Astor on 10 May, and spoke to the women members of the American Theatre Wing of the Allied Relief Fund in June, promising to tell Paris about the wonderful things they were doing. Leaving New York, he made public appearances in Salt Lake City, Chicago, San Francisco, Omaha, Cleveland, and Cincinnati, and he visited the British enclave in Los Angeles. While in the film colony, he stayed at the home of Cary Grant who, according to Charles Higham and Roy Moseley, was then working for British Intelligence.[11]

On his return to the East Coast in June, Coward reported to Lord Lothian his conviction that the young British actors who were remaining in Hollywood when Britain was in crisis were creating an unfavourable impression in the United States. The ambassador agreed and recommended to the secretary of state for war that they be urged to return to Britain and employed in the recreation and entertainment of troops and civilians.[12] Lothian was told that the National Services Act did not apply to British citizens living abroad and he should use persuasion to get young actors to go back and offer their services. This he did, though he also advised older British actors such as Cedric Hardwicke, C. Aubrey Smith, and Dame May Whitty to remain and champion the cause through Hollywood films.

Coward also did his share of meeting influential Americans at the dinner table and over drinks. In Washington he discussed the war and the political situation over dinner with the journalist Joseph Alsop, Supreme Court Justice Felix Frankfurter, and two senators, and then met with another leading journalist, Walter Lippmann. These encounters paled, however, in comparison with his two meetings with President Roosevelt. Paul Willert, an old friend of Eleanor Roosevelt, had given Coward a letter of introduction, and this led to an invitation to dinner at the White House. Before sitting down to dinner with Henry Morgenthau, secretary of the treasury, and others, he had a private conversation with the president about Chamberlain, Churchill, and the general European situation. After dinner, he entertained with several songs at the piano, including two renderings of "Mad Dogs and Englishmen" at the request of Roosevelt.

This dinner was repeated in June, shortly before Coward returned to Europe and just after the evacuation of Dunkirk. Consequently, on this occasion his conversation with the president was more serious, focusing on the stubbornness of the British character and the chances of repelling the anticipated German invasion of the British Isles. After dinner, Coward became Mrs Roosevelt's escort as she made an appearance at an agricultural students' dance at the Mayflower Hotel, and then he accompanied her on a moonlit visit to the Lincoln Memorial.

When Coward left the United States on the clipper on 9 June, he did so having put a wrong foot forward only once. Shortly after arriving in America, he had attended the first night of Robert Sherwood's strongly interventionist play, *There Shall Be No Night*, and was quoted next morning in the papers as having said to Edna Ferber: "I can go back to Europe tomorrow." In the view of the British Library of Information monitor, this was an "unfortunate" comment because it would feed isolationist paranoia.[13]

After a few weeks in England, Coward soon became as restless as he had been in Paris, and on 29 July he was back in New York. Upon his arrival, as he later wrote: "I was met by a hot and flustered gentleman from the British Information Services, who implored me breathlessly to tell the Press that I was arriving unofficially on my own theatrical business."[14] Coward had crossed the Atlantic on one of two ships carrying 372 British children who were being evacuated to the United States, and he was able to announce that sixty-eight of them were orphans in his personal charge who would be sheltered by the British acting community in Hollywood. Despite the pleas of the BIS official, he told reporters that he was "on a mission for Lord Alfred Duff Cooper and that he would be reporting to the British Ambassador the next day."[15]

Coward's return to the United States was indeed on the advice of Duff Cooper, who, concluding that he could be more useful there than in England, had given him a Ministry of Information ticket on a liner and a private letter to Lord Lothian. According to Coward, Duff Cooper's suggested mission was hazy and unspecified, but Foreign Office records indicate that it involved planning and establishing some form of public relations organization in America. Even as Coward was en route, however, the Foreign Office was being advised by a British Embassy official in Washington that he would be better employed doing something else:

Personally I am most anxious to utilise his undoubted gifts and large personal following. I do not consider his talents would be best employed as suggested, that is in connexion with planning and setting up of proposed organisation here but would like to propose that on his arrival it should be announced, if questions are asked, that he has come as private individual. I have in mind, that if after consultation it seems advisable, to ask him to investigate the possibility of the launching under suitable American auspices of a popular weekly publication on a commercial basis designed to expose propaganda methods of dictatorships in this country particularly as regards their actions in various publicity sectors. Such a publication is I feel greatly needed here and may score a considerable success. In refuting enemy propaganda, considerable opportunities would arise for presentation of our own case, from a standpoint which would disarm criticism which I am assured might otherwise be damaging. Whole scheme would be presented as a personal and patriotic contribution by Mr Coward ... If any means exist of communicating with him before arrival I should be grateful if he could be requested to make no statement until he has seen me and until we have been able to approve. If you could tell me the name of the boat on which he is travelling I will endeavour to prevent any misunderstandings on arrival and I trust that he will not arrive with a "Government Official" visa.[16]

On 1 August Lothian cabled the Ministry of Information that he had seen Coward and that he should remain in the United States for the next six weeks, ostensibly on his own business, and then they would decide how to use him. According to Coward, Lothian "assured me that I could be of considerable service if I travelled about the States for awhile and talked to key citizens, notably news editors and tycoons in the various cities, about England and the British war effort, so off I went by train and plane and talked at every possible opportunity."[17] Before leaving Washington, he told reporters that he would be staying in the United States for three or four months as a "goodwill ambassador."[18]

In *Future Indefinite*, Coward claimed considerable success as a goodwill ambassador at dinner parties, cocktail parties, lunches, and weekend parties, where he sang, spoke, and generally made himself an agreeable guest. In California, he met former president Herbert Hoover, who was attempting to deliver food to the starving populations of

Belgium and Holland, and he discussed politics with the editor of the *San Francisco Chronicle*. Back in Washington, he said, Lothian was grateful for his report on his travels, but Roosevelt and his adviser Harry Hopkins were even more interested.

What Coward's memoirs do not reveal is that, as a publicist for Britain, he became an immediate problem for his government. On the same day that he had first consulted Lord Lothian, he saw Roosevelt and suggested that the United States could help Britain by cutting off all food shipments to Europe. A day earlier, he had made the same point to the press, telling Americans: "Harden your hearts and close your ears. You will be asked to feed a starving continent and it will be your generous impulse to do so. It is an awful decision which must be made in the face of unimaginable suffering, but if you feed Hitler's victims you feed Germany herself. When the time comes, I beg you to harden your hearts and remember that liberty must not perish."[19]

Two days after Coward's plea, the British Library of Information telegraphed the Foreign Office a special survey report of the negative response in the American papers. "Can England pretend besides providing her with war material America must be deaf to [the] voice [of] humanitarianism?" asked New York's Italian-language daily, *Il Progresso*. In the American "melting pot" there were many immigrants from the conquered countries who would resent any attempt to deny aid to those in their homeland.[20]

On 5 August the Foreign Office cabled Lothian that Coward's repeated references to the starvation in Europe were arousing unnecessary discussion of the question in the United States. "Will you please inform Mr Coward and add that a considered telegram on the question will be sent by the Ministry of Economic Warfare in a few days time to you to be used at your discretion."[21] Several days later, Lothian replied that the substance of the telegram was being communicated to Coward, and he added that American correspondents in London who were calling attention to his statements should be told that "he is in this country on private business and that anything he may say represents his own views only."[22] Back in the Foreign Office, a memo questioned Coward's continued usefulness: "Mr Coward is receiving a very bad press both in the U.S. and here. He has had to be called to order by us over his statements about the food situation in Germany and German controlled territory."[23] An exasperated Balfour wrote more succinctly: "I assume M. of I. will answer for their protégé."[24]

The Ministry of Information did indeed have to answer for Coward's presence in the United States when questions were raised in the

House of Commons on 6 August. Sir Archibald Southby, the Conservative MP for Epsom, asked about Coward's mission – from what
minister he was receiving instructions, whether he had been asked to
seek an interview with the American president, and on whose authority he was making his statements regarding shipments of food to
Europe. Replying on behalf of the Minister of Information, Harold
Nicolson stated that Coward had gone to the United States with the
knowledge and approval of Duff Cooper and that he had called on
Roosevelt as a personal friend. Any remarks about the shipment of
food were merely an expression of his personal views.

Responding to a question from Labour MP Emmanuel Shinwell,
who had earlier questioned Coward's right to sail on ships of the
Royal Navy, Nicolson stated that the playwright's qualifications for
doing publicity in the United States were that he possessed "a contact
with certain sections of opinion which are difficult to reach through
ordinary sources." Another MP suggested that Coward proved that
someone with money and publicity value could easily get out of the
country when it was in crisis. The most damaging question came from
Edgar Louis Granville: "Does the Parliamentary Secretary recognise
that this gentleman does not appeal to democracy in America and
does not represent democracy in this country, and that he is doing
more harm than good, and will he bring him back to this country?"[25]

Outside the House, Granville's charge was being voiced more vigorously by an element of the British press. The *Sunday Express* wrote:
"The despatch of Mr Noel Coward as special emissary to the States
can do nothing but harm. In any event, Mr Coward is not the man
for the job. His flippant England – cocktails, countesses, caviar – has
gone." Similarly, the *Daily Mirror*'s Cassandra argued: "Mister Coward,
with his stilted mannerisms, his clipped accents and his vast experience of the useless froth of society, may be making contacts with the
American equivalents ... but as a representative for democracy he's
like a plate of caviar in a carman's pull-up."[26] Referring to the king
of Belgium's surrender to Germany on 28 May 1940, Coward's old
antagonist Hannen Swaffer asked, "What could Noel Coward do to
counteract the 'Leopold was right' argument?"[27]

Coward attempted to reply to his British critics by telling reporters
that one would think that Parliament might be more usefully occupied in such difficult times. "I came over here for the Minister of
Information, Mr. Duff Cooper, with a letter for our Ambassador ... It
seems to me to make horse sense to send someone who knows America well, rather than someone who doesn't. If the Government thinks

my contacts with the United States are good, so much the better."[28] Nevertheless, his work in America was being seriously undermined by the public criticism from British sources, as Pamela Frankau reported to the Foreign Office in November 1940: "The English in New York and the English press alike combine in questioning his good faith and his official status. Many New Yorkers have raised this subject with me thus: 'Why, if Noel Coward is on an official job, do the British treat him so badly?'"[29]

Most of the attacks on Coward in Britain came from left-wing MPS and journalists, but Philip Hoare suggests that there may have been a subtext to their protests, as implied in Joyce Grenfell's comment to her mother: "What do you think about Noel Coward going to America? ... I think it is a great mistake. Everyone knows his past history and altho' these things don't matter in one if merely writing stuff for the theatre, it is definitely a pity ... that the man who represents this country at a time like this should be famous as a 'queer.'"[30]

It may have been an exaggeration to say that Coward was "famous" as a queer, but there were certainly allusions to his homosexuality in the American press. Describing his appearance at the World's Fair at Flushing Meadow, Sylvia Taylor wrote: "[He] walked in with his characteristic easy stride, neat in his Bond Street suit of dark cloth, and ... I recalled his autobiography ... and how he had boasted of escaping service in the last war, and here he was escaping service in this war. I also recalled how he was worshipped by so many weak young men, who thought of him as their belle ideal of playwright, society darling and paragon of virtue."[31]

Coward's public attacks on the young British actors and others who were in the United States rather than in Britain also drew criticism from American commentators. Dixie Tighe, in the *New York Post*, wrote that Coward, "who is fast becoming Noel-fussbudget, is not making himself too popular with his New York British colleagues ... complaining about certain young Englishmen who are still in mufti. Noel is a little too quick to call some of his countrymen by his last name – a great deal of what he is saying in the theatrical district would sound better if he were in uniform over there and not in the well defined safety zone of New York."[32]

Coward also became a convenient whipping boy for hard-line isolationists. In an essay entitled "For a Free England" in the non-interventionist book *We Testify*, published in 1941, Frances Gunther pointed to Coward as an example of how far Britain had fallen into the cultural shallows in the twentieth century. "Have you ever thought," she asked, "that Elizabethan England, which possessed not a stitch of land beyond its own salt water girdle, produced Shakespeare, and that Georgian England with its Vast Empire Beyond the Seas, has produced only Noel Coward?"[33] In *America Is Worth Saving*, published in the same year, Theodore Dreiser commented sarcastically: "Englishmen exhaling the essence of English imperialism, like Noel Coward, dramatist of Mayfair 'smart sin,' are wandering about spreading poison."[34]

By October 1940 it was clear to British officials that the storm of adverse publicity had made Coward a public relations liability in the United States. Douglas Williams, director of the American Division of the Ministry of Information, advised Lord Hood, private secretary to Duff Cooper, on 14 October: "The Press there have not been kind to Noel in recent months. Do you not think it would be better if he refrained from any further public utterances there except on stage? As an unofficial spokesman from Britain he has not had success (probably not his fault)." Hood replied that no decision needed to be taken at that time, that American memories were so short that in three months Coward might be the right man for the job.[35]

Although Coward contributed to the British war effort on a number of fronts for the remainder of the war, his work in America became minimal. In October 1940, following a suggestion of Richard Casey, the Australian ambassador to the United States, he embarked on a tour of Australia and New Zealand to entertain the troops. Although London journalists sneered that the only news of the war in Britain that he could bring to the Empire was what he read in the papers, local officials reported to Duff Cooper that he made an excellent impression.[36]

When Coward left the United States for Australia, Lothian had intended to have him return to speak to Americans about the Australian war effort, to show how loyally the Empire was rallying around the Mother Country. In fact, when he flew back in early February 1941 he did little public speaking, and he left on the clipper for Lisbon and London on 31 March, telling the press that he would report to the British authorities and perhaps return to the United States later.

Six months after his return to Britain, Coward suffered an unexpected repercussion from the previous summer's American tour. A foreign currency law passed in August 1939 required that he should have declared his American currency holdings in his New York bank and his royalty earnings on American productions and that he should not have spent any of it. Since he had been travelling unofficially for the Ministry of Information and therefore not being paid by it, he had assumed that it would be acceptable for him to live off his American funds. In the eyes of the Finance Defence Department, however, he had committed a criminal offence and was liable to a sizable fine.

Coward's plight was an almost inevitable result of the loose arrangement by which British authors and other public figures were attached to the Ministry of Information, working on behalf of the war effort but not officially part of the ministry and therefore not on the government payroll. Such an arrangement had allowed the ministry and the ambassador in Washington to claim that he had been merely a private citizen, and now he was being punished for supporting himself as a private citizen. In court on 30 October, as Coward noted in his diary, the Ministry of Information had to own up to his having been one of their agents:

Gave my evidence quietly, and, I think, well. All the truth of my war activities came out except the secret stuff. Sammy Hood was in Court, presumably to protect the interests of the Ministry of Information. Prosecuting Counsel tried hard to prove that I was not sent to America officially by Duff. Fortunately M. of I. ticket was produced. Was cross-examined and kept my temper ... Magistrate asked Prosecuting Counsel what the British Government had expected me to live on, upon arriving in the U.S.A. with only £10.[37]

The magistrate clearly agreed that Coward had been working for the Ministry of Information and fined him £200 on one charge and nothing on the other two. Considering that the counsel for the prosecution had claimed that he was liable to a fine of £61,000, Coward was right to think that the verdict was a triumph.

From the beginning of the war Coward had wanted to do intelligence work, which was much more romantic and exciting than propaganda, and in 1941 it appeared that he would get his chance. Sir William Stephenson, head of British Security Co-ordination in the United States, wanted to give Coward an important intelligence assignment, but once again the writer was torpedoed by his public persona. In Bermuda, on his way back to London, he was given a telegram forwarded from Stephenson in New York:

April 2nd Following for Noel Coward (A) Regrettable publicity given to your visit London by entire British press which would increase on arrival unfortunately makes entire scheme impracticable (B) Complete secrecy is foundation our work and it would now be impossible for any of our people to contact you in England without incurring publicity (C) We are all very disappointed as we had looked forward to working with you but there are no further steps to be taken.[38]

The loss of a chance to work in intelligence with Stephenson was frustrating for Coward, but he continued to work for Britain – ironically, as Churchill had said he should, through entertainment. In 1941 he wrote the screenplay for a propaganda film, *In Which We Serve*, which became a popular success. In it, he played the central character, a naval captain based on his friend Lord Louis Mountbatten, and he co-directed the film with David Lean, who at the time was better known as a film editor. In 1943 he went on a lengthy Middle Eastern tour – to Malta, Cairo, Alexandria, Beirut, Tripoli, and Algiers – to entertain the troops, and in 1944 he made a three-month tour of South Africa to raise money for the Red Cross and Mrs Smuts's Comforts Fund. Leaving Africa, he performed for the troops in Ceylon, Burma, and India. From all indications, these tours were successful and useful contributions, and if Coward did not always appear in person, his work spoke for him. In two Victory Loan shows in Canada in 1944, for example, actors read his poem praising RAF bombers flying over the English Channel to Germany, "Lie in the Dark and Listen."

Coward returned to the United States only once more during the war, in December 1943, to do several radio broadcasts for Henry Morgenthau. This visit was supported by Minister of Information Brendan Bracken, and Coward was escorted to the *Queen Elizabeth* in Greenock by a ministry official. In New York he told the press that he was in America to enjoy himself, but he did two broadcasts for Morgenthau and another one for the Free French on Christmas Day. As well, he lunched at the White House with the Roosevelts and the Morgenthaus, and at a dinner party in New York he argued the Indian question with Clare Boothe Luce, then a Republican member of Congress, and the journalist John Gunther, whom he found "absolutely idiotic."[39]

Confronted by the security and relative luxury of wartime America, Coward felt "irritation, an unmannerly, irrational resentment."[40] This exasperation seems to have underlain his attitude to the United States throughout the war and to have led to several of his public relations gaffes. In late 1943 he was so annoyed by a young American officer proclaiming in Glasgow, "We're here to win the war for you!" that he wrote a poem for the British edition of the U.S. Army newspaper the *Stars and Stripes*. After praising the United States, he added:

> This is no opportunity
> For showing off; no moment to behave
> Arrogantly. Remember all are brave
> Who fight for truth. Our hope is unity.
> Do not destroy this hope with shallow words …
> Don't undermine
> The values of our conflict with a line,
> An irritating boastful phrase!

Referring to the year when Britain stood alone while the United States debated isolationism and intervention, he continued:

> It isn't lease or lend,
> Or armaments, or speeches that defend
> The principles of living. There's no debt
> Between your land and mine except that year.
> All our past omissive sins
> Must be wiped out.[41]

The poem, said Coward, was intended to improve British-American relations, but it is unlikely that its thin-skinned, self-righteous tone made American soldiers reading the *Stars and Stripes* feel any more warmly about Britain.

Another Coward wartime work, his 1943 song "Don't Let's Be Beastly to the Germans," elicited an unexpected negative response, particularly in the United States. He had become convinced that Germany had to be treated harshly, that it should be unconditionally defeated and then fragmented so that it could never again be a threat to European stability. His song was thus "a satire on a trend of thought that I felt was once more beginning to spread in the muddled minds of our moralists and sentimentalists":[42]

> Don't let's be beastly to the Germans
> When our victory is ultimately won,
> It was just those nasty Nazis who persuaded them to fight
> And their Beethoven and Bach are really far worse than their bite,
> Let's be meek to them –

And turn the other cheek to them
And try to bring out their latent sense of fun.
Let's give them full air parity –
And treat the rats with charity,
But don't let's be beastly to the Hun.

"Don't Let's Be Beastly to the Germans" became popular with a great many people, particularly Churchill and Roosevelt, both of whom insisted that its author perform it for them. But many others found it offensive – for strikingly different reasons. In Britain, listeners who missed Coward's irony denounced the song for delivering a pacifist, pro-German message. In America, on the other hand, where it was introduced by Celeste Holm on Mutual Radio, it was objectionable to many because of its call for tough, ungenerous treatment of Germany. "The storm of protest was aroused," wrote Gerald Savory in the *New York Times*, "not because it was thought that Mr. Coward was being serious but because he satirized and lampooned groups of citizens who do not believe that emulating the Nazis' brutality will prove any solution to the problem of what is to be done with Germany when victory is won."[43]

If the reaction to "Don't Let's Be Beastly to the Germans" was a storm, the American reaction to some of Coward's comments in *Middle East Diary* (1944) was a hurricane. His description of a group of visiting American senators as "uninspiring," "dull," and "an all-encompassing travelling rug" offended some people, but politicians were always fair game for ridicule. On the other hand, the comment that he was "less impressed by some of the mournful little Brooklyn boys lying there in tears amid the alien corn with nothing worse than a bullet wound in the leg or a fractured arm"[44] enraged New Yorkers and led to an explosion of negative publicity when it was highlighted in a *New York Times* review on 5 November.

Much later, it was explained to Coward that "Brooklyn boys" had been interpreted as a denigrating reference to Jewish American soldiers, but the remark was seen by many as directed at American soldiers in general. The *Brooklyn Eagle*'s headline screamed, "Borough Service Men Blast Coward for Slur," and the "Society for the Prevention of Disparaging Remarks about Brooklyn," established in 1936, posted Coward a Certificate of Dishonour. It proclaimed: "Noel Coward is held in the deepest contempt by those who have faith in the gallant men in the Service. Even a Coward dare not say that the

Unknown Soldier, whose memory typifies the spirit and bravery of American fighting men, was not a Brooklyn boy."[45] Five members of the Brooklyn council signed a resolution calling for a ban in New York of all Coward's books, songs, and plays, and Samuel Dickstein, the chairman of the House of Representatives' Immigration Committee, threatened to have him declared *persona non grata* in the United States.

Looked at retrospectively, the "Brooklyn boys" episode was the stuff of comedy, but in 1944 it was a matter of real concern to British officials. The British Information Services were made uncomfortable by the *Washington Post*'s editorial attack on Coward as "the kind of unofficial British propagandist who does damage to the British cause in America." Similarly, the *Chicago Tribune*'s headline "Don't Let's Be Beastly to Noel Coward" caused discomfort. "While this incident may seem intrinsically trivial," reported a BIS survey, "it is not to be laughed off, since it is of a kind which so swiftly undoes much of the constructive labours of those seriously engaged in the moulding [of] Anglo-American friendship."[46] Coward had planned to visit the United States in January 1945, but the British ambassador, the Earl of Halifax, recommended against this and he was supported by the Foreign Office, which agreed that a postponement would be "in Mr Coward's interest as well as that of British public relations as a whole."[47] Coward did not return to America during the war.

In itself, the incident was clearly trivial, but as the BIS survey shrewdly concluded, it brought to the surface residual American concerns about British imperialism:

Mr Coward's airy dementi has not helped. This outburst of feeling looks like an occasion for the expression of deeper and more general resentments, but the impression of Mr Coward now lodged in many Americans' minds has conjured up that traditional American caricature of the English gentleman, eyeglass, dinner jacket in the desert, cold contempt for, but no qualms about exploiting, inferior races including dreary and vulgar Americans, and all which lies at the root of so much anti-British feeling.[48]

The *Brooklyn Eagle* had said much the same thing when it called Coward "a quite useless member of society, a relic, a Dresden china ornament left over from another day, cracked and stuck together with mucilage."[49] Similarly, Edward Weeks, reviewing *Middle East Diary* in the *Atlantic Monthly*, complained that its author wrote as if he were a British naval officer, one who "seems to have been bitten by Kipling every time he thinks of the Empire."[50]

These comments explain why Coward was so unsuited to represent the British cause in the United States. Summing up his wartime role, Philip Hoare has written:

After the madcap Twenties and the bleak Thirties, the war redefined British-ness and served as an antidote to the disillusion and decadence of the inter-war period. Its revival of the values of empire and Britain's greatness was congenial to Coward ... His celebrity status between the wars led naturally to a role as unofficial ambassador during it. In his wartime travels to Europe, America, and the Middle and Far East, he represented the apparently undam-aged sway of the imperial power clad in Savile Row armour. Churchill's exhortation, to go and sing while the guns were firing, might have vexed Coward, but it was good casting, for his best contribution was his image, his representation of Englishness.[51]

Coward's redefined Englishness, however chameleonlike, appealed to the British and Empire troops he entertained in Cairo, Burma, or Beirut, and it was attractive to the anglophile populations in Austra-lia, New Zealand, and South Africa, where loyalty to Britain was little questioned. In the United States, however, he was on the one hand remembered as the frivolous and decadent performer of the twenties and thirties and on the other as the embodiment of the imperial Britain for which Americans did not want to fight. Americans might respond to the call to defend the Britain of the Magna Carta, Elizabeth I, Westminster Abbey, and Charles Dickens, but they were not pre-pared to fight for the Britain of the imperial and imperious Savile Row–clad gentleman.

If Noel Coward seemed to Americans to be the frivolous embodiment of imperial Britain, H.G. Wells was a thinker and an outspoken critic of the British political establishment. As novelist, journalist, sociolo-gist, and popular historian, he was one of the century's most influen-tial commentators on the shape of society, morals, philosophy, and religious beliefs. His early scientific romances – notably *The Time Machine* (1895), *The Invisible Man* (1897), and *The War of the Worlds* (1898) – had made him the first great science fiction writer in English; and his novels of social criticism such as *Kipps* (1905), *Tono-Bungay* (1909), *Ann Veronica* (1909), and *The History of Mr Polly* (1910) were popular successes. *The Outline of History*, published in 1920 and dis-missed by academic historians, was a best-seller for several decades. In all, he wrote about forty novels and volumes of short fiction, more than a dozen works analysing philosophic and social engineering, about thirty books of political and social prophecy, and numerous pamphlets treating such problems as armaments, nationalism, and world peace.

By the time the war broke out in 1939, Wells was seventy-two and had been losing his hold on the public imagination for some time. As his inventiveness declined, polemical books such as *What Are We to Do with Our Lives* (1931) and political economy studies such as *The Work, Wealth, and Happiness of Mankind* (1932) failed to find a wide audience. Nevertheless, though Wells's reputation may have been based on past achievements, he was still considered, with George Bernard Shaw, one of the most influential writers of the twentieth century. As late as 1944, Donald Brook summed him up quite simply: "The position of Mr Wells in the world of letters to-day is unique. There is nobody quite like him."[52] For many people, he was, in J.B. Priestley's words, "the great prophet of his time,"[53] and a man whose words still carried weight.

Unlike Coward, Wells had participated in both the public discussion of the conduct of the First World War and the British propaganda campaign. Too old to fight at the age of forty-eight, he had sat down on the day that war was declared in 1914 and written an essay called "The War That Will End War." This title became first the national slogan and then a source of bitter irony as the futility of that clash of arms became increasingly obvious.

In his essay Wells stated: "The ultimate purpose of this war is propaganda, the destruction of certain beliefs, and the creation of others. It is to this propaganda that reasonable men must address themselves."[54] Accordingly, a month after the outbreak of hostilities, he joined fifty-three other writers in signing an Authors' Manifesto, which was published in the *New York Times* on 18 September 1914. In March 1918 he wrote a "Memorandum on the General Principle of Propaganda,"[55] and in May he accepted Lord Northcliffe's invitation to take charge of the creation of propaganda literature aimed at Germany. Within two months, however, he had resigned in disgust over the infighting and bureaucratic inefficiency he observed in the propaganda agency.

At the beginning of the Second World War, Wells received the standard letter from A.D. Peters inviting him to stand ready to assist the Ministry of Information, and he replied angrily that he would not be a stalking horse for the Foreign Office again. The fact of the matter is that Wells had already come into conflict with the Foreign Office over an article he had written for the *News Chronicle* in the winter of 1938–39. There he described Hitler as a "certifiable lunatic" and said that it would be "a patriotic act if he were to be put away." When the German ambassador strongly complained that Wells's article went far beyond any legitimate criticism of a foreign head of state, Sir Robert Vansittart, who was then chief diplomatic adviser to the foreign secretary, arranged to see the *News Chronicle*'s chairman, Sir Walter Layton. Although illness prevented this meeting, the Foreign Office advised the paper, which intended to publish two further Wells articles, that so far as possible it should refrain from "gross attacks upon [Hitler], designed to bring him into hatred, ridicule or contempt."[56]

Such actions convinced Wells that the Chamberlain government did not intend to stop Hitler, and he believed that the Foreign Office was so riddled with Axis sympathizers that it would capitulate rather than fight.[57] Thus, when war broke out, he began writing letters to the *Times* calling for a debate on war aims, and in February 1940 he argued that the war should "end on German soil in unambiguous German defeat."[58] More stridently, he told the National Union of Students' congress at Leeds on March 28 that "everybody knows that our Government is grossly incompetent,"[59] and that Chamberlain and Halifax were just "playing about with the war."[60]

Wells was especially critical of Lord Halifax, the foreign secretary, who had encouraged the publication of a government-sponsored book, *The British Case*. A few months earlier Wells had been unsuccessful in persuading Lord Beaverbrook to publish his attack on it in the *Evening Standard*, calling it "the most damaging document that has ever been issued." "Halifax ought to go," he said. "I want to attack it *ferociously* in some conspicuous place."[61] Now, in Leeds, he told the students that *The British Case* showed clearly that Britain was fighting for the empire and imperialism, something that would damn it utterly in the eyes of neutral countries, especially the United States, and "if this is the stuff for which we are fighting, then it is foolish to fight."[62] On the subject of Halifax, Wells was blunt: "I invite you to read [*The British Case*] and then say whether Lord Halifax is or is not the proper person to be in charge of the Foreign Office."[63]

Wells's comments, of course, were ammunition for American isolationists looking for proof of Britain's imperial intentions, but they also created difficulties for British representatives in other countries. On 2 April 1940 the British Embassy in Chile wrote to suggest that such criticisms should not be telegraphed throughout the world, and two weeks later the British legation in Uruguay commented: "It is disheartening to work, often overtime, at our propaganda in all its aspects direct and indirect out here then to read of its being knocked down like a house of cards by someone like Wells, whose name naturally carries influence here."[64]

When these complaints reached the Foreign Office, some official noted with resignation on the file: "Cannot imagine that any power on earth will prevent Mr. Wells from expressing himself as he wants to."[65] He was right, of course, and six months later the Foreign Office was again attempting to put out fires started by the eminent author's pen. On 20 October 1940 the *Sunday Despatch* carried an article by Wells that called King Leopold of Belgium a traitor for having surrendered to Germany. "It is plain," said Wells, "that King Leopold has to be tried by his own people and the world for what many of us think was his deliberate treason to them and us, and either acquitted as a foolish weakling, unfit to govern brave people, or else condemned and executed."[66]

On the day after the publication of the article, the Belgian ambassador met with Lord Halifax and asked whether the British government could take legal action against Wells on the grounds that the article was harmful to the Allied cause. The foreign secretary apologized to the ambassador and agreed that the article was regrettable for political reasons, but he stated that Wells had done nothing illegal. Nevertheless, he wrote to the *Despatch*'s owner, Esmond Harmsworth, pointing out: "If anyone had wished to do a job of work for the Germans in Belgium, they could not possibly have done it better." Harmsworth replied that if he had known that parts of the article would offend the Belgian government and embarrass the Foreign Office, he would have had them deleted.[67]

By the time the *Sunday Despatch* article appeared, Wells had already created much more serious difficulties for the Foreign Office. On 3 October he had arrived in New York aboard the *Scythia* for a ten-week lecture tour, and before he had even set foot on the West Thirteenth Street Pier he had told reporters that the United States should not enter the war because its party politics would "swamp anything like a reasonable settlement" afterward.[68] Britons, he said, were divided on the issue of war aims and the conduct of the war, and "thinking Englishmen" were critical of "our appeasers, our Bourbons, some of them the satisfied landowners." Halifax, whom he thought exemplified the privileged classes, was "the man that all England wants to get out of office … the quintessence of all that patriotic Englishmen should be afraid of." Worse still, Wells declared: "I have a feeling, as a British citizen, that I have never before been so thoroughly misrepresented by anyone as by my present Foreign Minister."[69] Two days later, in an article in the *New York Times*, he wrote: "Nothing, I am convinced, stands between Britain and a complete and conclusive victory in the next year but our antiquated War Office and our antiquated, reactionary Foreign Office."[70]

Wells added that his criticism of Halifax might seem extraordinary since he "came here with the Foreign Office's permission,"[71] but in fact, although the Passport and Permit Office had granted him an exit permit, the Foreign Office had been unaware that he was going to the United States. When questions were raised in the House of Commons on 16 October, R.A. Butler, undersecretary at the Foreign Office, made inquiries and was told that Wells's application for an exit permit had been referred by the Passport Office to the American Division of the Ministry of Information. It had been returned, not by the American Division but by Martin Russell, the private secretary to the minister, Duff Cooper, with the following statement: "The Minister of Information has interested himself personally in Mr Wells' proposed visit to the U.S.A. and he would be most grateful if you could do all you can to enable Mr Wells to have his exit permit at once, so that he can start his journey without delay." Butler's response was: "The Foreign Office must be brought in, and I have so informed Mr. Osbert Peake. What is the value of the American Dept. of Miniform if ours be not consulted."[72]

The issue of Wells's exit permit had been raised in the House by Earl Winterton, Conservative MP for Horsham and Worthing. Noting that American politicians had protested against the author's engaging in political controversy while on American soil, he asked whether Wells had given any undertaking not to engage in propaganda "or make statements inimical to the national war effort before he went to the U.S.A." Osbert Peake, undersecretary of state for the Home Department, answered that lecturers were granted permits only on agreeing to return if required to do so, but that Wells had been granted a permit before this regulation had come into effect. "You will realise," he added, "that the general policy is to permit elderly persons and others who can render no useful assistance to the war effort to proceed overseas."[73]

Winterton continued his assault in the House several days later, charging that Wells had attacked the monarchy as a useless, medieval institution, that he had called the Christian religion a senseless, Judaic superstition, and that he had treated the structure of British society as rotten. "It is intolerable," said Winterton, "that this agnostic Republican, with his hatred of things upon which nine-tenths of his fellow countrymen place great store, should be permitted to lecture in the United States at the present time." He hoped that "the effect of this Debate will be to open the minds of the great American public to the true character of Mr Wells, so that he will not be accepted as a true representative of this country."

Wells was defended by Emmanuel Shinwell and Liberal MP Geoffrey Mander, who called him "a very great Englishman." Another MP supported Winterton, describing Wells as "an agnostic who is going past his best in his dotage" and "not so much a political judge as a first cousin to Old Moore's Almanac." When Peake resorted to the argument that it was important that as many dollars as possible be earned by British subjects, Winterton replied that, on those grounds, Sir Oswald Mosley should be released from jail to give a series of lectures in America. To Peake's claim that Wells could be considered "an invisible export," one member added, "But not inaudible."[74]

Wells was anything but inaudible in the United States, speaking without restraint on a number of sensitive subjects and eliciting a variety of responses from American commentators. Isolationists applauded his plea that the United States stay out of the war, but they resented his characterization of American party politics. His attacks on Lord Halifax disturbed some American politicians, notably John H. Delaney, who asked the House of Representatives to censure Wells, but many editorials praised his candour and his freedom to speak so critically of his own government. Commenting on the House of Commons debate, the *New York Times* wrote: "Lord Winterton leaves us cold ... We throw up our hats for a nation strong enough and civilized enough, in the middle of a life-and-death struggle, to permit a free discussion ... Mr Wells helps the British cause here more than an official spokesman ever could."[75]

Less well received was his statement at a press conference on 4 October that the only guarantee of peace in the world was an alliance between Britain, the United States, and Russia. Calling Russia "essentially peaceful" and not really a member of the Axis powers, he defended its attack on Finland on the grounds of necessary political defence. How would the United States react, he asked, if Staten Island was being held by a potentially hostile armed force?[76] Two days later, he made an even more inflammatory comment by arguing that by marching into Poland, Russia had merely taken back land awarded it by the Treaty of Versailles. To at least one reader of the *New York Times*, this position revealed the depths of British cynicism: "Such views cannot fail to arouse amazement and indignation when they are expressed by an Englishman – a member of the nation with which the Polish nation is united in a life-and-death struggle in defense of the principles of right, justice and liberty."[77]

Wells's brief for the Soviet Union also elicited a particularly hostile article in the *New York Sun* by George E. Sokolsky, who accused Wells of trying "to drive Soviet Russia down our throats." "It is not necessary," he said, "for Mr Wells to come over here to instruct us on the subject of the righteousness of Soviet Russia."[78] Writing in the *Journal American*, Benjamin De Casseres took the same line and warned his readers against being propagandized: "Mr Wells telling us before he gets off on the gangplank what we should do, and defending the Russian murder-machine is not doing the cause of his country any good ... As an international meddlemolly, Mr Wells has no equal. He is now scooping in our dollars on a lecture tour ... It might not be a bad idea ... to keep tabs on these 'lecturers' in order to see that we are not being PAISHED again."[79]

The Foreign Office also was concerned about Wells becoming another Sir George Paish, but for quite different reasons. Wells had used a press conference to dispute the statement of Columbia University's president, Dr Nicholas Murray Butler, that professors should resign if their convictions were different from the university's antitotalitarian stance. In response, Lord Lothian telegraphed the Foreign Office:

Dr Nicholas Murray Butler has started something resembling an anti-totalitarian heresy hunt in Columbia University and has been taken to task by H.G. Wells who has succeeded Paish as self-appointed interpreter of British thought in this coming crucial month. He has done some mischief by expounding his prejudices in home politics to American audiences and stating that the United Kingdom is not so united behind the war. These egoistic and somewhat half extinct prophets are much better kept at home where their importance is generally correctly estimated.[80]

Afraid that an uncontrollable Wells was damaging the British cause in the United States every bit as much as Paish had, the Foreign Office discussed with Lord Lothian what counter measures might be taken. Consideration was given to asking Wells to return to Britain, but Lothian feared the negative publicity that would ensue:

Whilst Lord Lothian said that Wells had done some mischief he considers that it would over-emphasise the importance of his utterances if we were to invite him to return home, which in the case of Sir George Paish proved a complete failure. The Ambassador considers that by far the best method of dealing with Mr Wells is to discredit him on the spot, by circulating back-stairs gossip and humorous remarks. Mr Childs, who is in charge of our publicity in the United States, is arranging for this to be done discreetly as he did in the case of Sir George Paish with marked success.[81]

Before this gossip campaign was initiated, British officials tried to reason with Wells. On 23 October Angus Fletcher called on him at his suite in the Ritz-Carlton and asked him to remember that Polish Americans hated the Soviet Union for its division of Poland, and American Catholics hated it for its atheism. Fletcher also told the writer that his attack on Halifax had been unfair, to which Wells replied that he had studied Halifax's life and concluded that it would have been impossible for him to have come to know the feelings of the ordinary Englishman. Although it was only by ruthlessly inter-rupting Wells that Fletcher was able to say anything, he reported to the British Embassy that Wells seemed to understand that "as a dis-tinguished British visitor at this time he should try to avoid unneces-sary criticism of British leaders or institutions and to keep clear of troubles with our foreign friends."[82]

Wells may have understood Fletcher's point, but he did not change his behaviour. At the end of October, he left New York for a tour of the American South and West in which he gave a lecture entitled "Two Hemispheres – One World" twelve times. In Los Angeles he reiterated that the Foreign Office was reactionary, that people were afraid of a "Vichy element" in Britain, and that the soldiers in Flanders had fought their way out in spite of the generals, who had let them down. In San Francisco he said that it was a sentimental pretence to say that Britain was united, adding that Britain had gone through a revolution but there still remained much mopping up to be done. In Phoenix he told his audience that Russia had shown more foresight than the British at Munich, and he claimed that the Vichy government was a direct result of Britain's "betrayal of Czechoslovakia and the legal government of Spain."[83] In Denver he once again attacked Halifax.

While many of these comments exasperated British government officials and may have undermined their effort to present a united and positive front in the United States, it was only Wells's left-wing views and his support of the Soviet Union that really alienated many Americans. More damaging was his personality which, this late in his life, was embittered, haughty, and curmudgeonly; and this was frequently noted by journalists. In Alabama a reporter, irritated by being denied an interview during a short stop in Birmingham, described Wells's walk to the washroom as a "rapid waddle like a pouter pigeon in a hurry."[84] In Los Angeles, according to a local newspaperman, four hundred people had gathered at a club dinner to hear him talk, but on being introduced, he claimed that he was not aware that he was expected to speak. He said that he had already conveyed his views on the war to local reporters and that his ideas on civilization in general could be found in his latest book. "With that," said the *Los Angeles Times*, "he sat down, the meeting adjourned and the general sentiment among the malefactors who moved into the bar was that Mr Wells and his blarsted Russians were just exactly what they'd always thought they were."[85]

In San Francisco the *Chronicle*'s widely read columnist Herb Caen recounted several incidents of similar lack of tact. When Wells arrived in the city and was welcomed with a bottle of champagne by a local dignitary, he declined the gift, explaining that his diabetes prevented him from drinking it. On arriving at his hotel room, with the dignitary present, he proceeded to call room service and order a large bottle of whisky.[86] A few days later, he told a woman who asked for his autograph: "I never give autographs – I only give them to the London Diabetes Society, and they use them to raise funds." As she turned away in disappointment, the woman glared at a nearby newspaper headline which read: "F[ranklin] R[oosevelt] Allots Half U.S. War Output to British!"[87]

Wells seems to have been no more successful as a lecturer than he was as a diplomat. Caen reported that hundreds of his San Francisco audience complained that they could not hear him, and after his Dallas lecture, the editor of the *Texas Weekly* wrote: "He is not a very attractive speaker."[88] Somerset Maugham, who had known Wells for nearly forty years, later painted a portrait of a man who had failed both on the lecture platform and in the personal encounter:

He came to lunch with me just before his return to England. He looked old, tired and shrivelled. He was as perky as ever, but with something of an effort. His lectures were a dismal failure. He was not a good speaker. It was odd that after so much public speaking he had never been able to deliver a discourse, but was obliged to read it. His voice was thin and squeaky and he read with his nose in his manuscript. People couldn't hear what he said and they left in droves. He had also seen a number of highly influential persons, but though they listened to him politely he could not but see that they paid little attention to what he said. He was hurt and disappointed.[89]

Maugham's summing up of Wells's American tour corroborates the conclusion reached by the British Press Service in its report of 25 November 1940. His popularity, it said, "has not increased since his arrival. Those who might agree with his ideas, apparently dislike his person, and many seem to dislike both ... He has symbolized Britain's tolerance, but he is rather a discredited prophet and as a personality does not appear to have been a help to the British cause."[90]

Wells left the United States for the last time on 18 December 1940 on the clipper, but even his return trip to Britain raised questions for the Foreign Office. On 6 December he had received a telephone call from J. Salter Hansen in Mexico City, who had Mexico's secretary of foreign affairs beside him. The secretary told Wells that the president of Mexico, Manuel Avila Camacho, was authorizing him (Wells) to take whatever steps he thought advisable to re-establish normal diplomatic relations between Mexico and Britain. Convinced that increasing German activities in Mexico posed a threat to the Allies, Wells had Hansen put the request in a letter, which was sent to his agent in New York.

When the clipper landed in Bermuda, Wells thought the matter of such urgency that he had the governor telegraph the Foreign Office. Anthony Eden, the foreign secretary, thought Wells's "unauthorised incursion into this question" important enough to write to Churchill to say that nothing should be done until they had seen Hansen's letter to Wells. He added that Wells was mistaken in assuming that German activity had increased in Mexico and that, in any case, it would be only a minor factor in the question of renewing diplomatic relations. The prime minister commented, "Good."[91]

Wells never returned to the United States, but he continued to write and speak about the way the war was being conducted. In doing so, he managed to continue to antagonize many Americans. In a report on public opinion in the United States in 1941, the British Information Services commented: "H.G. Wells is still stirring up trouble and there is a considerable amount of irritation shown against him."[92] On 30 August 1942 he published an article in the *Sunday Despatch* in which he stated that, in the fourth year of the war, "Anti-bolshevism, big business, and that long-cherished isolationism that still subordinates world affairs to party politics makes the role of America ... the cloudiest factor." According to Bruce Lockhart, Americans were furious.[93]

6

One God-Damned Thing after Another
W. Somerset Maugham

On 3 February 1941 Martin Charlesworth wrote to Sir Stephen Gaselee at the Foreign Office to bring his attention to a letter from an Englishman living in Rhode Island. It was necessary, said the correspondent, to send over capable British lecturers, to which Charlesworth added: "I only hope that this won't result in the sending of H.G. Wells or Bernard Shaw or other septuagenarians." Someone in the Foreign Office, with the recently returned Wells undoubtedly still fresh in his mind, scrawled across the file: "It is improbable that either Mr Wells or Mr Shaw would be sent to make propaganda in the u.s.a. on our behalf."[1]

Somerset Maugham, very nearly a septuagenarian at the age of sixty-six, was already in the United States, having gone there in October 1940 as the third of the well-known British authors sent by Duff Cooper. Unlike Coward and Wells, Maugham remained in America for the duration of the war, continued to be active in a variety of propaganda activities, and achieved a degree of success.

Like Coward, Maugham was a literary figure of remarkable versatility; but whereas Coward was seen as frivolous and superficial, Maugham was considered sober and serious. Among the fifteen novels he had written by 1940, *Of Human Bondage* (1915) was one of the most widely read books of the interwar period, mandatory reading for those who fancied themselves literate, while *The Moon and Sixpence* (1919), *The Painted Veil* (1925), and *Cakes and Ale* (1930) sold in large numbers. From 1908 to 1933 his thirty-two plays had made him one of the most popular playwrights on both sides of the Atlantic, and his hundred or so short stories – among which were such memorable tales as "Rain" and "The Letter" – had been a staple of magazines and periodicals. With the publication of his intellectual autobiography *The Summing Up*, in 1938, Maugham became the cosmopolitan gentleman in the parlour – like the aged writer Edward Driffield in *Cakes and Ale*, a Grand Old Man of English literature.

Wells, of course, was a venerated author of thoughtful and prophetic books, but he was self-dramatizing, polemical, and provocative. Maugham, on the other hand, was private, shy, and politically conventional. While Wells saw his writing as a way of presenting his ideas for changing politics and society, Maugham believed that the writer should focus on the artistry of his work rather than on topical social or political issues. And while Wells had briefly been employed in the First World War propaganda effort after spending most of the war writing from the outside, Maugham had been seriously involved in the more delicate business of espionage from 1915 to 1918.

Maugham had been forty at the outbreak of the First World War but had served as an interpreter with the ambulance corps during the first winter. A year later he was working in Switzerland for the British Intelligence Service, conveying information to and from agents, passing on orders, collecting and sending data, and paying the spies. In August 1918 he went to Russia, where he was the chief agent of the British and American intelligence services, with the mission of keeping the Russians in the war. According to Rhodri Jeffreys-Jones, Maugham was remarkably successful in carrying out his mandate, providing more accurate reports than those of other agents and embassy officials, and suggesting political and economic strategies that would help the Allies control events in East Central Europe. So perceptive were his analyses, says Jeffreys-Jones, that elements of them were used by Western European countries and the United States in their response to the invasion of Czechoslovakia and Poland in the late 1930s.[2]

Maugham wrote about his wartime experiences in his short story collection *Ashenden, or The British Agent*, published in 1928, though he had to leave out some material for fear of contravening Britain's Official Secrets Act. Four years later, with the shadow of another war looming, he seemed to step out of character when he wrote a deeply pacifist play, *For Services Rendered*. He was then, he said, trying "to protect the new youth of today from dying in the trenches or losing five years of their lives in a war that seems almost imminent."[3] The play is an angry attack on the jingoists and war profiteers of the earlier war and a warning to a new generation not to be similarly duped.

"Honour and patriotism," says one character, are "all bunk," and those who follow the "incompetent" leaders who will "muddle us all into another war" are "a lot of damned fools."[4]

In *Ashenden*, Maugham had written that patriotism was "in peacetime an attitude best left to politicians, publicists and fools, but in the dark days of war an emotion that can wring the heart-strings."[5] Perhaps it is not surprising, then, that in the dark days of 1939, even before the outbreak of hostilities, Maugham again offered his services to his country. During a visit to London in July, he consulted his brother Frederic, who was Lord Chancellor in Chamberlain's government, about the likelihood of war, and he made discreet inquiries about the possibility of doing more espionage work. In case British Intelligence considered him too old at sixty-five, he offered himself to the Ministry of Information as a propagandist.

Maugham received the standard A.D. Peters/Ministry of Information letter to authors in September, but because of the ministry's indecision it was some weeks before he was put to work, and then it was more in espionage than propaganda. On October 24 he wired his lover Alan Searle "to say that he was doing some of his old war work" and had "disappeared for the time being,"[6] and over the course of the winter he provided the British government with the same kind of detailed and shrewd advice about the conditions in France as he had earlier offered about Russia. He was particularly useful because he had lived in France for a dozen years, and his lifelong connection to the country in which he had been born gave him something of a native understanding of French thinking. Moreover, as a famous writer who was especially respected by the French and had connections with the French literary and social world, he had access to people and information that was available to few outsiders.

Maugham was also an author highly respected in Britain, one who, as a sensible Englishman living in France, could plausibly interpret the French situation and describe the French people's reactions. As such, he was more valuable as a propagandist, and by late November he was asked to write a series of newspaper articles on the French war effort. The Ministry of Information considered these pieces so effective that it commissioned Maugham's publisher, William Heinemann, to bring them out in book form as *France at War* in March 1940.

France at War quickly sold 100,000 copies, but with the collapse of French resistance in May and June the book was quickly withdrawn. Maugham himself was forced to flee to Britain on a coal ship in late

June, and within days of arriving at Liverpool he had begun broadcasting in both English and French on BBC radio. As well, at the request of the Ministry of Information, he wrote a series of five articles for the *Sunday Chronicle* on the French collapse and the current British war effort.

Maugham's articles were intended to raise morale within Britain, but for some months the Ministry of Information had been attempting to place some of his pieces in a prominent American periodical. On 8 April Sir Frederick Whyte had written the Foreign Office to say that "after much discussion and correspondence, the Ministry believe that they have secured the publication in *Collier's* magazine (circulation 3,000,000) of a series by Somerset Maugham."[7] For whatever reason, nothing ever appeared in *Collier's*, but in the autumn of 1940 another popular American magazine, *Redbook*, carried five of his articles, which described the fall of France, his escape to Britain, and the current conditions in Britain and Germany.

Maugham had not been back in Britain very long before the Ministry of Information, and particularly Duff Cooper, with whom he had a personal friendship, concluded that he would be more valuable in the United States delivering his message in person. As early as 31 July he was telling Gerald Kelly that he would be going to America to talk on the air.[8] To his American friend Bertram Alanson, he wrote on 19 August that he would be travelling to the United States very soon, but arrangements were apt to change. He added that he would have to settle in New York to do the work for which he was going to America.[9]

When Maugham finally did arrive in the United States on the clipper on 8 October, he told the reporters waiting at La Guardia Airport that he was there to reconstruct the manuscripts of two novels that had been lost in his hurried flight from southern France. Although he was careful to stress that anything he said was his own opinion, his statements closely reflected the line the British government was then taking with America – that Britain could win and was therefore worth backing and that the war was democratizing the country. "Optimism is not the word," he proclaimed. "I am absolutely positive of victory … Our soldiers are longing for an invasion. They feel that they can slaughter every one that comes over."[10] Similarly: "The only thing that we are quite sure of in England is that we shall all be ruined and the country shall be much more democratic than ever before. Some accept it with resignation, some with joy. I myself accept it with joy."[11]

To Alanson, Maugham confided that although he had come unofficially because the official agents who had come before had made a hash of things, in fact he was there on behalf of the government and would be getting in touch with Lord Lothian.[12] However, Lothian had returned to London until after the American presidential election, so Maugham consulted with a British Embassy official who went to New York to brief him.

It was not long before Maugham was put to work to present the British case. He helped sell books for the British War Relief Bookshop, and in his first month he gave at least three speeches, the first of which was to three thousand delegates at the *New York Herald Tribune*'s Forum on Current Problems held at the Waldorf-Astoria on 23 October. In a session devoted to the "Resources of the Creative Arts" as related to the general theme of "America's Second Fight for Freedom," Maugham appeared with American poet Archibald MacLeish and playwright Robert Sherwood, and stressed the intimate connection between the literatures of Britain and the United States. "And when, in this war," he added, "we British are defending our culture, the rich and fertile culture of the English-speaking peoples, we are defending, not only what is ours but what is yours."[13]

A week later Maugham joined Austrian writer Franz Werfel at an Emergency Rescue Committee dinner for fifteen hundred at the Hotel Commodore. There he guaranteed that Britain would survive with American help, and he looked to the day when both countries would be under one flag. He reiterated this idea of unification much more dramatically on 26 November when he spoke to three thousand people at a meeting to support a federal union of all democratic countries along lines proposed in Clarence Streit's book *Union Now*. Sharing the platform with Sherwood and the French playwright Henri Bernstein and actors Raymond Massey and Constance Collier, Maugham announced his conversion to a form of world government: "Do you wonder that I asked myself why if [federal union] has been a success in the United States of America, it shouldn't be a success in the United Democratic States of the world?"[14] Whether he or the many other Britons who supported Streit were really convinced of the value of a worldwide union of democracies, the movement's emphasis on the common goals of the English-speaking countries and the attacks on American isolationists usefully served British propaganda interests.

In part because of his literary reputation and in part because of his bearing, Maugham conveyed authority. Paul Horgan, who met him at this time recalls: "The presence of W. Somerset Maugham was, amazingly, powerful for such a small man. He was narrow-shouldered, carrying one shoulder higher than the other, slim, almost apologetic in bearing as though to state shyness."[15] Maugham's demeanour and performances pleased British officials in the United States, as indicated in the British Press Service September–November 1940 survey of the American press:

On his arrival Maugham was given widespread and favourable publicity. He is apparently well-liked by the Press. The *Daily Worker* was alone in presenting him as "the suave British novelist who has publicly confessed to being a British agent, a spy, for the British Empire," although R. Van Gilder [sic], literary critic of the *New York Times*, began his very favourable report on an interview with the remark, "Maugham is in this country as a British agent." He is widely quoted in out of town papers, and his article carried by the *Redbook* on the fall of France was quoted from by several editorials. Maugham emphasizes his confidence of ultimate victory, his conviction that the entry of the United States into the war would do Britain more harm than good, and his opinion that the end of the war will see a more democratic Britain "with no rich people and, I hope, I hope, no more poor."[16]

As Maugham had anticipated, he was soon employed giving radio broadcasts, this despite the lifelong stammer that made public speaking an ordeal. His first broadcast, which was an interview with Edward Weeks on NBC, revealed both the difficulties created by his impediment and his quick wit in facing them. When an unplanned three-minute hiatus led Weeks to ask an impromptu question about the source of the next great war novel, Maugham began to struggle: "Well, Mr Weeks, almost every novelist would rather write about defeat than victory. And j-j-just as the b-b-best novel about the First World War, *All Quiet on the Western Front*, came out of Germany's defeat, so I hope and b-b-believe that the best book about this war will come from the same source, and f-f-for the same reason!" It was, said Weeks, a bold answer in 1940 and it elicited an outburst of applause from the studio audience.[17]

In addition to his public appearances, Maugham was kept busy writing for American magazines. In March and April 1941 the *Saturday Evening Post* carried four articles about the French collapse and his journey from the Riviera to Britain and thence to the United States: "Novelist's Flight from France," "Little Things of No Consequence,"

"We Have Been Betrayed," and "Escape to America." These pieces were then put together with those carried in *Redbook* and published in book form as *Strictly Personal* in the United States in September 1941. As Maugham wrote to Edward Marsh, "It was written for American readers because I had certain things to say that I had a notion it would be useful for them to know, and I had no intention of publishing it in England."[18] Persuaded later that such a volume would also be of interest to British readers, Maugham consented to Heinemann bringing out a British edition in March 1942.

In all, Maugham wrote about twenty propaganda articles for American readers. In 1940, to emphasize that a common literary culture was one of the strongest links between his country and the United States, he wrote "Reading under a Bombing" for *Living Age* and "Give Me a Murder" for the *Saturday Evening Post*. As the war stretched on, he followed these pieces with "The Culture That Is to Come" (*Redbook*, August 1941), "Paintings I Have Liked" (*Life*, December 1941), "Reading and Writing and You" (*Redbook*, August 1943), "We Have a Common Heritage" (*Redbook*, August 1943), and "Write about What You Know" (*Good Housekeeping*, November 1943).

In June 1942 the American *Publishers' Weekly* carried Maugham's article "To Know about England and the English," in which he offered a brief list of historical books, memoirs, and fiction that would help Americans understand the British. For a portrait of life in wartime Britain, he recommended Phyllis Bottome's *London Pride*, Margaret Kennedy's *Where Stands a Wingèd Sentry*, Margery Allingham's *The Oaken Heart*, John Strachey's *Digging for Mrs Miller*, and Jan Struther's *Mrs Miniver*, all recently published in the United States. Playing one of the British propagandist's strongest cards at that time, Maugham especially urged Americans to read Philip Guedalla's *Mr Churchill: A Portrait* because Churchill "has the typical characteristics of the English in a pre-eminent degree."[19]

In 1943 Maugham reiterated the theme of a common language binding the literary cultures – and therefore the people – of Britain and the United States in an anthology that was only ever published in America, appearing first as *Great Modern Reading* and then as *Introduction to Modern English and American Literature*. Writing to G.B. Stern in April 1942, he had talked of doing research in the New York Public Library, not for any work of his own, but for an anthology he was preparing to be sold in the five- and ten-cent stores, a sort of get-together anthology, English and American, to suggest that Britons and

Americans are in fact one people.[20] In his introduction to the collection, his message was only slightly more indirect: "Some of the pieces are by English authors and some by American, but I have not sought in any way to distinguish them, for I think the time has passed when there was any point in speaking of English literature and American literature. I prefer now to speak of it as one, the literature of the English-speaking peoples."[21]

Anxious to work on his novel of Eastern mysticism, *The Razor's Edge*, which he had begun before the war, Maugham found it tedious to write propaganda. No one could imagine the things he was being asked to do, he wrote to Edward Marsh in 1943. At that moment he was racking his brains to think how to manufacture a readable article whose purpose was to persuade Americans to send vegetable seeds to England.[22] Maugham found the answer in professing to have before him letters of thanks from grateful ordinary Britons to "their unknown American friends." "They are badly spelled, the grammar is shaky and the handwriting is that of men who work with their hands and are unused to holding a pen," he said, but his sample excerpt does justice to the craftsmanship of a noted British author.[23]

Innately shy, Maugham found public speaking no more congenial than writing to order, commenting to Stern that he hated giving lectures to people, with all the preliminary tiresomeness of having to shake the hands of innumerable persons and saying if possible a few polite words to each![24] He nonetheless spoke frequently to American audiences in cities from New York to Los Angeles and San Francisco to Philadelphia. In March 1941 he addressed the Centennial Banquet of the New York University College of Medicine, and a month later he met William Lyon Phelps's students at Yale. In November 1942 he returned to Yale to give the Francis Bergen Memorial Lecture and to donate the manuscript of *Strictly Personal* to its library.

At least one of Maugham's lecture topics indicates the lengths to which he – and undoubtedly British government officials – were prepared to go in the propaganda campaign. In February 1941 Maugham told Lady Juliet Duff that he had to get out of a sickbed in Chicago to "give a lecture on of all subjects 'The English Family in War Time.'" "It may amuse you to know," he said, "that my discourse on 'Family Life in England' has been so successful that I have been asked to repeat it in the cities of the Atlantic Coast."[25]

The truth, of course, was that Maugham's experience of family life in England was extremely limited. Orphaned at ten, he grew up unhappily in a vicarage in Kent, had an unhappy marriage which led to divorce in 1929, and lived thereafter with his lover, Gerald Haxton, in the south of France. Maugham had always been discreet about his homosexuality, and unlike the more flamboyant Coward, he was viewed by most Americans as an orthodox divorcé. Thus it was not difficult to adopt the mask of the English family man.

Maugham was periodically briefed by the British Information Services in New York and the British Embassy in Washington, and he was careful to follow the official line. In Chicago, as he told Lady Juliet Duff, he was instructed to avoid antagonizing ardent isolationists through overstatement: "So strong was the feeling in Chicago that when I spoke over the air they wouldn't let me speak of the magnificent resistance of the British but only of their resistance and they wouldn't let me say the infinite courage of the people of London under the bombardment but only the courage."[26]

Maugham's demeanour and caution did not produce the kind of adverse publicity sparked by Coward and Wells, but neither did his lectures impress all his listeners. Among four speeches he gave in Chicago in March 1941 was one at the University of Chicago chaired by the British academic (and later member of the British Information Services) David Daiches. "I remember," said Daiches, "being very disappointed with his lecture, which consisted in explaining the fall of France on the grounds of the corruption of French officials exemplified by the fact that they very often short-changed you in French post offices. I thought that as a contribution to the political and military events of 1940 this was somewhat minimal."[27]

Maugham's analysis may have been overly simplistic for a university audience, but he was a novelist, more interested in the state of mind and behaviour of people than in the larger political and military issues. Moreover, his focus on the French national character as it appeared in 1940, which he dealt with at length in *Strictly Personal*, was an attempt to combat isolationist arguments that both France and Britain were doomed to lose to a more militarily powerful Germany and thus any American aid would be useless. By identifying the French surrender as having been the result of a failure of national character, Maugham was able to separate Britain from France in the eyes of Americans and suggest that the latter – which, under Churchill, did not lack character – was still worth supporting. Thus he wrote in *Strictly Personal* of the "ineptitude, insensibility to suffering and gross selfishness" of those in power in France, the widespread corruption among businessmen and politicians, and the military's lack of any real commitment to the war. There was, he claimed, "a general decay of morality, an insane craving for pleasure, and a cynical contempt for honour."[28]

Maugham was not alone in blaming the French military's collapse on moral decay. A month after his *Saturday Evening Post* articles on the fall of France appeared, the *New Yorker* published Kay Boyle's short story "Defeat," which won the O. Henry Prize for the best short story of the year. An American who had first-hand knowledge of life in France before its fall, Boyle wrote of the weeks following the surrender when soldiers trickled back to their homes, beaten, humiliated, and full of excuses. Convincing themselves that "a country isn't defeated so long as its women aren't,"[29] the men then watched as the women succumbed, on Bastille Day, to the attraction of a dance staged by the Germans. According to Boyle's biographer, Joan Mellen, "Defeat" was a vivid depiction of "the sting of moral defeat ... Not only had the officers and politicians betrayed their countrymen, but the French themselves – the women – had been corrupted."[30]

Boyle's story was a perfect dramatization of Maugham's thesis about the fall of France, and it captured the contempt which many people, particularly Americans, felt for the French in 1940. Two years later, however, when Maugham himself came to write a short story set in German-occupied France, the protagonist, a young French woman, was portrayed heroically. By then conditions had changed; the United States was in the war, an ally of de Gaulle's Free French, who had to be portrayed as useful comrades.

Maugham likely read Boyle's story, but it was one of Guy de Maupassant's tales, "Mademoiselle Fifi," set during the Prussian occupation of France in the Franco-Prussian War, that was Maugham's inspiration. It had been broadcast for propaganda purposes on the BBC on 30 October 1940 under the ironic title "The Defeated." Maugham was then in the United States, but he may well have heard its rebroadcast on the North American Service in February 1941; in any case, he was familiar with the story from his youthful reading of Maupassant. The title of his own story, "The Unconquered," published in *Collier's* on 10 April 1943 (and in book form in 1944), seems to have been a deliberate reversal of the titles of Boyle's story and the radio adaptation of Maupassant's.

"Mademoiselle Fifi" tells how a group of Prussian officers, barbaric in their defiling of the chateau they are occupying, bring in five prostitutes for their entertainment. "We are the masters! France belongs to us! ... All the women in France belong to us,"[31] boasts an officer, at which point one of the prostitutes stabs him to death and flees. When she is liberated at the end of the war and goes on to live a happy life, the implication is clear: so long as one woman does not belong to the conquerors, neither does the country.

In "The Unconquered" Maugham follows Maupassant in using the sexual violation of women to represent the violation of the country as a whole, and he too ends his story with a woman's violent response – in this case, one much more sensational than Maupassant's. Both the violation and the response were, in fact, so shocking that *Collier's* printed only an expurgated version of what later appeared in book form. In whatever form, "The Unconquered" was deliberate propaganda directed toward American readers, and it was not published in Britain until its inclusion in *Creatures of Circumstance* in 1947.

Hans, the German soldier who rapes and impregnates the young French woman, Annette, is initially described as stereotypically German: tall, slim, and broad-shouldered, with blond hair and blue eyes. Intoxicated by the ease with which the French army was routed, he is the conqueror, and conquerors take what they want. So his rape of the French woman is not an act of desire but an exercise of power.

Like the Belgian women of the notorious First World War propaganda posters, Annette is made to represent France itself. Hans is quick to notice that there is "a sort of distinction about her," with "a refinement that suggested the city-dweller rather than the peasant."[32] That refinement, writes Maugham, "that fine nose and those dark eyes, the long pale face – there was something intimidating about the girl, so that if he hadn't been excited about the great victories of the German armies, if he hadn't been so tired yet elated, if he hadn't drunk all that wine on an empty stomach, it would never have crossed his mind that he could have anything to do with her."[33] In other words, in normal circumstances, the barbaric German would have had nothing to do with refined French cosmopolitanism.

This contrasting of national stereotypes is reinforced by the portrayal of Willi, Hans's fellow soldier, and by Annette's fiancé, a teacher then in a German prisoner-of-war camp. Willi tries to dissuade Hans from assaulting Annette and then agrees to participate only because he does not want to be thought a "sissy." He is soft, concludes Hans, because he has spent two years as a dressmaker among the Parisian French: "A decadent people. It did a German no good to live among them."[34]

Annette's fiancé, she tells Hans, is "not strong and big like you, or handsome; he's small and frail. His only beauty is the intelligence that shines in his face, his only strength is the greatness of his soul. He's not a barbarian, he's civilised; he has a thousand years of civilisation behind him."[35] In contrasting the French fiancé with the German Hans so starkly, Maugham was following the practice of British propagandists since the beginning of the war – demonizing Germany, colouring the struggle as a black-and-white battle between civilization and light on the one hand and barbarism and darkness on the other.

Despite having sketched Hans so stereotypically, Maugham attempts something unusual in a short story in showing his character developing and changing when he learns that Annette is pregnant. He becomes attracted to the idea of fatherhood, of marrying Annette and settling on the farm; and in the reactions of Annette and her parents Maugham is able to allegorize the positions of both the resistance and the collaborators. As Hans ingratiates himself by providing hard-to-get foodstuff, the parents pragmatically accept the new state of affairs. When he suggests that he marry their daughter and manage the farm with new German machinery and stock, they are eager to assist him, offering the same argument as the Pétainistes did when making their peace with Hitler: "The best chance for France now is to collaborate."[36] In case the allegory is not clear enough, Maugham repeats the collaborationist argument in the form of editorial comments in Paris newspapers. "France," writes one, "must take the heaven-sent opportunity and by loyal collaboration with the Reich regain her honoured position in Europe."[37]

Annette, however, represents the younger French, those who were fighting in the Resistance and who might represent the future, and she drowns the newborn child rather than live with the offspring of a German-French liaison. The last image is of Annette collapsing in passionate weeping, having absolutely and finally rejected any involvement with Hans. Unlike the women in Boyle's story, she has remained unconquered.

Hans is anguished, giving the cry "of an animal wounded to the death"[38] because he is denied his dream of the German-French family and farm. But, one might ask, what of Annette, who has sacrificed her own child in an act of violence surpassing anything done by Hans? In the Maupassant tradition of the surprise ending, Maugham offered the unthinkable, a mother killing her own child, and in doing so he sacrificed credibility for allegorical purposes. The British under Churchill were committed to unconditional surrender, and they were always concerned that their allies – especially the Americans – might weaken and seek a compromising peace with Hitler. In "The Unconquered," Maugham represented victory in absolute terms, victory that could be achieved only at enormous and painful cost.

In speaking about France on the lecture platform and writing about it in *Strictly Personal* and "The Unconquered," Maugham was useful to the British cause in the United States in that, as a distinguished writer whose home was in France, he could interpret that country to Americans with authority. At the same time, in his persona as a famous British writer, he could describe the British response to the war with apparent authenticity. In this latter role, Maugham wrote two other works of fiction for propaganda purposes during his war years in the United States: a short story entitled "The Noblest Act" and a novel, *The Hour before the Dawn*.

"The Noblest Act," published in the American magazine the *Week* on 4 January 1942, is set in the familiar Maugham world of rubber plantations, colonial administrators, and expatriate Britons. Its protagonist, Mrs Farley, has lived in the Federated Malay States for thirty years and is now homesick for her country and the children she had left behind long ago. Most importantly, her doctor tells her that she must return to England or die within a year. Thirteen days before she is to set sail for England, her husband, a doctor, is asked to stay on so that the colony will not be without medical care. Since he does not want to be parted from his wife, she agrees to stay, knowing that it will mean her death.

In 1942 Maugham was best known for the fictional landscape he had created of the British colonies in the Far East, and in mobilizing his unique literary world in the war effort he was emulating James Hilton's propaganda use of Mr Chips or Jan Struther's employment of Mrs Miniver. Unlike them, however, he did not extend the ethos and behaviour of his colonial world into the war; he reversed them. He had always observed the British imperial presence with a cynical and unsentimental eye, and many of his colonial stories had dealt, not with nobility and sacrifice but with the weakness and decadence lying behind the spit-and-polish façade. Turning Kipling inside out, said V.S. Pritchett, Maugham more often than not revealed the white man's burden to be his wife's adultery.

There can be little doubt that Maugham's late reversion to a Kiplingesque homage to British colonial administrators was a stance temporarily adopted for propaganda purposes. British imperialism remained the most serious impediment to American commitment to the war in Europe, and it was necessary to portray the British colonial presence as benign. "The Letter," "The Outstation," or "Footprints in the Jungle," like almost all of Maugham's Far East stories, would have confirmed the worst American suspicions, but "The Noblest Act" argues for an archaic, nineteenth-century beneficent imperialism.

The Hour before the Dawn, written purely as propaganda for Americans, had a curious publishing history. On 1 March 1941 Maugham wrote to a friend that he was going to do a big propaganda picture,[39] and several weeks later he added that if British officials approved, he was going to write a film script for David Selznick about England in wartime.[40] By May, as he reported to his nephew Robin Maugham, *Redbook* magazine had agreed to publish his story in serial form, and the film studio would then turn it into a screenplay. He was off to California to work on the material, loathing the idea but realizing, as he said, that it was the sort of thing he was there for, so he had to do it.[41] When he finished the serial at the end of July, Maugham complained to G.B. Stern that he had hated doing it because he had no gift for describing action just for action's sake, besides which he had to work against time, and would have abandoned the job half a dozen times if the Ministry of Information had not wanted the project and thought it would be so useful.[42]

Maugham's mandate in *The Hour before the Dawn* was to portray a typical British family's response to the war, but his family is typical only of those who appeared in his comedies of manners on the London stage in the 1920s. The Hendersons live in a country house, complete with Italian statues, a tennis court, and a butler, on land "as far as the eye could reach."[43] The property has been in the family for two hundred years, and in the best tradition of the landed gentry "they were prepared to sacrifice themselves to hand down to their successors intact the land that they held in trust."[44]

Maugham populates this upper-middle-class family with what is meant to be a representation of various responses to the war. The patriarch, General Henderson, is too old for active service, but his son Roger works in counter-espionage at the War Office and his son-in-law

Ian is in the army. However, another son, Jim, has become a pacifist at Oxford, and his refusal to enlist distresses his family, though it respects his right as a Briton to do so. The youngest son, Tommy, is still at school but is eager to hear of the exploits of those in action. Mrs Henderson is the long-suffering, generous-spirited British mother; Roger's wife May is unhappy in her marriage and is in love with their friend Dick Murray; Ian's wife Jane is the plain-speaking comic member of the family; and Dora Friedberg is an Austrian whom Jim has secretly married.

The Hour before the Dawn begins the day before war breaks out and takes the reader through such events as the sinking of the *Athenia*, the evacuation at Dunkirk, and the London Blitz. Ian is wounded in action, and Roger, presumed dead, heroically escapes from France with the aid of a stereotypical little Cockney corporal, Knobby Clark. The theme of the classes working together in the common cause is repeated later when Roger and Jane take refuge in a bomb shelter along with Knobby, his wife, and children. Moreover, Mrs Henderson houses thirty working-class children evacuated from London, and one need only compare Maugham's cheerful picture of the results with that in Waugh's *Put Out More Flags* to see the difference between propaganda and satire.

Much of Maugham's emphasis is on the sacrifices of his English family, most of which involve their relationships. May is in love with Dick but decides to give him up because Roger is doing important war work and it would be selfish to pursue a divorce. Later, when Dick returns from action blinded, it is Roger's turn to be noble, and he tells May about her lover's wound so that she can go to care for him. Even infidelity, it seems, can be part of the war effort. Jim, too, makes a sacrifice when he abandons his pacifism and murders Dora, who is discovered to be a German spy who has contributed to the death of Tommy in a bombing raid. Jim then spares everybody the humiliation of flight or a trial by taking his own life.

At the end of the novel, when the Henderson family has taken its blows, it is left to the general to offer a valedictory speech on the passing of his class and the coming classless society created by the war:

We haven't always been wise, we landowners, and I dare say we've been complacent and high-handed, but on the whole we've been decent and honest and we haven't done badly by our country. Perhaps we've accepted the good things our happy lot provided us as though they were our due, but according to our lights we've tried, the best of us, I mean, and I think I may say most of us, to do our duty. But ... we've had a long innings ... The future belongs to the soldiers and sailors and workmen who will have won the war. Let's hope they'll make it a happier and better England for all the people who live in it.[45]

Following its serialization in *Redbook* from December 1941 to April 1942, *The Hour before the Dawn* was published in book form by Doubleday in June 1942. For the most part, the reviews were negative, finding that the people were "contrived [so that] one doesn't care two pins"[46] and that the dialogue in it sounded "pre-war, brittle, and trivial."[47] Incredibly, however, R. Ellis Roberts claimed in the *Saturday Review of Literature* that the novel showed Maugham at his best, that he effectively portrayed "the private and domestic tragedies in the light of the great public tragedy of the war."[48] Roberts's enthusiasm is perhaps understandable when one recalls that he was the British author and journalist who in 1939 arrived in the United States aboard the *Manhattan* with S.K. Ratcliffe and Cecil Roberts.

Maugham himself knew that *The Hour before the Dawn* was anything but his best work, and prefaced the Doubleday edition with an apologetic epigraph from Pope: "In every work regard the writer's end, / Since none can compass more than they intend." He urged friends not to read it and told Edward Marsh in 1943 that he would not publish it in Britain. He knew, he wrote, that it was poor, and he was miserable about it, preferring to think that it would be missed in England and forgotten in America.[49] *The Hour before the Dawn* was not published in Britain in Maugham's lifetime, and as late as 1968 his very close friend Sir Gerald Kelly confessed to me that he had never even heard of it.[50]

By the time Maugham had completed reworking the serial version of *The Hour before the Dawn* into a full novel in March 1942, the United States had already entered the war, and he felt that the story no longer served a purpose. He was dismayed to learn, however, that the American entry did not mean that his propaganda work was over: he was now expected not only to continue to work for Anglo-American cooperation but also to help the American war effort. Soon after his arrival in the United States, Maugham's reputation for espionage in the First World War had led Harold Guinzburg to consult him about the staffing of Bill Donovan's secret Co-ordinator of Information office. He had recommended the writer Jerome Weidman for the same reason that authors were useful to the Ministry of Information: "You're a freelance writer, which means that you can support yourself on royalties, so that an organization like the c.o.i., which has no funds for salaries, can use you without having to answer to Congress."[51] Now he was being asked to assist in War Bond drives, books for troops drives, and uso subscription drives. There was even talk of an assignment in Brazil in the spring of 1942, but this was eventually scrapped.[52]

By this point of the war, following nearly three years of writing propaganda and at the age of sixty-eight, Maugham was exasperated by the continued demands, which he characterized to Stern as one god-damned thing after another.[53] The worst of it, he wrote to Marsh, was that he would have to sit down and take what was coming to him without explanation or protest. But he said that it mattered only to him, and nothing really mattered except winning the war."[54] Having to take what was coming was, of course, a result of his arrangement with the Ministry of Information whereby he was allowed to live in the United States and draw on a portion of his American royalties in return for unofficially promoting the British cause. He had personal reasons for wishing to reside in America – his lover Gerald Haxton was not allowed to live in Britain – and the British Treasury was allowing him enough to live comfortably. So he continued to do propaganda work, though in diminishing amounts.

At the end of the war, Maugham's contribution to the British propaganda campaign in the United States was recognized by the Foreign Office in several ways. When he was devastated by Haxton's death in November 1944, Brendan Bracken, the minister of information, arranged for his nephew Robin to spend several months in America, ostensibly to do publicity for his armed services/civilian newspaper *Convoy* but in reality to deal with the old author's grief. Then, in the summer of 1945, when Maugham wanted another friend, Alan Searle, to come to the United States to act as his secretary, he donated the manuscript of *Of Human Bondage* to the Library of Congress in recognition, he said, of the kindness shown to Britons by Americans during the war. When he proposed that Searle personally bring the manuscript from London, Lord Halifax's private secretary wrote in support and the matter was considered by the secretary of state for foreign affairs, Ernest Bevin. J.C. Donnelly of the Foreign Office had written:

Mr Maugham is widely regarded in the United States as a major literary figure. I know that at one time he was working privately and unofficially as a propagandist for us in the United States. He was, I recollect, unpaid but allowed to retain funds for his subsistence from his dollar earnings. In any case, I think that the national interest requires us to regard Mr Maugham as in a special category ... and do whatever we reasonably can to help him. I think that Mr Searle should be granted an exit permit and that we should give him a moderate degree of priority in obtaining a sea passage.[55]

Searle arrived in the United States on Christmas Day 1945. Maugham and Searle returned to the south of France in May 1946, and in 1954 Maugham was made a Companion of Honour.

A Sad Story of Official Duplicity
Cecil Roberts

"I spent my money, I gave my services, I broke my health, and received from the British Government nothing but insult and injury."[1] Thus did an embittered Cecil Roberts sum up his nearly six years of speaking, writing, and making public appearances in the United States to promote the British war effort in the Second World War. The words are his epigraph to a lengthy file entitled "A Sad Story of Official Duplicity," included among his papers donated to the Churchill Archives Centre, at Churchill College, Cambridge. The file contains detailed documentation of Roberts's assertion, made public first in a guarded version in *And So to America* (1947) and then more explicitly in his volume of memoirs *Sunshine and Shadow* (1972), that the British government gladly exploited his services and then callously ignored him when he sought recognition and recompense for his sacrifice. Although his account of his experiences is coloured by self-puffery, it does illustrate the ambiguity engendered by the British government's use of writers as unofficial and seemingly arm's-length propagandists.

Cecil Roberts was born in Nottingham in 1892, and following his father's death when the boy was fifteen he and his mother endured five years of poverty. During the First World War, he was a naval correspondent with the Grand Fleet and then a correspondent for the Newspaper Society and Reuter's on the Western Front. Following the war, he became the literary editor and drama critic of the *Liverpool Post* and then served five years as editor of the *Nottingham Journal*, which made him the youngest editor in Britain – and of one of the country's oldest newspapers. He was reputed to be able to produce brilliant articles "as easily and rapidly as a tap produces water."[2]

In his twenties, Roberts began to publish slim volumes of poetry and tried his hand at playwriting, but he soon determined that much more substantial money was to be made in fiction. With the success of his first novel, *Scissors*, in 1923, he turned to full-time novel writing, though for some time he augmented his income as a freelance writer, contributing to *Sphere* and the *Daily Telegraph*. By the 1930s he had become a best-seller of light romantic novels such as *Pilgrim Cottage* (1933) and *Victoria Four-Thirty* (1937).

In 1920, at the age of twenty-eight, Roberts made a lecture tour of the United States, and its success led to four more tours in the inter-war period. On his second visit, in 1924 at the age of thirty-two, he gave the Commemorative Address at Washington and Jefferson University and was awarded an honorary Doctor of Letters.

At a dinner party in London in the spring of 1939, according to Roberts, he confronted Leslie Hore-Belisha, the secretary of state for war and president of the Army Council, about the impending war and the necessity of enlisting American aid. He offered his services as one who knew and understood America well. "Since official propagandists who were financially supported by their governments were banned by the [Neutrality] Act," he said, "there was one way to present our case. There were English authors known to the American public who could make lecture tours."[3]

When Roberts was referred to Major General Ian Hay Beith, director of information at the War Office, he provided a list of British authors who could conduct covert propaganda in the United States, and he pointed out that he himself was already booked for a tour beginning in October. Both Hay Beith and Hore-Belisha advised Roberts to go ahead with his American lecture tour, but nothing was done about his list of authors. Moreover, on 29 August Roberts was irritated to receive a typed form letter with his name written in from Hay Beith suggesting that he offer his services to S.D. Charles of the Civil Service Commission. Six days later, he was further insulted by another form letter, this time from the Ministry of Information's A.D. Peters, stating: "I am instructed to inform you that your name has been duly entered and that a further communication will be sent to you should the Ministry avail itself of your offer, which is gratefully noted."[4]

Roberts ignored both Charles and Peters and went directly to Sir Frederick Whyte, who also urged him to go through with his lecture tour and offered the assistance of the ministry. Years later, Roberts described Whyte as "an obscurantist and knighted dodo" running a department so disorganized that, two days before he left for the United States, he received a letter from Whyte's deputy director stating that he had heard from the Passport Office that Roberts was going to America and he would like to discuss his tour with him.[5]

Roberts arrived in New York aboard the ss *Manhattan*, along with Duff Cooper, S.K. Ratcliffe, I.A. Richards, R. Ellis Roberts, and Phyllis Bottome, and proceeded to make discreet contact with the British Library of Information. Several weeks later, he drove to Florida to speak in St Augustine, Miami, and Palm Beach to septuagenarians, stockbrokers, and members of societies interested in international affairs. In Winter Park, he joined poet Carl Sandburg, Countess Tolstoy, popular novelist Rex Beach, and the editor of the *New York Times* at a symposium at Rollins College. From there he went to a wintry and hostile Chicago to lecture at the English Speaking Union's annual dinner, the Women's Club, the Arts League, the Rotary Club, and the Executives' Club.

Despite Roberts's disdain for Whyte, he dutifully reported on his various lectures and public appearances in a letter he wrote to the director on 10 February 1940. Whyte replied on 5 March saying, "Your evidence straight from the front is valuable," and suggesting that Roberts consult Angus Fletcher at the British Library of Information about the possibility of continuing his speaking tour during the following winter.[6]

At the same time as he was being urged to remain in the United States, Roberts discovered that the British government, needing dollars with which to buy American armaments, required British subjects there to turn over all their American funds in exchange for British sterling, which was then immediately frozen. In his case, this meant selling seventy thousand dollars' worth of stocks and applying to the British Treasury for an allowance of twenty dollars a day from the proceeds. "It proved to be the most foolish act of my life," he later claimed. "I was to learn bitterly that no man should trust the promise of a Government. It has not the solidity of a soap bubble."[7]

In April 1940 Whyte informed Roberts that the Treasury had rejected his application for a dollar allowance, suggesting instead that he spend the summer months in the British West Indies, where he could draw on his English account. "In any case," added Whyte, "I hope that you will be able to remain on the other side and carry out your programmme."[8] When Duff Cooper, his fellow passenger on the

Manhattan the year before, became minister of information, he wrote Roberts saying: "I am sure you will be wise to stay in America at the present time and deliver lectures stating the British case. I found that even when I was there, they were quite willing to hear our case stated so long as they were not afraid that an effort was being made to drag them in."[9]

Roberts survived in the United States on various fees he received for lectures and articles, and on the kindness of friends and lion-hunting hostesses eager to add a British author to their guest lists. Although he cast envious glances at Somerset Maugham's suite in the Ritz-Carlton in New York, his own war years in the United States were hardly marked by deprivation. Both *And So to America* and *Sunshine and Shadow* describe comfortable stays in Palm Springs, Beverley Hills, Nantucket, and Bermuda; lunches at the Century Club, cocktail parties on Fifth Avenue, and concerts at Carnegie Hall; dinners with the Nelson Doubledays and New Year's parties with the Marques de Cuevas. Throughout his memoirs, the names drop as if from an autograph collector's album: Sergei Rachmaninoff, Emerald Cunard, Prince Windischgraetz, Archduke Otto of Hapsburg, Thomas Beecham, Lady Ribblesdale, Baron Maurice de Rothschild, and many more. Roberts might have had to sing for his supper, but the fare could hardly be called meagre.

James Hilton, then a successful and highly paid Hollywood screenwriter as well as an ardent propagandist for Britain, got Roberts a $3,000 commission to write a scenario based on a Maugham story. Although the film was never produced, the commission supported him for some time, and when Angus Fletcher heard that he was going to Hollywood he took the opportunity to give him a list of sixteen meetings that he wished him to address. By the time Roberts arrived in California, Hilton had arranged another seven lectures.

On his return to New York in September 1940 Roberts met with Fletcher, who told him that he was in demand as a speaker and that he hoped he would agree to another series of lectures: "I take this opportunity to say that the work you are doing in speaking yourself whenever opportunity occurs is valuable in meeting an urgent need. There are, alas, too many well-meaning but ineffective exponents of the Cause, and there are others who have to be paid $2,500 a time to be set in motion ... but neither meets the need as you do when you voluntarily harness your standing as an author."[10] From London, the new director of the American Division of the Ministry of Information,

Douglas Williams, added: "I have read with the greatest interest the account of your doings, and am delighted to see how well you are fulfilling a very important task."[11]

Roberts's "doings" involved making public appearances for such organizations as the British War Relief Society, Bundles for Britain, the British Red Cross, American Ambulances for the Allies, the U.S. Blood Bank, Refugees of England, and Soldiers' Canteens and Clubs. More important were his speeches to such groups as the Society of Colonial Wars, the American Institute of Decorators, the American Jewish Congress, the Princeton Club of New York, Columbia University, the New York Booksellers' League, and the American Association for Adult Education.

At first glance, Roberts would seem to have been a poor candidate for success on the American lecture stage. Harry Salpeter once commented, "Cecil Edric Mornington Roberts is, as his full name indicates, an Englishman ... tall, lithe, intense,"[12] and Roger Pippett called him "a survival from the eighteenth century ... an interesting amalgam of the snob and the man of feeling."[13] However, Lewis Richmond, who succeeded him as editor of the *Nottingham Journal*, claimed that "as a conversationalist there has been none to equal Cecil Roberts since Oscar Wilde ... As a lecturer he was equally successful; his description of places were spectacular and colourful; his wit never failed him and he was a master of epigram."[14]

Much of Roberts's success as a speaker seems to have been a result of his ability to turn his own Englishness to advantage. On one occasion, for example, he was speaking at an American Red Cross drive in New York, and following the foghorn American voices of the two previous speakers his English accent began to draw gibes from the tough Bronx audience. Roberts stopped, the hall grew silent, and he said: "I know what you have been laughing about. It's my English accent, the way I talk. May I remind you, ladies and gentlemen, that the men of the British 8th Army talk the way I do?"[15] It mattered little that few men in Montgomery's army, celebrated for its recent victory over Rommel in North Africa, spoke with an accent anything like Roberts's. The crowd cheered and listened intently for the rest of his speech.

In *Sunshine and Shadow*, Roberts claimed that he made five hundred speeches in forty-four states during the war, and even if this figure is somewhat exaggerated, he undoubtedly spoke widely and often. Some of his lectures – such as "The English Country House Tradition" and "Will the Home Survive?" – emphasized the historical and cultural traditions which, by implication, were threatened by Nazism. In "A Novelist at Home," declared the advertisement, Roberts talked about his cottage at Henley-on-Thames as a microcosm of British life: "This is the quintessence of England and English life, something that may have already vanished, to become a great legend. Around the cottage ... the novelist reconstructs with unforgettable characterization the men and women of England through five hundred years of its life."[16] His talk entitled "I Knew Six Cities: European Journey" examined London, Paris, Vienna, Rome, Venice, and Budapest – which Roberts called six "dead" capitals in the midst of the chaos of war.

Many other of Roberts's lectures were about the contemporary political situation. "The European Whirlpool," delivered in a number of places in the early months of 1940, traced Britain's relationship with Germany from the First World War to the Second, defending the Treaty of Versailles as "just, perfect, and moderate in demands in comparison with the treaty intended by the former German high command should they have won the last war." Sympathy for the defeated Germans, he claimed, had led to appeasement between the wars and to the military and psychological unpreparedness inherited by Chamberlain. The United States, he concluded, was facing the same dangers when it succumbed to "exploited peace propaganda" and the refrain of "Keep America out of war": "America's immunity is not ideological but geographical. Get rid of the 3,000 miles of Atlantic Ocean and America would be in the midst of the vortex."[17]

In "Torchbearers of Civilization," delivered often in 1942 and 1943, Roberts argued that the spiritual battle going on behind the actual fighting was for rebirth, as expressed by the thinkers, artists, writers, poets, and dramatists. Wars have ravaged the earth, but the vital torchbearers have been Homer, Shakespeare, Dante, Raphael, Goethe, Dumas, and Beethoven. Who, asked Roberts, guards the sacred flame today? "Mr Roberts," proclaimed the posters, "examines the field, looks towards this temple of refuge, the United States, and finds gathered here the immortal forces of creative genius that will renew a shattered Europe."[18]

On some occasions Roberts delivered a strongly political lecture in the guise of a literary or cultural talk. In September 1942, for example, when the failure of Sir Stafford Cripps's mission and Gandhi's civil disobedience made Britain's treatment of India the subject of much debate in the United States, Roberts was asked to speak to eight hundred people at an annual Neighbor's Night celebration in Nantucket, Massachusetts. "I chose the title of my lecture with deliberate duplicity," he later confessed. "'A Novelist Looks at His World.' Quite reasonably they expected a literary lecture; actually they were given a two-hour address on India."[19]

Roberts's Nantucket talk, which he repeated elsewhere throughout the autumn of 1942, was remarkably aggressive in defending British control of India. The old British Empire builders, he said, had found a country in total chaos as a result of internecine war, rape, and endless bloody quarrels between petty princes. The British presence there was "the natural expansion of an energetic people" – the same impulse, he was careful to point out, that had led white Europeans to subjugate North American aboriginals. Contemporary India, said Roberts, was ruled jointly by British and Indian civil servants through "a very large degree of Indian good-will and co-operation." India paid no taxes, direct or indirect, to Britain, had complete fiscal autonomy, and did not have conscription. Nehru's Congress Party represented only part of the huge population of India and was torn by internal divisions, and to turn the country over to its control would mean turning it into a dictatorship. Thus, Britain "must continue the Government through all the dangers of war now threatening India."[20]

Although patronizing toward India, Roberts's talk was detailed, carefully argued, and thorough; and it was printed in full in the *Nantucket Inquirer* and then reprinted in newspapers throughout the country. Roberts was careful to send copies both to Lord Halifax and to Brendan Bracken, the current minister of information. Halifax replied, "I have read with the greatest interest and admiration your clear and forceful exposition of the India problem," while Bracken wrote, "We think it a masterly performance. It is of immense service to us."[21]

Emboldened by the response to his lecture, Roberts became more strident about the Indian question as the autumn months wore on. On 2 December, in speaking to the Teaneck Masonic Lodge in Bogota, New Jersey, he was positively shrill. In November Wendell Willkie had attacked Churchill's assertion that Britain would not surrender its empire and had advocated the doctrine of self-determination of peoples. Roberts responded that India had in no respect shown itself capable of self-government, and it was "the duty of the white, English-speaking races to do a little dictating after the war by virtue of their military and economic sacrifices." "Attacking India with both fists," reported one newspaper, "Roberts asserted that it has contributed little or nothing to world civilization in government, philosophy, art, or architecture, and that the Indians are simply not yet equal to the white races." Any religion that permits a sacred cow to hold up the Delhi Express for eight hours was absurd, said Roberts, and there was little of value in Indian religions in general. He concluded this speech by carefully implicating the United States in the patriarchal control of much of the world. Calling its policy in the Pacific "imperial," he advocated its continuation for the good of all the peoples concerned.[22]

Despite the extremism of Roberts's statements, particularly when paraphrased by journalists, there is no record of their sparking a public outcry or of causing concern in the Foreign Office or the Ministry of Information. This may be because of the nature of the particular audiences he addressed, the manner of his delivery, or the fact that since Americans were by then in the war they were as concerned as the British that India not yield to Japan. In general, Roberts's lectures seem to have been successful, judging by the postwar comment of a *New York Times* reporter: "The best propaganda in the world is the British, and the most efficient expression we witnessed were the lectures held all over the U.S.A. by the noted author, Cecil Roberts. These lectures had never the flavour of propaganda but brought more goodwill towards Britain than anything else."[23]

Throughout the war Roberts used his pen as well as his voice in the British cause. When trouble developed between visiting British sailors and Americans who cut in on them at dances, he was commissioned to write a booklet entitled *Now You Are in the U.S.A.* which explained the American social habits to British servicemen. From time to time, he wrote articles for the American press about aspects of the British war effort: young gunners freshly over from the North African campaign, officers on tour from Libya, and members of the Army Film and Photographic Unit dodging bullets to get photographs. In the spring of 1941 Roberts edited and published *Letters from Jim*, a volume of correspondence sent to him by a young soldier who had been wounded in action behind German lines in northern Italy. In a review published a year later in the *Saturday Review*, he added his voice to those praising Philip Guedalla's adulatory biography of Churchill.

In addition to his American publications, in the early years of the war Roberts wrote articles analysing American attitudes, sending them back to Britain to be published in the *Telegraph and Morning Post*. Behind the scenes, he provided monthly reports – he estimated that he wrote about eighty during the war – to the Ministry of Information about American public opinion, the performance of other lecturers, and other aspects of the propaganda campaign.

Roberts's single most visible contribution to British propaganda, however, was his March 1941 poem "A Man Arose," which added to the mythology quickly growing around Churchill. Hitler and Mussolini had seized power, the poem began, because Britain had retreated into a "blind and happy isolation," but "in the dark, desperate hour, ringed with her foes, / God-given, to match the need, a man arose":

A man arose, in England sired,
And suckled by the young, free West,
Of lineage proud, of blood inspired,
That long gave England of its best –
Statesmen and captains, truculent, bold,
Hot in valour, in caution cold,
Masters of swift manœuvres, gay
With lightning thrust of speech and sword;
At Blenheim and at Malplaquet
Proud Fate bowed to her overlord
And granted, through contentious years,
To that far hour of perilous need,
One who promised "blood, sweat, tears"
To serve them as a conquering creed.

It mattered little that Churchill's arising, carefully orchestrated from his study at Chartwell and by his coterie of supporters, was about as spontaneous as that of Lazarus. Moreover, Roberts went on to call on Christ in Churchillian terms to save the country of tradition and courage:

O Lord enthroned, O pitying Christ!
Thou see'st a fair land sacrificed,
A valiant people holding breath
Beneath a screaming rain of death;
Unbowed, unbeaten in the hell
Of mine, torpedo, bomb and shell,
Around them ruin swiftly falls
On churches, towns memorials,
The loveliness a thousand years
Have touched with mellow grace of age;

And yet above the blood, sweat, tears,
They write for Time a deathless page,
Affirm the holy spirit of Man
Transcends his mortal heritage.[24]

Roberts enjoyed enormous success in the United States with this poem, first reading it to millions of listeners over the NBC radio network on 30 March, when he was introduced by Wendell Willkie, and repeating the performance five times in the next three months. Published in *Redbook* magazine in June 1941, an expanded version was reprinted in book form and, according to Roberts, sold 100,000 copies. The royalties went to the RAF Benevolent Fund, and his donation of the manuscript to the Library of Congress created even more publicity for Churchill and the country he had come to epitomize.

Like many other British authors involved in the propaganda campaign, much of Roberts's work was done in the social setting, among people in important positions who could influence public opinion. In 1941, like Noel Coward, he met with President and Mrs Roosevelt; having been introduced to the president's wife at a Bundles for Britain meeting in New York, he was invited to a small cocktail party at the White House to meet Roosevelt himself. The president, said Roberts, was particularly interested in the author's opinion of his American audiences.

While in Washington, Roberts consulted with Lord Halifax, who was proving to be notoriously out of touch with American public opinion. "His speeches," observed Roberts, "did not reveal any knowledge of American life and history, they lacked an intimate touch."[25] The writer offered to provide Halifax with background material on the places he visited and the people to whom he talked; and according to Roberts, he assisted in the preparation of forty-two of the ambassador's speeches over a three-year period. This, he later maintained, did much to make Halifax seem more human and more knowledgeable about American affairs. When Sir Gerald Campbell became director general of the British Information Services in 1941, Roberts similarly contributed material to his speeches.

Although Roberts had a tendency to exaggerate his contribution to the war effort, there is evidence that he was indeed working closely with the British Embassy in Washington. In the correspondence housed in Churchill College is a letter to him from C. Chetwynd, dated 11 May 1941, which explained that he was being sent the "Code

Ajax," which would be in use until further codes were supplied. "The Ambassador," the letter continued, "has given orders for you to receive the Confidential War Cabinet and Foreign Office reports each month. Owing to their highly confidential nature each copy must be returned to General Forbes. In no instance must the Code be returned in the same envelope. B.L.I. will be responsible for returning the reports by King's Messenger to Washington."[26] The provision of embassy codes suggests a close and trusting working relationship between the embassy and Roberts. Astonishingly, however, and unknown to him, Roberts was at the same time being viewed with suspicion by another branch of the British government.

Early in 1941 Roberts had continued his campaign to persuade the British Treasury to give him a comfortable allowance from the funds held for him in Britain. In February, Angus Fletcher had assured him that the British Library of Information had received only the most enthusiastic reports of his lecture tours and that it wished him to remain in the United States: "We have good reason to thank you for the great personal efforts you have made to undertake engagements which were significant to the British cause ... I still hope that some means may be found to enable you to stay here, not only because of your exceptional knowledge of the United States and your wide and representative contacts among Americans. Nobody knows better than we do the value of these personal relationships."[27] Yet a month later, Fletcher had to tell Roberts that the Treasury had turned down his request, and the Ministry of Information hoped that he would return to Britain for a brief visit so as to renew his authority to speak about life in wartime Britain.

On 6 March, when Roberts wrote to J.W. Pepper, a friend in London, to complain about his treatment by the British government, he used the pseudonym "C. Robins" and the return address of his New York agent, W.B. Feakins. Convinced that his belongings had been rifled by German agents in San Francisco the year before, Roberts may have adopted this subterfuge to foil the enemy. More likely, he wished to prevent the British authorities knowing that he was breaching confidentiality and airing his grievances to others.

Roberts had not counted on the diligence of the British government's Postal and Telegraph Censorship Department, which considered the contents of his letter sensitive enough to warrant the attention of the Foreign Office. Although it sent the letter on to Pepper, it characterized its author as "Englishman, lecturing on behalf of the British Government in the U.S.A." and paraphrased its content:

You would hardly believe it but I cannot get a penny to live on, no allowance even and depend on kindness of friends. The Chief here has cabled the F.O. three times and then sent me to the Embassy in Washington to see the Minister etc. All very sympathetic and powerless to do anything with the Treasury. So I said, I would go home. That let a storm loose. They beseeched me to stay and wrote such testimonials as you cannot imagine. Then on top of that fifteen heads of helping England organizations here bombarded our Ambassador saying I must be kept here as I was the No. 1 man, so I am awaiting news of another effort on the F.O. ...

I have a wonderful chief here in Sir Angus Fletcher and he paid me a very noble tribute when he wrote to Halifax, who I find rather a stuffed shirt. I completed my 236th speech last night and my 94th town ... I have written a tribute to Churchill ... it has swept America ... Never was I more wanted over here.[28]

Reading this in the Foreign Office, T. North Whitehead commented that while he was uncomfortable with using the Censorship Department as a means of betraying a man's correspondence to his superior, "Mr Robins looks to me like a dangerous fellow, not from ill will but from conceit & foolishness."[29] The paraphrase of the intercepted letter was therefore referred to Angus Fletcher, who replied on 13 May:

The writer's name is not Robbins and he is not in any way attached to the B.L.I., nor am I his "chief" in any sense. He is even more conceited than his letter suggests – he told me, for example, that if he had chosen another career he would by this time have been British Ambassador to the United States! However, at his best he does good work on the platform, and has gone out and done jobs at our request without payment as loyally as anyone, and in the past eighteen months he has been most useful. Latterly he seems to have been suffering from the nervous strain of uncertainty about funds (he is well off in Sterling) ... I have tried to make him realise that his lamentations about being penniless are not going down well, and I propose to take an early opportunity to tell him that he must be more careful in what he says, as he is in danger of being misunderstood. As it would be unwise to refer to his correspondence, we must be prepared to find that he continues to write in this hysterical way about himself, the Treasury and the Foreign Office.

Fletcher's letter effectively describes the relationship between the British authors working in the United States during the war and the government offices such as the British Library of Information and the Ministry of Information. Roberts was never officially employed at the

British Library, so Fletcher was never officially his superior. However, for eighteen months (i.e., the entire length of his stay to that point) Fletcher had found him "most useful" in working for the Library – and at his own expense. He went on to point out that the library had been handicapped in using people for publicity because it had had to rely on those, like Roberts, who could pay their own way. "The truth is," he said, "that we have had to use whatever human material there was at hand. We cannot complain of it, though we do so often wish we had 100% types rather than 2nd and 3rd best."

It is clear, moreover, that Fletcher believed that Roberts was still useful enough that he and the Foreign Office should be prepared to tolerate his continuing complaints. Even such carping by Roberts and others, he added cynically, had its publicity value: "We get a small dividend, however, because these grumbles are proof that H.M.G. is not throwing money about on propaganda over here." At the Foreign Office, North Whitehead and F.E. Evans apparently agreed with Fletcher to carry on using Roberts, both noting that "this seems to end the affair of Mr Robins."[30]

The Fletcher letter also discussed another of Roberts's concerns, one that he shared with many of the Britons who were doing propaganda work in the United States: anxiety about the effect that a lengthy stay in the United States was having on their reputation back in Britain. "He is very much afraid of being regarded by his friends in England as a runaway," said Fletcher. "I have told him that so long as he is earning dollars here, and doing some public speaking for the cause, and so long as he has not been asked to return to England ... he should not worry about his reputation. In practice not only he but all the British lecturers here feel rather uncomfortable on this question and are always asking to be reassured – a fact which I suppose is to their credit."[31]

Roberts did have reason to be apprehensive about how his American sojourn was being perceived back home. In *Testament of Experience*, Vera Brittain described an encounter with him on 5 April 1940, the day before she returned to Britain. When she suggested that there was room on her ship for him, he replied that it was impossible for him to leave, that he had a film script which he had to deliver personally to Hollywood. "Four years later," she observed sarcastically, "the author was still in America, but I had no impulse to join in the uncharitable comments on his prolonged absence. I had learned a bitter lesson during the reluctant flight from Europe with the children in 1938, and knew that I should never have been brave enough to live with the knowledge that I was afraid to return."[32]

Brittain does not identify Roberts, but there can be little doubt that he was the author in question. Roberts recognized himself in the passage, which he characterized to Phyllis Bentley as a "malicious attack" and a "highly actionable ... deliberate libel." His explanation of the incident was that since Brittain was returning home after a very controversial tour, he had been asked by the British authorities to make a report on her activities. He sought out Brittain and her husband at their hotel, told them about going to Hollywood to write the Maugham scenario without revealing that he was also going there to do propaganda work, and wrote a report which "played down her offence." For this, he complained, he was portrayed as "a cowardly poltroon who was staying out of his own country at such a time to make money."[33]

Although Fletcher's letter makes it clear that Roberts was not officially attached to the British Library of Information or the Ministry of Information, he spent the entire war and many more years convinced that he was working for the government. In Pamela Frankau's report to the Foreign Office on her American experience in 1940, she described Roberts as "an English lecturer with great opportunities. Has not been home since war began. But regards himself as officially a propagandist, in support of which he has a letter from the Minister of Information."[34] In a letter to Sir Godfrey Haggard at the Foreign Office, in February 1944, he wrote that he had gone to the United States "as the result of consultation with the Secretary of State for War in March, 1938 [sic], and with the Director of the American Branch of the Ministry of Information, in September, 1939."[35] In Donald Brook's *Writers' Gallery*, published in Britain in 1944, Roberts is described as "in America engaged in work of a semi-official nature."[36]

The British government certainly did little to convince Roberts that he was not working for it. Several months after the incident of the intercepted letter, Douglas Williams, director of the American Division of the Ministry of Information, wrote to tell him that it was not possible to fly him back to Britain for a brief visit. Although his renewed experience of the country in wartime would enhance his value as a lecturer, said Williams, "I fear you might find yourself stuck here when you should be on the lecture platform in America."[37] At about the same time, Fletcher was replaced by Charles Webster at what had by then become the British Information Services. According to Roberts, when Webster heard that he wished to return to Britain, he exclaimed: "For God's sake don't go! I'm told you are our best man here. What would you do if you went home? They need only soldiers and factory workers."[38] More succinctly, the Ministry of Information cabled: "We do very much hope you will stay."[39]

Following Pearl Harbor, Roberts, like Maugham, was convinced that isolationism was dead and that his job in the United States was done. However, Webster reminded him of the danger of Americans ignoring the European war in favour of the fight in the Pacific. It would be necessary for Roberts and others to insist that the war would be won or lost in Europe. Accordingly, when the writer gave his "Torchbearers of Civilization" speech to the Executives' Club in Chicago in March 1942, he pointed out that the enemy in the Pacific was seven or eight thousand miles away while the enemy in Europe was only three or four thousand: "Any sound strategist will tell you that we should act along the lines of the shortest communication, thereby conserving effort and transport. Our chances of knocking out Germany are infinitely greater, quicker and less costly. So I hope we shall not be diverted into what would be disastrous strategy. The collapse in Germany will be total and not long delayed. There will be no immediate collapse of Japan."[40] According to Roberts, the British consul general almost danced with delight: "That's the line! That's the line!"[41]

Roberts kept to the line for the remainder of the war, speaking and appearing in the United States on behalf of the British cause until the summer of 1945. As well, he worked for the American Treasury's War Bond Campaign. None of this prevented him from continuing to complain about his treatment by British officialdom. As late as February 1944, for example, he chastised Sir Godfrey Haggard for having remarked to an American lecture organizer that "Roberts should go home." "I am not an embusque nor a military service dodger," he wrote angrily. "In the past four years I have been in forty-seven states, over two hundred cities, and addressed over eight hundred meetings, all on behalf of British and Allied causes, receiving no fee whatsoever, my pen being my sole source of income ... The story, until recent times, of the treatment I have received at official hands has a particularly disgraceful chapter, to which you have now added a footnote."[42]

Long after the surrender of Japan, Roberts continued to wage his own war with the British government. In July 1947, wishing to repay American debts, he requested that the Treasury transfer the equivalent of $72,633 from his blocked sterling account to his bank in the United States, an amount which he calculated he was owed from his wartime activities in the United States. Since the Ministry of Information had by then been dissolved, Roberts sought testimonials from prominent figures in the propaganda campaign. Lord Halifax wrote appreciatively of his contribution to Anglo-American relations but mentioned nothing of his help in speech writing. Sir Gerald Campbell, on the other hand, commented on "the kind and generous way in which you responded from time to time to my appeals for information which would help to make my addresses more acceptable to American audiences through the introduction of items of local or national interest."[43] Brendan Bracken, the minister of information through the greatest part of Roberts' years in the United States, provided the warmest description of his work:

When the war broke out, he was encouraged by the British authorities to remain in America, for it was generally felt that by doing so he could render great help to our cause. British propaganda or publicity in the United States was a delicate and difficult matter in those days. As Mr Roberts was already a familiar and well-known figure there, he escaped the reproach of being a British propagandist. He had his audiences ready made, and he could speak for England without seeming to be a Government agent. There were, indeed, few Britons on the spot who combined his talents for the task with his freedom from official handicaps. His writings and speeches undoubtedly contributed to that marked rallying of support which was of priceless benefit to our cause during the blackest days.[44]

The Treasury turned down Roberts's request but pointed out that emigrants from Britain were permitted to withdraw a certain amount of their capital in yearly instalments. Interpreting this as a thinly veiled invitation to emigrate, he left Britain in bitterness, not for the United States but for Italy, living first in a villa overlooking the Mediterranean in Alassio and then in the Grand Hotel in Rome.

In 1960 Roberts was made an honorary citizen of Alassio, and six years later the City of Rome awarded him the Italian Gold Medal. In 1965 the city of his boyhood conferred on him the Freedom of the City of Nottingham. None of these honours, however, removed the sting of what he perceived to be a lack of recognition for his work during the war. He could not help noticing resentfully that Lord Halifax's autobiography, *Fulness of Days*, thanked Charles Peake for his contribution to his American speeches but made no mention of his own assistance. Similarly, Lord Birkenhead's 1965 biography of Halifax ignored Roberts and praised Peake, Angus Malcolm, and J.G. Lockhart. Four of Halifax's entourage were given knighthoods as well as pensions, the old writer noted bitterly. His own legacy was a recurring stomach ailment, which to the end of his life he called "my old enemy, my Treasury ulcer."[45]

8

Unheralded Ambassadors from England
British Non-Fiction Propaganda

Although the Ministry of Information spent the first five months of the Second World War indecisively wrestling with the problem of setting up an Authors' Planning Committee to give writers an administrative voice in the conduct of propaganda, it wasted no time in encouraging writers actually to put pen to paper in support of the war effort. In particular, the ministry recognized the need to use the written word in a wide variety of forms to enlist the sympathy and support of the United States.

An outline of the structure of the American Division framed in the months leading up to the war listed Basil Mathews as a "special officer" whose duties included "liaison with publishers in connection with publications in the u.s.a." A professor of theology and an author, who had chaired the Literature Committee of the Ministry of Information in the First World War, Mathews was familiar with the United States through his lecture tours there in the interwar period. For the first year of the war, he served as deputy director of the American Division, with the following duties: "Responsibility for all contacts with educational bodies, learned societies, and other cultural groups, including the Royal Institute of International Affairs, and with British organisations with Anglo-American contacts (eg. Rotary), for liaison with authors and publishers, and for all problems connected with churches and religious organisations (including the religious press)."[1]

From Washington, in the fall of 1939, Lord Lothian recommended the use of written propaganda, but only if it was not overt and heavy-handed. When his analysis was forwarded to the Ministry of Information, Sir Frederick Whyte wrote to the undersecretary of state: "The American Division agree with Lord Lothian that the Americans 'know the case very well already.' They accept his advice on articles and books by well known authors, and have been in constant consultation with the Home Publicity Division of the Ministry on this question. They hope that the result of two months' work will begin to show before long in the publication both in the United Kingdom and the United States of really useful books by writers whose names carry weight over there."[2]

The "two months' work" included arranging for the American firm Harper & Brothers to publish a book on the political crisis and the war, written by the *New York Times* journalist Harold Callender. Harper also agreed to publish Sir Norman Angell's *For What Do We Fight?*, which was followed by *America's Dilemma: Alone or Allied?* and *Let the People Know*. A contract was settled with Farrar and Rinehart for a popular edition of *The British War Blue Book*, a selection of documents about the events leading up to Britain's declaration of war. At the urging of W.H. Stevenson, Macmillan of New York was expected to bring out a volume by the Labour MP Arthur Greenwood. Ann Bridge agreed to write a book specifically for America, and in the winter of 1939–40 A.D. Divine was commissioned to produce a book about the various convoys, the Dover Patrol, minesweepers, and other subsidiary fleets supporting the navy's fighting ships. "The Ministry's main interest," it reported, "is primarily for the United States, and negotiations are already in hand commercially for publication in book form and for serialisation throughout the North American Newspaper Alliance."[3] Although Bridge's book never appeared, Divine went on to write nine more documentary books about British military units and battles. Negotiations were also underway for syndication in the United States of articles by J.B. Priestley.

By February 1940 the Foreign Office's T. North Whitehead could note an active Ministry of Information publication program: "The M of I provides British books and articles for American publication. It has 'close and confidential relations' with several American syndicates, literary agents, and publishers' representatives, as well as with British writers with American reputation. Results are now said to be showing in books and articles appearing in the U.S."[4]

As the war progressed, the Ministry of Information succeeded in placing a variety of articles in American periodicals, most notably in the *Atlantic Monthly, Harper's, Collier's,* and *Saturday Evening Post.* The *Atlantic Monthly,* with a circulation slightly over 100,000 and read by many business and influential social leaders along the East Coast of the United States, was particularly sympathetic to the British situation. In the first month of the war, its editors invited submissions on Britain's actions and aims; and through Ann Bridge, the Ministry of Information was able to arrange for articles by Harold Laski and Wickham Steed.[5]

Many of the British articles carried in American magazines were first-hand accounts of battles and military life, bringing the war closer to the American reader and putting a human face on the British struggle. Bartimeus (the *nom de plume* of a retired British sea captain) described the retreat at Dunkirk, the work of submarines, and other naval campaigns in a series of pieces for the *Atlantic Monthly*. Dunkirk was also treated by a writer with the pen name Taffrail, in the August 1940 issue of the *Saturday Evening Post*. In an article in the *New York Times* in November 1939, Sir Philip Gibbs told of the differences between life at the front in the two world wars (there was more camaraderie between classes in the Second World War, he said). In the *Atlantic Monthly* in July 1942, R.C. Hutchinson described an excursion to Norway; in the August 1944 edition of *Harper's*, Vernon Bartlett described the reactions of Britons to the first four days following D-Day; and in the January 1945 *Atlantic Monthly*, Charles Morgan reported on the European war.

C.S. Forester wrote articles such as "How the British Sank the Scharnhorst" and "How the Midgets Hit the Tirpitz," which were published in the *Saturday Evening Post*. As he told Roald Dahl in 1942, "I'm too old for the war. I live over here now. The only thing I can do to help is to write things about Britain for the American papers and magazines. We need all the help America can give us."[6] In the following year, as part of his war work, Forester wrote *The Ship*, a novel about a British light cruiser in action in the Mediterranean.

Articles on the political and social issues of the war always ran the risk of alienating Americans or providing ammunition to isolationists, but a number of authors could be trusted to write tactfully. Norman Angell had a monthly column in *Free World* and published also in the *Saturday Evening Post* and the *American Mercury*. Vernon Bartlett contributed to *Current History* and the *New York Times*, in which he wrote in 1944 that the division in the House of Commons was "between the few who hope to return to pre-war conditions with the special privileges they had enjoyed and the many, so largely responsible, who realise that social conditions in our country need reform and who hope to build a new world in which there is freedom from want and from fear."[7] Michael Arlen published "The People Write on Stone," an account of the democracy growing amidst an air raid on a Midlands city, in the *Saturday Evening Post* of December 1941.

In "The Armistice Period in British Fiction," carried in the *New York Times* in August 1941, Phyllis Bentley equated the interwar writers' search for consciousness and truth with the British battle against Hitler, and Harold Hobson told readers of the *Christian Science Monitor* of air raid damage to rare books. H.E. Bates, whose *Fair Stood the Wind for France* became a Book-of-the-Month Club selection in 1944, described the presence of American soldiers in Britain that year and concluded: "If there are finer, securer, deeper ties than this between the two people I do not know where you'll find them."[8] Hector Bolitho's "Britain's Darkest Hour" appeared in the *American Mercury,* James Hilton's "One Lamp Keeps Burning" in the *Los Angeles Times,* R.C. Hutchinson's "The Fire and the Wood" in the *Ladies' Home Journal,* and Storm Jameson's poignant "City without Children" in the *Atlantic Monthly.* Arthur Koestler wrote "Knights in Rusty Armour," "The Fraternity of Pessimists," and "On Disbelieving Atrocities" for the *New York Times* in 1943 and 1944.

While British authors generally exercised tact in writing for American journals and papers in the early years of the war, some were more aggressive once the United States became a participant, and one of the important questions became what the conditions of the peace would be when war ended. One such writer was Rebecca West, from whom the Ministry of Information had commissioned morale-raising articles for the British press and who had added a chapter to her *Black Lamb and Grey Falcon* at its request.[9] Throughout the war she contributed articles to the *New Yorker,* but nothing was as provocative as "The Hoover Frame of Mind," which she wrote for the *Atlantic Monthly* in June 1943.

West's essay was a fierce attack on *The Problems of Lasting Peace,* a book by the former American president, Herbert Hoover, and Hugh Gibson, a member of the American diplomatic corps. Strongly supportive of Roosevelt, West charged Hoover and Gibson with suggesting that the president had followed Woodrow Wilson's steps in leading his country into "an unnecessary and unprofitable war at the behest of a cloudy and intemperate idealism." She claimed: "The whole aim of the authors is to present the American voter with a picture of the war as a situation which ought to be left to stew in its own juices."[10] Moreover, she said, the book was poorly written, poorly researched, and full of pro-Axis propaganda.

"The Hoover Frame of Mind" generated a vigorous discussion in the letter pages of the following two issues of the *Atlantic Monthly*. Several writers defended West's right to speak about issues that affected the lives of Britons, and the noted American journalist Dorothy Thompson praised her for being "genuinely disinterested, philosophical, and historically minded."[11] Other correspondents, however, angrily attacked her for maligning a former president, who had organized food relief to Europe in the First World War. Calling the article "slander" and its tone that of "a didactic schoolteacher," one letter argued that West exhibited the English traits which Americans found most irritating: "Englishmen as sneering at Americans, as taking what we may have to give without gratitude, as supercilious and arrogant."[12] Another writer agreed that the piece would provide a focus for reawakened anglophobia and concluded: "The publication of an article reflecting so venomously on the quality of the greatest humanitarian now living is a great blot on the long, able record of the *Atlantic*."[13]

In July 1944 J.L. Hodson, who had spent the previous winter on a lecture tour of the United States, published "No Hard Feelings" in the *Atlantic Monthly*. The article was introduced by an editorial comment that "ever since 1940 the British in our midst have suffered in silence from the thoughtless or malicious criticism of Anglophobes. Here at last is an Englishman who speaks out, to strengthen – not weaken – the understanding of allies."[14] Hodson began by claiming that the United States, "mankind's most hopeful experiment to date," had endeared itself to him, but the rest of his article was a blunt counterattack on a wide variety of anti-British comments by both liberal and anglophobe Americans.

Like Maugham's "Why D'You Dislike Us?" which was published in the *Saturday Evening Post* in April 1942, and like Russell's "Can Americans and Britons Be Friends?" carried in the same magazine in June 1944, "No Hard Feelings" catalogued the charges against the British:

The English are high-hat and arrogant; Britain is going Red; Britain, on the other hand, is not a democracy, for she still has royalty, and the Old School Tie weights the scale in favour of fools when appointments are made; Britain has the smartest diplomats and businessmen in the world and their subtlety and Machiavellian methods outwit Americans; Britain always fights her wars with other folks' blood treasure; Britain draws great revenues from India and, despite what she has said, has no intention of getting out of India; England governs Canada, Australia, New Zealand, and South Africa – the suggestion that they are independent is just baloney and, anyway, what did Mr Churchill mean by saying he had not gone into office to liquidate the British Empire?

The English have no sense of humour, I have been told; the English accent is awful – nobody can tell what they say; the British didn't pay their war debts last time – they'll never be forgiven for that; for the second time the British have dragged Americans into war.[15]

Hodson systematically replied to each of these charges, arguing, for example, that Britain was not moving toward any political extreme, that it would leave India at the end of the war, and that although the English accent was offensive to Americans, the English were after all the original speakers of the language. His real worry, however, was that Americans would return to the position they had occupied after the First World War – isolated and sure that they had once more won the war for Britain: "Our appeasement of America leads you to feel that you are very noble to be fighting in Europe, that it is our war you are engaged in once more, that these awful English have taken you for a ride for a second time, and that when the fighting is done you will be entitled to withdraw once again to your mountaintop, then to look down, cold and aloof, on a hideous mad world."[16] If the United States adopted this position, concluded Hodson, its sons and those of Britain would one day do it all over again.

Surprisingly, "No Hard Feelings" did not provoke the kind of criticism that followed the West article. Subsequent issues of the *Atlantic Monthly* carried a firestorm of complaints about a Wallace Stegner article on Boston Catholics but nothing about Hodson's essay. Moreover, it was appreciated by the British Information Services, whose magazine survey reported that the article was "extremely effective" though "perhaps a little irritating" because it admitted no faults whatsoever in the British. In London a Foreign Office official rightly wondered whether irritation heightened effectiveness.[17]

One of the early results of the Ministry of Information's campaign to secure the publication of useful books in the United States was Josiah Wedgwood and Alan Nevins's *Forever Freedom*. Although more the work of Wedgwood than Nevins, it was a genuine Anglo-American production, an anthology of British and American prose and poetry edited and introduced by a British member of parliament and an American historian. It effectively bound the histories and futures of the two countries together by tracing the concept of liberty from the pronouncements of the Bible to the most recent speeches of Roosevelt and Churchill. "It is time," said Wedgwood, "to restate the case for England and Liberty; and it can best be done in double harness with those United States whose back is also against the wall."[18] The book ended with an undisguised invitation to Americans to intervene: Churchill's 4 June 1940 "We will fight on the beaches" speech to the House of Commons in which he declared, "Our Empire beyond the seas, armed and guarded by the British Fleet, would carry on the struggle, until, in God's good time, the new world, with all its power and might, steps forth to the rescue and liberation of the old." Beneath these words the editors added their own postscript: "To Be Continued."[19]

Wedgwood and Nevins were encouraged to assemble *Forever Freedom* by the Ministry of Information, and the manuscript was sent to the minister for approval prior to publication. The ministry advised the editors to ask the American firm of Scribner's to keep the price down to $2.00 or $2.50 so as to reach more readers,[20] but it appears that this arrangement did not suit Scribner's because the book was ultimately published in New York by Penguin.

A British publisher might produce books for the United States if necessary, but the Ministry of Information far preferred the books it solicited or encouraged to be published by American commercial houses. This arrangement suggested that just as British visitor/lecturers in the United States were paid by their hosts rather than by the British government, authors too were merely acting in their own professional interests. Negotiations were often left up to the writers, many of whom had long-standing contracts with particular publishers, and the arrangements had all the appearance of private professional deals. In some cases, authors were given the standard royalty, though the wartime currency regulations meant that they might have to wait for it; in other cases, the royalties were given to a war charity. The latter provision had the advantage of suggesting to American readers that not only were the writers contributing to the war effort both through pen and pocket but that they too, by buying the book, were joining the cause.

As a result of this arm's-length arrangement, suspicious Americans rarely succeeded in finding evidence that a particular book had been commissioned by the Ministry of Information. Sixty years later, when much more is known about the propaganda campaign in the Second World War, some of the evidence is still missing. The Ministry of Information files cited earlier do identify a number of commissioned books, but the ministry files in the Public Record Office are far from

complete, and not all arrangements left a paper record. In the case of
Somerset Maugham and *The Hour before the Dawn*, the only indication
that this novel was written at the request of the ministry is
Maugham's own memoirs. Similarly, the only evidence that Storm
Jameson's 1942 book *London Calling* was solicited by the ministry
comes from her autobiography.

Outside the Ministry of Information, there were other agencies
encouraging British authors to write for the British cause in the United
States. In the autumn of 1941 the Society of Authors' periodical the
Author reported that an organization called the American Outpost in
Great Britain had recently been formed with the goal of furthering
American aid to Britain and promoting mutual understanding between
the two countries. In addition to publishing a newspaper entitled *News
from the Outpost*, the group hoped "to expedite the publishing in America of lists of new British books including those calculated to throw
light on this country's traditions and culture," noted the *Author*. "The
recently formed British Books Committee in America is helping to
handle this side of the Outpost's work."[21]

The British Books Committee had been created by the British Library
of Information in New York in September 1940 under the chairmanship of Sir Robert Mayer. Its mandate was to bring the appropriate
British books to the attention of the American public, the reviewers,
and the literary editors of newspapers, and to make these books, many
of which had to be imported from Britain, more readily available. The
committee devised a list of recommended books called "Mrs Becker
Selects" and sent it to bookstores and newspapers throughout the
country. It also mounted displays of the books at various book fairs.
The exhibit was shown first at the American Institute of Graphic Arts
and then in the British Pavilion at the New York World's Fair. Sometimes accompanied by a reading by a British writer or by an actor such
as Maurice Evans, the display travelled to book fairs in such places as
Boston, Cleveland, Northampton, Jacksonville, Detroit, and Washington. According to the committee, these efforts resulted in "a real stirring of the book-buyer's consciousness towards a class of books which
in the ordinary way he is usually left to discover."[22]

In other ways too, the *Author* helped encourage British writers to
write for American readers as part of the war effort. In the spring of
1942 it quoted a "well-known writer at present in the U.S." who had
sent details of the writing market there:

There is still a place for English short fiction – ie. short stories – in the American magazine, and for novels, too, with the publishers; also "straight" war or adventure stories, with a war background; by "straight" I mean true stories, with no love interest or plot, if they are good enough or exciting enough. Essays or theses on political subjects are out for the moment – no one will touch them. All the major magazine editors over here are begging me to write them stories or serials about England at war, showing "people," men and women, under war conditions, with strong emotional colour.

As for the mechanics of publishing in the United States, the anonymous writer explained that a committee of authors, editors, and publishers called the Atlantic Panel had been set up in New York to facilitate publication by British authors. Those writers without an American agent could send their manuscripts to Carol Hill, a member of the panel, who would then place their work. Her 10 per cent commission went directly to the RAF Benevolent Fund. This report might seem to be merely professional advice, and the writer did admit that American publication could be lucrative. His or her conclusion, however, was that such writing would be of great political value because Americans could be reached and persuaded only really through their emotions.[23]

In the autumn of 1943 the *Author* carried a similar plea from Phyllis Bentley (who had recently returned from three months in the United States) to the American Division of the Ministry of Information. It was important that Americans know of British ideas and way of life, she said: "One of the simplest and most efficacious ways of making our ideas mutually known is the appearance of British-written articles and fiction in the American magazines, and vice-versa; it is especially efficacious in the case of American magazines because of their huge circulations. I was therefore distressed, and at first perplexed, to see what a small volume of British material appeared in the large-circulation American magazines." Part of the problem, she suggested, was the delay in the transport of manuscripts, but British authors could speed the process by sending synopses of articles before publication.[24]

Bentley was, of course, employed by the American Division of the Ministry of Information at the time she wrote the article, and one of her responsibilities was selecting and commissioning articles for *Britain* (the monthly bulletin issued by the British Information Services in New York) and for American magazines. If the report of her section for a three-week period in June 1943 is any indication, there was a steady stream of written material flowing to the United States. Fifty-one articles from the British press, forty original articles, and thirty-three articles prepared for other divisions of the ministry had been sent to *Britain* and to American publications. Seventeen articles designed especially for *Britain* had been commissioned from well-known authors and dispatched, including G.B. Stern's "No Place Like Home," Richard Church's "Poetry in Wartime Britain," Louis Golding's "Magnolia Street Goes to War," and Cecil Beaton's "These Men Build Navies." In the previous month, the report concluded, ninety-nine articles had been placed in American newspapers and magazines.[25]

On at least one occasion, the resources of the Society of Authors and the pages of the *Author* were used to convey an appeal to British writers from across the Atlantic. In the autumn of 1942 Curtice Hitchcock, president of the American publishing house Reynal and Hitchcock, paid an official visit to London in his role as special consultant to the American Office of War Information. With the United States in the war, his mission was to discuss with British authors, publishers, and booksellers and their representative organizations how Anglo-American relations could be extended and improved through the medium of literature.

On 13 November, Denys Kilham Roberts hosted a luncheon at the Ritz Hotel for Hitchcock and a number of the more distinguished members of the Society of Authors. "It is in no sense mere publisher's blandishments," Hitchcock told the writers, "when I suggest that at the present juncture in relations between Britain and America authors are particularly important. They are important, naturally, because they have reputations and popular influence."[26]

The main impetus for many of the books directed toward America, however, was the Ministry of Information, and in 1943 Cecil Day Lewis described how it put a writer to work: "He may be on the staff of one of the Service Departments as a writer, like H. St G. Saunders and Flight-Lieutenant H.E. Bates at the Air Ministry, or Major Eric Linklater at the War Office. Or he may be an outside author, commissioned to do one particular book. We've used in this way many first-rate writers – V.S. Pritchett, for instance, Tennyson Jesse, J.B. Priestley, Owen Rutter, David Garnett, J.L. Hodson."[27]

Priestley was responsible for two books published exclusively in the United States at the request of the Ministry of Information: *Britain Speaks*, his 1940 collection of radio talks, and *Britain at War*, released in 1942. Though issued by Harper in New York, the cover of the latter book was designed by the ministry's graphic artist E. McKnight Kauffer, and the copyright belonged to the Controller of H.M. Stationery Office. Moreover, the book offered a large number of statistics about such matters as enemy ships sunk, British troops stationed throughout the world, casualties among British forces, and planes made and flown by Britons. This data could have come only from British government sources.

Priestley's aim in *Britain at War* was to counter German propaganda claims that the British were letting everyone else – people from the Commonwealth, Allied European countries, and the United States – fight their battles and provide their armaments. The British habit of giving prominence to the parts played by Commonwealth troops, he said, had led Goebbels to claim that the British were hanging safely in the rear, when in fact 79 per cent of the casualties came from the British Isles. Producing a full-page chart, he argued that Britain sent out many more tanks and airplanes than it took in, adding pointedly that, relative to the populations of the two countries, Britain was manufacturing six times the number of weapons of war as the United States. Reiterating one of his favourite themes, he added that such production "could not even have been attempted if Britain were actually what some people overseas imagine it to be, merely a picturesque land of castles and thatched cottages, populated almost entirely by hunting squires and hat-touching villagers."[28]

Priestley was also concerned to dispel the impression created by German propagandists that democratic Britain was plagued by indecision and lack of conviction. There had indeed been considerable complaining, protesting, and grumbling about the war effort, he confessed (admitting that he had been among the most vocal), but this was motivated by a desire to create the most effective campaign possible. Such public outbursts showed that Britons were still thinking for themselves and had not been "bullied by wartime conditions into becoming members of a speechless herd, like the miserable Germans." "I declare to you," he thundered, "that the *British war effort has been prodigious, the greatest ever made by the people of this island, and perhaps the most remarkable national effort in all history*" (his italics).[29]

Another book commissioned by the Ministry of Information exclusively for American readers was *London Calling*, edited by the novelist and critic Storm Jameson and published by Harper in 1942. As noted earlier, Jameson had been considered for membership in the Ministry of Information's council, and when another candidate was preferred she had offered herself for future duties. Soon after America's entry into the war, the ministry invited her to consider what might be done to improve Anglo-American relations, and she suggested a volume of stories, essays, and poems by well-known British writers. It would be sold only in the United States, and the royalties would be donated to the United Services Organizations.

London Calling was a collection of brief pieces – short stories, poems, and essays – by some of Britain's most distinguished authors. Some of the essays were reminiscences, most with calculated references to America. Rebecca West's "The Man Who Came to Dinner" described a visit by the American man of letters Alexander Woollcott and how he brought a sense of the United States with him to a beleaguered country: "Out of his rich heart there flowed wordless assurances that we were still of value; and such assurances are sweet, when one has been made tatty by endurance of the war, its blitzes and its tediums … The scene around us, tarnished by our national misfortunes, was obscured by a screen of Americana, first transparent and wistful, then opaque and satisfying."[30]

Political scientist Harold Laski wrote "Lincoln as America," while the Leeds professor of English, Bonamy Dobrée, recalled an academic tour of the United States and praised American humane scholarship. Phyllis Bentley's essay thanked Fenimore Cooper for his portrait of America, and Mary Agnes Hamilton wrote admiringly of Frances Perkins, the first woman member of cabinet in United States history. In "The Making of England and the Making of New England," the historian G.M. Trevelyan drew a parallel between the migration of Anglo-Saxons to the British Isles in the fifth and sixth centuries and the migration of the English to North America centuries later. Only two essays – E.M. Forster's "The New Disorder" and Basil Liddell Hart's "A Page of Unwritten History" – did not deal with the United States.

As president of PEN during the war, Storm Jameson played a part in the publication in the United States in 1942 of selected papers that had been delivered at the PEN Congress in London the previous September. Writers from many parts of the world contributed pieces, but the volume, entitled Writers in Freedom: A Symposium, was slanted toward American readers. The American ambassador to Britain, John G. Winant, offered prefatory remarks, and Stephen Vincent Benét contributed to a section called "American Writers Salute Their Colleagues in England," wishing "all hope and strength to those writers who by word and deed in Britain are helping to make a free world."[31]

The British government had flown Thornton Wilder and John Dos Passos to London, and they both addressed the subject of the duty of the writer in times of political crisis. Storm Jameson, J.B. Priestley, and Rebecca West spoke for British authors. For Jameson, the question then facing writers was whether their work justified their ignoring a crisis that might lead to millions of deaths. A writer, she suggested, should support the state when it shared his or her values, and it was commonly agreed that in the present war "the values – resting on a Greek, Roman, and Christian base – of Western civilization are in danger ... In this war, the chance, only the chance, of renewing Western civilization, depends on the victory of England and her Allies."[32] Priestley argued that the political troubles of the previous decade had made the average person turn increasingly to the writer for guidance, and writers therefore had a greater responsibility than ever before. West defended nationalism as "an extremely noble force" because it represented the unique human experience that had always fascinated authors.[33]

Three British writers and one émigré author living there – Arthur Koestler – discussed the question of propaganda writing, but none suggested that anyone was doing anything more than identifying evil wherever it existed. Phyllis Bentley argued that propaganda was the dissemination of a particular doctrine or practice and that writers were entitled to declare their preference for a particular doctrine. B. Ifor Evans spoke of the need for writers to identify the prejudices and hatreds of nations as well as their ideals, and Arthur Calder-Marshall called for writers to be "going abroad to the United States, to the Soviet Union, to wherever men and women are producing and fighting to defeat Nazism."[34]

A more direct political appeal to Americans came from H.N. Brailsford's *From England to America: A Message*, published in 1940 only in the United States. An influential socialist writer and editor, he had gained credibility in the United States by having been a contributor to the *New Republic* since 1915. This, he argued, gave him the right to address Americans "as a candid friend, who is exempt from the charge of being a war propagandist, ... a citizen of the world, even though he is a patriotic Englishman." He had frequently disagreed with the British government's policy, he said, and for the present book he had "not consulted a single official person in England."[35] Brailsford may indeed have been operating independently of the Ministry of Information because his open plea for American entry into the war went far beyond government policy at the time.

From England to America was written in the perilous weeks of June and July 1940, and there is an urgency in its call for American intervention (Brailsford asked for a volunteer army of 500,000 Americans to liberate Europe in 1941 or 1942). He said that in the Duke of Marlborough's descendant, Winston Churchill, Britain had a "worthy captain," one whom history would rank among its great men. Under Chamberlain, however, the first eight months of the war had been conducted under the disastrous delusion that the Maginot Line would hold. Now, Brailsford argued, Americans were similarly deluded into assuming that the United States was impregnable to German attack. But "if England, like France, should go under, are not America's defenses compromised in much the same way? Strategically may not England be your Spain – only more so?"[36] Moreover, without a suitable base such as the British Isles from which to launch a counteroffensive, the United States would never be able to strike back at the Nazi empire.

The question, said Brailsford, was thus not merely the survival of Britain but the liberation of Europe and the peace of the Americas. Raising the stakes even higher, he claimed that a declaration of war by the United States would "transform the history of civilization": "On the day that it declares war upon this malignant principle, and sends out its volunteers to fight shoulder to shoulder with our young men, civilization has a future and mankind may dare to hope."[37]

In using Churchill as the modern Marlborough who could vigorously lead Britain and her allies against the Nazis, Brailsford was of course playing one of the British apologist's strongest cards after June 1940. So popular with Americans was the new prime minister that Philip Guedalla, the biographer and historian who had lectured in the United States early in the war and had worked for the Ministry of Information, wrote a biography, *Mr Churchill: A Portrait*, for publication on both sides of the Atlantic.

Guedalla had met Churchill before the war and on at least one occasion had served as his eyes and ears in the United States at a time when Churchill was out of office. On 20 April 1938 Guedalla had written him to say that he had just returned from a winter of lecturing in America and that his observations might be of use to Churchill. In Washington, he said, he had had a long interview with Roosevelt, who was almost embarrassingly pro-British, and he had attended two press conferences disguised as a reporter. Early in the year, he had found the general public in the United States to be sympathetic to Britain, but the attitude had changed sharply with Hitler's annexation of Austria in March:

The friendly tone was dissipated almost instantaneously and replaced by a feeling that H.M.G. had turned its back on the free peoples and decided to fraternize with the gangsters. Former Anglophobes attributed this to the constitutional inability of the British to run straight, and our friends, feeling themselves deserted, sank back into a hopeless feeling that Europe was just a mess which had best be left alone. British policy became an object not of uncertainty but of contempt ... But of course it is not easy for the Embassy at Washington, living on a little island surrounded by press-cuttings and isolationist Senators to know very much about the United States. Of course I put the whole of my information at their disposal for what it was worth.[38]

Guedalla was a skilled and experienced biographer, and his book is probably the best portrait that the times allowed of a man who was then in the midst of the most illustrious stage of his career. Aside from the general propaganda value of an adulatory picture of the leader of Great Britain, *Mr Churchill: A Portrait*, written before Pearl Harbor and published in the United States in December 1941, contained comments clearly designed to influence American readers. Writing at a time when Britain had no victories to boast of, Guedalla reminded readers of its glorious past:

All autocrats who seek to dominate the whole of Europe are faced, sooner or later, with Britain's enmity; and their stately figures join the long procession – King Philip pacing slowly under the grey bulk of the Escorial and flinging the whole weight of Spain and the Indies against an island Kingdom; the *Roi Soleil* holding the Continent in fee among the terraces and mirrors of Versailles; Napoleon ruling from Seville to the Polish marshes and thwarted of his last success by British squares upon a trampled ridge in Belgium; Kaiser Wilhelm in vain pursuit of victory from the gates of Paris to the quiet woods of Dorn.

Against "the maddest Mullah of them all," said Guedalla, Churchill joined the line to stand where Marlborough had stood.[39]

The prime minister, Guedalla was careful to point out, was an Anglo-American, implying that the combativeness so admired in the United States came from his American blood. In any case, the heroic British effort of 1940 had kindled the desire of Americans to help, and "there was a growing comprehension that the cause in which their help was needed was not exclusively British or even European ... They could see now that the American dream was not so different in essentials from the British aspiration to be free."[40] Referring to Churchill's meeting with Roosevelt at Placentia Bay, Guedalla asked, "What could be more American than their declaration of human rights 'that all the men in all the lands may live out their lives in freedom from fear and want?' And what could be more British?"[41]

Mr Churchill: A Portrait was the first biography of the British prime minister to be published in the United States, and it was widely reviewed and read. The remark of F.X Connolly in the *Commonweal* that "this biography of England's great leader is a purposeful book rather than an impartial study"[42] hinted at propaganda motives, but the great majority of reviews were positive.

With America's entry into the war, the emphasis of a number of writers turned to Anglo-American understanding. In 1943 Maurice Colbourne, an actor who had toured North America frequently in the interwar period with Barry Jones's company, published *America and Britain: A Mutual Introduction* with the assistance of the British Library of Information. The book was written in part, he said, because "the anti-British Isolationist opinion in America was not annihilated at Pearl Harbor, it was merely driven underground and temporarily silenced."[43] Among other things, Colbourne tackled the question of the old school tie, pointing out that Americans had their equivalent in the alumni, fraternities, sororities, "classes," "years," and other castes. On the question of the British Empire, he argued that every American holding beyond the thirteen original colonies was part of the United States' "empire."

Sir Philip Gibbs, who had lectured extensively in the United States in the days before Pearl Harbor, edited a collection of essays entitled *Bridging the Atlantic: Anglo-American Fellowship as the Way to World Peace*, which was published in London and New York in 1943. Gibbs's own piece was a recollection of his lecture tour of the United States in 1941–42, which he had written about at greater length in *America Speaks*. The English author Frank Swinnerton wrote about British and American novelists in "The Bridge of Ideas," and Sir Archibald Sinclair, Viscount Samuel, Megan Lloyd George, and others discussed such matters as the British Empire and British policy in Europe.

From the beginning of the Second World War, one of the genres of writing that was most effective in influencing American opinion was the personal report. From January to June 1941, Louis MacNeice sent a "London Letter" to the American periodical *Common Sense*, and from then until September 1943 the letters were written by Stephen Spender. From January 1941 to the summer of 1946, George Orwell contributed a regular London letter – more politically oriented than MacNeice's – to the *Partisan Review*, a very influential left-wing literary journal. On at least one occasion – when he referred to the possible lynching of German airmen landing in Britain – his work was censored in order to avoid alienating American readers.[44]

Mollie Panter-Downes's "Letter from London" columns in the *New Yorker*, which ran throughout the war, were a mixture of objective political commentary and detailed chronicling of the daily lives of Britons. When the first year's offerings were published in book form in the United States by the Atlantic Monthly Press in 1940, Diana Forbes-Robertson praised its immediacy and veracity: "After reading this book, it is possible to say of war-torn London: 'Now, I know what it is like.'"[45] The Foreign Office was made aware of the propaganda value of the columns by the report of the British Library of Information: "Some English women authors have contributed valuable material by writing with an apt and understanding humour of the English in their everyday life in a way which Americans find delightful. 'Letters From England' [sic], written each week by Mollie Panter-Downes to the *New Yorker*, are of this type."[46]

British women authors were in fact prominent in producing first-person accounts of wartime Britain, the literary equivalents of the reports given audiences in the United States by the visiting lecturers. Ruth Drummond, who had begun to contribute to the *Ladies' Home Journal* in the first year of the war and continued to do so regularly until 1942, published *A Woman Faces the War* in 1940. The book was written in the form of letters to an unnamed editor of a magazine, which having helped her as a housekeeper and mother, could now help her as a powerful friend of her country. "I am just a woman engaged in the difficult job of trying to rear a family under difficult circumstances," she claimed, "and am not in any way qualified to be a spokesman for the Allies and their cause, or a critic of England's aims and ambitions."[47] This did not stop her from occasionally commenting on the question of the empire or of Britain's fighting out of self-interest, or from referring to the war as one "in which we can feel thoroughly and righteously indignant at the acts of our opponents" because "we feel we are in the right."[48] Like so many other champions of beleaguered Britain, she underlined the new democratization of the country. After visiting a group of evacuee children, she wrote: "I went home, musing on the strange mingling of town and country people, low born, high born, all realizing for the first time the conditions under which others live. I cannot but feel that on the whole it is a good thing. Intolerance is fast breaking down, old prejudices are bound to disappear."[49]

For the most part, however, Drummond wrote of the effect of the war on her domestic life and family – of having, for example, to explain to her son that he must not hate Germans but only the way in which their soldiers marched into Poland. American reviewers appreciated her unpretentious and sincere approach, the *Books* reviewer calling it "a confidential report from behind spiritual lines that hold firm."[50] "There is a quiet courage and wholesome common sense about the book," observed the *Saturday Review of Literature*. "Mrs Drummond speaks a language universal among women."[51]

A more sophisticated picture of life in a small English village during the first eighteen months of the war was provided by Margery Allingham's *The Oaken Heart*, published by Doubleday, Doran in 1941. Known for nearly two decades as a writer of detective fiction with skilful character analysis and psychological insight, Allingham wrote sensitively of her village of Tolleshunt D'Arcy (which she called Auburn) in Essex, and of the reactions of her neighbours to the outbreak of war, the deprivation, and the bureaucracy which, though necessary in the crisis, frequently caused hardships.

The Oaken Heart was well received in the United States, to some degree because her earlier writing, like that of so many other authors, seemed to give her credibility. Iris Barry, in *Books*, observed that the book was "almost startlingly fresh, convincing, intimate and absorbing," adding: "Perhaps her effect is due, in part, from the fact that as a well known author of mystery stories she strikes us as wholly beyond suspicion; only a normal person writes murder mysteries, nothing highbrow or tendentious here."[52] In the *New York Times*, Katharine Wood wrote: "Americans who still cherish the delusion of a 'class-ridden' England and 'feudal' county society may brush the cobwebs from their eyes as they look at Auburn. For good and ill, this book's picture of Auburn is a picture of democracy."[53]

In early 1940 the author Margaret Kennedy, best known for her sentimental novel *The Constant Nymph* (1924) and its adaptation for both stage and screen, told a Society of Authors forum on the role of authors in wartime that "from the point of view of total war, little that they write is likely to be more valuable than the paper they waste ... Total war is not won by a brigade of authors."[54] Between the time she made this comment and July 1941, Kennedy's attitude changed dramatically, and she wrote *Where Stands a Wingèd Sentry* to argue Britain's case. Published only in the United States, the book, as its epigraph from Henry Vaughan signalled, was directed exclusively at Americans: "My soul, there is a country / Afar beyond the stars, / Where stands a winged sentry / All skillful in the wars."

Kennedy claimed that her book, constructed as a journal of the perilous months from May to September 1940, was not written for publication, but it reads very much as if it were concocted for American readers. She writes of the tragedy that the United States and Britain had fought the First World War together without ever understanding each other's version of democracy. She tackles anglophobia in the United States, the inevitability of that country becoming fascist if Hitler should win, and the proposition that wars – most notably the American Civil War – do settle things. She admits that "the traditional, bred-in-the-bone, dyed-in-the-wool British class distinctions stick in the American Gizzard,"[55] but argues that the old school tie is disappearing in Britain and that postwar England is going to belong to the common people, "a land fit for human beings."[56] Of Hitler, she says, "Human goodness has never been so challenged before, not even by Machiavelli,"[57] and about the destruction of ancient buildings in Britain and on the Continent, she points out that "it isn't a case of *ours* and *theirs*; that beautiful things in Europe are the common heritage of Western civilisation."[58]

Where Stands a Wingèd Sentry found a large readership in the United States and was reprinted five times in its first year. In the *Atlantic Monthly*, which in August 1941 had carried one of her journal entries, "Concert," Edward Weeks wrote: "If there is any strain in our present Anglo-American relations, it is, I think, owing to the lack of plain and reasonable talk between us. This book in its delightful way goes far to make up that omission."[59]

Phyllis Bottome, who had returned to Britain in June 1940, wrote a first-person account of conditions there in *Mansion House of Liberty*, published in the United States in 1941. She later recalled how she carried out "two activities simultaneously, speaking for the Ministry of Information for Britain during the bombing," while "writing at the same time for America a book on the war."[60] During the First World

War, she had done relief work in Belgium and had written propaganda articles; now, having lived in the United States for a few years from the age of nine on, she was well suited to writing about Britain through American eyes. In October 1940 she had begun this process by writing a letter to Upton Sinclair to be passed on to the *New Republic* in which she touted the flowering of democracy in Britain and the flourishing of the country's spiritual values.[61]

Aided by the resources of the Ministry of Information, *Mansion House of Liberty* provided a fairly thorough tour of wartime Britain: London and Liverpool after the bombings, the women's auxiliary services, the army, navy, and air force, the stately homes, and the lives of the common people. Bottome quotes the famous "this happy breed of men" speech from Shakespeare's *Richard II* and describes the damage to such venerable buildings as St Paul's, the Guildhall, and American author Henry James's Lamb Cottage at Rye. Alluding to the satanic elements of Milton's *Paradise Lost*, she characterizes the enemy as "Principalities and Powers" and describes the swastika as "an empty cross with hooks, rather than a cross with a Human figure on it drawing us not by force but by love." If Britain loses, she says, "there would be a world without human spirits."[62]

Bottome champions Churchill in reiterating the comment of American journalist Dorothy Thompson that "Churchill *is* England!" Bottome herself calls him "that horrid nightmare of Hitler's worst fears" who "at last stood astride the whirlwind!"[63] The awakened British social conscience appears frequently in her book, as in the comments of the mayor of a Liverpool slum district that had been heavily damaged by bombing: "Never again will the responsible citizens of England suffer our own people to live under such conditions!"[64] Britain is now acting and thinking in unison as it has never done before, concludes Bottome, and more people believe that good manners come from the heart rather than from a privileged education. Labelling the evacuee children "angels unawares," she writes that "wherever they go the children have soon become our treasures" who, deprived of parents and familiar surroundings, "re-settle and help bring up themselves."[65] Her concluding chapter, about the role of religion in the struggle, argues that "freedom is all men's religion," and she ends her book with a reminder to Americans of their own battle for freedom: "Perhaps Patrick Henry's test is the only safe one. 'Give me,' he once shouted, choked with his righteous anger, in the shortest of renowned speeches, 'Give me liberty – or give me death.'"[66]

Perhaps because Alistair Cooke was English and was familiar with the country described in *Mansion House of Liberty*, he was sceptical of Bottome's writing in his review in *New Republic*. "Her book," he wrote perceptively, "is stirring at first reading, disquieting thereafter. She is writing about the human spirit, but the way she goes around England in search of it is the newspaperman's artifice; she always finds it."[67] Many Americans might not have gone beyond a first reading, however, and Katherine Wood, in the *New York Times*, wrote of "the wise balance in this author's mind, seeing the cruel folly of appeasement and complacency, looking at the shortcomings of British democracy, writing with all the fine British incisiveness of self-criticism."[68]

A form of first-person wartime account considerably different from that of Drummond, Kennedy, and the others – and coming from a surprising source – was H.M. Tomlinson's *The Wind Is Rising* (1942). Born and raised in London's dockland, Tomlinson had become a journalist with the radical *Morning Leader* and was its war correspondent from 1914 to 1917, when it became the *Daily News*. He was withdrawn from the front by the Newspaper Proprietor's Association when Lord Northcliffe's representative complained that he was too "humanitarian." After the war, he became literary editor of the *Nation* and then a freelance author best known as a writer of the sea in the tradition of Joseph Conrad.

Tomlinson's "humanitarian" view of the First World War was expressed in two collections of essays, *Old Junk* (1918) and *Waiting for Daylight* (1922), and in 1935 he wrote a long antiwar tract, *Mars His Idiot*. In 1932 he undertook a lecture tour of the United States to argue the pacifist cause. It was therefore surprising to many observers in April 1940 that he began contributing a series of essays on the war to the *Atlantic Monthly*, essays which, as Frederick D. Crawford has pointed out, were intended to arouse the sympathy of Americans and convince them that they should not remain aloof from the struggle.[69]

Tomlinson wrote periodically for the *Atlantic Monthly* throughout the war, and in 1941 Little, Brown published seven of his articles, together with five additional pieces, as *The Wind Is Rising*. In one, "The Cliffs of England," Tomlinson explained that he still thought war "an obscene outrage on the intelligence,"[70] but this war was unlike any battle that had been fought before. A German statesman, he said, had vehemently proclaimed the first revolt against intellectualism since the French Revolution, and "the heritage of the Renaissance and the Reformation – the foundation of Christendom, if you like – will be either kept on the British coast or will perish in Europe."[71] If the Nazis had their way, he concluded, then nothing could be discussed. "Slavery is bearable, but the mind in chains is not. I know that some of our traditions and institutions may perish in resisting this subversion of the mind, but all will surely perish if no resistance is made. That is the choice we have."[72]

Tomlinson's essays are a skilful mixture of immediate detail of the London he loved and a careful, measured argument about the political and moral questions of the war. He writes of the old stones of London – St Paul's, the Guildhall, and other ancient buildings – and adds: "A Nazi in his teens roving the night, not sure of his whereabouts, but anxious to drop his load and get home, who knows nothing of history before 1933, and cares nothing, and nothing of the spirit except Hitler's, and wants to know no more, blasts to dust the best the centuries have given us."[73] The landscape is forever changed:

When we look for the comforting landmarks we knew, they are gone. Once a Cockney, idling out of Fleet Street into the wayside nook where once a stone told him, Here Lies Oliver Goldsmith; then contemplative over neighbouring rails with the tombs of the Crusaders below, under the walls of the church which had been there ten centuries; turning a corner, and recalling that in that house Coleridge dreamed, and there Elia was born, and down in that garden began the Wars of the Roses. And in that hall Shakespeare took wine; remembering that he himself had gossiped with one of its old guardians who used to watch Dickens stride in and out of its gates; and in fact that English literary history, literature and law had peopled this London sanctuary with ghosts and memories ... Today that place is rubble. The Nazi engines have been over it.[74]

American references – to Emerson, Melville, Whitman, Thoreau, and others – dot *The Wind Is Rising*, and Tomlinson praises Roosevelt and American assistance. One essay, "The Mayflower Sails East," talks of the American isolation envied by Britons who are now only a few minutes' flying distance from Europe: "We yearn for an isolation we shall never get."[75] But as he asks in reference to the German occupation of Greece, "If Mount Ida, why not Primrose Hill? Why not Bunker Hill?"[76]

Long after the publication of *The Wind Is Rising*, Tomlinson continued to contribute essays to the *Atlantic Monthly*, and he was one of the writers about whom its editor, Edward Weeks, wrote on his journalistic trip to Britain in 1943. Tomlinson's later essays, many concerned with the shape of the postwar world, were published in the United States in book form as *The Turn of the Tide* in 1945. As propaganda, they would have had little effect on the average American, but it is reasonable to assume that they influenced the politically sophisticated readership of the *Atlantic Monthly.*

In the autumn of 1940 Daphne du Maurier, whose novel *Rebecca* was a best-seller on both sides of the Atlantic, wrote *Come Wind, Come Weather* because, she said, "I wondered what I could do in the way of war service."[77] Aimed in the first instance at readers in Britain, where it sold 590,000 copies in the first four months, it was published the following year in Canada, Australia, India, Egypt, and the United States to enlist the support of those countries.

Tailoring the prefaces of the overseas editions to their particular readerships, du Maurier addressed Canadians as fellow combatants in the European struggle. Americans, however, had to be treated differently, and she declared that though they might never be involved in the war, they could not avoid "the battle against human selfishness." Moreover, she said, "In your country there are many replicas of the men and women in this little book. You will find them in your home town, in your street, possibly in your own house."[78] The implication was surely that Britons and Americans shared so much common heritage and so many characteristics that Britain's struggle was that of the United States.

Come Wind, Come Weather is made up of ten stories of how various people – a mother with sons in the navy, evacuee children, a shopkeeper, a miner, a Cockney, and others – overcome fear, selfishness, greed, and jealousy to help fight the Germans. Du Maurier's belief in Moral Re-Armament turns the stories into parables or sermons rather than realistic accounts, and this undoubtedly limited their appeal to American readers. "Some readers," observed the *Library Journal*, "will find in these stories and the epilogue an unrealistic amount of 'sweetness and light'; many will find them inspiring and exemplary of the gallant spirit that England is showing under severe trial."[79]

A more documentary and less moralistic portrayal of the British response to the war was presented in John Strachey's *Digging for Mrs Miller*, published in the United States in 1941. An economist, Evelyn John St Loe Strachey, had been a Labour MP from 1929 to 1931 and wrote a number of books on fascism, socialism, and economics in the 1930s. An "upper middle-class radical intellectual" whose political beliefs became increasingly left wing in the decade before the war, he considered that "his primary duty [was] to help defend England against the Nazis, without implying any change from his radical views."[80] By 1942 he was on active service in the RAF.

Subtitled *Some Experiences of an Air-Raid Warden*, his *Digging for Mrs Miller* is a slightly fictionalized account of the work of London's civil defence services during the worst of the German bombing. For the most part a carefully detailed chronicle of daily and nightly life in the Blitz, its understated description of death, destruction, and mutilation is very effective. Rather than indulging in the self-pity or self-congratulation found in some other British books of the period, Strachey lets the events speak for themselves.

Occasionally, Strachey's political beliefs are apparent, as for example when he describes a middle-aged worker surveying a bombed-out block of decrepit flats: "The Government tells me to hate Hitler. And I do, *and* need no need of telling. But I don't hate Hitler for this lot … Nothing ready; nothing done for the people. If they think we're going to hate Hitler for this, they're wrong. They'll find out their mistake some day, they will. Things won't ever be the same after this lot: nor they won't. It's time *we* had a say."[81] Later, Strachey reports the common fear that after the war "the blighting menace of renewed and intensified unemployment" will return and be met by another form of the dole. "Was it not," he wonders, "along the lines of a standing offer of alternative employment in a many-sided and permanent enterprise of Civil Reconstruction, instead of Civil Defence, that the challenge of Fascist Regimentation might be met?"[82]

Another genre of book that attempted intimately and personally to bring the wartime life of the Britain to American readers was the collection of letters. From the beginning of the war, the Ministry of Information recognized that an important conduit to concerned and influential Americans was personal correspondence, and it attempted to orchestrate even private British letter writing. In October 1939 the American Division reported: "Drafts are in preparation of notes to guide private correspondents in writing to the United States on various aspects of war activity."[83]

The extent of the Ministry of Information's influence on personal letter writing can never be known, but the outbreak of books of letters to America during the war suggests a propaganda campaign. Some volumes were in the form of exchanges of correspondence between British and American writers, suggesting conversations between allies, while others were compilations of letters from Britons of various classes and occupations. In both cases, the effect was of reading someone else's mail, of being allowed closely to see the anxieties and responses of those enduring the war.

One of the first of such epistolary books produced during the Second World War was F. Tennyson Jesse and H.M. Harwood's *London Front: Letters Written to America*, published in the United States in 1941. Jesse, whose father was a nephew of Tennyson, had worked for the Ministry of Information in the First World War and spent some time at the front as a freelance reporter. By 1939 she had built a reputation as a criminologist and novelist, best known for *The Lacquer Lady* (1929) and *A Pin to See the Peepshow* (1934). Her husband H.M. Harwood was a popular playwright from 1912 until the mid-1930s.

London Front was a series of letters from Jesse and Harwood to a group of American friends sympathetic to Britain: the playwright Sam Behrman; the literary critic Alexander Woollcott; Grace Hubble, wife of the famous astronomer Edwin Hubble; Carl Hovey, editor of *Metropolitan Magazine*, and his wife; and playwright John Balderston, author of *Berkeley Square*, and his wife. Sam Behrman later worked in the film section of an American propaganda organization called the American Union for Freedom. According to Jesse's biographer Joanna Colenbrander, Behrman passed the Jesse-Harwood letters to journalists working for the *New York Times* and the *New York Evening Post*, and "soon, other groups of people were attending regular readings, and were among those who later formed the kernel of a great variety of relief organizations and action groups of many and far-reaching kinds."[84] John Balderston became a member of the White Committee, a pressure group working in Washington to increase aid to Britain, and he broadcast on radio three times a week. Marion Balderston was heavily involved in various Aid to Britain organizations in California.

According to Colenbrander, the correspondence of *London Front* grew spontaneously out of Jesse's concern about the political developments in Europe and her love of letter writing, but many of the letters look more like polemical essays than communication between friends. Jesse did considerable work for the Ministry of Information during the Second World War, writing *The Story of Burma*, begun early in the war but owing to printing difficulties not published until 1946, and *The Saga of San Demetrio*, commissioned by the Ministry of Information for the Ministry of War Transport and published in the United States in 1942. In *London Front*, she also described being asked by a professor in a ministry (both unnamed but which must have been

Basil Mathews and the Ministry of Information) to write a pamphlet for publication in the United States. The subject was to be democracy in Britain in wartime. Jesse and Harwood responded that mild accounts of changes in civilian social life in Britain would pale beside the brutal news from Warsaw, and what Americans needed to know was that Britain would prevail and was worth backing. The project was dropped.

It seems that *London Front* did not always adhere to the guidelines for correspondence devised by the Ministry of Information. According to Jesse, the ministry objected to some comments in their letters to America – particularly Harwood's claim that for 150 years the Germans "have been a cancer in the world, and it is time they were removed"[85] – because such remarks opposed British government policy. On a number of points, the letters in *London Front* did stray from official policy, but many of the familiar themes were there. "This is not to be a war engineered by bankers, the city or the propertied classes," wrote Harwood in August 1939. "The leaders in public opinion in this matter are the 'little people.'"[86] "We are not fighting for England at all," proclaimed Jesse. "We are fighting for something greater and better ... its name is freedom ... We are not interested at this moment in preserving either the British Empire or the French."[87] Later, she announced that Britain was "fighting for what the Americans fought for in the War of Independence, but we are fighting for it not only for ourselves but for the whole world."[88]

London Front sold so well in the United States that Jesse and Harwood brought out a sequel in 1942 (though it had been intended for publication in the summer of 1941). It was entitled *While London Burns: Letters to America*. The *New York Times* praised it for its explanation of the evolving British attitude toward the war, and Cecil Roberts, ever busy with his own propaganda work, commended it in the *Saturday Review of Literature*. But two other Britons also working in the United States, Alistair Cooke and Diana Forbes-Robertson, both argued that the book would do little to persuade non-anglophile Americans. Cooke quoted Grace Hubble's comment that "of course, for Edwin and me, England is worth far more than all the rest of the world put together." Said Cooke: "It's a poor basis for American sympathy, and even aid to Britain, which is either a deliberate phase of American policy in the Atlantic or nothing."[89] Forbes-Robertson complained that the breathless reverence with which the American group treated every utterance of Jesse and Harwood created an expectation that frequently was met with only banal commentary.[90]

Forbes-Robertson was hardly a disinterested reader, having several months earlier edited, with Roger W. Straus, a very different kind of collection entitled *War Letters from Britain*. The daughter of the noted actor Sir Johnston Forbes-Robertson, she had grown up in England, married the American author Vincent Sheean, and was living in the United States. The book was her contribution to the British cause, with the royalties going to the British-American Ambulance Corps. Sheean contributed a foreword telling Americans that the British were fighting for survival but also "for the perpetuation of institutions which otherwise may perish from the earth."[91]

War Letters from Britain is an eclectic mixture of correspondence from the famous (Lady Diana Cooper, Rebecca West, Myra Hess, Alec Waugh, John Gielgud, the archbishop of York, and Cathleen Nesbitt) and the unknown (soldiers, BBC announcers, housewives, school-teachers, and children). Some of the letters were written in thanks to American aid organizations, some were sent to business associates, and many were addressed to friends and relatives. They described such wartime conditions as rationing, evacuation, blackouts, the Home Guard, and air raids.

Some of the letters were undoubtedly collected by the editors, but a number – like Alec Waugh's lengthy analysis of the retreat of the British Expeditionary Force to Dunkirk, which he wrote for his New York publisher – seem contrived for the occasion. "A Young Englishman" reminds a "Friend in America" that the European bombs are incendiary: "Not even all the water of the Atlantic can stop them from spreading if not quenched at the source ... I do not think that the one continent will be spared if another is sacrificed."[92] A ten-year-old boy, articulate beyond his years and his working-class background, tells the *New York Herald Tribune* that the working class appreciates what America is doing for Britain, and the English editor of *Harper's Bazaar* writes to her New York counterpart: "The people of Mayfair throw open the great houses to the East Enders, who quite candidly do not like the mansions of the great and swiftly return to the devastation of the bombed areas. Once more I have decided there can never be a revolution in this country. You just cannot have a revolution when the bulk of the people think their own place is beautiful beyond compare."[93]

Phyllis Bentley, having recently arrived in the United States for her lecture tour, promoted *War Letters from Britain* in a *Saturday Review of Literature* critique. It revealed admirably, she claimed, "the progress of the British spirit from sorrow and perplexity, through the agony of Dunkirk, to the 'grim exhilaration' and 'redoubled confidence' of today, when as one writer remarks, 'everyone is secretly delighted with the *privilege* of holding up Hitler.'"[94] Three months later Bentley was championing another book of correspondence, *Women of Britain: Letters from England*, introduced by Jan Struther and published in 1941 only in the United States.

Women of Britain was unique among the epistolary books in that it was composed entirely of letters from women: upper-middle-class Londoners, businessmen's wives, workers, housers of evacuee children, mothers, country dwellers, and the elderly. They wrote about such matters as the Blitz, children, food, money, morale, and the destruction of landmarks. At the core were repeated descriptions of the way in which the war was disrupting family life, separating husbands from wives and children from parents, and destroying familiar milieus. In her introduction, Struther pointed out that, for the first time in history, war had forced a dramatic change in the rhythm and pattern of the daily life of households throughout the country: "We certainly never imagined a war in which the homes themselves would be changed beyond recognition."[95] Now, she said, "the top floor attic is the front line, in which you are almost as likely to meet a war widower as a war widow, and in which the civilian's part is not so much to keep the home fires burning as to put out the incendiary bombs which threaten to burn down the homes themselves."[96] The women's reactions to this new civilian's war, commented Bentley, were especially valuable because they were unique in history.

British culture, tradition, and way of life, whose appeal to Americans was one of the strongest cards in the hand of the British propagandists, was the subject of the enormously successful Britain in Pictures series of books launched in March 1941. As Michael Carney has admirably revealed in *Britain in Pictures: A History and Bibliography*, the series, designed for use overseas, became one of the more subtle – and most effective – forms of literary propaganda produced by the British during the Second World War.

Britain in Pictures was the invention of Hilda Matheson, former director of talks and news at the BBC, who in 1939 became the first director of the Joint Broadcasting Committee for the Ministry of Information. The committee's mandate was to encourage beneficial publicity about Britain in foreign broadcasting, particularly that which would counter the negative perception of the British Empire, so Matheson was well aware of the need to present Britain positively to the world. In 1940 she set up an editorial committee that included the poet and journalist W.J. Turner, the poet Dorothy Wellesley, and herself, and created an advisory committee that included Sir Hugh Walpole and Sir Frederick Whyte.

Matheson's editorial committee created a format for short (forty-eight page) books with texts of 12,000–14,000 words in length, which would reveal British achievements in various areas of life. "The aim," said Carney, "was to present Britain in as many aspects as possible through the eyes of individual writers who would be free to interpret their subject, constrained only by the limitation on space and the need for ample pictorial illustrations."[97] Among the writers, who were paid only £50 per essay, were Vita Sackville-West, Edmund Blunden, Elizabeth Bowen, Graham Greene, Edith Sitwell, Sean O'Faolain, Rex Warner, Lord David Cecil, George Orwell, and John Betjeman.

The Britain in Pictures authors were given some guidance and terms of reference for their contributions, but they were encouraged to write in their own style keeping in mind that the series was to appeal to a wide audience. For the most part, they were to avoid lengthy descriptions of the war effort, but topical references occasionally crept in. Rose Macaulay's *Life among the English*, which sold 61,636 copies throughout the world, concluded with one of the more pointed depictions of wartime Britain and its new-found egalitarianism:

It was a life which tended to resolve class distinctions: taxi-drivers, dustmen, window-cleaners (this profession had naturally languished), shop assistants, hairdressers, and young ladies and gentlemen from expensive schools and universities, met and worked on level terms, addressing each other by nicknames. English social life is, in these curious, dark, troubled years, moving a few steps nearer that democracy for which we say we are fighting and have never yet had. Only a few steps; and whether these will be retraced or continued when the solvent furnace of war dies down, and we are left to grope a way through wreckage and smouldering ashes, we cannot yet know.[98]

The Britain in Pictures series, comprising 126 volumes, sold nearly 3 million copies, and its most useful effect was on readers in the United States and other parts of the world where people needed to be persuaded that Britain deserved to be saved. Reviewing the first of the books in March 1941, the *Listener* commented on the effectiveness of this kind of persuasion: "In these little books the propaganda is of the oblique and detached kind which so often succeeds where bare-faced trumpet-blowing fails. Britain's best 'case,' after all, is her culture, her character and her democratic institutions and it is upon these elements of our national life that this new series concentrates."[99]

It would be impossible to measure the effect that the Britain in Pictures series or the writing of Priestley, Jameson, Bottome, or Jesse had on the American public. At the very least, it would have reinforced Britain's case among those already sympathetic, and it may have reminded others of a tradition and culture that was more appealing than that of Nazi Germany. Writing in *London Calling* in July 1940, the publisher Stanley Unwin stated: "Our books are a multitude of unheralded ambassadors from England, and their vital message was never more essential than now. In them is enshrined all that England stands for."[100]

9

Thrilling and Dramatic Fiction
British Propaganda in Fiction and Poetry

Storm Jameson's *London Calling*, produced at the request of the Ministry of Information, did not consist only of essays and memoirs. It contained ten short stories, a genre more easily produced in the disruption and uncertainty of war than long fiction and one that flowered in the hands of Elizabeth Bowen, Rose Macaulay, Barbara Pym, Jean Rhys, and others during the Second World War. In Jameson's anthology, the form was well represented in tales by Sheila Kaye-Smith, Frank Swinnerton, Eric Linklater, Angela Thirkell, Kate O'Brien, Phyllis Bottome, H.E. Bates, and Lettice Cooper. The stories by Rose Macaulay and E.M. Delafield, however, were particulary interesting and well crafted.

Delafield, a novelist and short story writer best known in North America for *Diary of a Provincial Lady* (1931) and *The Provincial Lady in America* (1934), had volunteered her services to the Ministry of Information at the beginning of the war and became an effective propagandist on the home front. She wrote a thirty-page anti-Nazi booklet entitled *People You Love,* and contributed regular articles on wartime subjects to *Punch;* and she put her most famous creation to work as "The Provincial Lady in Wartime" in *Time and Tide* in the winter of 1939–40. *The Provincial Lady in Wartime* was published as a book in the United States by Harper in 1940.

Delafield's *London Calling* story, "Some Are Complicated," resembles Elizabeth Bowen's wartime tales of psychic aberration in the face of dislocation and loss. It tells of two precocious and imaginative young girls who are sent from London to the safety of the country during the Blitz. Self-contained, they entertain themselves, like two Bronte sisters, by inventing romantic sagas of survival; and when they are told by their fearful guardian that their parents have been killed in a bombing raid, they respond by beginning another fiction in which they are orphans in Siberia. Just as Bowen's protagonist in "Mysterious Kor" retreats under stress to the fictional world of a Rider Haggard novel, Delafield's girls deny their loss by fabricating their own imaginative escape.

Macaulay's story "Miss Anstruther's Letters" is a poignant tale of irretrievable loss in wartime Britain. Based on the author's own experience, it tells of Miss Anstruther losing all her possessions in a bombing raid, most notably her books and a cherished collection of letters from a former lover who had died earlier. Having lost him once, she has lost him again, this time without a trace, and she feels that she is now herself merely a drifting ghost.

Although some of the short stories in *London Calling* were set in wartime Britain, none were as overtly propagandistic as the essays and fragments of memoir. It would be a mistake, however, to underestimate the effectiveness of short fiction, particularly that which appeared in popular American magazines, in influencing American attitudes toward Britain. The Ministry of Information had been urged to take advantage of this form of literature in June 1940 in a report prepared by its own officials and Emery Reves, who managed press liaison in Paris and the Cooperative Press Service. "We must," the submission stated, "have a great number of fictions written by popular English and foreign writers, such as Somerset Maugham, Noel Coward, etc., etc. destined for the big American magazines. They must be thrilling and dramatic fictions, the stories of which would have to refer to the war and to outstanding military deeds, the heroic airmen, Nazi life in France, Belgium, Holland, etc., etc."[1]

Some British authors, such as H.E. Bates, who published both "The Earth" in the *Atlantic Monthly* and "Mr Penfold" in *Harper's* in January 1940, contributed simply by writing sensitive, humane stories of British life. Others, like Margery Sharp in "Night Engagement" and Alec Waugh in "First Stop Crewe" (both carried in *Collier's*) wrote more directly about wartime experiences.

Graham Greene, who joined the Literary Division of the Ministry of Information in April 1940 to help commission and encourage the production of books and pamphlets supporting the war effort, wrote his own propaganda story. "The Lieutenant Died Last," published in *Collier's* on 29 June 1940, tells of twelve Germans parachuting into a small English village with the intention of blowing up a vital railway line. The captured villagers can do nothing to prevent the sabotage, but the most unlikely figure, an old poacher who has been missed by the Germans, becomes a hero by shooting the enemy one by one. As Greene's biographer Michael Shelden points out, the ostensible message to American readers was that "because of the actions of one valiant Englishman, a daring raid is defeated, and the village can rest easy again, secure in the knowledge that their fellow citizens will fight for freedom with the same determination shown by Old Purves."[2]

Shelden goes on to deconstruct "The Lieutenant Died Last" and demonstrates that the artist in Greene made him an imperfect propagandist. The "hero," Purves, is the village drunk, a poacher with an illegal firearm, who escapes the notice of the Germans only because he is hiding on a local aristocrat's estate. A week after his heroism, he is jailed for a week for poaching. The Germans, on the other hand, who are polite and humane in their treatment of the villagers, do not shoot to kill a young man who attempts to escape. Moreover, although Shelden does not comment on it, the story concludes with Purves feeling remorse as he looks at a photograph of a naked baby on a hearthrug – the child of the lieutenant he has killed.

According to Shelden, "If a subtle German propagandist had written the story, he could not have done a better job of making England look bad to the American public."[3] Norman Sherry, on the other hand, calls Greene's showing of sympathy for the enemy "commendable moral courage in wartime."[4] In the summer of 1940, that sympathy would have appealed to many readers in the United States. At the same time, even though this story of heroic British resistance and successful repelling of the invaders came from the most unlikely source, it carried the "island fortress" message which the Ministry of Information was sending to the United States in the perilous months following the fall of France.

In April 1942 *Collier's* was also the outlet for a propaganda story by Eric Knight, whose highly successful 1941 novel, *This Above All*, had attacked the class-ridden, old-school-tie Britain. In "The Rifles of the Regiment," Knight reverses his position and writes in praise of the Colonel Blimpish kind of officer caricatured in the United States. His Colonel Heathergall, "Old Glass-eye" to his Loyal Rifle Regiment, has served at the Somme, in India, and in Palestine, and he believes that "fear is a cad – you just don't recognize the bounder." Trying to lead his regiment to safety a fortnight after Dunkirk, he is visited by Fear, who says: "All your arrogant, aristocratic, British life you've snubbed me and pretended you didn't know me ... You too have courage, in your own way. The huntin'-shootin'-fishin' sort of courage. The well-bred, polo-field kind of courage. But that's got nothing to do with *this* kind of war."[5] The point of the story, however, is that even in this kind of war the old-school-tie brigade has its value.

One Briton whose propaganda writing led to a career as a professional author was Roald Dahl, who in the postwar years became famous for his short stories and his books for children. A member of the RAF, he suffered serious injuries in a plane crash in Libya and in 1942 was assigned to the British Embassy in Washington as an assistant air attaché. Loosely associated with the British intelligence services, the attractive young pilot gathered what information he could from such informed people as columnist Drew Pearson and journalist Ralph Ingersoll. C.S. Forester, writing propaganda for the British, urged Dahl to let him describe his flying experiences in the *Saturday Evening Post* because, as Jeremy Treglown has pointed out, the British at that time had so few victories to advertise that the embassy decided that propaganda should focus on past triumphs, especially those of the RAF.[6] "You are now in America," Forester told him, "and because you have, as they say over here, 'been in combat,' you are a rare bird on this side of the Atlantic."[7]

Forester intended that Dahl should provide him with notes about his flying days in Libya, but he was given instead an evocative article entitled "A Piece of Cake." Forester immediately arranged to have it published in the *Saturday Evening Post*, where in August 1942 it appeared anonymously as "Shot Down over Libya." Dahl went on to write eleven short stories over the next two years, and all were published in popular American magazines, including the *Saturday Evening Post*, *Ladies' Home Journal*, *Atlantic Monthly*, *Harper's*, and *Town and Country*.

Two of Dahl's stories, "They Shall Not Grow Old" and "Death of an Old Old Man," were such poignant tales of the horror of battle that they were not published until the final months of the war. The remainder, argues Treglown, all contributed to the British war effort, reiterating the message that British defiance in the face of the German onslaught remained unshaken: "Each one of Dahl's stories which found a publisher during the years most dangerous for the Allies contained some overt propaganda."[8] "Katina," set during the British evacuation of Greece, had an RAF pilot telephoning a German counterpart to declare, "One day we will come back,"[9] and it ended with a Greek girl being killed while shaking her fists at Messerschmitts flying past. In another story, an Englishman's servant in Dar es Salaam reacted to the outbreak of war by killing a farmer in the former German colony.

The theme of determined retaliation against German attack appeared even in Dahl's "Gremlin Lore," his children's story of mythological creatures who sabotaged RAF missions. Moreover, the text included a scene in which Hitler, "sputtering a flood of unintelligible German," complained to Goering and Goebbels that the credit given to the gremlins was robbing the Luftwaffe of their glory. The Fuhrer was then interrupted by Mussolini, "looking pretty battered [and] holding his hands up sort of like an Italian chef describing a dish of spaghetti."[10]

Dahl completed "Gremlin Lore" within a few months of arriving in Washington and submitted it for approval to the British Information Services, which sent it to Walt Disney. Disney bought the script and arranged to have it published in *Cosmopolitan* in December 1942 under the pseudonym Pegasus. Disney then began to work on a film version, though this project was abandoned within a year; but Random House published a picture book edition of *The Gremlins* in 1943.

While short fiction was highly effective in engaging the sympathies of American readers, it was the novel that had the greatest impact. "Most readers," Curtice Hitchcock told British authors in 1942, "when moved by a great novel, do feel a genuine sense of gratitude to the writer who created it and of a personal bond with him. There follows inevitably a sense of trust on which in times like these an author in all sincerity and humility can draw for worthy purposes ... Make us feel in personal and human terms your problems, your dreams, and what you are like as human beings."[11]

Ironically, the work of fiction which had the greatest influence on American wartime readers, and which spoke in "personal and human terms," had already appeared and was not intended to be propaganda. In the late 1930s Jan Struther, a writer of poems and small pieces for *Punch*, the *Spectator*, and the *New Statesman*, was asked to write some short, light pieces for the Court page of the *Times*. They were to be about "an ordinary sort of woman who leads an ordinary sort of life – rather like yourself."[12]

Struther's creation, Caroline Miniver, was anything but ordinary, at least in the sense of resembling anything like the average British woman. From the upper-middle class, she and her architect husband Clem have a house in fashionable Chelsea, a cottage in the country, a son at Eton, and a maid, a cook, and a gardener. Her life is comfortable, her children are nearly angelic, her husband agreeable, and her days are filled with leisure, shopping, and dinner parties. Not for nothing had Struther named her protagonist Miniver after the white fur used for ceremonial robes.

As Struther's pieces went on in the winter of 1938–39, intimations of the coming war began to unsettle the Minivers' world. Outside her newsagent's shop, she notices a hoarding blown by the wind so that only the word "JEWS" showed, and she concludes that "however long the horror continued, one must not get to the stage of refusing to think about it."[13] Collecting gas masks for her children, she thinks: "It was for this ... that one had boiled the milk for their bottles, and washed their hands before lunch, and not let them eat with a spoon which had been dropped on the floor."[14] Three weeks into the war, she writes to a friend: "We're all so buoyed up just now with the crusading spirit, and so burningly convinced of the infamy of the Government we're fighting against (this time, thank goodness, one doesn't say 'the nation we're fighting against')."[15]

The Miniver pieces appeared every few weeks, and they drew such a wide readership that, in October 1939 they were brought out in book form in Britain as *Mrs Miniver*. Although they had popular appeal, they were seen by many intellectual readers as superficial and smug. The reviewer for the *Listener* summed up the complaints of many people:

Much of the sensitivity is a product of a four-figure income ("a car, nowadays, was such an integral part of one's life"), little morals snugly close each column, the book is immensely flattering to people like Mrs Miniver, and by them it will be warmly welcomed. It ministers both to their self-satisfaction and their sense of superiority ... Sensitiveness to chrysanthemums and friendship is no substitute for the Morality of intelligence. Mrs Miniver is superior about Left Wing and Right Wing without showing that she has the least idea of what all the fuss is about; and her views on war and crisis are sentimental and muddled. Miss Struther presents her heroine with considerable deftness and skill; but the main effect of her creation will be to confirm the smug in their comfortable assurances that their smugness is a virtue.[16]

Mrs Miniver may have dismayed thoughtful Britons, but when it was published in the United States in the summer of 1940 and was made a Book-of-the-Month Club selection, it became a best-seller. A year later, fifteen hundred copies were being sold in a day. The familiarity that seemed to breed contempt in many British reviewers was generally absent in their American counterparts, who found in the Minivers a charm and decency worth preserving. The *New York Times* headed its review "Qualities in English Life That Must Survive,"[17] and the *New Yorker's* Clifton Fadiman declared that Mrs Miniver's touch, "the touch of Lamb, even of Shakespeare in a minor mood, is one of the indefinable things, quite unimportant, that Englishmen and Englishwomen are fighting and dying for at the moment."[18] "There isn't much war in 'Mrs. Miniver,'" said Lewis Gannett in the *Boston Transcript*. "But you can't help thinking of bombs falling in Kent, and on London, as you read it ... The book wasn't written for America; there isn't a word of propaganda in it. Yet reading it, you understand why the poets have written so many of their loveliest lines about 'this England.'"[19]

While *Mrs Miniver* may not have contained a word of overt or recognizable propaganda, it was nonetheless effective in enlisting American sympathies. Seeing the force of her creation when she arrived in the United States in 1940, Struther became much more than an inadvertent propagandist and put the Minivers to work for the war effort. In a new edition of *Mrs Miniver* brought out shortly after Pearl Harbor, she included a new piece called "Mrs Miniver Makes a List," written originally in 1939 for *The Queen's Book of the Red Cross*. Many American readers, she said, who were experiencing separation from their families in the first Christmas of their war would see the same dislocation in Caroline Miniver's account of shopping for Christmas gifts.

In August 1942 Struther wrote a piece for the *New York Times* called "Mr Miniver" in which she described how the first three years of the war had affected Clem and "most of the other men of his age and position in the British Isles, whether their names happen to be Miniver, MacDonald, Morgan, or Micklewaite." Being an architect, he had seen the bottom fall out of his business and was then attached to the Ministry of Works and Buildings, designing hostels for munitions workers. Living on half his prewar salary, he shared an apartment in London with a co-worker, and since the maid, cook, and gardener had all been drafted, he had to do the work at the cottage on weekends.

"The days of $6,000 a year, the small car, the well-filled cellar, and the vacations in Scotland" were over. Clothes rationing meant that

Clem wore old, ill-fitting suits and shoes, and razor blades were almost impossible to find. He had lost fifteen pounds from digging up the garden and tennis court to plant vegetables, and his diet consisted of tea without sugar, toast with margarine and a teaspoonful of jam. Pressure of work and then evenings at his ARP post until midnight meant no more tennis or cocktail parties. Clem reacted to all of these deprivations as he did to his volunteer work during the Dunkirk evacuation: "Of this experience he speaks very little."[20]

Struther seems not to have realized how little Clem Miniver represented the average British man, and a lengthy editorial in the *New York Times* questioned the accuracy of her claims about his income. Only recently, it pointed out, the British chancellor of the exchequer had stated that men in Clem's position had seen their income fall by only a third.[21] Several weeks after the editorial appeared, a reader wrote to analyse what Clem was able to get – as Struther described it – for his £1,500 ($6,000) income in the prewar period. "Can any American family," she asked, "live so excellently on less than $20,000 or $25,000 a year, or four times what it cost in England prior to the war?"[22]

Despite its portrayal of a privileged and materially comfortable Britain – or perhaps because of it – *Mrs Miniver* continued to win American sympathies. Struther fostered this affection by donating the original proofs of the book to the Library of Congress in August 1942. When, in the same year, Metro-Goldwyn-Mayer's film version of *Mrs Miniver* won the Academy Award for best picture and attracted large crowds of filmgoers, the influence of Struther's story became very much greater. It is said that Roosevelt stated that it had considerably hastened the United States' entry into the war, and that Churchill commented that Struther's words had done more for the Allies than a flotilla of battleships.[23]

Struther did not limit her wartime writing to the Minivers. In 1941 she contributed an introduction to *Women of Britain: Letters from England*, and in October 1942 the *Atlantic Monthly* carried her "Traveling America," a long poem describing the echoes of England to be found in many parts of the United States. Another poem, "Wartime Journey," appeared in the same periodical in February 1944. In August 1943 she wrote an article for the *New York Times* summing up the four years of the British war effort. A reminder to Americans of the hardships and sacrifices already endured by the British, it also repeated the familiar theme of change and democratization in Britain. In

Struther's view, the reconstructed country which Priestley and other left wingers had long been demanding had already arrived: "Under their feet, under their hands, while they worked, the Britain of which people had dreamed has grown up ... Advances and reforms for which the practical men – the 'starry-eyed idealists' – had been working for years are emerging through all the turmoil of war and becoming part of the national life, as though, having sat for so long with the motor switched on, someone – or perhaps forty-seven million people – had suddenly decided to press down the accelerator."[24]

One of the severest critics of *Mrs Miniver* was Eric Knight, a Yorkshireman who had been living in the United States since the age of twelve. Knight's cynicism about British society was forcefully portrayed in his own novel, *This Above All*, one of only two other wartime works of British fiction that came close to the popularity of Struther's book in the United States.

When *This Above All* was published in the United States in 1941, the Harper dust jacket touted it as "the first important novel to come out of the war." Knight, however, preferred to call it "the last book to come out of World War I."[25] What lay behind this remark was his four years of service in the First war – he had enlisted in a Canadian unit – and the death of both his brothers on the same day in that war. His father, a Quaker, had been killed in the Boer War when Knight was only a few years old, leaving him to support himself by working in the Yorkshire mills at the age of twelve. He went on to create a reputation as a writer – author of *The Flying Yorkshireman* (1938), *The Happy Land* (1940), and the very popular *Lassie Come Home* (1940) – and when he saw Europe embroiled in yet another war, he wrote a novel that questioned the reasons for another generation of young men to fight and die.

This Above All is set in England in the summer and autumn of 1940, and its protagonist, Clive Brooks, having fought courageously with the British troops who retreated from Dunkirk, has come to doubt whether the country is worth fighting for. An illegitimate child born and raised in an industrial slum, he meets and has an affair with Prudence Cathaway, a middle-class young woman unfamiliar with the life of the working class. Anticipating the class conflict of John Osborne's *Look Back in Anger*, Knight uses the lovers to represent the clash of the two Britains – the underclass and the privileged – and in one lengthy argument between them Clive explains why he will no longer fight for the country.

At Dunkirk, says Clive, young men were dying because the foreign policies of a series of hollow, smug British governments had betrayed them. The leaders preferred to appease Hitler out of fear of communism, "a blind unreasoning fear that British labour might come up from the stink of the dole and revolt."[26] To working-class people like him, Clive declares, England "means walking around until your boot soles are thin, and hoping against hope that the next place you go there'll be a job. It means taking any old job, no matter how ugly or distasteful or incompatible with your hopes and ambitions of youth. It's meant a furtive childhood – when life most of all should have been splendid and strong."[27]

No longer, says Clive, will he risk his life or anyone else's for colonies in Africa or for Shell Petroleum or Incorporated Rubber Industries: "I'll fight for a hope of a new Britain with its unknown virtues, but not for the Britain whose vices I know."[28] The government, he says, "are perverting the goals of this war. They could only make it a true crusade by stating our goals and aims. What *are* we fighting for? A new world? A better world? Wisdom in world order – or to be the bully of the schoolyard again?"[29]

Clive's speech is a scathing attack on the British class system and the war he thinks is being fought to preserve the privileges of the upper classes. Writing in the left-wing *New Statesman and Nation*, Tom Paine praised the novel for discussing sincerely "the sort of questions which many people ask themselves privately and scarcely dare to discuss in public."[30] The *Times Literary Supplement* called it "a tribute to the continued liberty of thought and speech which makes its appearance possible."[31] Among the political old guard, however, especially at the Foreign Office, it could not have been palatable reading.

In the United States, many reviewers echoed the comment of *Boston Transcript*'s Olga Owens: "You cannot say, any longer, that no great novel has come out of the second World War. Eric Knight has written one."[32] In particular, Knight was applauded for his willingness to discuss the weaknesses in British society and for his call for social reconstruction. Although he had confided to friends that he wrote the novel to promote Anglo-American understanding, no one accused him of propaganda. In the *New York Times*, Marianne Hauser declared: "*This Above All* is no propagandist book. It is the gripping, unforgettable story of England's battle and of a man's inner battle both fighting with their backs to the wall."[33] R.B. West, in the *Saturday Review of Literature*, similarly noted: "It is not propaganda. It seems to me to be a sincere, but hurried piece of work by an admirable writer, and a British patriot."[34]

Despite its harsh criticisms of British society, *This Above All* does indeed finally come down on the side of patriotism. In countering Clive's disillusionment, Prue argues for the Britain of culture and history:

If I said it was Shakespeare – and thatched roofs – And the countryside, you could mock … If I said it was – speakers in Hyde Park free to say what they wish – and polite bobbies on the corner – and these cliffs here, and Drake alive in memory – you could curl your lip superciliously.

If I said it meant the Magna Carta and all that went into it – and the freedom of the common man that sprang from it – and speaking your mind without fear, and the knowledge that your own home, no matter how wretched is still your castle, and all the heritage of liberty that man in this age has found – you would laugh because it's been said before.

If I said England was the thump of a bat at cricket, and the New Forest deep in fern and holly trees standing tall; if I said it was the larks that will sing here tomorrow and for ever – if I said it was the shout of a newsboy on the corner, or the sound of a taxi horn, or the quick clipped cheerful talk of a cockney passing in the dark, or the age and dignity of our cities – of the fog and the green grass and softness of voice and skin – or the sense of fair play that we've given the world – if I said it was all those, you could mock.[35]

Clive does mock Prue's hymn of praise to traditional England, but he nonetheless returns to the struggle and is killed during a raid. The novel ends with Prue, pregnant by him, envisaging an England in which the child will inherit what they both believed in: "But you're going to have a better time of it than he did. You're going to have a better England to live in! Because we were both right. Both right! We have to fight now for what I believe in. And after that, we'll have to fight for what he believed in. We'll win this war because – because we can stick it. And then, God help us, we're going to win the peace, too."[36]

In his debate with Prue, Clive had repeatedly demanded that she have a realistic attitude to the country, and it is this insistence that makes *This Above All* almost unique among the popular British novels of the Second World War. As Paul Rotha has pointed out, it also gave the novel a special credibility with American readers: "It was credited with doing more to cement Anglo-American understanding in the United States than any piece of conscious propaganda because it represented to the American public Britain's ability to examine her own faults and virtues with equal objectivity. Written only as a piece of personal soul-searching, it put Eric Knight in the position of being one of Britain's most ardent protagonists in the U.S. and Canada."[37]

Knight himself worked hard to win the war and in particular for the British cause. After the success of *This Above All*, which went through four editions, he went back to Britain so that he could lecture in the United States as someone who had "been there." He also wrote a number of articles for the *Saturday Evening Post* with titles such as "The British Eat to Win" and "Sam and His Yankee Allies," and for *Collier's* he wrote "The Rifles of the Regiment," his story of the heroism of an upper-class officer whom Clive Brooks would have despised.

On his return journey from Britain to the United States in March 1942, Knight stopped off in Canada and gave a radio talk, "They Don't Want Swamps and Jungles," for the Canadian Broadcasting Corporation. Although nominally addressed to Canadians, its message – that the battle against the Axis powers mattered as much to North Americans as it did to Britons – was also aimed at the many American listeners in the northern states: "I am asking you to understand a new and bloody kind of world conquest that threatens the free life of a Canadian and American just as surely as it does the free life of a Briton."[38] The talk was so well received that it was rebroadcast twice and the Director of Public Information in Canada had it published as a pamphlet.

In 1942 Knight joined the U.S. Army, rising to major in the Film Unit of the Special Services Division. Together with Anthony Veiller, he wrote the screenplays for the first two films in Frank Capra's *Why We Fight* series, as well as *Know Your Ally, Britain*. In 1943 he wrote *A Short Guide to Great Britain* – the explanatory booklet that was given to American soldiers stationed in Britain. Addressing Irish Americans in particular, Knight argued that this was not the right time to fight old battles, and to the general reader he claimed that British democracy might actually be even more effective than the American version: "The important thing to remember is that within this apparently old-fashioned framework the British enjoy a practical working twentieth century democracy which is in some ways even more flexible and sensitive to the will of the people than our own."[39] In early January 1943 Knight was killed in a transport plane crash in Dutch Guiana. Shortly before, he had written to his publisher to say that "the big thing [was] to win this war by killing Germans, not by writing books."[40]

Another British novel that remained high on the best-seller lists in the United States in 1941 was James Hilton's *Random Harvest*, which was reprinted four times in its first month of issue. It is the story of an Englishman, Charles Rainier, whose shell shock suffered in the First World War caused him to lose all memory of the two years of his life from 1917 to 1919. In the next two decades, he built the family business into an international success, became a member of parliament, and married his secretary. In talking to his latest secretary, the narrator of the novel, he recovers his memory and realizes that during the lost period he had married a beautiful young actress named Paula. He is now willing to give up everything to find her, and as the novel ends, Hilton pulls the strings and reveals that Rainier's wife is actually Paula, who had remained with him in the hope that he would recover his memory of her. Rainier recognizes her and they are reunited with her words: "It may not be too late."[41]

Although *Random Harvest* is about a First World War veteran, it is clearly meant to be an allegory of events leading up to the Second World War. The epigraph, supposedly from a German report – "According to British Official Report, bombs fell at Random" – repeated a folkloric tale coming out of the raids of 1940. Moreover, the novel begins on Armistice Day in 1937; Charles first met Paula on Armistice Day 1918, and the story ends as German tanks cross the border into Poland in 1939. As the second war begins, Paula observes: "We're terribly unready. We missed our ways years ago and found a wide, comfortable road, fine for sleepwalkers, but it had the major drawback of wandering just anywhere, at random ... There's nothing we can do about it now, is there." When the narrator asks "Are you talking about – er – the country – or – er –," she replies: "Both, in a way."[42]

Hilton seems to be using Rainier's loss of memory of the most vital relationship of his life – and his subsequent years of business aggrandizement, of mechanically performing as a member of parliament, and especially of living in a marriage that was no more than one of convenience – to represent the British political somnambulance of the interwar period. Just as Rainier can regain his memory and his passionate love of Paula, so too, Hilton seems to be saying, can the country regain its commitment to action.

Allegory, like irony, can be elusive and easily missed. Judging by the responses of reviewers, few Americans saw any allegorical implications in *Random Harvest*; they were far more interested in the story simply as one of love lost and regained. There was some propaganda value in the essential decency of the central figures and in references to "the utter destruction of civilization" threatened by the Nazis,[43] and in talk of "a simpler England after the war ... not so rich and not so snobbish,"[44] but the core of Hilton's novel went unrecognized.

The fourth British novel to capture a wide readership in the United States in 1941 was Helen MacInnes's *Above Suspicion*, published in July and reprinted eight times in the next two months. MacInnes, whose husband Gilbert Highet worked for Sir William Stephenson's British Security Co-ordination in New York, was a strong advocate for the British cause and, together with Highet, had presented a detailed analysis of British counterintelligence needs to the Ministry of Information in 1940.[45] *Above Suspicion* was her first novel, and in the postwar years she went on to establish a solid reputation as a writer of spy novels.

Above Suspicion is an espionage thriller about an Oxford don and his pretty wife who are asked to travel to Germany as tourists in the summer of 1939 in order to learn about the fate of an anti-Nazi agent. In the process, they witness the fear and paranoia pervasive in Nazi Germany, and MacInnes misses little opportunity to paint the Nazis as ruthless automatons prepared to beat, torture, and kill. She even employs heavy irony, as in the German agent's reply to the comment that all people – Germans, Jews, Czechs, or Poles – should have their *Lebensraum*:

It is just such thoughts as these which have weakened Britain. In the last twenty-five years, she could have established herself as ruler of the world. Instead, she makes a Commonwealth out of an Empire, and they won't even fight to help her when she has to fight. She leaves the riches of India untapped; she urges a representative government on Indians who were about to refuse it. She alienates Italy with sanctions. She weakens herself all the time, and she thinks it is an improvement.[46]

MacInnes brings the question of isolationism, neutrality, and the United States into her story through an American character, Henry M. Van Cortlandt of High Tor, New York. A journalist working in Europe, he initially articulates the American scepticism of British foreign policy and adopts a position of neutrality. Drawn into the espionage intrigue and repelled by the brutal methods of the Nazis, however, he becomes a fighter, explaining his evolution to an English friend:

My stories were going to be a model of detachment. Can you imagine that? My angle was that the Germans had a tough time of it. If only they had gotten a square deal ... all that hash. It only took me a few weeks to find out that every deal was square if it benefited Germany, and to hell with the rest ... They are always in the right, and the rest of us just misunderstand them. Criticism is just another stab in the back from Jews and Communists. They've kidded other people so long now that they've started kidding themselves.[47]

Among other British novels published in the United States in 1941 was the ubiquitous Phyllis Bottome's *London Pride*. It dramatized the wartime life of the working class, which was seen only in recollection in *This Above All*. Set like Knight's novel in the summer of 1940, *London Pride* concerns the life of an East End London family during the Blitz: the charwoman mother, the dockland communist father, and the four children. The protagonist, seven-year-old Ben, has significantly been named after Big Ben, one of the most powerful and widely recognized symbols of Britain. As the novel progresses, he sees his parents wrestle with the difficult decision of sending two of their children to the country; his house is destroyed in a raid, the neighbouring family is killed, and he himself is injured by the bombing. As the novel ends, Ben has been sent to the relative peace and pastoral calm of the southwest coast of England.

London Pride benefited from the research Bottome was able to do for *Mansion House of Liberty*, revealing a detailed knowledge of the customs, humour, problems, laws, and beliefs of London's dockland. However, Bottome did not have a working-class background, and her novel is marred by the patronizing treatment of her subject, which was common in British literature prior to the 1950s. Her use of phonetic spelling is, for example, acceptable when she represents the Cockney accent – but not when she concocts a letter from an evacuated Cockney child in which the words are spelled phonetically. As Diana Forbes-Robertson noted in *Books*, the reader is made to observe the remarkable actions of the East Enders much as they would the behaviour of monkeys, and one laughs at them rather than with them.[48]

The other weakness of *London Pride* is its sentimentality. As the *Atlantic Monthly* pointed out, all the novel's characters behave courageously in the Blitz and we know that this is not true to human nature: "Nervous systems are shattered, brave men and women run screaming in circles."[49] This sentimentality is signalled in its dedication in the British edition to "the Children of Bermondsey and Bethnal Green" and its accompanying stanzas from William Blake's "Jerusalem." There is no indication in the novel that the poet's call for a new equitable society has been heard by anyone in authority. The slum children experience "England's green and pleasant land" only through being evacuated to a country estate run by an upper-class woman (who is so august that she is called only "the Vision") and through Ben's being sent to the south coast. Looking across the water from there, Ben visualizes London, and Bottome provides a lyrical vision of the heart of the city, not a picture of the squalid slums of the East End to which Ben will eventually return:

It was as if he saw instead, his own river Thames, flowing between two measureless darknesses of sea and sky. Above the river's silver floor, shot up the towers of Westminster. These were the palaces of freedom, the halls of kindly kings, the Abbey of a merciful God. Flames and vampire bats tried to drag down these towers night after night; but Ben saw them again, standing there in placid security, as if nothing could ever shake or destroy them. He had only to listen, to hear within his heart the long reverberating strokes of Big Ben.

London had been made for people – and by people – like Ma and Dad, Flossie and Bert; and even Em'ly. For Em'ly had the courage of those ancient towers. London had not sprung from its great buildings; it had made them, out of its shabby, arrogant, defiant, hopeful and astute old heart.[50]

A book written from a patronizing and sentimental point of view, while flawed artistically, may nevertheless be effective in reaching the readers' sympathies, and London Pride was reprinted twice in its first month of publication in the United States. Despite her reservations, Forbes-Robertson praised the novel for its authentic details of East End life, and Clifton Fadiman concluded that "the book gets you … Her pictures of air-raid shelters, looting, evacuations, and so forth have a sharp veracity."[51]

In her other wartime novel, Survival, published in the United States in 1943, Bottome moved away from detailed description to intellectual inquiry into the causes of the war. Told in diary form, it is the story of an Austrian psychiatrist of Jewish descent who becomes a refugee in England and gets involved with the lives and passions of a group of English people. Although there are some vivid descriptions of treating the wounded during an air raid on Plymouth, the excessive Adlerian analysis frequently smothers the vitality of the story.

Speaking as though she is a foreigner in Britain allows Bottome to comment about the country and its people, but since she is not entirely successful in hiding her own voice, these remarks smack of disingenuous and exaggerated self-praise. Shortly after arriving in England, for example, the narrator sums up the entire population: "Every one of these forty-two million Islanders thrills to a risk, and they thrill in common. Down go their class barriers, their blind arrogance of privilege; even the smug selfishness of the rich! The people of Great Britain thrill together, aim together, face in skilled unison together, the Beast of Prey that threatens their homes and the inner freedom of the hearts that built them."[52]

The theme of Britain changing and becoming more democratic through the war is given various iterations: "The ideals of the British people may change faster than the static minds of their ruling class. This is indeed, whether the British yet realize it or not, everybody's War; and it must lead to everybody's peace. But if it is to be a democratic peace, not Totalitarian State Slavery, we must first arrive at something better and more generally advantageous than the fake democracy now practised for the good of the few at the expense of the many."[53]

Survival repeats the veneration of Churchill found in Bottome's American speeches and in her earlier writing – "Churchill *is* England!" proclaims the narrator after Dorothy Thompson – and Roosevelt is "that man of infinite courage and astuteness."[54] Like many other British wartime novels, it brings in an American character, in this case a vivacious young woman with the freshness and openness of the New World, who is fought over by three Englishmen. At the end of the novel, the narrator proposes to his own young woman at the Mayflower Monument in Plymouth, from where the Plymouth Fathers sailed, because "it was a great venture … and a happy one. They were driven forth into exile, a persecuted group, and it is to their descendants that England now looks for bread and hope. I thought it would be nice to meet where they had stood looking out, as we do now, into the unknown." The narrator tells this young woman (and readers of any nationality): "You've got to choose to-day between being a person who hates, a Hitlerite, or his chief enemy, a person who loves, a lover of Life!"[55]

The device of viewing Britain through the eyes of a foreigner who has ultimately to choose between it and Germany had already been used more simplistically by the Scottish author and cousin of Robert Louis Stevenson, Dorothy E. Stevenson. Her novel *The English Air*, published in New York by Farrar and Rinehart in early 1940, tells of a young German, Franz, who is sent to England in the spring of 1938 in order to learn about British attitudes and practices. His mother, now dead, had been English born, and he is sent to live with her cousin at a country house called Fernacres. After a year in the English "air" – an atmosphere presented as casual, humorous, warm, and benign – Franz becomes an anglicized "Frank" and rejects Hitler's plans for Germany. The product of an unhappy marriage between a vital young English woman and a formal German man, he concludes that "the air of England is very wholesome."[56]

Stevenson misses few opportunities to paint Nazi Germany as contrastingly unwholesome. She describes how Franz's mother was psychologically destroyed by the rigidity of German society and how his Aunt Anna has become gripped by paranoia in the face of the Nazi regime. Where young people at Fernacres are relaxed and informal, those in Germany belong to regimented youth groups, who sing ideological songs in place of those of Schubert, Brahms, and Strauss. Where young German soldiers enlist for personal glory, Franz concludes, Britons have built their empire by self-sacrifice: "They left their comfortable homes thousands of miles behind them and fought and suffered in deserts under burning suns, and, because this was bred in their bones, they wanted no fuss. It was their duty, that was all."[57]

Written in early 1940, *The English Air* even treats Neville Chamberlain – who a few months later is vilified as a weak and naive leader – as a heroic, peaceful man confronting a ruthless enemy. Through Franz's eyes, Chamberlain is seen driving to Downing Street after the Munich Crisis "like a victorious general,"[58] and to Franz the declaration of war is a moving and understated call to arms: "Mr Chamberlain spoke to the people. He did not make a speech, he just spoke to the people of Britain quietly and from a full heart, and the people of Britain listened. There was no excitement, there was no waving of banners, but there was determination. The people of Britain were at one in their determination to fight against aggression in the cause of liberty and justice – it was in this spirit that Britain took up arms."[59]

Stevenson suggests, moreover, that the fight against Nazi Germany is a battle between Christian values and barbarism. Anna tells her nephew: "Hatred blinds us to all that is beautiful ... and so it is with the Fatherland which was full of so much goodness and beauty. People are being taught to hate. Jesus Christ taught us to love."[60] At the novel's end, Franz, who much earlier has joined those opposing Hitler within Germany, concludes that he may never return to his homeland because the Germany he admired really only existed in his imagination.

The English Air received mixed reviews in the United States. The literary critic of the *New Yorker* spoke for many in arguing that Stevenson's unqualified praise of everything English robbed her novel of any credibility: "Miss Stevenson's sugar-coating seems irrelevant, immaterial, and a mite silly."[61] On the other hand, as the comments of Olga Owens in the *Boston Transcript* suggest, some readers found the novel convincing: "Her book is not propaganda, but the genuine outpouring of individual belief and experience. In no current novel have we found the ideas and ways of living implicit in the word 'democracy' so delicately yet sharply implied."[62]

Susan Ertz's 1943 novel *Anger in the Sky* also presents an outsider to Britain who is forced to choose, but in this case it is an American who is confronted by the question whether or not to participate in the war, and his choice represents that of his whole country. Ertz was an Anglo-American novelist born in England to American parents, and she spent her early years there until moving to the United States with her family. She returned to Britain to work in the First World War and spent most of her adult life in London, occasionally revisiting the United States, as she did in a coast-to-coast lecture tour in 1937. From 1922 on, she was known as a writer of novels of domestic problems.

Like Maugham's *The Hour before the Dawn*, Ertz's *Anger in the Sky* is about the wartime life – in this case, from 1940 to 1942 – of a large country house and the representative characters who populate it. Meddenhall belongs to Oliver and Ruth Anstruther, who inherited it unexpectedly, and they rule over it with open and unpretentious generosity. Oliver, an army officer, is absent throughout the novel, and Ruth has to manage the household affairs on her own, as well as supporting her two daughters. Stacy is a lively, inquisitive, generous seventeen-year-old who gets killed in an air raid while touring London's East End to see what the working class are enduring. Her older sister Viola, a nurse in a London hospital, is embittered because her lover has suffered a head wound which has rendered him virtually a vegetable. Their brother Lennox is in the RAF.

Among the other characters for whom Meddenhall is a temporary home are thirty evacuee children who, with one exception, adapt well to the benign setting. Madame Vibourg is a refugee from France whose concern for self-preservation makes her sympathetic to Germany. Her husband, however, leaves Vichy France in disgust and joins their daughter in London to work for the Free French. Mr Redcliffe, the butler, performs his duties stoically throughout the Christmas period, even though his beloved nephew has been killed in action. Lord and Lady Monkhorton, who live nearby, are stiff and pompous aristocrats who are described as anachronisms (Lady Monkhorton is even called Dodo) in the changing, more egalitarian Britain.

The most important outsider at Meddenhall is Elliott Tully, a visiting American who aggressively voices all the isolationist arguments of the pre-Pearl Harbor period. "It simply beats me," he says, "why Europe can't settle its troubles without wars ... I don't want Germany to win. It's just that it isn't our war and we've got to keep clear of it."[63] As the novel progresses, Tully and Viola fall in love, and like many of his countrymen at the time, he develops considerable sympathy for Britain without joining the fight. When he proposes to Viola, she rejects him on the grounds that his and America's nonintervention in the war will create a permanent gulf between them. "We haven't got private lives any longer," she says, elevating each of them to symbols of the two countries:

After this war is over, if you're with us, we can begin to try to make a better world. I've seen enough of America to realize that it can't be done without you because you're too vital to the success of any such plans. If you keep aloof, aloof from the war and the world after the war, I don't see how we, the peoples who are fighting Nazism, and you who didn't fight it, can ever come together. Or not for a hundred years. Even if I were very much in love with you, instead of being what I am, very, very fond of you, I don't think I'd marry you as things are. We'd always have to try not to speak of the war.[64]

When the Japanese bombing of Pearl Harbor brings the United States into the war, the barrier between Tully and Viola is removed, though neither Viola nor Ertz seems aware that the attack has meant that neither the man nor the nation has had to make the decision to fight.

In addition to the central argument about isolationism, Ertz treats many of the familiar themes of British propaganda. Ruth Anstruther, for example, appeals to the members of a Women's Institute meeting to work together because, although they may come from different classes, they have "the same traditions, the same heritage, the same blood" in their veins.[65] Another character defends the British Empire by claiming: "These islands are a sort of blood transfusion centre. We pump the blood from our arteries into other entities, and when they're strong enough to stand alone, they either come in and join the family circle or go their own ways, profiting, let's hope, by our virtues as well as our mistakes."[66]

The theme of Nazi barbarism threatening Allied civilization also is woven throughout *Anger in the Sky*. The First World War, thinks one character, "had been a war like many other wars, but ... this one was a turning point in the story of civilization."[67] And Lennox tells Tully: "If we lose it, everything is lost. Civilization will get a setback it may not recover from for centuries."[68] In Ruth Anstruther's concluding thoughts at the end of the novel, Ertz manages to make London the world's first line of defence against the disease of Nazism: "And here in unlovely, battered, paintless London she felt she was at the core, at the very core and firm centre of the world's resistance to the sickness that had been so nearly fatal to it."[69]

In some respects its strong emphasis on American isolationism would have made *Anger in the Sky* much more useful to the British cause two years before its publication. Isolationism, however, had not ended with the American entry into the war, and it was still important to keep Americans focused on the European conflict. Richard Match, for example, while rightly complaining in the *New York Times* that the characters were simply embodiments of various attitudes toward the war and the peace to come, praised its picture of embattled Britain: "An American reader can only be impressed and sobered by the universality of war in England, the apparent determination of most Britons that some more just and peaceful way of life shall come out of this conflict. Miss Ertz's book should help unbombed Americans to understand their point of view."[70] In the *Atlantic Monthly*, Edward Weeks described the novel as "a constant endeavour to light up the understanding between Britain and the United States," though he remained suspicious of Britain's new-found egalitarianism: "The strength of this story lies in its warm-blooded picture of that classless community which England has (temporarily?) become in its own defense."[71]

When Storm Jameson assembled *London Calling*, she did not forget the poets; among the contributions were poems by Walter de la Mare,

Edith Sitwell, Dorothy L. Sayers, Cecil Day Lewis, Edmund Blunden, and the poet laureate John Masefield. In 1941 Masefield, who also did radio broadcasts, lectured in hospitals, and later read his poetry at American army camps in Britain, wrote *The Nine Days Wonder*, a prose account of the Dunkirk evacuation, and four short poems in honour of the fallen soldiers.

Although poetry is the literary form least accessible for the ordinary reader, it has always flourished in wartime, and the Second World War saw the work of a number of British poets used in the propaganda campaign in the United States. The *Atlantic Monthly* carried Richard Aldington's "For Armistice Day, 1939" in its November 1939 issue, and as the war went on it published two poems by Jan Struther. "Travelling America" (October 1942) takes the reader on a rail trip through part of the United States, suggesting that much of it is little different from regions of the British Isles. A clapboard house in Massachusetts reminds the poet of a weatherboard one in Essex, the Chesapeake Bay woods resemble those in Devon, the stony fields of Kentucky call to mind the stunted crops of Scotland, and the light in the Blue Ridge Mountains hints at that in the Malvern Hills. Only in the American Southwest can Struther find no British counterpart, and for this reason she prefers it because there is no suggestion of wartorn Britain. "Here, and here alone, I can walk unhaunted," she says. "I shall stay here long. Strangeness, at last brings peace."[72] "Wartime Journey" (February 1944) details a rail trip through a United States that was by then at war: the old railway cars brought back into service, soldiers on the move, lonely young women writing to men overseas. As one voice says, "This war – seems like it's everybody's war."[73]

The Anglo-American alliance was celebrated also by Alfred Noyes, then living in the United States, in a poem written for the navy and Total Defense Day in October 1941. Called "Atlantic Charter," this verse tribute to the meeting between Churchill and Roosevelt at Placentia Bay in Newfoundland was read by the author on national radio in the United States on 27 October and printed in the *New York Times* the following day.

In the critical month of June 1940, T.S. Eliot contributed a poem to a Britain at War exhibition mounted by the Museum of Modern Art in New York. A collection of photographs, drawings, paintings, cartoons, and posters, the exhibition was assembled by Sir Kenneth Clark, who was identified as the director of the National Gallery but in fact was working for the Ministry of Information. When in May

1941 the museum published *Britain at War,* a book based on the show, Eliot's poem, "Defense of the Islands," was included, along with an introduction to British artists written by the poet and critic Herbert Read. Calling on tradition, Eliot wrote of British soldiers "changing nothing / of their ancestors' ways but the weapons" and of demonstrating to past and future generations that "we took up / our positions."[74]

James Hilton penned a short poem called "Young and Old" for the *Atlantic Monthly* in September 1944. In four stanzas, he contrasted young men flying hazardous four-hundred-mile bombing missions to Cologne and old men walking two benign miles for a pint at the local pub:

> Hard duties, warm desires
> Make hours go slow or fast,
> Till young men leave their fires
> And old men down their last.[75]

British poetry also appeared in a number of collections published in the United States during the Second World War. In December 1941 B.H. Bronson edited a volume for the British War Relief Association of Northern California containing English poems which he said were "expressive of various ways of national feeling – of devotion to country, of pride in England's history and her glorious dead, of noble self-dedication and high hope."[76] Included was the verse of Chaucer, Shakespeare, Browning, Arnold, Tennyson, Wordsworth, Kipling, Bridges, Shelley, and Owen. The epigraph, from Milton, was clearly aimed at an America not yet in the war:

> I cannot praise a fugitive and cloister'd vertue, unexercised and unbreath'd, that never sallies out and sees her adversary, but slinks out of the race, where that immortall garland is to be run for, not without dust and heat.

After the American entry into the war, the emphasis in collections of poetry shifted to that of the common struggle. George Herbert Clarke's *The New Treasury of War Poetry: Poems of the Second World War,* published in 1943, focused on verse from Britain and America, and to avoid favouritism it used American spelling for American poets and British for the British and Canadian writers. Jan Struther's "Travelling America" found its way into the volume, as did poems by Clemence Dane, Laurence Binyon, John Masefield, Stephen Spender,

Patric Dickinson, Mervyn Peake, Ivor Brown, A.L. Rowse, Edwin Muir, and others.

The year 1943 also saw the publication of *War Poems of the United Nations*, edited by Joy Davidman for the League of American Writers. Among the hundred and fifty contributors from twenty countries were the British or British Empire poets J.R. Ackerley, John Cornford, James Hilton, C. Day Lewis, Hugo Manning, John Pudney, Haydon Weir, Gordon LeClaire, Diana Buttenshaw, and Megan Coombes-Dawson. Not included, explained Davidman, were the poets from Britain whose views were less than positive: "The section from the British Empire has been deliberately limited by us in order to exclude certain defeatist and appeaser elements which are fortunately losing their quondam influence on renascent British poetry."[77]

British poetry and fiction published in the United States during the Second World War served as "unheralded ambassadors from England," to borrow Stanley Unwin's term, as effectively as the non-fiction articles and books. Appealing more to the imagination and the emotions, they presented a picture of wartime Britain and Nazi Germany which although frequently propagandistic was persuasive because it was offered in the guise of a thriller, a psychological study, or a coming-of-age story set in the political upheaval of Europe. Through their pages many Americans vicariously shared the adversities faced by Britons, and their sympathies were inevitably enlisted.

A Friendly Intruder
in a Non-Belligerent World
Writers in British Radio Propaganda

Within weeks of the outbreak of the Second World War, the North American representative of the British Broadcasting Corporation observed that radio might turn out to be decisive in "effecting American participation" in the war.[1] At the same time, Lord Lothian was advising the Foreign Office of the importance of presenting the British case on the three American radio networks, but only if it did not smack of propaganda:

These three systems are only too ready to cooperate provided they cannot be accused of propagandizing. If the British Government can secure, or encourage the radio system to engage the services of the most popular and competent broadcasters and enable them to say interesting things, things which Americans want to listen to, they will get into the air, and will be widely listened to all the time. But they won't relay propaganda or dull stuff. There is no other way to this vast public except through the most expert and adept and dramatic broadcasters and programmes.[2]

Radio did indeed prove to be one of the most effective means of influencing American public opinion, though it was nearly a year into the war before the BBC began to aim its programs specifically at the United States. Among the scriptwriters and broadcasters who best met Lothian's requirement of presenting wartime Britain and the British case without seeming to be propagandists were British authors.

In the prewar years, if Americans heard British radio voices they were being broadcast on the BBC's Empire Service, created in December 1932. Five zones of the Empire were served by directional aerials, one of which was Canada, and in many parts of the northern United

States people with short-wave radios were able to receive the signal. As Nicholas Cull has pointed out, the BBC's discovery that it was receiving more correspondence from Americans than from Canadians suggests that it had a considerable number of listeners in the United States.[3]

The Empire programs were initially created to keep expatriates and other anglophiles in touch with the "old country," though in 1935 the BBC added that the Empire Service had "the further mission of putting the British outlook" before the world.[4] As a result, American listeners were cast in the role of eavesdroppers overhearing the conversations of a neighbour and its overseas relative talking about family matters. And that conversation, though in English, seemed nonetheless carried on in another language: the formal, stiff delivery of the traditional Oxford BBC voice.

The fact that it did not directly address American audiences in the 1930s reflected the policy of the Foreign Office, which was concerned that Britain should not appear to be broadcasting propaganda to the United States. In 1934, when the BBC proposed a series of commentaries on British affairs to be broadcast on American radio, both the British Library of Information and the British Embassy in Washington objected. Since the American public saw the BBC as the official voice of the government, claimed Angus Fletcher, such broadcasts would immediately be construed as propaganda: "We know from past experience that this sort of 'hands across the sea' propaganda is extremely disliked by an important section of the American public ... The majority of people in the United States believe that [the BBC] is HMG. Hence there is a possibility of an outcry against what may be regarded as *direct* propaganda by His Majesty's Government and an attempt thereby to influence public opinion in the United States."[5]

Several weeks later, Sir Robert Vansittart, the permanent undersecretary for foreign affairs, warned the BBC's director general, Sir John Reith: "Our view is that the important thing, from the point of view of our relations with the United States of America, is to avoid talks put on by the BBC having the appearance of being directed expressly 'at' the United States."[6]

Ironically, on the outbreak of war and throughout the winter of 1939–40, when Lothian, the Foreign Office, and the Ministry of Information began to suggest that radio broadcasts to the United States might be important, it was the BBC that was reluctant to tailor its programs to an American audience. At the Foreign Office in November

1939, for example, B.E.T. Gage commented: "We know that Americans are bored by the tone of voice of the BBC announcers, which they think is affected and lacks pep. The suggestion has been made that we should in our overseas broadcasts substitute American or Canadian announcers but this might smack of propaganda. A Scotsman, a Yorkshireman (not too colloquial) or any Englishman minus Oxford accent would, however, be an improvement. The technique of some of our football commentators is perhaps what's required."[7]

The BBC, however, was unwilling in either the form or the content of its Empire broadcasts to depart from the mandate given it in 1932 to speak to Britons in the outposts. In December 1939 Frank Darvall, at the Ministry of Information, complained that the BBC "is always emphasising the fact that short-wave programmes are intended chiefly for Empire listeners and that the isolated Englishman in the remoter parts of Empire, who is more Blimpish than Col. Blimp himself, would be horrified if the dignity of the BBC were to be exchanged for the snappy radio techniques of the Americans."[8]

With the end of the phony war in April 1940, and especially with the fall of France in June, the BBC's attitude to broadcasting to the United States changed dramatically. Churchill, who by then was prime minister, had made Alfred Duff Cooper minister of information, and Duff Cooper pushed the BBC to restructure its North American broadcasting. It did so by replacing the old Empire Service, directed solely at Canada, with a North American Service that would appeal to both Canadians and Americans. A Canadian, Ernest Bushnell, the general program organizer of the Canadian Broadcasting Corporation, was temporarily seconded to help reshape the service to make it appeal to Americans. A few months later another Canadian, H. Rooney Pelletier, became the North American program organizer.

The North American Service was formally launched on 7 July 1940, and on 29 September it was expanded to a 6$^1/_2$ hour continuous evening schedule, beginning at 5:20 PM New York time and lasting until midnight, with news bulletins being carried during the day. In addition, by the fall of 1940, about 90 American medium-wave stations were rebroadcasting BBC programs, and this number increased to about 130 by June 1941. The Mutual Broadcasting System transmitted the BBC news twice a day, and once a week it carried two of the BBC's most important programs: *Britain Speaks* and *Radio Newsreel*.

On opening the expanded North American Service in September, the director general of the BBC, F.W. Ogilvie, stated that the network "aims to move and entertain by 'human front-page' stuff the average American listener; it speaks as a friendly intruder in a non-belligerent world."[9] It would have been more accurate to say that the service spoke as a friendly but persuasive intruder, as suggested in an August 1940 memorandum by Gerald Bullett, a novelist, poet, and biographer, who was serving as a talks organizer in the Overseas Service.

When recruiting A.P. Herbert – a fellow author, who had been on the staff of *Punch* since 1924 – to appear on *Britain Speaks*, Bullett wrote: "The idea is that you should tell them, as persuasively as possible, whatever you think will confirm our American supporters in their good opinion of us, fortify the waverers, and win over the timid and the hostile. We try, naturally, to wrap up the pill of propaganda in the sugar of entertainment, so far as this is possible."[10] The following January, when asked to speak on *Democracy Marches*, Herbert received similar guidelines from Alan Melville: "The speakers are left to choose their own subjects, as long as these subjects fit in with the main aim of the series, which is to put the British point of view before the American people and to do something to further Anglo-American relations."[11]

In spite of Ogilvie's characterization of the BBC's American listeners, they were anything but "average," and the corporation knew it. According to Cull, in campaigning for a North American service, Duff Cooper had been encouraged by the argument of the noted American broadcaster Edward R. Murrow that although the number of Americans who owned short-wave radios was small, they would be influential listeners who would sway many of those around them.[12] This thesis was later borne out by studies carried out in the United States during the war. In January 1941 a survey of short-wave listening made by the American Institute of Public Opinion for the Princeton Listening Center revealed that one out of every three Americans owned a radio capable of receiving short-wave signals. Ten per cent of respondents reported that, during the previous month, they had listened to at least one British program on short wave or through rebroadcast on American networks.

The Listening Center concluded that the total audience for all short-wave broadcasts lay between 5 and 10 per cent of the adult population. More importantly, anyone who made the effort necessary to hear the programs was almost certainly a committed and active student of politics. "Most significantly," observed Charles J. Rolo in *Radio Goes to War* (1942), "in almost every case short-wave listeners are more keenly interested and active politically than non-listeners. Thus the ultimate influence of short-wave broadcasts on American opinion is much greater than the actual number of listeners would indicate."[13]

Similarly, in his 1942 essay "Britain Speaks," Daniel Katz pointed out that to assume that the intellectual nature of the BBC short-wave programs had limited the size of its audience and had therefore been ineffective was to misunderstand the nature of propaganda: "One of the most important functions of propaganda is to reach the small group of persons who are already sympathetic, to keep up their enthusiasm and interest and to furnish them with arguments and interpretations so that they can convert others."[14]

One way in which the BBC attempted to reach this audience was through its British equivalent: those patrons interested and literate enough to subscribe to its magazine, the *Listener*. An article in its August 1940 issue outlined the programs in the new North American Service and concluded: "That is the fare, and while its popularity depends very largely on its own merits, something depends too on the extent to which these programmes can be made known in America. Those of us who have friends across the water will know how to 'pass the word.'"[15]

The early programs of the North American Service clearly reflect an awareness of the relative sophistication of the American audience. The first broadcaster, Vernon Bartlett, an Independent Progressive MP and a diplomatic correspondent, spoke unapologetically of his mission: "I am going to talk to you three times a week from a country that is fighting for its life. Inevitably I'm going to get called by that terrifying word 'propagandist.' But of course I'm a propagandist. Passionately I want my ideas – our ideas – of freedom and justice to survive."[16] His passion notwithstanding, Bartlett's many broadcasts throughout the war were intellectual discussions of international affairs aimed well above the average man or woman in the street. The talks of Wickham Steed, historian and former editor of the *Times*, were equally complex, as were those of George Slocombe, author of books on international affairs, and other political commentators. In a medium in which words were pre-eminent, the North American Service employed a wide variety of authors – among whom were A.G. Macdonnell, Ian Finley, Hugh Walpole, J.B. Priestley, Somerset Maugham, James Stephens, Rose Macaulay, Richard Llewellyn, S.P.B.

Mais, John Brophy, John Lehmann, Storm Jameson, Louis MacNeice – but their broadcasts were literate and sophisticated and designed to appeal to the well-educated American public.

Even when the BBC handed the microphone to working-class broadcasters such as Herbert Hodge or William Holt, it did not expect them to speak to their American counterparts. Hodge was a London cab driver who had developed such a reputation as a raconteur among his fellow cabbies that the BBC put him on the Home Service and then on the North American Service, where he became one of the corporation's most famous "characters." William Holt was a man of many parts – a weaver from Todmorden in Yorkshire, a lumberman, journalist, war correspondent, and author.

Holt's first broadcast for the BBC was a North American Service talk on the reactions of ordinary Londoners to the Blitz. When the American press wrote about his program, and *Life* and *Time* magazines carried interviews with him, he became a celebrity in Britain and a regular broadcaster both in his own country and in the United States. His weekly North American broadcasts focused on the contribution to the war effort made by ordinary working-class Britons: the sixty-five-year-old Norfolk fisherman who, as a volunteer lifeboat coxswain, had saved seven hundred men from the North Sea; the first ATS woman to be killed in action, complete with descriptions of her mother, fiancé, and pet dog; or the only Cockney woman still living on her bombed-out East End street.

Many of Holt's broadcasts emphasized the common theme of British propaganda that the war had brought about a social levelling, a democratization, and a liberation of those who formerly had been kept down. In October 1942, for example, he described the changes in a young working-class woman in the industrial north who had been lifted from the narrowness of a factory job to a more independent life. "After this war," concluded Holt, "the men will see that the women who have stood by them, even at the guns, will have their prospects opened up."[17] In September 1943 he attempted to explain the fierce independence of the British working man who, he said, had never really been understood by Americans:

What he will do in the future cannot be foretold in detail. He does not know himself. He is more interested in principles than in cut-and-dried plans. In fact, he abhors committing himself to specific actions in detail in advance, and I think quite rightly so. Because who knows exactly what the future will bring? This does not mean that he is opposed to social planning, but unless such planning is aimed truly at increasing the security of his personal freedom he will not have it.[18]

This presentation of the working-class response to the war reflected the strong emphasis in British propaganda in the period following Dunkirk when the threat of invasion loomed: that all classes were united to defend what Priestley called "this island fortress." Holt's talks elicited a large number of letters from Canadians. One wrote: "We feel very badly about what you were going through – we shouldn't feel it so much if you were not putting up such a good show."[19] But some American observers were more cynical. In "Britain Speaks," Katz suggested that speakers such as Hodge and Holt were being used on the one hand to demonstrate to liberal Americans that the BBC was democratic and on the other to show right-wing Americans that the British working class was not Bolshevik. In either case, the argument was being made to American intellectuals: "They demonstrate that the English, self-conscious in their new-found democracy, have not objected to some representatives of those who have not been in public school. That Hodge and Holt carried any genuine appeal for the American masses is doubtful, but they have satisfied upper-class Americans that the English can be democratic without being vulgar or communistic."[20]

The heavy reliance of the North America Service on authors as broadcasters may have originated, at least in part, with the writer who was to become the service's most effective speaker: J.B. Priestley. In a conversation in early July 1940 with Anthony Weymouth, the assistant coordinator of Empire talks, Priestley argued that the BBC could make much more use of writers than it had been doing, "that the air was the one medium left for authors." Because of the paper shortage created by the war, said Priestley, fewer books were being written and published. Newspapers were now published in shorter editions which, by necessity, focused almost entirely on news and news commentaries rather than on feature articles and human interest items. As a result, many authors were freer than they ever had been to go before the microphone and use their words in the war effort.[21]

Priestley had already been broadcasting both within Britain and to North America on the Empire Service on the programs *This Land of Ours* and *Britain Speaks*. On 5 June 1940 he had begun a series of *Postscripts*, short programs on current events, carried on the Home

Service immediately following the nine o'clock news, and he soon had a regular listening audience unmatched by anyone except Churchill. Between 5 June and 20 October, Priestley made nineteen broadcasts, building up an average audience of 31 per cent of all adults in Britain for each program. In Graham Greene's words, "He became in the months that followed Dunkirk a leader second only in importance to Mr. Churchill ... unmistakably a great man."[22]

According to Asa Briggs, Priestley's appeal lay in both the sound of his voice – which the *Yorkshire Post* said "England finds so welcome and reassuring" – and his message, which together made him seem like "a man of the people."[23] In his autobiographical *Margin Released*, Priestley made light of the *Postscripts*, calling them "nothing more than spoken essays, designed to have a very broad and classless appeal."[24] In fact, though he had broadcast very little before the war, he proved to be very skilful, employing an experienced playwright's sense of timing and providing his listeners with simple but concrete details which conveyed much about the ordinary Briton's response to the crisis. According to fellow Yorkshireman John Braine, Priestley "had the perfect microphone voice: warm, relaxed, with a slight Yorkshire intonation. The latter is important. Priestley is often described as having a strong Yorkshire accent ... *Intonation* is the correct word, or perhaps *flavour* would be nearer."[25]

As appealing as Priestley's intonation was to the British ear, it was in the United States that it best served British propaganda. One of the most difficult problems for the North American Service, recalled its director, Maurice Gorham, was the American dislike of the standard BBC voice: "Unfortunately, the sort of English voice then most often heard on the BBC was not easily understood across the Atlantic, and it was not liked. Peoples have their own standards in these things, and the Oxford-Cambridge-Temple-Whitehall accent seems to most Americans silly and stuck-up. Most 'cultured' voices were unsuitable for my service, many English women's voices were impossible, and even the most virile English types tend to avoid using a virile voice."[26]

The Foreign Office, too, was aware of the voice problem. In April 1940, V. Bentinck wrote of the need for the BBC to use announcers with more masculine voices, even though they might be less refined than the usual ones. "I am told," he said, "that the BBC announcers are largely looked upon as a standing joke in the United States and Canada." T. North Whitehead confirmed Bentinck's view, saying that from his own experience in the United States "the usual epithet for the BBC voices is 'pansy.' I have never yet met an American who did not pour contempt on the BBC announcers."[27]

In the United States in February 1940, J.C. Furnas wondered in a *Saturday Evening Post* article why the BBC had not taken "the next logical step of hiring a good Hoosier drawl for their news bulletins aimed at the United States, … it would help."[28] The Foreign Office had, of course, earlier rejected the suggestion of employing Americans or Canadians for fear of the old accusation of broadcasting propaganda, though it thought that a Scotsman might be appropriate. Priestley was not a Scot, but his Yorkshire speech was robust and down to earth, and it did not take American listeners long to respond to it. In July 1940 *Time* magazine spoke of the new North American Service as a vast improvement over the "stodgy stuff" of the Empire Service and at its best when Priestley spoke: "Compact as a beer mug, with a voice as mellow as ancient ale, Priestley has a pronounced Yorkshire accent which falls more pleasantly on American ears than the nasal whinnys of Oxford."[29]

With the beginning of the North American Service, Priestley was broadcasting to the United States three times a week. Since the BBC was convinced that Americans would respond better to the immediacy of live performances, this meant sitting before the microphone in the early hours of the morning. On Sundays, when Priestley was also doing a *Postscript* for the Home Service, he would write both scripts during the afternoon, deliver one in the evening and the other at 2:30 AM. None of his producers could recall that he ever needed to revise the scripts.

Like many of those working in the North American Service, Priestley often slept in the BBC building, arriving late on a Saturday night with suitcase and typewriter. J.L. Hodson, a regular contributor in 1941–42, later described the routine: "Turned in at 11.30 pm in a basement with eight or ten beds in two tiers, and with a ventilator roaring like a small ship. They gave me a sleeping bag made out of a sheet – excellent idea; and three blankets. Roused at 1.45 am, spoke at 2.30; back to bed, slept till eight, had a bath (they gave me two fragments of soap and a clean towel); then to the BBC canteen, where I had a fine bowl of porridge."[30]

Unlike Hodson or William Holt, Priestley never went to bed before his North American broadcasts, claiming that being hauled out of bed in the early morning completely destroyed the atmosphere of speaking to New Yorkers at 8:30 in the evening. Instead, he arrived at Broadcasting House about midnight, had a drink with senior BBC officials, did his broadcast, and then slept there. Holt's solution to the "atmosphere" problem was to suggest to a BBC chief that one of the studios should be fitted up as an American cocktail bar, with murals of Manhattan on the walls. Broadcasters would then feel that they were really among the Americans to whom they were speaking, rather than sitting in a cramped room with a glass of water and a microphone, while people slept in the corridors.[31]

Priestley's broadcasts to North America were a clever mixture of stories of the courage and determination of the ordinary man in the street or the woman in the factory and of sophisticated arguments about politics and morality. And despite his claim that he spoke without any government strings attached to him, many of his themes were those promoted by the British propaganda chiefs.

One of Priestley's recurrent contentions, for example, was that the war was not, as American isolationists claimed, a political quarrel between two European competitors, but a simple battle between good and evil. On 30 May 1940 he argued that the reported Nazi slaughter of refugees showed that Germany was no longer a civilized European power, that the conflict was now "a fight to the death between the old civilisation of Christendom and this new evil empire of machines and robots." The Nazi threat, he said, "is simply gigantic insane gangsterism ... It is no more simply European than typhoid fever is simply European, and like a plague, if it is not stopped here, then it will spread all over the world." In the fight against this disease, he told his American listeners, "the American frontier is the English Channel."[32]

In another talk, Priestley spoke of the war as being clearly different from the First World War, which Americans still saw as a struggle between quarrelling European powers. The new struggle, he said, "is no more a European issue than a world outbreak of cholera would be."[33] People should see it as "a final conflict between a projected Nazi-Fascist world and a world in which liberal civilisation is still possible."[34] In this battle, he concluded, Britain was "the hope of humanity and trustee of the faith of the civilised world."[35]

Having been to the United States in the period between the wars, Priestley understood Americans, and he was careful to bring in American references to implicate the American listener in the European struggle. In talking of the efforts of the volunteer defence workers, he quoted the poetry of Walt Whitman, and in describing the moral indignation of the average Briton he added: "We share this strain of thoughtless but genuine moral idealism, of course, with the

Americans."[36] Speaking on American Independence Day in 1940, Priestley said that it was a good time "to realise all over again that now we mean what we say just as Americans meant what they said nearly a hundred and seventy years ago."[37] A few days later, he shrewdly referred to Roosevelt's Independence Day speech in which he had outlined the five freedoms that people must have – freedom from fear and want, freedom of religion, information, and expression – and pointed out: "The Nazis represent the denial of all those freedoms ... That is why it is vitally important that people in the New World should not be lured into believing that this is just another European War."[38]

In response to American isolationism, Priestley pointed out that before September 1939 there had been many isolationists in Britain, and they believed that Britain could ignore European politics. Two years later, he said, Americans were in danger of repeating the blunder, of foolishly thinking that Hitler had no interest in the United States and that the Atlantic was a sufficient barrier. If Hitler was not eyeing America, why did he have such an elaborate espionage network there? "It is a world conflict," Priestley charged in July 1940. "To imagine that the United States has no direct interest in this world upheaval is like pretending in an earthquake that you may only be feeling a trifle giddy."[39]

In the summer of 1940, when the British government was concerned to emphasize that Britain could take it, that the United States would not therefore be aiding a losing cause in offering material assistance, Priestley frequently claimed that there was no shortage of essential foodstuff. In late June he managed simultaneously both to thank Americans for sending food parcels and to argue that knowledgeable people were aware that there was not "the slightest need of food parcels from America or anywhere else."[40] The British people, he later assured his listeners, were not waiting for anyone to rescue them.

Priestley's broadcasts reiterated a number of other British propaganda concerns. In June he warned that German propaganda would soon be blaming the British blockade of the Continent for starvation in the defeated countries, and a month later he claimed that the blockade was still "the best weapon the world possesses with which to resist this vast threatening tyranny."[41] Similarly, in describing the height of the London Blitz in September, Priestley played heavily on the theme of the destruction not just of buildings but of tradition and civilization – a tradition and civilization shared by America. Even hardened young Nazi airmen, he said, must be troubled by glimpses below them of the destruction of "the mighty ancient capital city whose contributions, by way of government and law, arts and sciences," to the world's civilization had been incalculably vast. St Paul's Cathedral, left standing amidst the destruction all around it, was "a symbol, with its unbroken dome and towering cross, of an enduring civilisation of reason and Christian ethics against a red menacing glare of unreason, destruction and savagery."[42]

In September 1940 Priestley even tackled the question of his being a propagandist over the airwaves. In the sense that he was not, nor ever had been, neutral about Nazi Germany, he explained, he *was* a propagandist; but in the sense of being part of some general government publicity campaign, he was *not* one. "No official tells me what to say," he claimed. "So long as I do not give information that might be useful to the enemy, I am free to say what I please. I am simply a private person giving his impression of what is happening."[43]

In claiming to be simply a private person speaking his own mind, Priestley was of course being disingenuous. Like the other BBC overseas broadcasters, he was regularly advised by the Ministry of Information and the Foreign Office about what points should be made. Broadcasts to the United States, especially before its entry into the war, were always a delicate matter, and by the second year of the war the BBC's North American Service had itself become very attuned to events and public opinion in America. Oxford Professor and historian Denis Brogan, who could "often tell you not only why something had happened but what was going to happen next,"[44] served as its intelligence adviser on American affairs. His weekly reports on American opinion were widely read throughout the BBC, and they guided producers and broadcasters as they shaped their material to appeal to a particular American concern or at least to avoid offending American sensibilities.

In February 1941, for example, Priestley was advised that Churchill was anxious to scotch a story going around the United States that he had stated that America should never have got into the First World War and should not get into the present conflict. Could Priestley introduce the matter into his talk by saying something along the lines of "Another example of the kind of 'whopper' which is told in wartime is so-and-so ... a whopper so monstrous that it led to the Prime Minister's denial in these words"?[45]

In the same month, the Ministry of Economic Warfare asked Priestley to give a direct response to Herbert Hoover's campaign to provide food to the occupied countries. The Ministry of Information gave its approval, the Ministry of Economic Warfare provided data, and Priestley wrote a script for *Britain Speaks* which was approved by both ministries. At the last minute, however, the Foreign Office vetoed the talk because its American monitors reported that while the Lend-Lease bill was being discussed, any attack on Hoover would look like interference in American politics. After some discussion, Priestley agreed to repeat a talk on Dover that he had given on the Home Service.[46]

In March 1941 Duff Cooper, as minister of information, required two changes to one of Priestley's *Britain Speaks* talks because German propagandists were trying to frighten Americans with the claim that Britain was going completely Bolshevik. Duff Cooper thought that some of Priestley's comments about the social levelling of the war and the increased democratization could be twisted to prove the German point. Priestley disagreed, arguing that his sources told him that at least as many Americans thought Britain was going crypto-fascist as those who thought it was going Bolshevik. He agreed, nevertheless, to delete a sentence about the landed gentry not being the England that was fighting the war.[47]

Priestley was hardly alone in having his broadcasts altered. When, in May 1940, E.M. Forster spoke on *This Freedom*, a program on the Overseas and Empire Service, he was required to remove the word "propaganda" from his script, even though the director of the Empire Service, R.A. Rendall, had insisted that "the purpose of this series is propagandist."[48] He could do propaganda, but he was not to use the word on the air. In April 1942, J.L. Hodson was told that he could not tell North American listeners that the Indian troops tramping north from Burma were suffering from cholera; he was to say only that they were sick. "As it's known all over the world," he later observed, "I thought this lunatic, and omitted the sentence altogether."[49]

On occasion the censor's discussions of scripts went beyond lunacy into a kind of surrealistic comedy. In February 1941, Phyllis Bottome was scheduled to broadcast to North America on the *Democracy Marches* program, and she decided to use Disney cartoon characters as metaphors. Asking for a second rewriting of her script, a BBC official stressed that it was terribly important that she should not say anything to the United States at that time which was not "absolutely right from every point of view." In her characterization of the cartoons, he suggested, lay some propaganda pitfalls:

Page 1. I think it is absolutely right to take comfort from the way the hollow Disney ogres are crumpled to pieces but I think it is, on the other hand, extremely dangerous to suggest that we identify ourselves with a mouse faced by a boa constrictor or with a water baby keeping its toes out of reach of a shark. I would suggest cutting these two images altogether.

Page 2. I find myself now that I come to read the script in its new form in some doubt as to whether Donald Duck is really on our side or on the other. I *think* that you will find that in most people's minds, he is taken as a prototype of the Mussolinis of the world: after all, Donald's main contribution to the Disney films is that of making a frightful nuisance of himself, flying into Hitlerian rages and showing his helplessness in long passages of quack, quack invective.

Similarly, I think it is dangerous for us to identify ourselves with the little piglets and then suggest that they are "often misled by their unsuitable ambitions" and that they "come squealing home." I suggest that you might care to leave out these qualifying phrases and also leave out the word "insignificant" on the same page.[50]

Bottome agreed to the changes, and it was apparently left to Disney himself to send Donald Duck off to fight for the Allies on the movie screen.

Of all the media used by British propagandists during the Second World War, BBC radio broadcasts were the most easily and closely controlled. Some potential speakers such as H.G. Wells and George Bernard Shaw were rejected by BBC senior officials because the Ministry of Information or the Foreign Office considered them troublesome. Anyone working for the BBC was given a security check by MI5, which had the authority to reject a candidate or, as in the case of Cecil Day Lewis in 1940, to approve the use of his material but not allow him to appear before the microphone himself.[51] Day Lewis, under suspicion presumably because of his earlier membership in the Communist Party, might speak out of line on the air, but his scripts could be carefully scrutinized and laundered.

Even those speakers who were approved had to provide a typescript of their talk in advance, for approval by the Ministry of Information or the Foreign Office, and no deviation from the written material was permitted in the broadcast. In part, this procedure was intended to prevent someone unwittingly providing useful information to the enemy (about, for example, the extent of damage in a particular raid), but it was also a means of ensuring that political arguments were consistent with government policy. In October 1943, for example, Vernon Bartlett was advised by George Barnes, director of talks, that the alterations to one of his scripts was made in order "that it should conform to the precise official guidance on the subject of King Victor Emanuel and Marshall Badoglio."[52]

Although he adhered to the censorship rules, albeit reluctantly, Priestley eventually ran afoul of the government officials because of what he said on the air. Ironically, it was not his broadcasts into the politically sensitive atmosphere of America that caused the problem but his talks to his fellow Britons. By September 1940 senior Conservative politicians had begun to complain about Priestley's emphasis on the virtues of the lower-middle and working classes and his call for a new classless Britain. He voluntarily ended his series of *Postscripts* on 20 October 1940, saying publicly that it was time for a different voice, though privately expressing frustration with government policy. When he began a new series on 26 January 1941, his talks were, he said later, more "aggressively democratic in feeling and tone,"[53] and the complaints about his left-wing bias became more vociferous. Churchill complained to Duff Cooper that the first of the new *Postscripts* had expressed views on war aims that differed from his own, and a delegation from the 1922 Committee protested Priestley's reappearance on the air.[54] Sir Archibald Southby himself went before the microphone to attack his broadcasts.

Priestley delivered eight *Postscripts* in the new series and then was taken off the Home Service. He later recalled receiving letters from the Ministry of Information and the BBC, each blaming the other for the decision to end his broadcasts. "While blaming each other," he said, "I think both of them were concealing the essential fact – that the order to shut me up had come from elsewhere."[55] This suspicion is borne out in A.P. Ryan's minute to Walter Monckton at the Ministry of Information on 18 March 1941: "Priestley series stopping ... on instructions of Minister."[56]

Duff Cooper argued publicly that Priestley had a right to broadcast but that no one should deliver more than six *Postscripts*. Earlier, however, he had confided to BBC officials that he considered Priestley "a second-rate novelist, who had got conceited by his broadcasting success."[57] Duff Cooper clearly shared Anthony Eden's view of Priestley when it was suggested to him, as foreign secretary, that Priestley write the response to *Life* magazine's attack on Britain: "Priestley fills me with horror!"[58]

Priestley objected to the ending of the *Postscript* series, pointing out to Ryan: "From a propaganda point of view, it is a bad move. Rightly or wrongly, there will be a certain uneasiness all over the English-speaking world." Only that morning, he said, he had received a cutting from the *New York Post* in which Samuel Grafton hailed his return to the air in Britain: "This is more than the return of a particular speaker to the BBC microphones. It is the recapturing of a mood. Something of hope went out of England when Mr Priestley, sick at heart over what he considered to be his country's moral apathy, left the studios in October. Something of hope has come back with his return." Moreover, as an Edinburgh housewife said to the *New York Times*, "He speaks for us."[59]

Silencing Priestley on the BBC did indeed present a serious propaganda problem for the British in the United States. By the fall of 1940 he had attracted a large and loyal following in America, and letters to the BBC clearly indicated that he was its most effective speaker. A listener from Ohio wrote: "His voice seems particularly adapted to radio – deep and clear – and the text of his message was to the point and most convincing – not a single word, much less a sentence, wasted. His voice reached us so clearly that he might have been sitting alongside us; so clearly, indeed, that I have never listened to anything from overseas to match it." A writer from New York said: "The broadcasts by Mr J.B. Priestley in *Britain Speaks* are of the finest ... next in importance to the news itself." From North Carolina a listener commented: "In a world where the rules of decency and veracity no longer exist except with the Anglo-Saxon race, it is quite refreshing to hear informed men of character and international reputation, such as ... J.B. Priestley, Wickham Steed and others talk to us in America. The BBC is doing America a real service, and one is comforted by the fact that one has the facts, be they good or bad." Similarly, "We have taken Mr Priestley into our hearts and home, and read all his books," said a letter from Michigan, "we love them."[60]

Priestley's success in the United States was to some degree achieved at the expense of his popularity elsewhere in the overseas network. When an Australian complained that his talks, many of which were also carried on the Empire Service, were always aimed at North America, Empire talks organizer Marjorie Wace replied that "that was the intention of the series."[61] America was the primary target, and as Sir Stephen Tallents reported to J.C.S. MacGregor of the Ministry of Information in December 1940, the series was a triumph:

Priestley's talks in "Britain Speaks" have been the outstanding success with audiences overseas, especially, but by no means exclusively, in the U.S.A. During the difficult months of June, July, and August in particular, he did a fine job, for he sounded always confident of victory and must have reassured any American listeners who were doubting our resolve and ability to carry on the struggle. Thousands of appreciative letters addressed to him and to the BBC, as well as many Press references, make this clear.[62]

So important was Priestley to the North American Service that when his *Britain Speaks* series ended on 1 January 1941, the Mutual Network stopped rebroadcasting BBC programs.

Priestley's reputation with American listeners meant that, at the same time that he was being removed from the British air waves, he was being urged to continue to speak to the United States. In part, BBC officials were worried that his absence would be interpreted as censorship of free expression. In October A.P. Ryan had warned that Priestley might have to be handled carefully lest he quit and create a public relations disaster: "The balance of evils is the danger of Priestley dropping some brick, against the certainty that, faced with censorship at this end he would resign, thereby robbing American listeners of one of our most popular speakers, and further leading to a great deal of stink about the British suppression of one of their most independent and articulate spokesmen."[63] Indeed, when Priestley ceased speaking on the Empire and North American services in January 1941, the British survey of the Canadian Press indicated that many Canadians believed that "old school tie" prejudice was responsible. So concerned was E. Rawdon Smith, of the Dominions Office, about this perception that he asked to speak privately with the director general, F.W. Ogilvie, at the Athenaeum club.[64]

Needing Priestley's voice and needing to avoid unfavourable publicity in the United States, the BBC got him to agree to broadcast on the North American Service every Monday for three months, beginning in February. Following his removal from the Home Service in March, however, he refused to begin yet another American series on the grounds that it would be dishonest to broadcast to the United States at the same time that he was "denied the air at home": "I cannot and will not say things to America that I am not allowed to say here." Priestley's mind was changed when he was offered what R.A. Rendall characterized as a "carte blanche on the Empire Talks side." Said Rendall: "As Empire Talks is so urgently in need of Priestley's service (and his listening public in the United States is so enormously greater than that of any other speaker), I am anxious to do anything I can to secure his return."[65]

By late August 1941, Priestley was demanding even more freedom in his North American broadcasts. He was being given plenty of material about the Home Front, he complained, but nobody in the United States was any longer interested in such matters. He wanted to speak more directly and candidly to Americans, doing everything to enlist their aid short of telling them when they should come into the war. Rendall supported Priestley, arguing: "He is our star overseas broadcaster ... and I think that the M of I and the BBC between them ought to be prepared to take more trouble than has been done in the past to build up such a speaker with material, facilities, etc."[66]

Priestley carried on broadcasting to the United States until June 1943. According to Briggs, he gave forty Britain Speaks talks in 1942, as well as one Christmas Day broadcast, one New Year Resolution, five Answering You talks, two feature programs – St George and the Dragon and The Ships – and one Radio Newsreel. He continued to be criticized by Conservative politicians in Britain – as in July 1942, when he was attacked in the House of Commons for broadcasting to America that the Nazi party was different from the rest of the German people.[67]

Throughout his broadcasts to the United States, Priestley was given more freedom – and indeed encouragement – to say to Americans things that had led to his banishment from the microphone in his own country. In May 1942 he spoke about "The Life and Death of Colonel Blimp," interpreting the famous David Low caricature as representing myopic upper-class Englishmen who were being forced to change and yield power because of the war. In a later broadcast entitled "Democratic England Has Arrived," Priestley spoke of the confusion of an American woman who could not reconcile his talk of a new Britain without class distinctions with a letter from an English woman living in country house with a large garden. The latter had complained about the shortage of servants and looked forward to the postwar period when high unemployment would guarantee an abundance of staff.

In arguing that his new democratic Britain, rather than that of the upper-middle-class woman, was the real one, Priestley pointed out that he had a much better knowledge of the country than she did. No lady in a country house could match his wartime experience, he claimed, because she would then no longer be a lady in a country house; she would be out doing some useful war job. The landed gentry blindly considered the war only a brief interruption in their quiet, settled existence. They were like the last of the dinosaurs, still crashing and blundering about the place but really on their way to extinction:

After Hitler is defeated *things aren't going to be the same as they were before the war*. If we have fought and toiled and suffered so that democracy shall survive, it is going to be a real democracy, and there is not going to be a lot of unemployment in order that women in country houses should have plenty of cheap labour to employ, and if women in country houses don't like it they can lump it ... Nobody can reasonably expect the ordinary folk of this island to go deliberately back to an economic and social system that had ceased to function properly before the war.[68]

It was probably no accident that Priestley made this argument to American listeners shortly after the film version of *Mrs Miniver* had become so popular in the United States. While the American response had been very positive, there was a danger that the film might be seen to be showing that the war was being fought to preserve the comfortable middle-class lives of people like Caroline Miniver. For those Americans who saw her simply as a middle-class woman with whom they could identify, the film would succeed in enlisting their sympathies with Britain; for those repelled by the idea that she represented comfort and privilege, Priestley's talk would offer other reasons to support the British war effort.

A year before *Mrs Miniver*, Priestley had objected to another enormously popular artistic work that had done much to gain American sympathy for Britain, Alice Duer Miller's 1940 poem *The White Cliffs*. Written from the point of view of an American, it glorified an anglophilic view of traditional England, its villages, history, and people. Capturing the imagination of many Americans, the poem sold 300,000 copies in book form, was frequently broadcast, and was performed in a musical recording by Jimmy Dorsey.

On 9 March 1941 Priestley protested to his American listeners that the Britain of *The White Cliffs* was not the one that was fighting the war:

This Christmas card caricature of England couldn't fight this war a couple of days. This is a war of machines and of men who make and drive these machines. They don't make 16-inch guns or Hurricanes or Spitfires down in the old family place in Devon ... It is an industrial England that is fighting this war ... It is these towns who've produced most of the wealth that enabled the other fancy little England to have its fun and games; and it is this other big England that is having to take it in this war. The bombs fall on Coventry, Sheffield, Birmingham, Manchester, not on the old family place in Devon.[69]

To find a "Christmas card caricature" of Britain against which to place his gritty, realistic, working-class picture, Priestley would not have had to look as far as American productions such as *Mrs Miniver* and *The White Cliffs*. The BBC's North American Service had its own share of broadcasters who evoked the Britain of quaint villages, charming customs, cultural traditions, and colourful history. The American listening audience was not homogeneous; it was made up of a wide spectrum of political and social beliefs, and the British programs needed to appeal, at different times, to different parts of that spectrum.

In the early days of the North American Service, Sir Hugh Walpole was suggested specifically as a contrast – and indeed as competition – to Priestley. On 10 July 1940 a BBC official asked if Walpole had been approached to talk on *Britain Speaks*, pointing out: "He has, as of course you know, a big public in America, he is an attractive speaker and an experienced broadcaster, and (as I happen to know from conversations with him in the North) Priestley puts him in a mood of extreme, though friendly rivalry, and in any broadcast to the States Walpole would, I feel sure, be very much on his mettle. His manner and method are so different from Priestley's that it might be a very effective contrast, and I think he would be keen to broadcast."[70]

Walpole had in fact already been engaged by the North American Service, and from then until his death in June 1941 he was one of its most effective broadcasters. A series of romantic novels – notably, *The Cathedral* (1922) and the four-volume *Herries Chronicle* (1930–33) – had made him one of the most popular British novelists among American readers, and he had lectured frequently and successfully throughout the United States. In July and August 1940 Walpole did a number of *Britain Speaks*, in October and November he appeared frequently on *Within the Fortress*, and from February to March 1941 he had his own series entitled *Hugh Walpole Talking*.

Like Priestley, Walpole was a quick and confident worker. Anthony Weymouth described how he "came on from the party, arriving about half-past eleven, and was due to go on the air at 1:30 AM. In under an hour he had dictated the talk, and in five foolscap pages of typescript there was only one sentence which needed correction."[71] His scripts, added Weymouth, would be ready for broadcasting with only enough time to be reviewed by the censor.

For the most part, Walpole's talks gave American listeners a picture of England much like that presented in his novels. In July 1940 he spoke as if from his house in Wordsworth's Lake District: "It is half-way up a little mountain, has a lake at its feet, has a lawn on which the fattest and tamest of thrushes strut like archbishops, has a rose garden, a rock garden, bees, and a library of 15,000 books." In this retreat, after hearing grim war news, he was consoled by listening to a Beethoven trio on the radio, looking at his Utrillo, and reading an excerpt from *David Copperfield*. "I hope," he was careful to add, "when this war is over, that there will be a new England, and that every man will have his acre."[72]

Priestley, of course, was also calling for a new Britain of equality, but where he seemed to speak for the underclass, Walpole spoke from above. As patronizing as it may have been, it was a theme which Walpole repeated in various ways in a number of broadcasts. On the 24 July 1940 *Britain Speaks*, he argued that in the First World War no one had visualized any social change once hostilities ceased, whereas everyone agreed that the high purpose of the present war was the birth of a better order. "That means at once an equality. We have suffered for years in England from class snobbery, neglect of the very poor, indifference to what was going on in the street next to ours. For the first time in 400 years in England there's beginning to be an absolute equality, an equality created by the imminent threat of the loss of freedom of all of us ... The world after the war is going to be a people's world."[73]

In one of his last broadcasts, in April 1941, Walpole dissociated himself from Priestley and others whom he called "Theorists," those who demanded that "we set up a New Order to rival Hitler's New Order." Claiming to be a "man in the street," he argued that the postwar world would be no paradise, that there would be social lev-elling and social cohesion because no one would be well off: "These two foul and horrible wars have achieved one great thing, namely, that the Two Worlds, as Disraeli called them, of the rich and the poor cannot remain ignorant of one another any more. They have already coalesced. When this war is over there will not be the two worlds of the Haves and the Have Nots. There will be, in England, at any rate, only one world – the Have Nots ... My point in all this is that this second war will complete the awakening of the social conscience which ever since the Reform Bill of 1832 has been stirring."[74]

Walpole's popularity as a speaker on the North American Service led the BBC to change its copyright policy on broadcast talks. The standard contract stipulated that talks were not to be printed within three months of delivery, but in early October 1940 Ronald Boswell reported that the BBC's North American representative had asked whether speakers would have any objection to their talks being published in the American press. Since the BBC considered that "this would definitely be in the national interest," said Boswell, he hoped that Walpole would agree to grant publication rights for a period of three months from the date of broadcast.[75]

Ironically, it was Priestley's talks that most prominently appeared in print in the United States. Throughout the war, his pieces were periodically reprinted in the *New York Times*, the St Louis *Post Dispatch*, the *Oakland Tribune*, and other newspapers. More importantly, in December 1940 his New York publisher, Harper, brought out *Britain Speaks*, a volume of his transatlantic broadcasts. The title page mistakenly stated that the book was being published in Britain under the title *Postscripts*, but in fact the talks had all been transmitted on the North American Service and they were never published in Britain. Priestley later described them as "a collection of radio talks I gave – usually at 2.30 am – during 1940. As they were recorded they were transmitted all over the world – to 80 stations in the U.S. – Canada, Australia, New Zealand, South Africa, India, etc. etc. As these talks were addressed to people overseas, the book was not published in Britain."[76]

Anthony Weymouth's *The English Spirit*, a collection of twenty talks presented on the Empire Service, was published in Britain in 1942, but it was also sold in the United States. Among its contributors were Priestley, Walpole, Maugham, H.E. Bates, Sir Philip Gibbs, Clemence Dane, Philip Guedalla, and William Holt. Many of the broadcasts made by writers were also printed in the BBC's overseas magazine *London Calling* and in this way reached many American subscribers.

Priestley and Walpole, along with Louis MacNeice, were the British authors who worked most effectively in the North American Service, but there were many others who contributed in varying degrees. From time to time, talks given by Maugham, Coward, and others for the Home Service were rebroadcast across the Atlantic. E.M. Forster, who had joined the war effort because he believed it "a writers' and artists' war more strongly than [he had] in 1914,"[77] broadcast three talks called *The Nazis and Culture* in which he discussed what a victorious Hitler would do to the culture of the English-speaking world. On 3 July 1940 Storm Jameson did a *Britain Speaks* program that was directed specifically to the New York branch of PEN. S.P.B Mais, novelist, essayist, freelance journalist, and regular speaker on the BBC in the 1930s, broadcast weekly to the United States in the winter of 1942–43 on *What I See Going Around and About*. H.V. Morton spoke in a number of *Life at Home* programs, which were intended to give overseas listeners an idea of the day-to-day conditions of living in the British Isles; and Dorothy Sayers, who did a number of religious broadcasts on the Home Service during the war, was carried on the North American Service at least once in early 1941.

Rose Macaulay, nearly sixty but driving an ambulance at night and pedalling through the hazards of London streets on her ancient bicycle by day, disliked the national boast of "We can take it" and took a different approach to her American listeners in a January 1941 broadcast:

My talk to America is about "Consolations of the War." I am mentioning ruin-seeing, the beauty of the black nights and the moonlit ones, the romantic scenes during raids (fire lighting the sky, etc.) increased companionableness, shelter life, the pleasure of waking up still alive each day. The foreigners among us, and the sympathy of Americans. Some one just home from New York told me that Americans didn't like us to be so pompous and grand about the war, so I've tried not to be. People too often are, with all this "Christian civilization" business and self-praise. I've tried to sound humble, and not once said "we can take it."[78]

Ironically, four months after making this broadcast, Macaulay's optimism was severely tested by the bombing raid that destroyed all her books and papers and led to her short story "Miss Anstruther's Letters."

The Welsh novelist and playwright Richard Llewellyn had achieved his greatest success, *How Green Was My Valley*, in the first year of the war, both in Britain and in the United States, where it sold more than 100,000 copies in 1940. A lyrical account of the difficulties of a common Welsh mining family in the late nineteenth century, it was filmed by Hollywood a year later. Llewellyn took his Wales to North America in such programs as *War in the Rhondda Valley*, broadcast by the Canadian Broadcasting Corporation in September 1940, and as a regular contributor to *Democracy Marches* on the North American Service in early 1941. He also served as chief transport officer for ENSA (Entertainments National Service Association) before rejoining the army as a captain in the Welsh Guards.

Monica Dickens was a student nurse in Windsor in the early months of the war, then worked for a year in an aircraft factory repairing Spitfires before going back to another hospital for the remainder of the war. The great-great-granddaughter of Charles Dickens, she had written the very successful *One Pair of Hands* (1938), an autobiographical novel about her experiences working in kitchens. In the midst of her war work in 1940, she published another novel, *The Moon Was Low*. In 1942 the North American Service commissioned Dickens to write a program on the role of women in the British war effort for its series *Britain to America*. According to the BBC's overseas magazine, *London Calling*, the government let her leave her job as an inspector of supercharged aero engines only for twenty-four hours, so she wrote all night and all the next day and then was back at work at seven the next morning.[79]

James Hanley, whose 1943 novel *No Directions* was one of the best evocations of the surrealism of the Blitz to come out of the war, broadcast *Civilian's War* on the North American Service in September 1941. Hanley focused on a sailor's home, described as being in one of Britain's great ports, where sailors of all nations gathered between voyages.

Novelist and playwright Clemence Dane, whose 1919 novel *Legend* was a stage success as *A Bill of Divorcement* in 1921 and then was an acclaimed film of the same name in the United States in 1932, worked extensively for the BBC during the war, sometimes on the North American Service. According to Noel Coward's companion, Cole Lesley, Dane's focus was on the great and heroic tradition in British history and culture. "Winifred [Clemence Dane] was endlessly engaged in writing scripts for radio or films, all directly or indirectly helping towards the war effort by calling up the spirit of England, so that the shades of Shakespeare, Henry V, Drake, Nelson, Queen Elizabeth, Alfred the Great and all our national heroes were never far away when you were in Winifred's company."[80] This spirit was invoked, for example, on 19 July 1940, the day on which Hitler was widely rumoured to be going to launch his offensive against the British Isles. Recalling that it was also the anniversary of the day in 1588 when the news reached England that the Spanish Armada had set sail, Dane spoke on "The Old Armada and the New."

A typical Dane broadcast was her reading of a poem entitled "The Heart" on 23 March 1942, the anniversary of the death of Elizabeth I.

The poem tells of a small boy finding the heart of the legendary queen in a broken urn in Westminster Abbey, and of her spirit returning to earth to help Britain in its present crisis. "Clemence Dane's experience as an actress," observed Anthony Weymouth, "stands her in good stead when the subject of her broadcast, as in this instance, demands pathos. And, speaking lines she herself had written, gave her every opportunity to impersonate the great queen and to stress her stalwart love of England."[81]

Another playwright and novelist, Cosmo Hamilton, broadcast frequently to the United States in the early years of the war. In an October 1940 talk entitled "Americans and Ourselves," he attempted to dispel the distorted impressions Americans had gained of Britons through the works of P.G. Wodehouse and Coward. "We were a race," he said, "which sat on sit-sticks, wore the old school tie. We were a people who used a language which gave you great offence. We were conceited and supercilious, and our women had large feet." Most importantly, Americans thought the British cowardly: "We were fascists and appeasers, conscientious objectors, and wavers of white flags. These were fixed ideas. It was a 'phoney' war." But things had changed, claimed Hamilton, since Britain had "stood up to Germany."[82]

Although Michael Arlen had been forced to resign his position as civil defence public relations officer and had left for the United States, the North American Service broadcast his play *Lady, Here's a Flower* in August 1941. *London Calling* advertised it as "a play about the curious kind of everyday life that most of us are living in the midst of war."[83]

By 1943, with the United States in the war and with Russia an ally, it seems that MI5's doubts about Cecil Day Lewis vanished, and he was allowed to broadcast a talk on the North American Service entitled "Books of the People, for the People." In it he described how the Ministry of Information had invited or commissioned books on various aspects of the war experience from a wide variety of authors. All over London, said Day Lewis (and, by implication, as should be occurring in America), people were queuing to buy copies of *Front Line*, *Battle of Britain*, *Bomber Command*, *Coastal Command*, or *Roof over Britain*.

Reviews and discussions of books provided the BBC with an excellent means of reminding American listeners about the common linguistic and cultural tradition and of discussing the contemporary political issues without seeming to be heavy-handed. L.A.G. Strong, who spoke about English village life on the North American Service on such programs as *People of Britain* and *In England Now*, talked regularly about such authors as W.B. Yeats, W.W. Jacobs, Eden Philpotts, Dr Johnson, and Cecil Day Lewis on *Books and People*. On 29 November 1940 he discussed "The Writer's Task Today: Literature as an Instrument of Civilisation" on the series *In My Opinion*. The gulf between people of different nationalities can be bridged by literature, he claimed: "Nothing can so surely promote real understanding between the nations as the free circulation of honestly written novels and short stories among them."[84]

The most prolific reviewer on the North American Service was John Brophy, who had joined the army at the age of fourteen in the first year of the First World War and had seen action when he was sixteen. Between the wars, he became a published novelist – best known in the United States for *Gentleman of Stratford* (1939), editor of *John O'London's Weekly*, and a strong antifascist. According to his son-in-law, Sir Michael Levey, "nobody was more pacific by nature, though also patriotic in an unjingoistic way. I suspect that the core of his attitude was a hatred of fascism, his awareness of which may have been sharpened by travelling in Europe during the 1930s."[85] When war broke out, Brophy wasted little time in offering to do a "books to be read in wartime" series for the BBC.

Brophy was used extensively on the Home Service, on the Forces Radio, the Empire and Overseas Service, and on the North American Service. In March 1941 he appeared on *Britain Speaks*, and in the winter of 1942–43 he was a regular member of *Answering You*, a program in which a panel answered questions from America. At the same time, he had his own series, *Writing and Fighting*, in which he discussed books dealing with the war and political issues. In August 1942 he echoed Priestley's complaints about the picture of Britain presented in the film version of *Mrs Miniver*, arguing that the British depicted therein hardly counted at all: "They belong to the past ... Believe me, the real revolution in Britain is not concerned with trivialities like flower shows and prize roses." This revolution, Brophy added, was being documented by exciting lesser-known writers such as Pamela Hansford Johnson, Gerald Kersh, Frank Tilsley, and Leo Walmsley – "good writers, who picture the real life of Britain today."[86]

Brophy's reviews were also an excellent way of drawing attention to particular American books that supported the British cause. In December 1942, for example, he discussed *The British Empire, 1815–1939*, by Paul Knaplund, a professor of history at the University of Wisconsin. He began by reminding his American listeners that they would know more about Wisconsin than he, particularly that it was in the middle of the American Midwest where, of course, no one could expect to find a pro-British bias. "I do earnestly hope," he said, "it will be studied by all those politicians, editors, journalists, authors, and broadcasters whose business it is to try to influence public opinion in the United States."

Knaplund's book, Brophy pointed out, traces the British Empire from 1815 – the year in which Britain finally overthrew Napoleon after a long and exhausting struggle – to 1939, the year in which Britain began the battle against an even more powerful and ruthless despot. It demonstrates that the British Empire is no longer the empire of George III – a network of exploited colonies run by an oligarchy of undemocratic statesmen in London. Moreover, had there been no imperialism in the past, "North America would now belong exclusively to the Red Indian, the grizzly bear, and the bison."

The introduction to *The British Empire, 1815–1939* was written by Denis Brogan, a Ministry of Information official who was adviser to the BBC on American matters. Brophy found nothing incestuous about quoting him with approval. British policy, said Brogan, had increasingly been directed by liberal-minded men, so that not only had Canada, Australia, New Zealand, and South Africa been granted independence, but democratic institutions had been set up in every part of the empire. Moreover, concluded Brophy, American listeners should remember that the political system of the United States emerged directly out of the two-party political structure in Britain. "We have both gone a long way since the days of George the Third."[87]

In its campaign to persuade Americans of the natural kinship of the English-speaking peoples, the most useful authors were those, like Priestley and Walpole, who had first-hand experience of the United States. One such writer was A.G. Macdonnell, known for his novels, satires, and detective fiction. Having written *England, Their England*, a witty study of British manners and customs, in 1933, he toured the United States the following year and penned *A Visit to America* (1935). At the height of the Blitz in the fall of 1940, Macdonnell commented on the news three times a week on the North American Service. "I don't see much chance of having a book ready for the autumn," he told his editor Lovat Dickson. "At the moment my war work consists of broadcasting to America at two in the morning, which leaves me a little jaded after breakfast on the same day!!"[88] Seven months later, Macdonnell was killed in an air raid on Oxford.

Phyllis Bottome, who had spent the first winter of the war lecturing in the United States, offered her experience to the BBC in 1941. Following a talk on "Democracy Marches" in February, she was asked to broadcast to Austria and did so only when she was assured that it would not prevent her from doing further work on the North American Service. In November, Elsie Bowerman of Overseas Liaison recommended further programs because "Miss Bottome is a first-rate lecturer and has done a lot of speaking for the M of I: she has a special knowledge of the United States and Germany." However, on the advice of Norman Collins, who had not liked her interpretation of Donald Duck and reported that Bottome was a poor speaker at the microphone who needed much coaching and rehearsal, the BBC limited its use of her to an *Answering You* program in February 1942.[89]

Like Bottome, Pamela Frankau had toured the United States extensively in 1939–40, and soon after her return to Britain in November 1940 the BBC enlisted her to speak fortnightly on the North American Service's *Democracy Marches*. On 29 January, the day of her first broadcast, she reported to Sir David Scott at the Foreign Office: "I had a fairly satisfactory morning with the Ministry of Information, and I broadcast to America on the short wave at 4 am to-day."[90] Though somewhat abrupt and clipped in her delivery, Frankau performed well enough to be invited to speak weekly, which she did until May. She then joined the ATS but continued to work periodically for the BBC, primarily in the Home Service but on occasion on *Answering You* to North America.

Frankau spoke to Americans as one who had been among them and with whom she shared a culture. For example, when describing an air raid on London viewed from twenty miles away, she found a way of mentioning a copy of *John Brown's Body* that she had brought back from the United States and had almost worn out with reading and rereading. To capture the violence of the scene, she looked to the American poet Stephen Vincent Benét: "A new age curdles and boils in a hot steel cauldron ... / Steel is being born like a white-hot rose / in the dark smoke-cradle."[91]

Robert Henriques, author of *No Arms, No Armour, Captain Smith and Co*, and *Death by Moonlight*, was a colonel in the British army, and in 1942 he landed with American troops on the beaches of Casablanca. From there he went to New York and then back to Britain, where a year later he broadcast a paean to the cooperation between British and American forces, a program aimed simultaneously at listeners in points as far apart as San Diego and Sheffield. Misunderstandings still existed in the homes and legislatures of the Allied countries, said Henriques, but in the battle zones the British private and the American doughboy respected the other's fighting ability: "You read now in the Press about American senators; about speeches from politicians, on both sides of the Atlantic, asking who is going to pay for what. All this talk about inter-Allied understanding, Lease-Lend and reverse Lease-Lend. There is not much Lease-Lend either way in a battle; you are just very glad to see American tanks coming up on your left and British Spitfires overhead."[92]

Louis MacNeice's experience in the United States in 1940, as well as his literary skills, led to his recruitment by the BBC, where he became one of its most prolific and effective propagandists. In March 1940, while MacNeice was still at Cornell University, T. Rowland Hughes of the BBC's Features and Drama Section wrote to say that he had been discussing with Val Gielgud and Laurence Gilliam the possibility of MacNeice writing for radio: "I wonder if some aspects of Nazism and its influence or its victims would appeal to you as the theme of a Radio programme. What I have in mind, of course, is something in the style of MacLeish's 'Fall of the City' and 'Air Raid.' We in this country have not yet been able to secure a first class poet for such radio programmes and I feel convinced that your lines would speak well."[93]

On his return to Britain at the end of 1940, MacNeice contacted F.W. Ogilvie, the director general of the BBC, and in early January he agreed to write scripts for both British and overseas listeners, first as a freelance writer and then as a staff member. Although he had always professed a loathing of propaganda, he now believed that his work would simply be to break down the stereotypical views that Britons and Americans had of each other:

Apart from news commentaries and political talks the BBC are now properly conscious of the value of presenting Britain *as it is* to Americans. It is high time that ordinary individuals on both sides of the Atlantic should realize what their counterparts on the other side are like. From my own experience I think there is little to choose – for unreality – between the popular British conception of Americans and the popular American conception of the British. I am not saying that these conceptions are uncomplimentary; the point is that they are quite fantastic.[94]

One of MacNeice's first programs was a fifteen-minute play called "Cook's Tour of the London Subways," broadcast to North America in March 1941. Borrowing from American literature, it tells of the first visit to London since 1930 of a Mrs Van Winkle Brown and her tour of Underground railway stations now functioning as air-raid shelters. There, in Jon Stallworthy's words, "she and thousands of American listeners are introduced to the voices of a London down but not out, not downcast, not defeatist."[95]

MacNeice used his dramatic skills in a similar fashion in 1942 in his "Three Years of War," a program in the highly successful *Britain to America* series, which was broadcast both on the North American Service and on the American Blue Network. *London Calling* described MacNeice as "one of the most prominent young poets and critics of pre-war days and … one of the BBC's most exciting wartime finds … The sympathetic understanding of America that he learnt in the months he spent lecturing there in 1940 (he arrived back at the height of the blitz) gives extra force to his *Britain to America* features. He can see Britain through American eyes with uncanny precision."

What MacNeice saw through those "American" eyes was a Britain still led by the stereotypical old-school-tie Tory, an image he attempted to destroy in the introduction to his chronicle of three years of war:

NARRATOR: Hullo, America. Can you hear me? Hullo, America!

AMERICAN TOUGH: Hiya fellow, Who are you?

NARRATOR: I'm one of those stuffed shirts Britishers – you can tell that by my voice. I'm one of those chaps with old school ties and a monocle. I can't really do any work. So that's why they gave me this job. They want me to tell you about our British war record.

AMERICAN TOUGH: You tell *us* about *your* war record?

NARRATOR: Exactly.

AMERICAN TOUGH: Ain't you the guy that Hitler caught with his pants down?

NARRATOR: Well, er …

AMERICAN TOUGH: And you took on a world war as though it were a game of pea-knuckle?

NARRATOR: Pea-knuckle?

AMERICAN TOUGH: Hitler drove your B.E.F. out of France?

NARRATOR: Yes.

AMERICAN TOUGH: And a bit later he smashed you up in Greece?

NARRATOR: Yes.

AMERICAN TOUGH: And in Crete?

NARRATOR: Yes.

AMERICAN TOUGH: And then the Japs took a turn and they knocked the blue-hell out of you way out there in Malaya?

NARRATOR: Yes.

AMERICAN TOUGH: And you're the dope that lost Singapore?

NARRATOR: Yes.

AMERICAN TOUGH: And you lost Burma.

NARRATOR: Yes.

AMERICAN TOUGH: And you let the *Scharnhorst* and the *Gneisenau* sail down your own little gutter right past your own front doorstep?

NARRATOR: Yes.

AMERICAN TOUGH: And now you've been had for a sucker in Libya and Rommel's gotten you tied up there in Egypt?

NARRATOR: Yes ... Yes ... your facts are quite correct.

AMERICAN TOUGH: I'll say they're correct. And, granted they're correct, what I'm asking you right now is – get to hell off the air.

NARRATOR: Please, don't shout like that. You make me drop my monocle, supposing I had a monocle. Listen my friend. You're only one American, and maybe you're not representative. Well, I'm only one Britisher and maybe I'm not representative, but I'm here today to compere a radio programme telling you about Great Britain. And I want you to let me tell you.

AMERICAN WOMAN: Let him tell you, honey. He can't help his accent.

NARRATOR: We've been at war three years. I needn't tell you where we fell down; *you* know that as well as I do. All I want to do is to take you back ...[96]

Both before and after the United States' entry into the war, MacNeice was assigned a number of programs directed specifically to America. In July 1941, when the Ministry of Information wanted a public expression of Britain's gratitude for the fifty destroyers transferred to it from the U.S. Navy, MacNeice was sent out on patrol on the North Atlantic with Francis Dillon. The result was "Freedom's Ferry – Life on an ex-American Destroyer," a program about the rescue of survivors from a torpedoed British merchant ship broadcast on 16 July. Later, MacNeice did "Halfway House," a program about the U.S. Expeditionary Force in Ireland, and "Salute to the U.S. Army." On 12 October 1942 his "Christopher Columbus," a radio play celebrating the 450th anniversary of Columbus' discovery of America, was broadcast on the North American Service. A fusion of prose and poetry, it had forty-nine speaking parts, a cast headed by Laurence Olivier, and musical accompaniment by the BBC Chorus and Symphony Orchestra conducted by Sir Adrian Boult. It was, says Stallworthy, "a resounding success."[97]

MacNeice's most substantial contribution to the BBC's American propaganda campaign came before America's entry into the war in a weekly series of fifteen-minute programs described in *London Calling* as "constructed around historical buildings in London and other parts of Britain which have suffered damage or destruction from German bombs." British officials, including Churchill, had become convinced that few things were more likely to elicit American support than the destruction of famous historical British buildings, structures that symbolized some part of the shared Anglo-American heritage. In his *America and Britain: A Mutual Introduction*, Maurice Colbourne wrote of the American reverence for certain British buildings: "Britain's feudal relics have an especial significance for Americans. Are they not part and parcel of themselves? An integral part of their history before America was budded from Britain? When an American tours Britain he is more than sightseer. He is sharing in riches that are his own right of ancestry. As Alicia Street has said: 'To Americans, the Pantheon in Paris is a sight; Westminster Abbey is a shrine.'"[98]

In the spring of 1941 MacNeice had already written about one such shrine in the first of five "London Letters" for the American leftist periodical *Common Sense*, edited by Selden Rodman and Alfred M. Bingham. "The Church of St Clement Danes in the Strand," he said, "one of Wren's elegances in Portland stone, looks none the worse for having had its windows blown out; outside it in the churchyard, just beyond the apse, a statue of Dr Johnson still stands among the debris, unconcerned and pawky, with an open book in his left hand, looking up Fleet Street."[99] On 5 May he carried the theme of the indestructible man of letters into "Dr Johnson Takes It," the first program in the series *The Stones Cry Out* (to which the announcer always added: "but the people stand firm!"). Here MacNeice took his listeners to Johnson's bomb-damaged house in Gough Square, where Johnson had written his dictionary. As Stallworthy points out, Johnson had become a symbol of British tenacity and a celebration of the common language of the British and American people.[100]

The Stones Cry Out was carried weekly on the North American Service until the end of 1941, and MacNeice wrote most of the scripts. Among other landmarks visited were the Guildhall, Madame Tussaud's, St Paul's, the Drury Lane Theatre, the Old Vic Theatre, Llandaff Cathedral, Chelsea Hospital, and St James's Palace. The Old Bailey was treated as a symbol of democracy in the civilized world, and the barbican in Plymouth was, American listeners were reminded, where the *Mayflower* set sail and where in 1919 the first aircraft (an American seaplane) to cross the Atlantic arrived.

No building featured in *The Stones Cry Out* embodied the richness of British tradition more than Westminster Abbey, and MacNeice's description of it became a catalogue of political and cultural eminence:

PREACHER: Let us now praise famous men and our fathers that begat us ...

1ST SPEAKER: Who lie under the nave and the transepts and the chapel behind the sanctuary.

PREACHER: Such as did bear rule in their kingdoms –

1ST SPEAKER: Edward the Confessor, Henry the Third, Edward the First, Edward the Third, Richard the Second, Henry the Fifth, Henry the Sixth and Henry the Seventh.

2ND SPEAKER: Edward the Sixth and Mary Tudor, Queen Elizabeth and Mary Queen of Scots.

PREACHER: ... men renowned for their power, giving Counsel by their understanding –

1ST SPEAKER: William Pitt, Earl of Chatham, Pitt the Younger and Charles James Fox –

PREACHER: Leaders of the people by their counsels –

2ND SPEAKER: William Ewart Gladstone and Benjamin Disraeli –

PREACHER: And by their knowledge of learning meet for the people, wise and eloquent in their instructions –

1ST SPEAKER: William Wilberforce and Richard Cobden, Sir Isaac Newton and Charles Darwin –

2ND SPEAKER: And the early Abbots and doctors of divinity –

PREACHER: Such as found out musical tunes –

1ST SPEAKER: Handel and Henry Purcell –

PREACHER: And recited verses in writing –

2ND SPEAKER: Chaucer, Spenser, Dryden, Tennyson, Browning, Kipling, Hardy.[101]

MacNeice reached even farther back in history in his "Greece Lives," a program carried on the North American Service on 28 October 1941. After the fall of France, Greece had been Britain's only ally outside the Commonwealth, and it had fought gallantly against the invading Germans until the British were forced to withdraw in April

1941. American isolationists seized on the evacuation as another Norway, another sign that Britain could not win a battle and therefore
was not worth saving.

The Greeks had fought well, and were continuing a resistance to
the German occupation, a defiance which MacNeice compared to the
Greek resistance to Persia ten thousand years earlier. According to
London Calling, the ancient and modern Greeks had set an imperish-
able example for people in the modern democracies:

Today the people of Greece by their superb courage in the face of overwhelm-
ing force have proved again the truth of the immortal words of Pericles,
"Happiness is Freedom and Freedom is Courage." This is the theme which
Louis MacNeice, one of England's leading poets, has taken for this programme, in which parallels are drawn between ancient and modern Greece,
ancient Persia and modern Germany, between ancient Thermopylae and
modern Crete, between the Greek ideal of freedom and the ideal for which
Britain and her allies are fighting now.[102]

MacNeice continued to write for the BBC for the remainder of the
war, producing scripts both for the Home Service and the North
American Service. He remained with the corporation until two years
before his death in 1963, becoming one of the most successful writers
of radio plays in BBC history.

As with the other forms of propaganda employed by the British in
the Second World War, the effectiveness of the radio broadcasts of
MacNeice, Priestley, Walpole, and the many other British authors can
never be determined with certainty. However, the volume of correspondence from Americans received by the BBC during the war, and
the frequency with which the press in the United States cited North
American Service broadcasts, suggests that they were important
shapers of American attitudes to Great Britain. According to Asa
Briggs, the BBC did not bring the United States into the war, but it
helped prepare the American public for the Anglo-American cooperation necessary after Pearl Harbor: "There was a real sense in which
Anglo-American understanding had been canvassed with more
warmth to the British people before the United States entered the war
than Anglo-Russian understanding was officially canvassed even
after the USSR came into the war."[103]

The Most Gigantic Engines of Propaganda
British Writers and Film Propaganda

Three months before the entry of the United States into the Second World War, pressure from isolationists caused the U.S. Senate to create a subcommittee to investigate alleged propaganda in the American motion picture industry. Its chairman, Gerald P. Nye, charged Hollywood with encouraging intervention in the European conflict "At least twenty pictures have been produced in the past year all designed to drug the reason of the American people, set aflame their emotions, turn their hatred into a blaze, fill them with fear that Hitler will come over here and capture them, that he will steal their trade. ... [The movies] have become the most gigantic engines of propaganda in existence to serve war fever in America and plunge the Nation to her destruction."[1]

Behind the overheated rhetoric of Senator Nye, who could not actually remember the names of the offending films, lay the truth that a number of films produced since the beginning of the war had indeed attacked Nazi Germany, promoted assistance to Britain, and even suggested American intervention. Some films were made in Britain, some were made in Hollywood with British encouragement, and many relied on the books and screenplays of British authors.

British propagandists in the First World War had used film very effectively, and on the outbreak of the Second World War one of the divisions of the Ministry of Information was devoted to film. Unfortunately, its first director, Sir John Ball, was chosen because he had been in charge of Conservative Party film propaganda. He was viewed with suspicion by Labour and Liberal party members, and with detestation by many in the literary and cultural establishment. After several months of seeming inertia in the Films division and much public criticism, Ball was replaced in December 1939 by Sir Kenneth Clark, whose experience with "pictures" had been limited to the sort that hung on the walls of the National Gallery. Like Ball, Clark headed the division for only a few months, but he managed to develop a program for film propaganda which defined the roles for feature films, documentaries, and newsreels.

In April 1940 Clark was replaced by Jack Beddington, whom the British director Michael Powell later called "one of the most unjustly forgotten men of the war."[2] Beddington brought to the division a knowledge of public relations gained through serving as director of publicity for the Shell Group, whose Shell Film Unit had successfully produced informational films during the 1930s. According to film historian James Chapman, Beddington's policy was to find a balance between making documentaries and encouraging commercial feature films. To the latter end, he made Sidney Bernstein, a respected businessman who had developed the Granada chain of cinemas, an adviser to the Films Division. Bernstein's familiarity with the United States and his friendships with such important Hollywood figures as Walter Wanger were to serve the division well.

At the beginning of the Second World War, British documentary filmmakers were better suited to propaganda work than those making feature films. In the 1930s the British government had sponsored the creation of a great many documentaries on various social issues. In particular, the General Post Office Film Unit, headed by John Grierson, had developed a team of skilled filmmakers that included Alberto Cavalcanti, Basil Wright, Humphrey Jennings, Arthur Elton, and Paul Rotha. In 1940 the British government requisitioned Pinewood Studios and renamed the GPO film unit the Crown Film Unit.

In addition to their considerable expertise, the documentary filmmakers had the advantage of being able to make short films in a matter of days, whereas it could take half a year to make a feature film. Moreover, the nature of their work had taught them how to get closer to the ordinary person and the events they were describing. As well, in the early years of the war the Ministry of Information appeared to consider the feature film as merely escapist entertainment while the documentary was the instrument of propaganda and education.

Throughout the war the Crown Film Unit and other official units produced hundreds of documentaries, most of which were intended for use in the British Isles, on such subjects as storing vegetables indoors, the psychological readjustment when a soldier returns home, and the prevention of blackout accidents. The scripts for a number of these films were written by noted British authors. Graham Greene, in 1940, did *The New Britain*, a demonstration of Britain's social achievements between the two world wars; that same year Emlyn Williams wrote *Mr Borland Thinks Again*, which stressed the importance of silage to farmers; and in 1942 Gilbert Frankau scripted *Give Us More Ships*. In 1940 J.B. Priestley summed up the spirit of his country after Dunkirk in *Britain at Bay*, and two years later he surveyed the strength of the Soviet armies in *Our Russian Allies*. A.G. Macdonnell wrote the script in 1941 for *From the Four Corners*, in which Leslie Howard discussed with soldiers from Canada, Australia, and New Zealand their reasons for fighting in the war.

In 1942 Arthur Koestler provided the screenplay for *Lift Your Head, Comrade*, a short film about one of the companies of German and Austrian antifascists fighting against Hitler. *The Great Harvest*, an account of how the harvest of 1942 was brought in by the cooperative efforts of farm workers, children, and British and American soldiers, was written by A.G. Street and narrated by Rex Warner. Warner also contributed to the script of *They Speak for Themselves*, a 1942 film which recorded a group of young people's views on the war and the future. In 1943 J.L. Hodson provided the commentary for *Desert Victory*, an hour-long explanation of the desert campaign from El Alamein to Tripoli. At the end of the war, E.M. Forster wrote the script for *Diary for Timothy*, a film that dramatized an imaginary diary of child born during the final months of the conflict. Perhaps because of the work of the author of *A Passage to India*, young Asian filmmakers and film students were fascinated by *Diary for Timothy* when it was shown in India in 1969.[3]

Most of the British documentary films made during the Second World War were designed for domestic consumption, and few were ever screened in the United States. In 1943, however, Paul Rotha made a forty-six-minute film about the growing, harvesting, and marketing of food, the way the British people were managing under wartime rationing and price controls, and the need for more equitable distribution of food in the postwar world. Based on an idea of Eric Knight, who wrote two thirds of the script, *World of Plenty* was financed by the Ministry of Information and was made with the cooperation of the novelist Arthur Calder-Marshall, who was a script editor in the Films Division. According to Clive Coultass, it was originally intended for American audiences in order to appeal to the spirit of the New

Deal and the sentiments of the Atlantic Charter.[4] When it was shown to three hundred delegates at a World Food Conference in Hot Springs, Virginia, a delighted British Information Services cabled Rotha: "It was received with prolonged applause and excited much comment and enthusiasm. We have requests for the film from Chinese, Egyptian, and American official delegates."[5]

In the early months of the war the role of feature films in the propaganda campaign was less clearly defined than that of documentaries. The first feature film produced solely for propaganda purposes was Alexander Korda's jingoistic version of the early events of the war, *The Lion Has Wings*, a project initiated by Korda but supported by the Ministry of Information and shot in three weeks. In 1941 the ministry also partly financed Korda's *The 49th Parallel* (released in the United States as *The Invaders*), the story of a group of German submariners who are stranded in Canada and eventually captured. At the end, the last and most formidable German is stopped by a Canadian soldier while trying to cross the American border at Niagara Falls. In case this did not implicate American audiences in the conflict, one of the American customs officials who refuses entry to the German was given the line: "We've all got to do our duty, soldier."

After an uncertain start, the British feature film industry began to produce many films intended primarily to raise morale and stiffen the country's resolve and, secondarily, to make its case abroad. Integral to many of these productions were original stories or screenplays provided by British authors.

The indefatigable J.B. Priestley provided the narrative for *The Foreman Went to France* (1942), a very successful Ealing Studies film, which showed that the ordinary civilian who was manufacturing materials for the war was as important and as engaged in the fight as the soldier at the front. In 1943 Ealing also made *San Demetrio, London*, a tribute to the British Merchant Navy, which was based on F. Tennyson Jesse's *The Saga of San Demetrio*, written for the Ministry of War Transport.

Graham Greene's short story "The Lieutenant Died Last," published in the United States for propaganda purposes, was filmed as *Went the Day Well?* by Ealing Studios in 1942. Greene had written a script for a film about the Gestapo in England which was never produced, but the screenplay for *Went the Day Well?* was commissioned from John Dighton, Diana Morgan, and Angus MacPhail. By 1942 the concerns of the Ministry of Information had changed, and the film retained only the essentials of Greene's plot, focusing on the danger of complacency about invasion, the dangers of fifth column activity, and various ministry domestic campaigns.[6]

Several years into the war, the playwright Terence Rattigan was seconded from the RAF, where he had served as an air gunner and wireless operator, to write a number of screenplays. *The Day Will Dawn* (1942) dealt with the resistance movement in Norway, while *Uncensored* (1942) treated the efforts of the Belgian underground to counter German propaganda with a resistance newssheet. In 1945 Rattigan wrote scripts for two films about the RAF, the first of which was *Journey Together*, a feature-length documentary about the training of aircrews, produced by the RAF film unit. In the same year he collaborated with Anatole de Grunwald on the screenplay for the Ministry of Information–sponsored *The Way to the Stars* (*Johnny in the Clouds* in the United States), which highlighted the main events of the war in the air from 1940 to 1944.

Although Rattigan's RAF films were primarily about British pilots and the effects of the air war on those close to them, each contained elements clearly aimed at American audiences. *Journey Together* treated the issue of British class differences by presenting the friendship between an upper-middle-class Cambridge undergraduate and a working-class cockney. Moreover, their training takes them to a flying school in the United States, where they have to adjust to differences in language and social customs. The film's title is apt, as James Chapman has pointed out, in several ways: "A journey is undertaken together by people from different class backgrounds, by the bomber crew all with different but equally essential duties to perform, and not least by the British and Americans."[7]

The importance of mutual understanding and respect between Britons and Americans is more strongly underlined in *The Way to the Stars*, in which American pilots are shown arriving at a British air base in 1942. The tension between two groups, each with little comprehension and sympathy for the other eventually dissolves when the Americans realize the difficulties of bombing Germany and the British begin to appreciate the sacrifices of the Americans. After the death of an American pilot who had continued to fly because he thought that the United States had entered the war too late, the film ends with a formerly antagonistic pair of American and British pilots walking together back to the base.

The Way to the Stars formed a sort of military trilogy with two other films for which noted authors provided screenplays: *In Which We*

Serve (1942) and *The Way Ahead* (1944). *In Which We Serve* was the creation of Noel Coward – indeed, he was its scriptwriter, director (with David Lean), producer, composer of the score, and principal actor. At the urging of Filippo del Giudice, managing director of Two Cities Films, he wrote a fictionalization of the story of the sinking of HMS *Kelly*, commanded by Lord Louis Mountbatten, in the Battle of Crete. It was not a story that the Ministry of Information could approve, said the Films Division's Jack Beddington: the sight of one of His Majesty's ships being sunk was not the kind of propaganda to be showing abroad.

With the support of Mountbatten and the Admiralty, however, Coward completed the film, which became a popular success on both sides of the Atlantic. According to Dilys Powell, he had taken "a handful of typically British men and women and made from their stories, ordinary in themselves, a distillation of national character."[8] This distillation clearly appealed to audiences in the United States, where it earned $ 1.8 million, was nominated for an Academy Award for best original screenplay, and ultimately was given a special Academy Award. The *New York Times* called it "one of the most eloquent motion pictures of these or any other times. There have been other pictures which have vividly and movingly conveyed in terms of human emotion the cruel realities of this present war. None has yet done it so sharply or so truly."[9]

So successful was *In Which We Serve* that the minister of information, Brendan Bracken, asked Coward to make a similar film about the army. Coward declined because he knew much less about the army than the navy, and the job of writing the screenplay for what became *The Way Ahead* (1944) fell to Peter Ustinov and Eric Ambler, who were then both in uniform. Across the Atlantic, Hollywood was busy filming Ambler novels – *Journey into Fear* (1942), *Background to Danger* (1943), and *Epitaph for a Spy* (1944) – but Ambler himself was writing documentary scripts for the army. He wrote and directed *United States*, which explained American customs to British soldiers, and with Ustinov he wrote the script for *The New Lot* (1943), a film about the induction and training of conscripts, which was rarely used because of its dramatization of conflict between the men and a sergeant.

In *The Way Ahead*, Ustinov and Ambler portray an army of conscripted civilians, from different classes and backgrounds, who come together – as both officers and men – in a common cause and begin to understand each other. With its emphasis on a more egalitarian army fighting for the promise of social and political change in the future, *The Way Ahead* should have been effective propaganda in the United States. But it was not released in America until the final months of the war, and its effect was thus limited to influencing the postwar attitudes of Americans to Britain.

As important as documentary films were in educating the British public and as valuable as British feature films were in raising the country's morale, Nicholas Cull has observed that "arguably, film remained the weakest element in British propaganda to the United States throughout the war."[10] In fact, the films that most effectively drew Americans to the British struggle came from Hollywood, whose studios, unlike those in Britain in 1939, were wellfunded, firmly established, and influential. The American cinematic picture of Britain was almost always sentimental and archaic, but in a country where three-quarters of the people saw a movie each week, it touched the sympathies of millions of Americans. Aware of the power of the Hollywood motion picture, the Ministry of Information worked behind the scenes with filmmakers, and a community of British actors, directors, and writers in Hollywood carried the flag in film after film.

The importance of the American feature film to British propaganda was first enunciated by Lord Halifax, the foreign secretary, in October 1939:

I am rather disturbed at our total failure to use the film weapon effectively. It is in fact the most effective of the lot ... Documentaries are all very well in their way, but they appeal at best to a public that can be counted in tens of thousands. But a big film deal is a dead loss unless it is seen by a rock bottom minimum of sixty million people, and success consists in being seen by a minimum of something nearer two hundred million people. Moreover, the real effect of films only comes by getting at the emotions. Documentaries of course can never do that. There are plenty of people in Hollywood who would be delighted to make films which would work our way, if they were provided with the material. Many of the leading actors would give their services for nothing or practically nothing.[11]

At the outbreak of the war, there was a talented colony of British actors – Sir Cedric Hardwicke, Dame May Whitty, C. Aubrey Smith, Edmund Gwenn, Alan Mowbray, Basil Rathbone, Cary Grant, Brian Aherne, Herbert Marshall, Roland Young, Nigel Bruce, Ronald Colman, and others – all prepared to work for the British cause. According to

Sheridan Morley, the attitudes and activities of this group of expatriates was nearly a parody of British colonial life at the height of the empire. Smith (who was knighted in 1944) was its unofficial viceroy, and the pecking order was as carefully arranged as that of the Raj. On Sundays there was cricket, followed by a tea party restricted to the British, and Nigel Bruce was once heard to remark to Gladys Cooper in a tone of outrage: "Gladys, there's an American on your lawn."[12]

Hardwicke had been the last British officer to leave France at the end of the First World War, and when war broke out again, he applied to resume his commission; but he was told that he was too old at forty-six. He then formed a liaison committee with Aherne, Rathbone, and Colman to monitor developments in the film community for the British consul general in Los Angeles and to raise money for Britain. A production of Coward's *Tonight at 8.30* mounted in 1940 raised over $50,000 for the War Relief effort.

With the end of the phony war and the emergence of a real threat of invasion in Britain in the spring of 1940, the British actors in Hollywood were inevitably called shirkers by some of their counterparts at home. Noel Coward urged the British ambassador to order them back to Britain, and J.B. Priestley broadcast to the United States that they were deserters. In London, Sir Seymour Hicks claimed that the British in Hollywood were "gallantly facing the footlights," and he proposed a new film for Charles Laughton, Alfred Hitchcock, and Herbert Marshall to be called *Gone With the Wind Up*.[13]

In the end, younger actors such as David Niven, Laurence Olivier, and Vivien Leigh returned to Britain, but the older ones were officially instructed to remain in California. Lord Lothian cabled Lord Halifax to argue for their value in the American film industry: "The maintenance of a powerful British nucleus of older actors in Hollywood is of great importance to our own interests, partly because they are continually championing the British cause in a very volatile community which would otherwise be left to the mercies of German propagandists, and because the production of films with a strong British tone is one of the best and subtlest forms of British propaganda."[14]

Hitchcock, who had gone to Hollywood in 1939, was reminded by two senior British officials that he was to work for "the better representation of British characters in Hollywood produced films." In Hollywood, he kept in contact with the British consul general, assuring him that he planned to amend his screenplays to include "secondary characters whose representation will tend to correct American misconceptions regarding British people."[15] When Michael Balcon later accused Hitchcock of deserting Britain, says John Russell Taylor, he was "unofficially informed that Hitch, like Korda, was continuing film-making in America at the express request of the British Government."[16]

Alexander Korda had gone to America in the autumn of 1939 to promote *The Lion Has Wings* and to form an alliance with United Artists. By the war's end, he had been accused of running an espionage and propaganda agency for the British (a charge made at the Senate Foreign Relations Committee hearings into Hollywood films), and he had also been put on the Nazi list of those to be dealt with after the war. There is strong evidence that Korda was indeed associated with Sir William Stephenson's British Security Co-ordination in New York, as was Cary Grant, who was asked to report on Hollywood activities and attitudes.[17]

The Foreign Relations Committee also accused the British director Victor Saville of being a British spy. There can be little doubt, says Charles Higham, that Saville was at least reporting on film productions in Hollywood to the Ministry of Information and influencing Metro-Goldwyn-Mayer to make pro-British pictures.[18] One of his first achievements for the British cause seems to have been to persuade Metro-Goldwyn-Mayer to film Phyllis Bottome's *The Mortal Storm*. Written in 1938 and based on first-hand observation, the novel dealt with the rise of Nazism and its effect on a Jewish professor and his family. The script was prepared by the British screenwriters Claudine West and Andersen Ellis and the German author George Froeschel, and when it was released in June 1940 it became one of Hollywood's first anti-Nazi films.

In an oblique way, *The Mortal Storm* also became the first American film to deal with the treatment of Jews in Germany, though the Roth family is referred to only as "non-Aryans" rather than "Jews." Their "problem" is explained as Professor Roth's refusal to withdraw his scientific findings that there is no difference between Aryan and non-Aryan blood. His classes are boycotted, his books destroyed, and he is sent to his death in a concentration camp. By then his two stepsons have joined the Nazis and repudiated him, and the film ends with Roth's daughter, Freya, being shot in an attempt to flee to Switzerland with her antifascist lover, Martin. The viewer is left with the implication that fascism will destroy people like the Roths unless the Martins of the world fight back. The fact that one stepson, Otto, comes to recognize the real nature of the Nazi party and rejects it suggests that there are good Germans who can fight the Nazi grip on their country.

Despite its reluctance to use the word "Jew," *The Mortal Storm* was a provocative film to make in the propaganda-sensitive atmosphere of the United States at the beginning of the war. The *Motion Picture Herald* recognized this at its preview, stating: "A few months or weeks ago this Hollywood press audience would have used the word 'propaganda' to describe the film and speculated on the policy prompting its manufacture." Shown on 10 June, with France collapsing and Italy entering the war, criticism was muted,[19] and the *New York Times* reviewer, Bosley Crowther, welcomed its message: "There is no use mincing words about it: *The Mortal Storm* falls definitely into the category of blistering anti-Nazi propaganda. It strikes out powerfully with both fists at the unmitigated brutality of a system which could turn a small and gemutlich university community into a hotbed of hatred ... As propaganda, *The Mortal Storm* is a trumpet call to resistance."[20] Joseph Goebbels was said to have been so incensed by this trumpet call that he ordered Hollywood films banned in countries under German control. Years later, Basil Wright wrote: "It must be recognized that a film like this, despite overblown sentimentality, did play a part in getting across to people the real nature of Nazi racism and anti-Semitism."[21]

The opening of *The Mortal Storm* was followed two months later by *Foreign Correspondent*, an equally anti-Nazi but even more interventionist film. Directed by Hitchcock, it tells of a naive American correspondent who is sent to Europe to investigate the political situation but becomes involved in a conspiracy. On one level *Foreign Correspondent* is a Hitchcock thriller; on another, it is a political allegory directed at isolationist America. According to film historian Roger Manvell, the script by the British writers Charles Bennett and James Hilton, as well as by Joan Harrison, Robert Benchley, and Hitchcock, was deliberately written "to shake the United States into awareness of what must threaten her if she turned her back on Europe."[22] As the film opens and the correspondent is asked about the situation in Europe, he answers, "What crisis?" At the end, after he has seen fascism at first hand, he broadcasts a virtual call to arms to his fellow Americans from a London radio studio: "The lights have gone out in Europe! Hang on to your lights, America – they're the only lights still on in the world! Ring yourself around with steel, America!"

Man Hunt, based on the English author Geoffrey Household's novel *Rogue Male* and directed by Fritz Lang in 1941, was similarly anti-isolationist and strongly anti-Nazi. Walter Pidgeon plays a big-game hunter who aims his rifle at Hitler in his mountain retreat, not to kill him but for the thrill, and is subsequently captured and beaten by the Gestapo. In escaping and being chased back to England, he learns the truth about the German regime and realizes that he cannot avoid fighting Nazi Germany. He joins the British army, and as the film ends, he is being parachuted back into Germany to hunt his quarry for real. "Once again," points out Roger Manvell, "a thriller becomes a vehicle for significant propaganda."[23]

In directing *Foreign Correspondent*, Hitchcock was certainly promoting the British cause, but no British writer in Hollywood did more for his country than James Hilton. A novelist well known in the United States for *Lost Horizon* (1933) and *Goodbye, Mr Chips* (1934), Hilton had moved to Hollywood to work in the film industry in the late 1930s, and when war broke out he became one of the most active champions of the British war effort in California. In November 1940 the *San Francisco Chronicle* observed: "For a man who has never seen Hitler's buzzards, he is astonishingly well informed about the progress of pulverization."[24] Hilton's home became the meeting place for those working for Britain – for example, Victor Saville, John Balderston, R.C. Sherriff – and for visiting British lecturers such as Cecil Roberts and J.L. Hodson.

Early in 1940 Hilton wrote the script for *Lights Out in Europe*, a documentary film directed by Herbert Kline about the darkness being created by the spread of Nazi power. Hilton also wrote a revised version, *Not Peace but a Sword*, for Canadian audiences, and in September 1940 he joined Dorothy Thompson, Robert Sherwood, and Alexander Woollcott on Canadian radio to talk about the British war effort, democracy and totalitarianism, and international relations. In November he wrote "One Lamp Keeps Burning," an article for the *Los Angeles Times* in which he claimed to see a unity growing among everyone who was fighting for democracy.

Hilton was best known in the United States for the highly successful 1939 film version of *Goodbye, Mr Chips*, for which Robert Donat won an Academy Award, and he was not above putting his most famous character to work for the war effort. Speaking on 14 November 1940 about how "Mr Chips Looks at the World," he told an audience at San Francisco's War Memorial Opera House that his sentimental schoolteacher and his class-conscious society represented qualities that could still save Britain: "Chips represents a British attitude which has been good in the past and still holds. He symbolizes the sticking power of tried institutions against hysterical jingoism. The British people today are a composite of Chips. London is Chips ... Londoners are ex-English schoolboys, and while they can hardly ignore the war, they are certainly not losing morale ground to it."[25] Chips went back to work after the Americans had entered the war, appearing in *A Welcome to Britain*, an educational film for American troops commissioned from the Ministry of Information by the U.S. War Office in 1943. As played by Felix Aylmer, the old schoolmaster gave his audience a useful lesson in British geography.

Film historian Colin Shindler has called Hilton "the architect of MGM's Britain"[26] because of his work on *Foreign Correspondent, Mrs Miniver* (1942), and *Random Harvest* (1943). In addition, his membership in the Hollywood Writers' Mobilization, an organization of writers for the screen, radio, and newspapers working for the Allied cause, led to his playing a major role in planning the 1943 Writers' Congress, which was attended by twelve hundred delegates. Hilton himself spoke there about "The Obligation of the Writer – Today and in the Future," and there was a strong representation of British authors working in propaganda. John Masefield and John Strachey, president and chairman of the Society of Authors, sent greetings from Britain, as did Storm Jameson on behalf of PEN. Hilary St G. Saunders cabled a plea for films that more accurately represented Britain and the United States. Not surprisingly, J.B. Priestley urged writers to speak out for the common people and "absolutely refuse to act as a mouthpiece or otherwise cut capers for disguised Fascists, privilege hounds, and stuffed shirts." Equally predictably, Cecil Day Lewis called for greater use of poetry in film – "moving words for motion pictures." Phyllis Bentley, in the United States for the Ministry of Information, spoke about cultural changes in Britain, the work of British authors in the war, and the role of writers in the postwar period.

The screenplay for *Goodbye, Mr Chips* had been written in part by the British playwright R.C. Sherriff, and before the war was over his contribution to American films supporting Britain came to equal Hilton's. Wounded at Ypres during the First World War, Sherriff became well known on both sides of the Atlantic in the 1930s for *Journey's End* (1928), an enormously successful play about life in the trenches in 1918. At the beginning of the Second World War, the

Ministry of Information invited him to write propaganda articles, thinking that *Journey's End* gave him a particular authority, but Sherriff found the work disagreeable.

In the summer of 1940 he was invited to accompany Alexander Korda to Hollywood to make films which The Ministry of Information believed would be good propaganda. "The sort of pictures they had in mind," said Sherriff, "would relate valiant episodes in Britain's not too distant past that would serve to counteract enemy propaganda and do a lot of good in neutral countries, provided they didn't wave the British flag too obviously and had genuine entertainment value."[27]

Sherriff's first Hollywood film, written with Walter Reisch and produced and directed by Korda, was *Lady Hamilton* (*That Hamilton Woman* in the United States), which featured Vivien Leigh and Laurence Olivier. Described by Korda as "propaganda ... with a very thick coating of sugar,"[28] it was a costume drama about the affair between Admiral Nelson and Emma Hamilton, and it offered many opportunities to underline the parallels between Britain's battle against Napoleon and its current struggle against another European tyrant. In one scene Sir William Hamilton explained to Emma the need for Britain to oppose ambitious Continental dictators, and in another Nelson argued against appeasement in a speech to the Admiralty:

Gentlemen, you will never make peace with Napoleon. He doesn't mean peace today. He just wants to gain a little time to re-arm himself at sea and to make new alliances with Italy and Spain – all to one purpose. To destroy our Empire! ... Napoleon can never be master of the world until he has smashed us up – and believe me, gentlemen, he means to be master of the world. You cannot make peace with dictators. You have to destroy them. Wipe them out!

In New York showings of the film, the last lines never failed to draw a round of applause. It is hardly surprising that *Lady Hamilton* led to accusations that Korda was working for British propaganda and espionage. Neither is it surprising that Churchill saw the film half a dozen times, most notably with Roosevelt at their Atlantic Conference, and that Korda was given a knighthood a year later.

Sherriff's next assignment, for which he was never credited, was to provide dialogue for *Mrs Miniver*, the most influential film about Britain's struggle to come out of the Second World War. The idea of making a screen version of Jan Struther's popular heroine seems to have originated with Louis B. Mayer, who discussed it with Sidney Bernstein (then working for the Ministry of Information) for three hours in the summer of 1941. Since the book had taken the Minivers only to December 1939, the script had to be considerably amplified to include the momentous events of 1940. To do the rewrite, Mayer brought in George Froeschel and four British writers: Claudine West, James Hilton, the playwright Arthur Wimperis, and Sherriff.

Despite, or perhaps because of, the strong presence of the British writers, *Mrs Miniver* portrays Britain as it never had existed, Britain as anglophile Americans wanted to see her – the Britain, in fact, that they were accustomed to seeing in Hollywood films. The opening legend, accompanied by a muted playing of "Land of Hope and Glory," clearly sets the scene in a quaint village England remote from coal mines, steel mills, unemployment, or starvation: "This story of an average English middle-class family begins with the summer of 1939; when the sun shone down on a happy, careless people, who worked and played, reared their children and tended their gardens in that happy, easy-going England that was so soon to be fighting desperately for her way of life and for life itself."

The implication is that, except for the exterior threat of Germany, life in prewar Britain was nice. In fact, says Colin Shindler, "the problem with *Mrs Miniver* is that everyone is terribly nice."[29] The Minivers, who are anything but representative of the average British family, live in a large house on the river, have a maid and a cook, own a boat, and are able to buy the latest luxury automobile. Lady Beldon, who represents the aristocracy, is initially presented as a snob who complains, "I don't know what the country's coming to – everyone trying to be better than their betters – mink coats and no manners – no wonder Germany's arming." She is adamantly opposed to the marriage of her granddaughter Carol and the Minivers' son Vin, and she is determined to win the rose competition – as she has always done since it began – at the annual Flower Show. By the end, however, she has melted, welcoming the marriage and reversing the judges' decision at the show so that the working-class stationmaster, Ballard, can win the first prize. Both decisions are given added meaning when Ballard and Carol are killed in an air raid.

The familiar British propaganda strategy of casting the war as a conflict between Christian virtues and Nazi barbarism is employed prominently in *Mrs Miniver*. The announcement of war is made to the villagers while they are assembled in the parish church, with Lady

Beldon and Carol segregated in the Beldon family pew. Later, alluding to Hitler's Germany, Ballard observes that those who do not understand that the Bible contains the most profound ideas can never win the war.

The final scene takes place in the church, now battered and roofless from the raids, when the community is mourning its dead. The vicar explains why the innocent have died: "Because this is not only a war of soldiers in uniform. It is a war of the people – of all the people – and it must be fought not only on the battlefield but in the cities and in the villages, in the factories and on the farms, in the home and in the heart of every man, woman and child who loves freedom ... This is a people's war! It is our war! We are the fighters!" Vin, who had earlier railed against the class system, crosses to the Beldon pew and together with Lady Beldon joins the congregation in singing "Onward Christian Soldiers." As the credits roll, the martial hymn is replaced by the swelling sound of "Land of Hope and Glory."

Addressed nominally to the fictional English congregation, the vicar's speech was also directed to the American audience, which was not yet in the war when the film was being made. Roosevelt liked the speech so much that, once his country was in the war, he had thousands of copies of it dropped over Occupied Europe. The film itself was a great success in the United States, attracting a million and half viewers in the first ten weeks of its run at Radio City Music Hall. It won four of the five most coveted Academy Awards: best picture, best director (William Wyler), best actress (Greer Garson), and best supporting actress (Teresa Wright). Perhaps most importantly, *Mrs Miniver* won the Academy Award for best screenplay.

Mrs Miniver was also popular with British audiences, but not with British reviewers and commentators. John Brophy, broadcasting to North America, complained that it sustained the American conception of Britain as a land of ancestral lawns, stately homes, and Gothic cathedrals. The Minivers, he said, "are dead wood, even if they don't know it yet. They are being left behind by the steady onrush of millions of very different British people who haven't time to look picturesque because they are getting on with their jobs."[30] Eric Knight complained to Paul Rotha that *Mrs Miniver* "stinks. It's tremendous. It's hogwash. It makes people cheer ... Films here are sloppy, bad, unrealistic. *Mrs Miniver*s are still the tempo. They still think of Britain as circa 1912 – or just as bad, circa 1939."[31] The reviewer for the *New Statesman*, William Whitebait, even coined a new term, "Miniveration," to describe the falsification of Britain in films.[32]

Distaste for *Mrs Miniver* extended even to the British Embassy in Washington, and Sidney Bernstein, who had approved Louis B. Mayer's original idea, was summoned to answer for it by Lord Halifax. The embassy, he was informed, believed that the film presented a "shocking and distorted picture of Britain." Unconvinced, Bernstein had a Gallup poll done of the attitudes of people who had seen *Mrs Miniver*, *Eagle Squadron*, and *This Above All*, and he learned that those who had seen these British films were 17 per cent more favourable to Britain than those who had not.[33]

Eighteen months after Bernstein's summons, British government officials had come to recognize that, false though its picture of Britain might be, *Mrs Miniver* was good propaganda. In a paper on publicity and policy in the United States dated December 1943, the director of the American Division of the Ministry of Information, R.J. Cruikshank, wrote: "No film in recent years has had a greater success than 'Mrs Miniver.' It made a great many people in America feel kindly towards the British, although it had the defect of perpetuating the legend that this is a semi-feudal society, wrapped round in the lace and lavender of charm."[34] Roosevelt is said to have commented to Wyler that the sympathy engendered by the film made it easier for him to aid the British.

No other American film did as much for the British cause in the Second World War as *Mrs Miniver*, but there were others to which the British authors in Hollywood contributed. In 1942 Sherriff wrote the screenplay for Knight's *This Above All*, which was directed by Darryl Zanuck and starred Tyrone Power and Joan Fontaine. Power's clean-cut film persona itself guaranteed that the novel's bitter protagonist would be more positive and heroic on the screen, and unlike the original, his Clive does not die. Heavily bandaged at the end, he calls for a united defiance of the enemy. There is also no premarital pregnancy, and the novel's strong condemnation of the Church of England is muted. Moreover, Prue is given a hymn of praise of Britain – claimed to be the longest speech ever delivered by a woman in a film – in which she declares, "We won't be beaten. We won't. We just won't."

Knight's reaction to the film version of his story is reflected in his comment to Paul Rotha about *Mrs Miniver*: "My wife says it's a picture she's glad she saw, because now she thinks even *This Above All* wasn't really so putrid."[35] Knight's judgment is rather harsh since, for a mainstream film of its time, it still contained a number of iconoclastic rants and some suggestion from Prue of a need for a more egalitarian

Britain. K.R.M. Short rightly notes that despite the "comfortable mis-interpretations" available to jingoists, "the message of the film was in fact the same as that of the book: *Clive was not converted; it was Prue.* Clive was prepared to fight for what Britain currently represented, but only to save it for post-war reformation."[36] In this sense, *This Above All* was similar to the 1944 film version of Alice Duer Miller's *The White Cliffs*, for which Claudine West was one of three screenwriters.

Eagle Squadron (1942), the third of the films surveyed by Gallup, was based on a C.S. Forester story about young American pilots flying in the RAF. Forester, by then working for the British Information Services, had earlier written a screenplay based on his Hornblower novels which had definite propaganda overtones. On 20 May 1940 he wrote to Angus Fletcher saying: "For the last fourteen weeks I have been at work for Warner Brothers in Hollywood making a screenplay of my novel 'Captain Horatio Hornblower.' The novel itself had a slightly satirical and even faintly pacifist flavour, which of course I was prepared to eliminate in the script. I succeeded in doing this."

It seems remarkable that Forester could believe that his tale of British heroism on the high seas would not have propaganda value for Britain, which was then under threat of invasion. Certainly, as John Balfour told Sir Frederick Whyte, both he and T. North Whitehead, his colleague at the Foreign Office, considered the story of great value: "Whitehead and I, who have read the novel, regard it as a patriotic and artistic masterpiece, and there seems to us to be no foundation whatever for the author's own diffident judgement that it was written with a slightly satirical and even faintly pacifist flavour."[37]

Much of the pressure on Forester to produce a script "with a very strong pro-British flavour" came from Warner Brothers, who hoped that the British government would be moved to allow them to take out of the country any revenues they earned in Britain. Whyte, however, guessed that there would be a guaranteed market for a Hornblower film in the United States and that Warners would not stop production merely because their British profits were frozen. He guessed wrong, and the film was not made until 1951. Forester nonetheless went on to write the story for *Eagle Squadron* and *Commandos Strike at Dawn* (1943), and to contribute to *Forever and a Day* (1943).

In 1942 Claudine West and Arthur Wimperis wrote the screenplay – which was nominated for an Academy Award – for MGM's film adaptation of Hilton's novel *Random Harvest*. Ronald Colman played the part of the officer who suffers amnesia during the First World War, and Greer Garson was Paula, the woman who helps him recover his memory. According to Short, "the only contribution made to blunting American prejudices was to stress the egalitarian nature of the hero,"[38] but the American Office of War Information nonetheless criticized a scene in Parliament because it did not include Labour MPs "wearing baggy and unpressed trousers, denim shirts open at the neck and exposing hairy chests and that sort of thing."[39] "Miniveration," it seems, was not the only stereotype to be imposed on films about British life.

In their "Memorandum on British Counter-Propaganda," produced for the Ministry of Information in 1940, Gilbert and Helen Highet stated: "Films are always welcome; they need not be blatantly bellicose, although 'The Lion Has Wings' has had considerably [sic] popularity here. 'South Riding,' with its pure statement of some of the finest British ideals, was very valuable indeed."[40] In 1943 Helen Highet (as Helen MacInnes) had two wartime novels made into Hollywood films. *Assignment in Brittany* featured Jean-Pierre Aumont as a member of the French Resistance whose best weapon is his resemblance to one of the Nazi leaders. The very popular *Above Suspicion* was produced by Victor Saville for MGM, with a screenplay written in part by the English author Keith Winter. The roles of the Oxford don and his English wife were improbably played by Fred MacMurray and Joan Crawford, and that of the German agent by Basil Rathbone. Though essentially a thriller, *Above Suspicion* did retain some of MacInnes's anti-Nazi material, particularly the use of medieval torture instruments as metaphors for Hitler's regime. The fingernail remover is termed "a totalitarian manicure" and the "Iron Maiden" is called "the German Statue of Liberty."

The most British of all American films made during the Second World War – at least in terms of participation – was RKO's *Forever and a Day* (1943), whose title was meant to symbolize Britain and the empire. The brainchild of Hardwicke, who called it "a patriotic piece of wartime sentiment to which a multitude of people gave their talents,"[41] it told the story of a London house and its inhabitants from 1804 to the Blitz. Among its seven producer/directors were Hardwicke, Saville, Herbert Wilcox, and René Clair, and its list of twenty-one co-writers was the longest in cinema history. Among the authors were those experienced in propaganda films – Forester, Hilton, Winter, Bennett, Sherriff, West – as well as Christopher Isherwood and the well-known British playwright Frederick Lonsdale. The cast was the largest collection of prominent British actors ever assembled, including Anna Neagle, Claude Rains, C. Aubrey Smith, Charles Laughton, Herbert Marshall, Merle Oberon, Dame May Whitty, Edmund Gwenn, Nigel Bruce, Robert Coote, Donald Crisp, Reginald Owen, Elsa Lanchester, Gladys Cooper, and Hardwicke himself.

For the English critic James Agate, the producers of *Forever and a Day* had assembled "one of the most brilliant casts of modern times … to bolster up one of the poorest pictures."[42] Artistry has never been essential to propaganda, however, and when the film was shown throughout the Allied countries it raised more than a million dollars for charity. A group of Hollywood's British filmmakers presented a print of *Forever and a Day* to Roosevelt at the White House, and Hardwicke and Smith went to Ottawa to give one to the Canadian governor general.

"Wartime sentiment," as Hardwicke called *Forever and a Day*, best describes Hollywood's portrayal of Britain during the Second World War. For the most part, the film industry in the United States had always been a "dream factory" providing Americans with the mythical Britain they wanted to see. During the war the British film colony, and particularly writers such as Hilton, Sherriff, Forester, and West, happily contributed to the "Miniveration" of their country as part of the war effort. What did it matter if America was mobilized to help a Britain that had never existed so long as it helped preserve the one that did exist?

Conclusion

In his conclusion to *Desperate Deception: British Covert Operations in the United States 1939–44*, Thomas Mahl writes that "Britain's World War II influence-shaping campaign in the United States was one of the most important and successful covert operations of history."[1] Through "black" propaganda (what one British agent termed "subversive propaganda" in 1941) and the creation of American front organizations, and by rigging public opinion polls, orchestrating campaigns to discredit isolationist politicians, and feeding slanted material to American newspaper columnists, Britain's intelligence agency was able to support an interventionist Roosevelt and draw the United States into the war. Moreover, argues Mahl, "the destruction of the isolationist opposition paved the way for the post–World War II bipartisan foreign policy that diplomatic historians have so marveled at."[2]

As Nicholas Cull has demonstrated in *Selling War*, however, the British campaign to bring the United States into the war required much more than intelligence schemes and covert propaganda. It needed a far-reaching, multifaceted program that would influence both the average American citizen and those in positions of authority. Moreover, this campaign of overt – or "white" – propaganda had to be conducted very delicately so as not to alarm a country that was sensitive to manipulation by foreign agents. "To have done less to cultivate American public opinion might have proved disastrous," says Cull, "because Britain could not afford to squander one iota of American sympathy. Yet had the British done more, had their efforts peaked earlier, or had it sought to bypass the trusted channels of the United States' own press and broadcasting system, Britain might inadvertantly [sic] have provided powerful ammunition for the isolationists."[3]

The program of overt, discreet propaganda provided a credible interpretation of events on BBC overseas newscasts, mounted an effective display at the New York World's Fair, and disseminated information about Britain through the British Library of Information in New York. In addition, it used the resources of the American print media – newspapers, magazines, and books – the BBC's North American Service, and the feature film industry. And, finally, it encouraged moderate and tactful Britons with good reputations in the United States to tour the country lecturing and speaking privately about the British cause.

Although the focus of Cull's study is on the period before Pearl Harbor, the British propaganda campaign did not end with the American declaration of war on Germany; it continued until the end of hostilities as Britain attempted to focus American attention on the European campaign rather than on the fighting in the Pacific. In the final months before the surrender of the Axis powers, the British propagandists were particularly concerned to position their country favourably in the postwar world.

Given the complex political, economic, and military circumstances of the Second World War, it is difficult to assess accurately the British propaganda campaign in the United States. Particularly hard to gauge are the effects of the work of the many British authors who wrote for American publication and for the screen, or who spoke from the lectern or over the radio waves. How does one measure the influence of their appeal to the emotions or to a common linguistic, literary, and cultural tradition? To what degree were the votes in the American ballot box, in Congress or the Senate, or in corporate boardrooms, affected by a sympathy for Britain engendered by a book, film, or radio broadcast? Were they all only reactions to news reports and objective self-interest?

In *The War of Words* Asa Briggs argued that British radio propaganda had helped elicit American understanding and sympathy before Pearl Harbor forced the two nations into an alliance, and that this served to make for better relations for the remainder of the war. Frances Thorpe and Nicholas Pronay, in *British Official Films in the Second World War*, have further suggested that the international respect for Britain in the postwar world was the result of the propaganda campaign:

It is only when we compare the years following victory in 1918 with those following victory in 1945 that there seems to be good reasons to argue that something very important was achieved by the propagandists, overt and covert. In the First World War British military, naval economic power had played the decisive role in the victory. In the Second World War this was not the case. Yet, Britain enjoyed a much greater fund of prestige, respect and even affection everywhere in Europe and even in the United States after 1945 than in 1918. British institutions, and the admirable aspects of the traditions of her system of government and culture, had never before been so well known and so much admired.[4]

Thorpe and Pronay made this observation in 1980, but the nearly twenty-five years since have not proved them wrong. Of course, the Cold War landscape of the four and a half decades following the Second World War was very different from that of the period after 1918, and the international terrorism of the new millennium has radically changed the shape of world politics. Even allowing for these differences, though, the absence of American scholarly and journalistic recriminations of British Second World War propaganda is notable. Nowhere has there been an indictment comparable to James D. Squires's *British Propaganda at Home and in the United States from 1914 to 1917* or H.C. Peterson's *Propaganda for War: The Campaign against American Neutrality, 1914–17*. Neither has there been any of the anglophobia, any of the accusations of British haughtiness and diplomatic cunning, which was widespread in the America of the 1930s.

If, as Gore Vidal has alleged, the British were engaged in "the largest, most intricate and finally most successful" conspiracy directed at the United States in the twentieth century, they carried it out in such a way that few Americans have ever objected to it. No one could point to the kind of lurid excesses – mutilated Belgian babies – that marked the British First World War propaganda campaign. In part, at least, this success is surely attributable to the use of British authors to remind Americans of their common literary and cultural history. And, by implication, their common political goals.

Notes

PREFACE

1 Nicholas, *Britain and the United States*, 32–3.
2 Vidal, "The Eagle Is Grounded," 3.
3 Buitenhuis, *The Great War of Words*, 8.
4 As quoted by Buitenhuis, "British Authors and Propaganda in the Second World War," 91.
5 Ibid., 94.
6 Greene, "Through American Eyes," 94–5.
7 Vidal, "The Eagle Is Grounded," 3.

CHAPTER ONE

1 As quoted by Adler, *The Isolationist Impulse*, 335.
2 Adams, ed., *The Works of John Adams*, 505.
3 Washington to Patrick Henry, 9 October 1795, in Padover, ed., *The Washington Papers*, 392.
4 Fitzpatrick, ed., *The Writings of George Washington*, 234.
5 Richardson, ed., *A Compilation of the Messages and Papers of the Presidents, 1789–1902*, 301.
6 As quoted by Williams, Current, and Freidel, *A History of the United States since 1865*, 364.
7 Richler, *Writers on World War II*, xix.
8 Sherwood, *The White House Papers of Harry Hopkins*, 129.
9 Jonas, *Isolationism in America 1935–1941*, 28. I am indebted to Professor Jonas for the brief survey of historical studies presented here.
10 Bausman, *Facing Europe*, 321.

11 As quoted by Adler, *The Isolationist Impulse*, 258.

12 Villard, "Issues and Men: Neutrality and the House of Morgan," 555.

13 Jonas, *Isolationism in America 1935–1941*, 23.

14 Roberts, *Sunshine and Shadow*, 269.

15 Wheeler-Bennett, *Special Relationships*, 130.

16 Gibbs, *The Pageant of the Years*, 500.

17 As quoted by Jonas, *Isolationism in America 1935–1941*, 125.

18 Villard, *Our Military Chaos*, 45.

19 Brittain, *Testament of a Peace Lover*, 18.

20 Davenport, *Too Strong for Fantasy*, 252.

21 Thomas, "The Pacifist's Dilemma," 68.

22 Jonas, *Isolationism in America 1935–1941*, 41.

23 As quoted by Cole, *Roosevelt and the Isolationists: 1932–1945*, 435.

24 Lavine and Wechsler, *War Propaganda and the United States*, 35

25 Hyde, *The Quiet Canadian*, 90.

26 Viereck, *The Kaiser on Trial*, xv.

27 Cantril, ed., *Public Opinion 1935–1946*, 968.

28 Ibid., 1185.

29 Ibid., 1160, 971.

30 As quoted by Langer and Gleason, *The Challenge to Isolation 1937–1940*, 192

31 Bailey, *A Diplomatic History of the American People*, 796.

32 As quoted by Cole, *America First*, 193.

33 Ibid., 194.

34 See Nicholas, ed., *Washington Despatches 1941–1945*.

35 Adler, *The Isolationist Impulse*, 319.

36 Sherwood, *The White House Papers of Harry Hopkins*, 443.

37 Public Record Office (PRO), FO 371/34129.

38 Nicholas, ed., *Washington Despatches 1941–1945*, 456.

39 Ibid., 154.

40 Ibid., 160.

41 Ibid., 180.

42 Lockhart, *Diaries*, 2:242.

43 PRO, INF 1/371, Darvall to Tree, 13 December 1941.

44 Lockhart, *Diaries*, 2:239.

CHAPTER TWO

1 Clark, *Less than Kin*, 1.

2 Cantril, ed., *Public Opinion 1935–1946*, 956.

3 Allen, *Conflict and Concord*, 209.
4 Tree, *When the Moon Was High*, 187.
5 Grafton, *An American Diary*, 5.
6 Payne, *England: Her Treatment of America*, xiii, xiv.
7 Ibid., 292–3.
8 Priestley, "Let Us Say What We Mean," 6.
9 Cohen, "Blaming the British," 406.
10 Grafton, *An American Diary*, 85.
11 Clark, *Less than Kin*, 71.
12 MacNeice, *The Strings Are False*, 25.
13 Angell, "What the British Empire Means to America," 101–02.
14 Clark, *Less than Kin*, 73.
15 As quoted by Jonas, *Isolationism in America 1935–1941*, 227.
16 Ibid., 228–9.
17 Ibid., 230.
18 Ibid., 231.
19 Dreiser, *America Is Worth Saving*, 41, 42, 43.
20 Cole, *America First*, 35.
21 "Lindbergh Sees a 'Plot' for War," *New York Times*, 12 September 1941. 2.
22 Nicolson, *Diaries and Letters*, 2:207.
23 As quoted by Churchill, *The Hinge of Fate*, 218.
24 *New York Times*, 28 September 1942, 9.
25 Davenport, "An Open Letter from the Editors of *Life* to the People of England," 34.
26 PRO, FO 371/30672, 8 October 1942.
27 Bartlett, *Life*, 26 October 1942, 24.
28 PRO, FO 371/30671, W. Ridsdale minute, 13 October 1942.
29 As quoted by Gilbert, *Churchill*, 734.
30 "Willkie Demands Frank Discussion of War Aims," *New York Times*, 17 November 1942, 1.
31 Clark, *Less than Kin*, 77.
32 Nicolson, *Diaries and Letters*, 2:310.
33 Nicholas, *Washington Despatches: 1941–1945*, 418.
34 Ibid., 533.
35 Empson, "Passing through the U.S.A.," 429.
36 Cole, *America First*, 35.
37 Davenport, "An Open Letter from the Editors of *Life* to the People of England," 34.
38 Cooper, *Old Men Forget*, 268.
39 Cantril, ed., *Public Opinion 1935–1946*, 1075.

40 Cooper, *Old Men Forget*, 271.

41 Davis, "Is England Worth Fighting For?" 35.

42 Ibid., 36.

43 Gibbs, *America Speaks*.

44 Empson, "Passing through the U.S.A.," 428.

45 PRO, FO 371/26170, November 1940.

46 Nicolson, *Diaries and Letters*, 2:222.

47 Ibid., 2:226.

48 *New York Times*, 8 December 1941, 6.

49 As quoted by Elliott and Hall, *The British Commonwealth at War*, 5.

50 As quoted by Sherwood, *The White House Papers of Harry Hopkins*, 442.

51 Nicholas, *Washington Despatches 1941–1945*, 199.

52 Ibid.

53 Visson, "Suspicions Old and New," 66.

54 Nicolson, *Diaries and Letters*, 2:310.

55 Adler, *The Isolationist Impulse*, 292.

56 Empson, "Passing through the U.S.A.," 430.

57 Maugham, "Why D'You Dislike Us?" 31.

58 PRO, FO 371/38518.

59 Maugham, The *Letters of William Somerset Maugham to Lady Juliet Duff*, 36.

60 PRO, FO 371/26215, Elizabeth P. Tibbals to Winston Churchill, 4 March 1941.

61 PRO, FO 371/26215, British and Allied Lecturers (1941).

62 Maugham to Lady Juliet Duff, in Maugham, *The Letters of William Somerset Maugham to Lady Juliet Duff*, 38.

63 Maugham, "Why D"You Dislike Us?" 60.

64 Harry Ransom Humanities Research Center mss, Maugham to G.B. Stern, 25 April [1942].

65 Russell, "Can Americans and Britons Be Friends?" 14.

66 Ibid., 37.

67 Ibid., 58.

68 Ibid., 57.

69 PRO, FO 371/38505, AN 430/6/45.

70 PRO, FO 371/38504, A33/6/45.

71 Lockhart, *Diaries*, 2:291.

72 Hodson, *The Sea and the Land*, 260.

CHAPTER THREE

1 Lavine and Wechsler, *War Propaganda and the United States*, 89.

2 Buitenhuis, *The Great War of Words*, 54.

3 Marett, *Through the Back Door*, 89.
4 As quoted by Buitenhuis, *The Great War of Words*, 67.
5 As quoted by Jonas, *Isolationism in America 1935–1941*, 136–7.
6 Hillenbrand, "If War Comes Will Moscow Be Our Ally?" 294.
7 Peterson, *Propaganda for War*, 330.
8 As quoted by von Kries, *Strategy and Tactics of the British War Propaganda*, 88.
9 Ibid., 91.
10 Cole, *Roosevelt and the Isolationists*, 501–2.
11 Nock, "A New Dose of British Propaganda," 482–3.
12 Roberts, *Sunshine and Shadow*, 257.
13 Empson, "Passing through the U.S.A.," 426.
14 As quoted by Lavine and Wechsler, *War Propaganda and the United States*, 92.
15 Cooke, "British Propaganda in the United States," 605.
16 Monroe, "British Propaganda," 51.
17 As quoted by Cull, *Selling War*, 35.
18 As quoted by McLaine, *Ministry of Morale*, 12.
19 PRO, FO 395/648, P3227/105/150, "Report on the British Service of Information in the U.S. in Time of War," 20 July 1939.
20 Macgowan, "Fights for the U.S. on News Front," 12.
21 PRO, INF 1/848, "Publicity in the United States," Policy Committee Paper no. 2, 22 January 1940.
22 PRO, FO 371/22839, "British Publicity in the United States."
23 PRO, FO 371/24228, "British Publicity in the United States," 8 April 1940.
24 Ibid.
25 British Library, Add. Ms 63351, Society of Authors, Kilham Roberts to Wolfe, 27 January 1939.
26 Ibid., Wolfe to Kilham Roberts, 9 March 1939.
27 Ibid., Kilham Roberts to Wolfe, 13 March 1939.
28 Keyishian, *Michael Arlen*, 118.
29 As quoted by Day-Lewis, in *C. Day-Lewis*, 124.
30 William Ready Division of Archives, McMaster University, Vera Brittain Papers.
31 Lockhart, *Diaries*, 2:41.
32 PRO, INF 1/229, 1939 Committee on Authors, Walpole to Macmillan, 5 September 1939.
33 Wells, "The Honour and Dignity of the Free Mind," 607.
34 Raymond, *Please You Draw Near*, 69.
35 Young, *Francis Brett Young: A Biography*, 242.

36 PRO, INF 1/229, 1939 Committee on Authors, R. Needham, "Proposes Substitution of Authors Advisory Panel for Existing Authors Planning Committee."

37 PRO, INF 1/32, "Staff Organisation: Literature and Art Division," Waterfield to Wolfe, 8 September 1939.

38 Ibid., Wolfe to Waterfield, 11 September 1939.

39 PRO, INF 1/32, Storm Jameson to Macmillan, 29 September 1939.

40 Ibid., Peters to Waterfield, 29 September 1939.

41 Ibid., Peters to Waterfield, 10 October 1939.

42 PRO, INF 1/229, memorandum from H. Walpole.

43 Ibid., Waterfield to Hilton, 11 October 1939.

44 PRO, INF 1/32, "Staff Organisation: Literature and Art Division," Peters to Waterfield, 10 October 1939.

45 PRO, INF 1/229, Wolfe to Waterfield, 14 November 1939.

46 As quoted by Hart-Davis, *Hugh Walpole*, 415.

47 PRO, INF 1/229, Stevenson to Waterfield, 22 November 1939.

48 Ibid., Faber to Waterfield, 13 December 1939.

49 Ibid., Waterfield to Hilton, Carr, Hodson, Bevan, and Stevenson, 27 December 1939.

50 "Authors and the War," *Author*, Summer 1940, 93.

51 As quoted by Brome, *J.B. Priestley*, 257.

52 Jameson, *Journey from the North*, 80.

53 "Brevities," *Author*, Spring 1942, 59.

54 Letter to the *Author*, Autumn 1943, 57.

CHAPTER FOUR

1 Rogerson, *Propaganda in the Next War*, 149.

2 PRO, FO 371/24227, Lothian to Scott, 15 January 1940.

3 "Sir George's Indiscretion," *Time*, 9 September 1940, 12.

4 Ibid.

5 Ibid.

6 PRO, FO 371/24244, BPS report no. 78 – 1940; FO 371/26216, British Lecturers in the United States, August and September 1941.

7 PRO, FO 371/26171.

8 PRO, FO 371/26216, British Lecturers in the United States, Fletcher to American Division, Ministry of Information, 19 August 1941.

9 Ibid., Granville-Barker to Harold Nicolson, 1 May 1941.

10 PRO, FO 371/24228, A2094/26/45, Allied Lecturers in the United States.

11 PRO, FO 371/22839, British Publicity in the United States, 24 November 1939.

12 PRO, FO 371/24247, British Publicity.

13 PRO, FO 371/24227, Lothian to Scott, 15 January 1940.

14 PRO, INF/6, Seventh Weekly Report on the Activities of the Ministry of Information, October 23–30 1939.

15 Cooke, "British Propaganda in the United States," 611.

16 Gibbs, *America Speaks*, 167.

17 Horgan, "Luncheon for Somerset Maugham," 99.

18 Newman, *American Journey*, 82–3.

19 Roberts, *And So to America*, 36.

20 Churchill Archives Centre, Cecil Roberts Papers, Whyte to Roberts, 13 September 1939.

21 PRO, FO 371/22840, British Publicity in the United States, Whyte to Lothian, 28 October 1939.

22 Roberts, *Sunshine and Shadow*, 258.

23 PRO, FO 371/24228, One Speaker's Experience: October 1939 to April 1940.

24 PRO, FO 371/24227, British Publicity, 18 December 1939.

25 Lavine and Wechsler, *War Propaganda and the United States*, 19.

26 PRO, FO 371/26215, Preliminary Report on the Demand for and Supply of British Lecturers in the United States.

27 PRO, FO 371/26215, British and Allied Lecturers, 1941, Gaselee to Charlesworth, 5 February 1941.

28 Stallworthy, *Louis MacNeice*, 270.

29 MacNeice, *The Strings Are False*, 26.

30 Salmon, *A Secret Life*, 287.

31 Ibid., 287.

32 Ibid.

33 Salmon, ed., *Granville-Barker and His Correspondents*, 296.

34 Salmon, *A Secret Life*, 288–9.

35 The Public Record Office catalogue lists "Lecture Tour of the United States, Views on U.S. Attitude Towards Great Britain," A5009/1292/45, but I have been unable to locate this file.

36 Bottome, *The Goal*, 229.

37 Monroe, "British Propaganda: 1940 Version," 15.

38 PRO, FO 371/24240, Lecturers in the U.S., 12 June 1940.

39 Lavine and Wechsler, *War Propaganda and the United States*, 174, 180–1.

40 *San Francisco Chronicle*, 8 November 1940, 15.

41 As quoted by Brittain, *Testament of Experience*, 218.

42 Berry and Bostridge, *Vera Brittain*, 390.

43 PRO, FO 371/24244, Reporting of Lecturers September–November 1940.

44 William Ready Division of Archives, McMaster University, Vera Britain Papers, Brittain to Peters, 10 September 1939.

45 Ibid., Diaries, 12 September 1939.

46 Brittain, *Testament of Experience*, 229.

47 PRO, FO 371/24245, Charles Peake to Mr Scott, 2 January 1940.

48 *New York Sun*, 19 January 1940.

49 As quoted by Frank Reid, *Brooklyn Eagle*, 18 January 1940.

50 *Oneonta Star*, 14 March 1940.

51 As quoted by Helen Corman, *Michigan Daily*, 9 March 1940.

52 Toronto *Evening Telegram*, 14 March 1940.

53 PRO, FO 371/24245, British Publicity, 7 February 1940.

54 *Parliamentary Debates*, House of Commons, 21 February 1940.

55 William Ready Division of Archives, McMaster University, Vera Brittain Papers, unidentified correspondent to Catlin, 4 April 1940.

56 Brittain, *Wartime Chronicle*, 46.

57 PRO, FO 371/24227, Darvall to Rowe-Dutton, 18 May 1940.

58 Ibid., North Whitehead to Darvall, 11 November 1940.

59 Ibid., Bamford to Newsam, 25 November 1940.

60 Angell, *After All*, 334.

61 "Holds Lindbergh Errs," *New York Times*, 9 August 1940, 2.

62 Miller, *Norman Angell and the Futility of War*.

63 PRO, FO 371/22839, British Publicity in the United States, 13 November 1939.

64 PRO, INF 1/102, Reorganisation of the Ministry of Information (American Division), Cooper to Guedalla, 25 November 1940.

65 Alfred Noyes, letter to the *Times*, 16 December 1939, 6.

66 "Catholic Church Held World Hope," *New York Times*, 20 January 1941, 7.

67 "Topics of the Times," *New York Times*, 2 April 1942, 20.

68 "Catholic Church Held World Hope," *New York Times*, 20 January 1941, 7.

69 "Morale Stressed as Victory Factor," *New York Times*, 10 April 1942, 12.

70 "Topics of the Times," *New York Times*, 2 April 1942, 20.

71 Ambler, *Here Lies*, 156.

72 Ibid., 156.

73 Van Gelder, "Jan Struther, Who Created Mrs Miniver," 2.

74 PRO, FO 371/24244, BPS report no. 78 – 1940, Reporting of Lecturers, September–November, 1940.

75 "Women Emphasize Morale in the War," *New York Times*, 2 March 1942, 13.

76 PRO, FO 371/26170, Notes and Observations Made in America 1940.

77 Ibid., T. North Whitehead, 6 January 1941.

78 PRO, FO 371/26215, British and Allied Lecturers, Scott to Frankau, 12 February 1941.

79 Bentley, "O Dreams, O Destinations," 217.

80 Ibid., 218.

81 Latham, My Life in Publishing, 169.

82 Ibid., 221.

83 PRO, FO 371/26216, Frankau to Sir David Scott, 4 June 1941.

84 Bridge, Facts and Fictions, 70.

85 PRO, INF 1/229, 1939 Committee on Authors, 14 November 1939.

86 Van Gelder, "An Interview with Ann Bridge, Novelist," 2.

87 Bridge, Facts and Fictions, 124.

88 Lewis, "Charles Morgan," 27.

89 Van Gelder, "An Interview with Charles Morgan," 24.

90 "Influence of France after War Stressed," New York Times, 10 January 1942, 13.

91 BBC Written Archives Centre, Charles Morgan File, Bazley memorandum, 8 July 1940; R.A. Rendall memorandum, 11 July 1940.

92 Latham, My Life in Publishing, 156–7.

93 Alistair Cooke to R.L. Calder, 16 October 1991, personal communication.

94 PRO, FO 371/30679, Cooperation between Britain and U.S. on Education, R. Butler to Anthony Eden, 24 March 1942.

95 PRO, FO 371/26215, Beith to Eden, 30 April 1941.

96 "Britain Sends Men to Take Ships Back," New York Times, 21 September 1941, 12.

97 Gibbs, America Speaks, 91.

98 Gibbs, The Pageant of the Years, 502.

99 Gibbs, ed., Bridging the Atlantic, 10.

100 Frank W. Richardson, letter to the Times, 13 August 1942, 8.

101 Newman, American Journey, 2.

102 Ibid., 144.

103 Ibid., 33.

104 Hamilton, Up-Hill All the Way, 109.

105 Ibid., 113.

106 Hodson, And Yet I Like America, 290.

CHAPTER FIVE

1 PRO, FO 371/26259, United States July/October 1940.

2   Hoare, *Noel Coward*, 139.

3   Beaton, *The Glass of Fashion*, 153.

4   Hoare, *Noel Coward*, 140.

5   As quoted by Lesley, Payn, and Morley, *Noel Coward and His Friends*, 123.

6   As quoted by Coward, *Future Indefinite*, 51.

7   Ibid., 52.

8   Ibid., 102.

9   Ibid., 113.

10 PRO, FO 371/24228, Bentinck to Balfour, 15 April 1940.

11 Higham and Moseley, *Cary Grant*.

12 PRO, FO 371/24240, Lothian to Secretary of State for War, 8 June 1940.

13 PRO, FO 471/24240, BLI report no. 224, 20 May 1940; Leonard Lyons article, *New York Post*, 1 May 1940.

14 Coward, *Future Indefinite*, 155–6.

15 "Two British Liners Bring 372 Children," *New York Times*, 30 July 1940, 3.

16 PRO, FO 371/24230, Childs to Foreign Office, 25 July 1940.

17 Coward, *Future Indefinite*, 156.

18 "Noel Coward Is 'Goodwill Ambassador,'" *Daily Express*, 9 August 1940, 1.

19 PRO, INF 1/849, Ministry of Information Policy Committee, Reuters Report, New York, 31 July 1940.

20 PRO, FO 371/24230, British Library of Information New York Survey, 2 August 1940.

21 PRO, FO 371/24231, Foreign Office to Lothian, 5 August 1940.

22 PRO, FO 371/25201, Lothian to Foreign Office, 8 August 1940.

23 PRO, FO 371/24240, Perowne minute, 6 August 1940.

24 PRO, FO 371/24231, Balfour minute, 6 August 1940.

25 *Parliamentary Debates*, House of Commons, 6 August 1940.

26 As quoted by Lesley, *The Life of Noel Coward*, 242.

27 "War Is Not a Bottle Party," *Daily Herald*, 8 August 1940, 2.

28 "Noel Coward Replies to MP Critics," *Daly Express*, 9 August 1940, 1.

29 PRO, FO 371/26170, Notes and Observations Made in America, 1940.

30 Hoare, *Noel Coward*, 313.

31 As quoted by Hoare, *Noel Coward*, 313–14.

32 As quoted by Hoare, *Noel Coward*, 314. Tighe's article was also the subject of a British Library of Information special survey telegram, PRO, FO 371/24230.

33 Schoonmaker and Reid, eds., *We Testify*, 137–8.

34 Dreiser, *America Is Worth Saving*, 70.

35 PRO, INF 1/543, Lecturers for Empire Publicity: Noel Coward, Williams to Hood, 14 October 1940.
36 Ibid., Cranbourne to Cooper, 18 March 1941.
37 As quoted by Lesley, *The Life of Noel Coward*, 250–1.
38 As quoted by Lesley, *The Life of Noel Coward*, 244.
39 Coward, *The Noel Coward Diaries*, 23.
40 Coward, *Future Indefinite*, 270.
41 "Let Us Be Friends, Noel Coward Pens," *New York Times*, 10 October 1943, 29.
42 "Noel Coward Firm on Anti-Nazis Song," *New York Times*, 25 October 1943, 3.
43 Ibid.
44 Coward, *Middle East Diary*, 52–3, 106.
45 Iddon, "Noel Coward Gets 'Scroll of Dishonour,'" n.p.
46 PRO, FO 371/38521, Noel Coward's Reception in America, 18 November 1944.
47 Ibid., Halifax to Ministry of Information, 15 November 1944.
48 PRO, FO 371/38521, Noel Coward's Reception in America, 18 November 1944.
49 As quoted by Hoare, *Noel Coward*, 352.
50 Weeks, "The Peripatetic Reviewer," 129.
51 Hoare, *Noel Coward*, 329.
52 Brook, *Writers' Gallery*, 154.
53 MacKenzie and MacKenzie, *The Time Traveller*, 446.
54 Wells, *The War That Will End War*, 91.
55 PRO, INF 4/9, memorandum on the General Principle of Propaganda, 21 March, 1918.
56 PRO, FO 371/22988, article in the *News Chronicle* Insulting Herr Hitler, 5 January 1939.
57 MacKenzie and MacKenzie, *The Time Traveller*, 410.
58 Wells, "Bringing the War Home to Germany," 9.
59 "Mr Britling Sees It Through," *Yorkshire Post*, 29 March 1940, 3.
60 "H.G. Wells Denounces Chamberlain Regime," *New York Times*, 29 March 1940, 4.
61 House of Lords Record Office, Beaverbrook Papers, Wells C321, Wells to Beaverbrook, 4 January 1940.
62 Ibid.
63 PRO, FO 371/24182, Havas Press Release, 28 March 1940.
64 PRO, FO 371/24182, Wells's attack on Halifax and Chamberlain in speech in Leeds, April 1940.

65 Ibid.

66 PRO, FO 371/24286, *Sunday Despatch*, 20 October 1940, n.p.

67 PRO, FO 371/24286, attack by Mr H.G. Wells on King Leopold, 21 October 1940.

68 PRO, FO 371/24243, comment on H.G. Wells, October 4–25th, BPS report no. 12 – 1940, New York 26 October.

69 "H.G. Wells Here Suggesting U.S. Stay Out of War," *New York Herald Tribune*, 4 October 1940, 1.

70 "Wells Says Nazis Would Embroil Us," *New York Times*, 5 October 1940, 2.

71 Ibid.

72 PRO, FO 371/24232, Passport and Permit Office to Butler, 14 October 1940.

73 "H.G. Wells in U.S.," *Daily Express*, 17 October 1940, 17.

74 *Parliamentary Debates*, House of Commons, 16 October 1940.

75 PRO, FO 371/242443.

76 "Wells Urges Soviet Pact," *New York Times*, 5 October 1940, 2.

77 Theodore Abel, letter to the *New York Times*, 16 October 1940, 22.

78 "These Days," *New York Sun*, 18 October 1940

79 PRO, FO 37124244, H.G. Wells: American Utterances. BPS report no. 66 – 1940, New York, 25 November, *Journal American*, 25 October, 1940, n.p.

80 PRO, FO 371/24232, Activities of Mr H.G. Wells, Lothian telegram, 8 October 1940.

81 PRO, FO 371/24232, Foreign Office to Miss Davies, Home Office, 22 October 1940.

82 PRO, FO 371/24232, Fletcher to Press Counsellor, British Embassy, 23 October 1940.

83 "H.G. Wells Confident Russia Won't Join Allies," *New York Herald Tribune*, 14 November 1940, 6.

84 PRO, FO 371/24243, Comment on H.G. Wells, October 4–25th.

85 "By the Way," *Los Angeles Times*, 18 November 1940, 2.

86 Herb Caen, "It's News to Me," *San Francisco Chronicle*, 7 November 1940, 13.

87 Herb Caen, "It's All News to Me," *San Francisco Chronicle*, 11 November 1940, 11.

88 Peter Molyneaux, *Texas Weekly*, 14 November 1940, n.p.

89 Maugham, *The Vagrant Mood*, 228.

90 PRO, FO 371/24244, H.G. Wells: American Utterances. BPS report no. 66 – 1940, New York, 25 November.

91 PRO, FO 371/24216, Possible Re-Establishment of Diplomatic Relations with Mexico and Transmission by H.G. Wells of a Letter, December 1940.

92 PRO, FO 371/26171, 1941 Opinion in U.S.
93 Lockhart, *Diaries*, 2:193.

CHAPTER SIX

1 PRO, FO 371/26215, British and Allied Lecturers (1941), Charlesworth to Gaselee, 3 February 1941.
2 Jeffreys-Jones, *American Espionage*, 100.
3 "Why Mr Maugham Wrote It," *Daily Express*, 3 November 1932, 11.
4 Maugham, "For Services Rendered," 164.
5 Maugham, *Ashenden*, 46.
6 Special Collections, Stanford University mss, Searle to Bertram Alanson, 24 October 1939.
7 PRO, FO 371/24228, Whyte to Scott, 8 April 1940.
8 British Library mss collection, RP2505, Maugham to Kelly, 31 July [1940].
9 Stanford University mss, Maugham to Alanson, 19 August 1940.
10 *New York Times*, 9 October 1940, 27.
11 "Maugham Plans Four Novels, Sure Britain Is Safe," *New York Herald Tribune*, 10 October 1940, 21.
12 Stanford University mss, Maugham to Alanson, 13 October [1940].
13 *New York Times*, 24 October 1940, 8.
14 "Democracy Union Urged at Meeting," *New York Herald Tribune*, 27 November 1940, 16.
15 Horgan, "Luncheon for Somerset Maugham," 100.
16 PRO, FO 371/24244, BPS report no. 78 – 1940, Reporting of Lecturers September–November 1940.
17 Weeks, *Writers and Friends*, 21–2.
18 Maugham, *Strictly Personal*, v.
19 Maugham, "To Know about England and the English," 2192.
20 Harry Ransom Humanities Research Center mss, Maugham to Stern, 25 April [1942].
21 Maugham, *Introduction to Modern English and American Literature*, xv–xvi.
22 Berg Collection mss, New York Public Library, Maugham to Marsh, 1 March [1943].
23 Maugham, "Hands – and Seeds – Across the Sea," 4.
24 Harry Ransom Humanities Research Center mss, 20 July [1941].
25 Maugham, *The Letters of William Somerset Maugham to Lady Juliet Duff*, 29, 30.
26 Ibid., 30.

27   David Daiches to R.L. Calder, 27 September 1976, personal communication.
28   Maugham, *Strictly Personal*, 73, 148.
29   Boyle, "Defeat," 46.
30   Mellen, *Kay Boyle*, 260.
31   Maupassant, "Mademoiselle Fifi," 14, 15.
32   Maugham, "The Unconquered," 463, 466.
33   Ibid., 469.
34   Ibid., 463.
35   Ibid., 476.
36   Ibid., 479.
37   Ibid., 480.
38   Ibid., 486.
39   Fales Library, New York University, mss, Maugham to Margot Hill, 1 March 1941.
40   Stanford University mss, Maugham to Alanson, 17 March 1941.
41   Harry Ransom Humanities Research Center mss. Maugham to Robin Maugham, 23 May 1941.
42   Harry Ransom Humanities Research Center mss, Maugham to Stern, 20 July 1941.
43   Maugham, *The Hour before the Dawn*, 8.
44   Ibid., 9.
45   Ibid., 302.
46   Littell, "Outstanding Novels," viii.
47   "Other New Books," *Newsweek*, 22 June 1942, 71.
48   Roberts, "The Art of Somerset Maugham," 6.
49   Berg Collection mss, Maugham to Marsh, 1 March 1943.
50   Gerald Kelly to R.L. Calder, 1968, personal communication.
51   Weidman, *Praying for Rain*, 225.
52   Harry Ransom Humanities Research Center mss. Maugham to Robin Maugham, 4 June 1942.
53   Harry Ransom Humanities Research Center mss, Maugham to Stern, 25 April [1942].
54   Harry Ransom Humanities Research Center mss, Maugham to Marsh, 1 April 1942.
55   PRO, FO 371/44582, Donnelly minute, 14 September 1945.

CHAPTER SEVEN

1   Churchill Archives Centre, Cambridge, Cecil Roberts Papers 4/3, "A Sad Story of Official Duplicity."

2 Brook, *Writers' Gallery*, 126.

3 Roberts, *Sunshine and Shadow*, 233.

4 Roberts Papers 4/3, Peters to Roberts, 4 September 1940.

5 Roberts, *Sunshine and Shadow*, 244, 247.

6 Roberts Papers 4/3, Whyte to Roberts, 5 March 1940.

7 Roberts, *Sunshine and Shadow*, 274.

8 Roberts Papers 4/3, Whyte to Roberts, 16 April 1940.

9 Roberts Papers 4/3, Cooper to Roberts, 29 August 1940.

10 Roberts, *Sunshine and Shadow*, 291.

11 Roberts Papers, Williams to Roberts, 19 December 1940.

12 As quoted in Kunitz and Haycraft, eds., *Twentieth Century Authors*, 1180.

13 Ibid.

14 As quoted by Brook, *Writers' Gallery*, 126.

15 Roberts, *Sunshine and Shadow*, 360.

16 Roberts Papers 5/4, "A Novelist at Home."

17 As quoted by Lee Rogers, "Visiting Englishman Warns of Dangers Ahead for America," January 1940 (newspaper not identified).

18 Roberts Papers 5/4, lecture advertisement [1943].

19 Roberts, *Sunshine and Shadow*, 355.

20 "A Novelist Looks at His World," *Nantucket Inquirer*, 5 September 1942, n.p.

21 Roberts, *Sunshine and Shadow*, 356.

22 "Roberts Backs Britain's Stand on Imperialism," *Bergen Evening Record*, 3 December 1942, n.p.

23 Roberts, *Sunshine and Shadow*, 414.

24 Roberts, "A Man Arose," 15, 84.

25 Roberts, *Sunshine and Shadow*, 348.

26 Roberts Papers 4/2, Chetwynd to Roberts, 11 May 1942.

27 As quoted by Roberts, *Sunshine and Shadow*, 314.

28 PRO, FO 371/26215, Postal and Telegraph Censorship, submission no PO/14604/41, 27 March 1941.

29 Ibid., Whitehead minute.

30 PRO, FO 371/26215, Fletcher to F.E. Evans, 13 May 1941; North Whitehead and Evans minutes, 6 June 1941.

31 Ibid.

32 Brittain, *Testament of Experience*, 246.

33 Roberts Papers 2/4, Roberts to Bentley, 18 December 1962.

34 PRO, FO 371/26170, P. Frankau, Notes and Observations Made in America, 1940.

35 Roberts Papers 4/3, Roberts to Haggard, 15 February 1944.

36 Brook, *Writers' Gallery*, 120.

37 Roberts Papers 4/3, Williams to Roberts, 25 July 1941.

38 Roberts, *Sunshine and Shadow*, 318.

39 Ibid., 319.

40 Roberts Papers 5/4, "Torchbearers of Civilization."

41 Roberts, *Sunshine and Shadow*, 346.

42 Roberts Papers 3/3, Roberts to Haggard, 15 February 1943.

43 Roberts, *Sunshine and Shadow*, 400.

44 Roberts Papers 4/3, Bracken letter, 24 July 1946.

45 Roberts Papers 2/4, Roberts to Bentley, 18 December 1962.

CHAPTER EIGHT

1 PRO, INF 1/29, American Division.

2 PRO, FO 371/22840, British Publicity in the United States, Whyte to Undersecretary of State, 4 November 1939.

3 PRO, INF 1/848, Book Activities of the General Division, 18 April 1940.

4 PRO, FO 371/24227, North Whitehead note, 13 February 1940.

5 PRO, INF 1/6, Sixth Weekly Report on the Activities of the Ministry of Information from October 16 to October 23 1939.

6 As quoted by Dahl, "Lucky Break: How I Became a Writer," 195.

7 Bartlett, "The Old Britain Is Gone Forever," 9.

8 Bates, "My Grandfather's Farm," n.p.

9 Glendinning, *Rebecca West*, 171.

10 West, "The Hoover Frame of Mind," 50.

11 Dorothy Thompson, letter to *Atlantic Monthly*, August 1943, 30.

12 W.R. Castle, letter, to *Atlantic Monthly*, August 1943, 28.

13 Ibid., 30.

14 Hodson, "No Hard Feelings," 81.

15 Ibid., 82.

16 Ibid., 86.

17 PRO, FO 371/38511, extract from Survey Magazine Digest report no. 53 of 5th July [1944].

18 Wedgwood and Nevins, eds., *Forever Freedom*, 15.

19 Ibid., 216.

20 PRO, INF 1/848, Book Activities of the General Division, 18 April 1940.

21 "Brevities," *Author*, Autumn 1941, 13.

22 PRO, FO 371/26243, XC 326, British Books Committee, Report of Activities, 28 February 1941.

23 "Brevities," *Author*, Spring 1942, 59, 60.

24 Phyllis Bentley, *Author*, Autumn 1943, 57.

25 PRO, INF 1/102, Report of Section 6, June 10th to July 1st, 1 Article Section, 30 June 1943.

26 "Anglo-American Relations," *Author*, Autumn 1942, 19.

27 Day Lewis, "Books of the People, for the People," 17.

28 Priestley, *Britain at War*, 69.

29 Ibid., 15, 18.

30 West, "The Man Who Came to Dinner," 27.

31 Benét, "American Writers Salute Their Colleagues in England," 5.

32 Jameson, "The Duty of the Writer," 13, 14.

33 Priestley, "The Duty of the Writer," 21.

34 Calder-Marshall, "Propaganda and the Temptations of the Writer," 73.

35 Brailsford, *From England to America*, vi, vii.

36 Ibid., 57.

37 Ibid., 95, 109.

38 Winston Churchill's Britain at War Experience, Tooley Street, London Bridge, London, Guedalla to Churchill, 20 April 1938.

39 Guedalla, *Mr Churchill*, 321.

40 Ibid., 318–19.

41 Ibid., 321.

42 Connolly, *Commonweal*, 35.

43 Colbourne, *America and Britain*, 13.

44 Shelden, *Orwell*, 365.

45 Forbes-Robertson, *Current History and Forum*, 2.

46 PRO, FO 371/24242, BLI report no. 391, 30 August 1940.

47 Drummond, *A Woman Faces the War*, 156–7.

48 Ibid., 158.

49 Ibid., 46.

50 *Books*, 30 June 1940, 13.

51 *Saturday Review of Literature*, 9 November 1940, 20.

52 *Books*, 28 September 1941, 6.

53 Wood, "An English Village Sees It Through," 8.

54 "Authors and the War," *Author*, Spring 1940, 59.

55 Kennedy, *Where Stands a Wingèd Sentry*, 159.

56 Ibid., 232.

57 Ibid., 13.

58 Ibid., 220.

59 Weeks, "The Atlantic Bookshelf," n.p.

60 Bottome, *The Goal*, 230.

61 Bottome, "England's Fighting Strength," 527.

62 Bottome, *Mansion House of Liberty*, xiii.

63 Ibid., ix.
64 Ibid., 21.
65 Ibid., 154, 157.
66 Ibid., 264.
67 Cooke, "Experience of War," 261.
68 Woods, *New York Times*, 23 March 1941, 3.
69 Crawford. *H.M. Tomlinson*, 151.
70 Tomlinson, *The Wind Is Rising*, 44.
71 Ibid., 29.
72 Ibid., 45.
73 Ibid., 128.
74 Ibid., 202–3.
75 Ibid., 220.
76 Ibid., 200.
77 du Maurier, publisher's note in *Come Wind, Come Weather* (Toronto edition).
78 du Maurier, *Come Wind, Come Weather* (New York edition) vi.,vii.
79 *Library Journal*, 15 January 1941, 79.
80 As quoted by Kunitz and Haycraft, *Twentieth Century Authors*, 1355.
81 Strachey, *Digging for Mrs Miller*, 25.
82 Ibid., 142.
83 PRO, INF 1/6, Seventh Weekly Report on the Activities of he Ministry of Information from October 23 to October 30 1939.
84 Colenbrander, *A Portrait of Fryn*, 211.
85 Jesse and Harwood, *London Front*, 1.
86 Ibid., 1.
87 Ibid., 10, 31.
88 Jesse and Harwood, *While London Burns*, 371.
89 Cooke, "Experience of War," 260.
90 Forbes-Robertson, *Books*, 17.
91 Forbes-Robertson, *War Letters from Britain*, vii.
92 Ibid., 57.
93 Ibid., 71, 185.
94 Bentley, "Stereopticians to a War," 21.
95 *Women of Britain*, 8.
96 Ibid., 6.
97 Carney, *Britain in Pictures*, 30.
98 Macaulay, *Life among the English*, 48.
99 As quoted by Carney, *Britain in Pictures*, 30.
100 Unwin, "Books as Ambassadors," 13.

CHAPTER NINE

1 PRO, INF 1/535, British Propaganda in North and South America.
2 Shelden, *Graham Greene*, 286.
3 Ibid., 288.
4 Sherry, *The Life of Graham Greene*, 37.
5 Knight, "The Rifles of the Regiment," 56.
6 Treglown, *Roald Dahl*, 52.
7 Dahl, "Lucky Break: How I Became a Writer," 195.
8 Treglown, *Roald Dahl*, 65.
9 Dahl, "Katina," in *Over to You*, 114.
10 Treglown, *Roald Dahl*, 65.
11 "Anglo-American Relations," *Author*, Autumn 1942, 19, 21.
12 Peter Fleming, as quoted by Grove, Introduction to *Mrs Miniver*, x.
13 Struther, *Mrs Miniver* 72.
14 Ibid., 63.
15 Ibid., 122.
16 "The Listener's Book Chronicle," *Listener*, 7 December 1939, 1138.
17 "Qualities in English Life That Must Survive," *New York Times Book Review*, 28 July 1940, 5.
18 Clifton Fadiman, *New Yorker*, 27 July 1940, 65.
19 Lewis Gannett, *Boston Transcript*, 25 July 1940, 11.
20 Struther, "Mr Miniver," 4.
21 "Topics of the Times," *New York Times*, 2 September 1942, 22.
22 Marion Mills, letter to the *New York Times*, 20 September 1942, 4.
23 Grove, introduction to *Mrs Miniver*, xi.
24 Struther, "There Is Nothing They Fear Now," 27.
25 Knight, *Portrait of a Flying Yorkshireman*, 168.
26 Knight, *This Above All*, 293.
27 Ibid., 303.
28 Ibid., 296.
29 Ibid., 318.
30 Tom Paine, *New Statesman and Nation*, 13 December 1941, 98.
31 *Times Literary Supplement*, 15 November 1941, 565.
32 Olga Owens, *Boston Transcript*, 12 April 1941, 7.
33 Marianne Hauser, *New York Times*, 13 April 1941, 6.
34 R.B. West, *Saturday Review of Literature*, 5 April 1941, 6.
35 Knight, *This Above All*, 300–1.
36 Ibid., 473.
37 Knight, *Portrait of a Flying Yorkshireman*, 168.

38 Knight, *They Don't Want Swamps and Jungles*, 10.
39 As quoted by Short, "Cinematic Support for the Anglo-American Detente, 1939–43," 134.
40 As quoted by Kunitz, *Twentieth Century Authors*, first supplement, 528.
41 Hilton, *Random Harvest*, 327.
42 Ibid., 321.
43 Ibid., 166–7.
44 Ibid., 325.
45 PRO, INF 1/484 xc199499, memorandum on British Counter-Propaganda.
46 MacInnes, *Above Suspicion*, 23.
47 Ibid., 290.
48 Forbes-Robertson, *Books*, 30 November 1941, 5.
49 R.E.D., "The Atlantic Bookshelf," *Atlantic Monthly*, December 1941, 23.
50 Bottome, *London Pride*, 252.
51 Clifton Fadiman, *New Yorker*, 29 November 1941, 104.
52 Bottome, *Survival*, 26.
53 Ibid., 164.
54 Ibid., 49, 203.
55 Ibid., 334, 337–8.
56 Stevenson, *The English Air*, 101.
57 Ibid., 65.
58 Ibid., 130.
59 Ibid., 235.
60 Ibid., 191.
61 *New Yorker*, 13 July 1940, 66.
62 Olga Owens, *Boston Transcript*, 29 June 1940, 1.
63 Ertz, *Anger in the Sky*, 77, 78.
64 Ibid., 291.
65 Ibid., 24.
66 Ibid., 184.
67 Ibid., 59.
68 Ibid., 81.
69 Ibid., 337.
70 Richard Match, *New York Times*, 12 December 1943, 28.
71 Weeks, "The Peripatetic Reviewer," *Atlantic Monthly*, March 1944, 125.
72 Struther, "Travelling America," 57.
73 Struther, "Wartime Journey," 84.
74 Eliot, "Defense of the Islands," 8.
75 Hilton, "Young and Old," 109.

76 Bronson, *That Immortal Garland*, ix.
77 Davidman, *War Poems of the United Nations*, vii.

CHAPTER TEN

1 BBC Written Archives Centre, R61/6, Rowse memorandum, 20 September 1939.
2 PRO, FO 371/22839, Lothian to Foreign Office, 28 September 1939.
3 Cull, *Selling War*, 11.
4 BBC *Annual 1935*, 131, as quoted by Paulu, *British Broadcasting*, 384.
5 As quoted by Taylor, *The Projection of Britain*, 74.
6 Ibid., 75.
7 PRO, FO 371/22839, Gage note, 24 November 1939.
8 PRO, FO 371/24227, Darvall to Foreign Office, 18 December 1939.
9 PRO, INF 1/173, British Broadcasting Corporation Analysis of Foreign and British Broadcasting for the American Listener, 9 October 1940.
10 BBC Archives, Herbert File, Bullett to Herbert, 1 August 1940.
11 Ibid., Melville to Herbert, 24 January 1941.
12 BBC Archives, R61/3/2, Eckersley to Whyte, 28 May 1940.
13 Rolo, *Radio Goes to War*, 123.
14 Childs and Whitton, ed., *Propaganda by Short Wave*, 115.
15 *Listener*, 22 August 1940, 262.
16 As quoted by Cull, *Selling War*, 85.
17 Holt, "Lola Set Father a Problem," 5.
18 Holt, "In Defence of the Working Man," 4.
19 As quoted by Hodson, *Before Daybreak*, 6.
20 Katz, "Britain Speaks," 114.
21 Weymouth, *Journal of the War Years*, 1:277.
22 Greene, *Reflections*, 87, 89.
23 Briggs, *The War of Words*, 211.
24 Priestley, *Margin Released*, 220.
25 Braine, *J.B. Priestley*, 108–9.
26 Gorham, *Sound and Fury*, 114.
27 PRO, FO 371/24228, Bentinck and Whitehead note, 15 April 1940.
28 Furnas, "The War of Lies and Laughs," 69.
29 *Time*, 9 July 1940, 49.
30 Hodson, *Home Front*, 7.
31 Ibid., 6.
32 Priestley, *Britain Speaks*, 4.
33 Ibid., 90.

34 Ibid., 65.

35 Ibid., 91.

36 Ibid., 64.

37 Ibid., 84.

38 Ibid., 89.

39 Ibid., 120–1.

40 Ibid., 37.

41 Ibid., 124.

42 Ibid., 216.

43 Ibid., 232.

44 Mansell, *Let Truth Be Told*, 194.

45 BBC Archives, Priestley File III, Unidentified correspondent to Priestley, 3 February 1941.

46 Ibid., Sir Stephen Tallents memorandum, 23 February 1941.

47 Ibid., Tallents memorandum, 9 March 1941.

48 BBC Archives, Forster Papers, Rendall to Forster, 1 February 1940.

49 Hodson, *Home Front*, 7

50 BBC Archives, unidentified correspondent to Bottome, 23 February 1941.

51 Day Lewis, *C. Day Lewis*, 131.

52 BBC Archives, Bartlett File I, Barnes to Bartlett, 13 October 1943.

53 Priestley, *All England Listened*, xviii.

54 BBC Archives, A.P. Ryan memorandum, 29 January 1941.

55 Priestley, *Margin Released*, 221.

56 Home Board minutes, 21 March 1941, as quoted by Brome, *J.B. Priestley*, 251.

57 BBC Archives, Priestley File I. Tallents memorandum, 21 December 1940.

58 PRO, FO 371/30672, Eden note, 11 October 1942.

59 Grafton, *An American Diary*, 89.

60 "Letters from Listeners," *London Calling*, 5 October 1940, 2.

61 BBC Archives, Priestley File I, Wace to Priestley, 13 December 1940.

62 Ibid., Tallents to MacGregor, 24 December 1940.

63 Ibid., Ryan memorandum, 21 October 1941.

64 Ibid., Smith to Ogilvie, 17 January 1941.

65 Ibid., E.T.M. memorandum to F.T.D., 15 May 1941.

66 Ibid., Rendall memorandum, 25 August 1941.

67 Briggs, *The War of Words*, 618–19.

68 Priestley, "Democratic England Has Arrived," 3, 4; italics in the original.

69 As quoted by Katz, "Britain Speaks," 117.

70 BBC Archives, Walpole File, C. Conner memorandum, 10 July 1940.

71 Weymouth, *Journal of the War Years*, 1:307.

72 Walpole, "The Haven of the Arts," 12.

73 Walpole, "After the War – What?," 9.

74 Walpole, "We Cannot Expect a Paradise After the War Is Won," 8.

75 BBC Archives, Walpole File, Boswell to Walpole, 3 October 1940.

76 As quoted by Day, *J.B. Priestley: A Bibliography*, 21.

77 BBC Archives, Forster File. Forster to Rendall, 4 February 1940.

78 Macaulay, *Letters to a Sister*, 121.

79 "The Story behind 'Britain to America,'" *London Calling*, 1 November 1942, 21.

80 Lesley, *The Life of Noel Coward*, 255.

81 Weymouth, *Journal of the War Years*, 2:99.

82 Hamilton, "Americans and Ourselves," 7.

83 *London Calling*, 10 July 1941, 18.

84 Strong, "Are Writers Needed in Wartime?" 14.

85 Sir Michael Levey to R.L. Calder, 2 September 1993, personal communication.

86 Brophy, "The World Today," 11.

87 Ibid.

88 British Library, Add. mss 54963, Macdonell to Dickson, 3 August 1940.

89 BBC Archives, Bottome File, Bowerman memorandum, 25 November 1941.

90 PRO, FO 371/26215, British and Allied Lecturers (1941), Frankau to Scott, 29 January 1941.

91 Frankau, "Anything Realer than War," 518.

92 Henriques, "We're Beginning to Get the Thing Clear," 4.

93 Stallworthy, *Louis MacNeice*, 287.

94 MacNeice, *Common Sense*, 111.

95 Stallworthy, *Louis MacNeice*, 292.

96 "The Story behind 'Britain to America,'" *London Calling*, 1 November 1942, 21.

97 Stallworthy, *Louis MacNeice*, 315.

98 Colbourne, *America and Britain*, 25.

99 MacNeice, *Selected Prose of Louis MacNeice*, 102.

100 Stallworthy, *Louis MacNeice*, 295.

101 As quoted by Stallworthy, *Louis MacNeice*, 296–7.

102 *London Calling*, 25 September 1941, 19.

103 Briggs, *The War of Words*, 402.

CHAPTER ELEVEN

1 As quoted by Roffman and Purdy, *The Hollywood Social Problem Film*, 215.
2 Powell, *A Life in the Movies*, 383.
3 Wright, *The Long View*, 201.
4 Coultass, *Images for Battle*, 137.
5 Knight, *Portrait of a Flying Yorkshireman*, 222–3.
6 Aldgate and Richards, *Britain Can Take It*, 130–1.
7 Chapman, *The British at War*, 156.
8 Powell, *Films since 1939*, 28.
9 *New York Times*, 24 December 1942, 18.
10 Cull, *Selling War*, 48.
11 PRO, FO 371/22839, Halifax memorandum, 21 October 1939.
12 Morley, *Gladys Cooper*, 197.
13 Moorehead, *Sidney Bernstein*, 174.
14 As quoted by Hardwicke, *A Victorian in Orbit*, 200.
15 Cull, *Selling War*, 18.
16 Taylor, *Hitch*, 163–4.
17 McCann, *Cary Grant*.
18 Higham, *Merchant of Dreams*, 268.
19 Shindler, *Hollywood Goes to War*, 20.
20 Bosley Crowther, *New York Times*, 21 June 1940, 25.
21 Wright, *The Long View*, 178.
22 Manvell, *Films and the Second World War*, 35.
23 Ibid., 36.
24 "London Gets Its Morale from 'Mr. Chips,'" *San Francisco Chronicle*, 14 November 1940, 11.
25 Ibid.
26 Shindler, *Hollywood Goes to War*, 15.
27 Sherriff, *No Leading Lady*, 321.
28 Barker, *The Oliviers*, 179.
29 Shindler, *Hollywood Goes to War*, 48.
30 Brophy, "The World Today," 11.
31 Knight, *Portrait of a Flying Yorkshireman*, 214, 218.
32 Whitebait, "The Movies," 288.
33 Moorehead, *Sidney Bernstein*, 142.
34 PRO, FO 371/38505, AN 430/6/45, Publicity and Policy in the United States, December 1943.
35 Knight, *Portrait of a Flying Yorkshireman*, 214–15.

36 Short, "Cinematic Support for the Anglo-American Detente, 1939–1945,"
    132; emphasis in the original.
37 PRO, FO 371/24230, Forester letter, 20 May 1940; Balfour to Whyte,
    26 May 1940.
38 Short, "Cinematic Support for the Anglo-American Detente, 1939–1945,"
    127.
39 As quoted by Koppes and Black, *Hollywood Goes to War*, 137.
40 PRO, INF 1/484, XC199499.
41 Hardwicke, *A Victorian in Orbit*, 206.
42 As quoted by Short, "Cinematic Support for the Anglo-American
    Detente, 1939–1945," 137.

CONCLUSION

1 Mahl, *Desperate Deception*, 186.
2 Ibid., 178–9.
3 Cull, *Selling War*, 200.
4 Thorpe and Pronay, *British Official Films in the Second World War*, 13

Bibliography

UNPUBLISHED AND ARCHIVAL SOURCES

Berg Collection of English and American Literature, New York Public Library

British Broadcasting Corporation Written Archives Centre, Caversham Park, Reading

British Library, London, Society of Authors Papers

Churchill Archives Centre, Churchill College, Cambridge. Cecil Roberts Papers

Department of Special Collections, Stanford University. W. Somerset Maugham Papers

Fales Library, New York University

Harry Ransom Humanities Research Center, University of Texas, Austin. W. Somerset Maugham Papers

House of Lords Record Office, London. Lord Beaverbrook Papers

Newspaper Library, British Library, Colindale

Public Record Office, Kew, London

INF 1, General correspondence and records of the Ministry of Information, 1939–45

FO 371, Foreign Office correspondence and records, British publicity in the United States

FO 395, News Department

Society of Authors, London. Archives

William Ready Division of Archives and Research Collections, McMaster University, Hamilton, Ontario. Vera Brittain Papers

PUBLISHED SOURCES

Adams, Charles F., ed. *The Works of John Adams*. Vol. 2. Boston: Little, Brown 1856

Adler, Selig. *The Isolationist Impulse: Its Twentieth-Century Reaction*. New York: Abelard-Schuman 1957

Aldgate, Anthony, and Jeffrey Richards. *Britain Can Take It: The British Cinema in the Second World War*. London: Basil Blackwell 1986

Allen, H.C. *Conflict and Concord: The Anglo-American Relationship since 1783*. New York: St Martin's Press 1959

Allen, Trevor. "Cecil Roberts." *Books and Bookmen*, October 1960

Allingham, Margery. *The Oaken Heart*. New York: Doubleday Doran 1941

Ambler, Eric. *Here Lies: An Autobiography*. London: Weidenfeld and Nicolson 1985

Angell, Norman. *After All*. London: Hamish Hamilton 1951

– "What the British Empire Means to America." *Saturday Evening Post*, 17 June 1944, 19, 101–2

Bailey, Thomas A. *A Diplomatic History of the American People*. New York: F.S. Crofts 1944

Balfour, Michael. *Propaganda in War, 1939–1945*. London: Routledge and Kegan Paul 1979

Barker, Felix. *The Oliviers: A Biography*. London: Hamish Hamilton 1953

Bartlett, Vernon. *And Now, Tomorrow*. London: Chatto and Windus 1960

– "The Old Britain Is Gone Forever." *New York Times Magazine*, 15 October 1944

Bates, H.E. "My Grandfather's Farm." *This Week*, 15 July 1944

Bausman, Frederick. *Facing Europe*. New York: Century 1926

Beaton, Cecil. *The Glass of Fashion*. London: Weidenfeld and Nicolson 1954

Benét, Stephen Vincent. "American Writers Salute Their Colleagues in England." In *Writers in Freedom: A Symposium*, ed. Hermon Ould. New York: Hutchinson 1942

Bentley, Phyllis. *"O Dreams, O Destinations": An Autobiography*. New York: Macmillan 1962

– "Stereopticians to a War." *Saturday Review of Literature*, 8 February 1941

Berry, Paul, and Bostridge. *Vera Brittain: A Life*. London Chatto and Windus 1995

Bonham-Carter, Victor. *Authors by Profession*. Vol. 2. London: Bodley Head 1984

Bottome, Phyllis. "England's Fighting Strength." *New Republic*, 14 October 1940

– *The Goal*. London: Faber and Faber 1962

– *London Pride*. Boston: Little, Brown 1941

– *Mansion House of Liberty*. Boston: Little, Brown 1941

– *Survival*. Boston: Little, Brown 1943

Boyle, Kay. "Defeat." In *Wave Me Goodbye: Stories of the Second World War*, ed. Anne Boston, 41–50. London: Penguin 1989

Brailsford, H.N. *From England to America*. New York: Whittlesey House 1940

Braine, John. *J.B. Priestley*. London: Weidenfeld and Nicolson 1978

Bridge, Ann. *Facts and Fictions: Some Literary Recollections*. New York: McGraw-Hill 1968

Briggs, Asa. *The War of Words*. London: Oxford University Press 1970

Brittain, Vera. *Testament of a Peace Lover*, ed. Winifred and Alan Eden-Green. London: Virago Press 1988

– *Testament of Experience*. London: Virago 1979

– *Wartime Chronicle: Vera Brittain's Diary 1939–1945*, ed. Alan Bishop and Y. Aleksandra Bennett. London: Gollancz 1989

Brome, Vincent. *J.B. Priestley*. London: Hamish Hamilton 1988

Bronson, B.H., ed. *That Immortal Garland*. Berkeley: Gillick 1941

Brook, Donald. *Writers' Gallery*. London: Rockcliff 1944

Brophy, John. "The World Today." *London Calling*, 3 September 1942

Buitenhuis, Peter. "British Authors and Propaganda in the Second World War: The End of an Era." *English Studies in Canada* 20 (March 1994): 91–103

– *The Great War of Words*. Vancouver: University of British Columbia Press 1987

– "J.B. Priestley: The BBC's Star Propagandist in World War II." *English Studies in Canada* 26 (December 2000): 445–72

Calder-Marshall, Arthur. "Propaganda and the Temptations of the Writer." In *Writers in Freedom: A Symposium*, ed. Hermon Ould, 71–3. New York: Hutchinson 1942

Cantril, Hadley, ed. *Public Opinion: 1935–1942*. Princeton: Princeton University Press 1958

Carney, Michael. *Britain in Pictures*. London: Werner Shaw 1995

Chapman, James. *The British at War: Cinema, State and Propaganda, 1939–1945*. London: I.B. Tauris 1998

Childs, Harwood L., and John B. Whitton, eds. *Propaganda by Short Wave*. Princeton: Princeton University Press 1942

Churchill, Winston. *The Hinge of Fate*. Boston: Houghton Mifflin 1950

Clark, Kenneth. *The Other Half*. London: Longman 1977

Clark, William. *Less than Kin: A Study of Anglo-American Relations*. Boston: Houghton Mifflin 1957

Clarke, George Herbert, ed. *The New Treasury of War Poetry*. Freeport, N.Y.: Houghton Mifflin 1943

Cohen, David. "Blaming the British." *Atlantic Monthly*, April 1942

Colbourne, Maurice. *America and Britain: A Mutual Introduction*. London: Dent 1943

Cole, Wayne. *America First*. Madison: University of Wisconsin Press 1953
- *Roosevelt and the Isolationists: 1932–1945*. Lincoln: University of Nebraska Press 1983
Colenbrander, Joanna. *A Portrait of Fryn: A Biography of F. Tennyson Jesse*. London: Andre Deutsch 1984
Connolly, F.X. *Commonweal*, 27 February 1942
Cooke, Alistair. "British Propaganda in the United States." *Fortnightly* 153, ns 147 (June 1940): 605–13
- "Experience of War." *New Republic*, 25 August 1941
Cooper, Duff. *Old Men Forget*. London: Hart-Davis 1954
Coultass, Clive. *Images for Battle: British Film and the Second World War, 1939–1945*. London: Associated University Presses 1989
Coulton, Barbara. *Louis MacNeice in the* BBC. London: Faber and Faber 1980
Coward, Noel. *Future Indefinite*. London: Heinemann 1954
- *Middle East Diary*. London: Heinemann 1944
- *The Noel Coward Diaries*, ed. Graham Payn and Sheridan Morley. London: Macmillan 1982
Crawford, Frederick D. *H.M. Tomlinson*. Boston: Twayne 1981
Cull, Nicholas John. *Selling War: The British Propaganda Campaign against American "Neutrality" in World War II*. Oxford: Oxford University Press 1995
Curran, James, and Vincent Porter. *British Cinema History*. Totowa, N.J.: Barnes and Noble 1983
Dahl, Roald. "Lucky Break: How I Became a Writer." In *The Wonderful World of Henry Sugar*, 605–13. New York: Knopf 1977
- *Over to You*. New York: Reynal and Hitchcock 1945
Daiches, David. *A Third World*. Sussex: Sussex University Press 1971
Dallas, Philip. "Cecil Roberts at Eighty." *Books and Bookmen*, June 1972, 16–18
Darlow, Michael, and Gillian Hodson. *Terence Rattigan: The Man and His Work*. London: Quartet 1979
Davenport, Marcia. *Too Strong for Fantasy*. London: Collins 1968
Davenport, Russell. "An Open Letter from the Editors of Life to the People of England." *Life*, 12 October 1942
Davidman, Joy, ed. *War Poems of the United Nations*. New York: Dial Press 1943
Davis, Elmer. "Is England Worth Fighting For?" *New Republic*, 15 February 1939
Day, A.E. *J.B. Priestley: A Bibliography*. New York: Garland Publishing 1980
Day Lewis, Cecil. "Books of the People, for the People." *London Calling*, 22 April 1943
Day-Lewis, Sean. *C. Day-Lewis: An English Literary Life*. London: Weidenfeld and Nicolson 1980

Divine, Robert A. *The Reluctant Belligerent: American Entry into World War II.* New York: John Wiley and Sons 1965

Dreiser, Theodore. *America Is Worth Saving.* New York: Modern Age Books 1941

Drummond, Ruth. *A Woman Faces the War.* New York: H.C. Kinsey 1940

du Maurier, Daphne. *Come Wind, Come Weather.* New York: Doubleday, Doran 1941; and Toronto: Heinemann 1941

Eliot, T.S. "Defense of the Islands." In *Britain at War.* New York: Museum of Modern Art 1941

Elliott, W.Y., and H.D. Hall, eds. *The British Commonwealth at War.* New York: Knopf 1943

Empson, William. "Passing through the U.S.A." *Horizon*, June 1940: 425–30

Ertz, Susan. *Anger in the Sky.* New York: Harper 1943

Fisher, Clive. *Noel Coward.* New York: St Martin's Press 1992

Fitzpatrick, John C., ed. *The Writings of George Washington*, Vol. 35. Washington: Government Printing Office 1931

Forbes-Robertson, Diana. *Books*, 25 May 1941 and 30 November 1941

– *Current History and Forum*, 26 November 1940

Forbes-Robertson, Diana, and Ralph Straus, eds. *War Letters from Britain.* New York: G.P. Putnam's Sons 1941

Frankau, Pamela. "Anything Realer than War." *Listener*, 10 April 1941

– *Pen to Paper.* London: Heinemann 1961

Furhammer, Leif, and Isaksson, Folke. *Politics and Film.* Trans. Kersti French. New York: Praeger 1971

Furnas, J.C. "The War of Lies and Laughs." *Saturday Evening Post*, 3 February 1940, 16–17, 68–70, 72

Gibbs, Philip. *America Speaks.* New York: Doubleday, Doran 1942

– *The Pageant of the Years.* London: Heinemann 1946

– ed., *Bridging the Atlantic: Anglo-American Friendship as the Way to Peace.* New York: Hutchinson 1943

Gilbert, Martin. *Churchill: A Life.* London: Heinemann 1991

Glendinning, Victoria. *Rebecca West: A Life.* New York: Knopf 1987

Gorham, Maurice. *Sound and Fury.* London: Percival Marshall 1948

Grafton, Samuel. *An American Diary.* Garden City: Doubleday, Doran 1943

Graves, Harold. *War on the Short Wave.* New York: Foreign Policy Association 1941

Greene, Graham. "The Lieutenant Died Last." *Collier's*, 29 June 1940

– "Through American Eyes." In *Reflections*, ed. Judith Adamson. Toronto: Lester & Orpen Dennys 1990

Guedalla, Philip. *Mr Churchill: A Portrait.* New York: Reynal and Hitchcock 1942

Hamilton, Cosmo. "Americans and Ourselves." *London Calling*, 31 October 1940

Hamilton, Mary Agnes. *Up-Hill All the Way*. London: Jonathan Cape 1953

Hardwicke, Cedric. *A Victorian in Orbit*. London: Methuen 1961

Hart-Davis, Rupert. *Hugh Walpole: A Biography*. London: Macmillan 1952

Henriques, Robert. "We're Beginning to Get the Thing Clear." *London Calling*, 16 December 1943

Hickman, Tom. *What Did You Do in the War, Auntie?* London: BBC Books 1995

Higham, Charles. *Merchant of Dreams: Louis B. Mayer, MGM, and the Secret Hollywood*. New York: Donald I. Fine 1993

Higham, Charles, and Roy Moseley. *Cary Grant: The Lonely Heart*. New York: Harcourt Brace Jovanovich 1989

Hillenbrand, M.J. "If War Comes Will Moscow Be Our Ally?" *America* 57 (July 1937): 294–5

Hilton, James. "One Lamp Keeps Burning." *Los Angeles Times*, 17 November 1940

– *Random Harvest*. Boston: Little, Brown 1941

– "Young and Old." *Atlantic Monthly*, September 1944

Hoare, Philip. *Noel Coward: A Biography*. New York: Simon and Schuster 1995

Hodson, James Lansdale. *And Yet I Like America*. London: Gollancz 1945

– *Before Daybreak*. London: Gollancz 1941

– *Home Front*. London: Gollancz 1944

– "No Hard Feelings." *Atlantic Monthly*, July 1944

– *The Sea and the Land*. London: Gollancz 1945

Holt, William. "In Defence of the Working Man." *London Calling*, 7 October 1943

– *I Still Haven't Unpacked*. London: Harrap 1953

– "Lola Sets Father a Problem." *London Calling*, 5 November 1942

Horgan, Paul. "Luncheon for Somerset Maugham." *American Scholar* 62 (Winter 1993): 98–102

Hyde, H. Montgomery. *The Quiet Canadian*. London: Constable 1989

Iddon, Don. "Noel Coward Gets 'Scroll of Dishonour.'" *Daily Mail*, 15 November 1944

Jameson, Storm. *Journey from the North*. London: Collins and Harvill 1970

– "The Duty of the Writer." In *Writers in Freedom: A Symposium*, ed. Hermon Ould, 13, 14. New York: Hutchinson 1942

– ed. *London Calling*. New York: Harper 1942

Jeffreys-Jones, Rhodri. *American Espionage: From Secret Service to CIA*. London: Collier Macmillan 1977

Jesse, F. Tennyson, and H.M. Harwood, *London Front: Letters Written to America*. New York: Doubleday 1941

– *While London Burns: Letters Written to America*. New York: Doubleday 1942

Jonas, Manfred. *Isolationism in America 1935–1941*. New York: Cornell University Press 1966

Katz, Daniel. "Britain Speaks." In *Propaganda by Short Wave*, 109–49. Princeton: Princeton University Press 1942

Kennedy, Margaret. *Where Stands a Wingèd Sentry*. New Haven: Yale University Press 1941

Keyishian, Harry. *Michael Arlen*. Boston: Twayne 1975

Knight, Eric. *Portrait of a Flying Yorkshireman: Letters from Eric Knight in the United States to Paul Rotha in England*, ed. Paul Rotha. London: Chapman and Hall 1952

– "The Rifles of the Regiment." *Collier's*, 15 August 1942

– *They Don't Want Swamps and Jungles*. Ottawa: Director of Public Information [1942]

– *This Above All*. New York: Harper 1941

Koppes, Clayton R., and Gregory D. Black. *Hollywood Goes to War*. London: Collier Macmillan 1987

Kries, Wilhelm Von. *Strategy and Tactics of the British War Propaganda*. Berlin: German Information Service 1941

Kunitz, Stanley, ed. *Twentieth Century Authors*. First supplement. New York: H.W. Wilson 1955

Kunitz, Stanley, and Howard Haycraft, eds. *Twentieth Century Authors*. New York: H.W. Wilson 1942

Langer, William L., and S. Everett Gleason. *The Challenge to Isolation: 1937–1940*. New York: Harper 1952

Latham, Harold. *My Life in Publishing*. New York: E.P. Dutton 1965

Lavine, Harold, and James Wechsler. *War Propaganda and the United States*. New Haven: Yale University Press 1940

Lesley, Cole. *The Life of Noel Coward*. London: Penguin 1978

Lesley, Cole, Graham Payn, and Sheridan Morley. *Noel Coward and His Friends*. New York: William Morrow 1979

Lewis, Eiluned. "Charles Morgan: A Memoir," in *Selected Letters of Charles Morgan*. London: Macmillan 1967

Littell, Robert. "Outstanding Novels." *Yale Review*, ns, 32 (Autumn 1942): vi–xii

Lockhart, Robert Bruce. *Diaries*. Vol. 2: *1939–1965*, ed. Kenneth Young. London: Macmillan, 1980

McCann, Graham. *Cary Grant: A Class Apart*. New York: Columbia University Press 1997

Macaulay, Rose. *Letters to a Sister*, ed. Constance Babington Smith. London: Collins 1964

– *Life among the English*. London: Collins 1942

Macgowan, Gault. "Fights for the U.S. on News Front." *New York Sun*, 9 October 1939

MacInnes, Helen. *Above Suspicion*. Boston: Little, Brown 1941

MacKenzie, Norman, and Jeanne MacKenzie. *The Time Traveller: The Life of H.G. Wells*. London: Weidenfeld and Nicolson 1973

McLaine, Ian. *Ministry of Morale: Home Front Morale and the Ministry of Information in World War II*. London: Allen and Unwin 1979

MacNeice, Louis. *Common Sense*, April 1941

– *Selected Prose of Louis MacNeice*, ed. Alan Heuser. Oxford: Clarendon Press 1990

– *The Strings Are False*. London: Faber and Faber 1965

Mahl, Thomas E. *Desperate Deception: British Covert Operations in the United States, 1939–1944*. Washington: Brassey's 1998

Mansell, Gerald. *Let Truth Be Told*. London: Weidenfeld and Nicolson 1982

Manvell, Roger. *Films and the Second World War*. London: J.M. Dent 1974.

Marett, Robert. *Through the Back Door*. London: Pergamon Press 1968

Maugham, W. Somerset. *Ashenden, or The British Agent*. New York: Doubleday, Doran 1941

– "For Services Rendered," In *The Collected Plays of W. Somerset Maugham*. Vol. 3. London: Heinemann, 1952

– *France at War*. London: Heinemann 1940

– "Hands – and Seeds – across the Sea." *New York Times*, 21 March 1943

– *The Hour before the Dawn*. New York: Doubleday, Doran 1942

– *Introduction to Modern English and American Literature*. Philadelphia: Blakiston 1943

– *The Letters of William Somerset Maugham to Lady Juliet Duff*, ed. Loren Rothschild. Pacific Palisades, Calif.: Rasselas Press 1982

– "The Noblest Act." *This Week*, 4 January 1942

– *Strictly Personal*. New York: Doubleday, Doran 1941

– "To Know about England and the English." *Publisher's Weekly*, 13 June 1942

– "The Unconquered." In *The Complete Short Stories of W. Somerset Maugham*, 2:461–86. New York: Doubleday 1952

– *The Vagrant Mood*. New York: Doubleday 1953

– "Why D'You Dislike Us?" *Saturday Evening Post*, 11 April 1942

Maupassant, Guy de. "Mademoiselle Fifi." In *Short Stories of the Tragedy and Comedy of Life*. Akron: St Dunstan Society 1903

Maynard, Richard A. *Propaganda on Film*. New Jersey: Hayden Book Company 1975

Mellen, Joan. *Kay Boyle: Author of Herself*. New York: Straus and Giroux 1994

Miller, J.D.B. *Norman Angell and the Futility of War.* London: Macmillan 1986

Monroe, Kenneth. "British Propaganda: 1940 Version." *Scribner's Commentator,* 9 November 1940

Moorehead, Caroline. *Sidney Bernstein: A Biography.* London: Jonathan Cape 1984

Morgan, Charles. *Selected Letters,* ed. Eiluned Lewis. London: Macmillan 1967

Morley, Sheridan. *Gladys Cooper: A Biography.* London: Heinemann 1979

Muggeridge, Malcolm. *The Infernal Grove.* New York: William Morrow 1974

Newman, Bernard. *American Journey.* London: Robert Hale 1943

– *Speaking from Memory.* London: Herbert Jenkins 1960

Nicholas, H.G. *Britain and the United States.* London: Chatto and Windus 1963

– *Washington Despatches: 1941–1945.* Chicago: University of Chicago Press 1981

Nicolson, Harold. *Diaries and Letters.* Vol. 2: *The War Years,* ed. Nigel Nicolson. New York: Atheneum 1967

Nock, Albert Jay. "A New Dose of British Propaganda." *American Mercury* 42 (December 1937): 482–6

Padover, Saul K., ed. *The Washington Papers.* New York: Harper 1955

Paulu, Burton. *British Broadcasting: Radio and Television in the United Kingdom.* Minneapolis: University of Minnesota Press 1956

Payne, G.H. *England: Her Treatment of America.* New York: Sears 1931

Peterson, H.C. *Propaganda for War: The Campaign against American Neutrality, 1914–1917.* Norman: Oklahoma University Press 1939

Powell, Dilys. *Films since 1939.* London: Longmans, Green 1947

Powell, Michael. *A Life in Movies.* New York: Knopf 1987

Priestley, J.B. *All England Listened.* New York: Chilmark Press 1967

– *Britain at War.* New York: Harper 1942

– *Britain Speaks.* New York: Harper 1940

– "Democratic England Has Arrived." *London Calling,* 28 May 1942

– "The Duty of the Writer." In *Writers in Freedom: A Symposium,* ed. Hermon Ould, 19–20. New York: Hutchinson 1942

– "Let Us Say What We Mean." *Sunday Express,* 22 September 1940

– *Margin Released.* London: Heinemann 1962

Raymond, Ernest. *Please You Draw Near.* London: Cassell 1969

Reid, Robert W. "When Priestley Talks to America." *Radio Times,* 18 October 1940

Reynolds, David. *The Creation of the Anglo-American Alliance 1937–1941.* Chapel Hill: University of North Carolina Press 1982

Rhodes, Anthony. *Propaganda: The Art of Persuasion. World War II.* London: Chelsea House 1976

Richardson, James D., ed. *A Compilation of the Messages and Papers of the Presidents, 1789–1902*. Vol. 8. Washington: Bureau of National Literature 1904

Richler, Mordecai, ed. *Writers on World War II: An Anthology*. New York: Viking 1991

Roberts, Cecil. "A Man Arose." *Redbook*, June 1941

– *And So to America*. New York: Doubleday 1947

– *Sunshine and Shadow*. London: Hodder and Stoughton 1972

Roberts, R. Ellis. "The Art of Somerset Maugham." *Saturday Review of Literature*, 27 June 1942

Roffman, Peter, and Jim Purdy. *The Hollywood Social Problem Film*. Bloomington: Indiana University Press 1981

Rogerson, Sidney. *Propaganda in the Next War*. London: Geoffrey Bles 1938

Rolo, Charles. *Radio Goes to War*. New York: Putnam's 1942

Russell, Bertrand. "Can Americans and Britons Be Friends?" *Saturday Evening Post*, 3 June 1944, 14–15, 57–9

Salmon, Eric. *A Secret Life*. London: Heinemann 1983

– ed. *Granville Barker and His Correspondents*. Detroit: Wayne State University Press 1986

Sargent, Porter. *Getting Us into War*. Boston: Porter Sargent 1941

Schoonmaker, Nancy, and Doris Fielding Reid. *We Testify*. New York: Smith and Durrell 1941

Severn, Derek. "A Minor Master." *London Magazine* (18 February 1979): 47–58

Shelden, Michael. *Graham Greene: The Man Within*. London: Heinemann 1994

– *Orwell: The Authorised Biography*. London: Heinemann 1991

Sherriff, R.C. *No Leading Lady*. London: Gollancz 1968

Sherry, Norman. *The Life of Graham Greene*. Vol. 2: *1939–1955*. New York: Viking 1994

Sherwood, Robert. *The White House Papers of Harry Hopkins*. London: Eyre and Spottiswoode 1948

Shindler, Colin. *Hollywood Goes to War: Films and American Society, 1939–1952*. London: Routledge and Kegan Paul 1979

Short, K.R.M. "Cinematic Support for the Anglo-American Detente, 1939–1945." In *Britain and the Cinema in the Second World War*, ed. Philip M. Taylor, 121–4. New York: St Martin's Press 1968

– *Film and Radio Propaganda in World War II*. London: Croom Helm 1983

– "'The White Cliffs of Dover': Promoting the Anglo-American Alliance in World War II." *Historical Journal of Film, Radio and Television*, 2 March 1982, 3–25

Squires, James D. *British Propaganda at Home and in the United States from 1914 to 1917*. Cambridge: Harvard University Press 1935

Stallworthy, Jon. *Louis MacNeice*. New York: Norton 1995

Sternlicht, Sanford. *C.S. Forester*. Boston: Twayne 1981

Stevenson, Dorothy E. *The English Air*. New York: Farrar and Rinehart 1940

Strachey, John. *Digging for Mrs Miller: Some Experiences of an Air-Raid Warden*. New York: Random House 1941

Strong, L.A.G. "Are Writers Needed in Wartime?" *London Calling*, 12 December 1940

Struther, Jan. Introduction to *Women of Britain: Letters from England*. New York: Harcourt, Brace 1941

– "Mr Miniver." *New York Times*, 30 August 1942

– *Mrs Miniver*. New York: Harcourt, Brace 1940

– "'There Is Nothing They Fear Now.'" *New York Times Magazine*, 29 August 1943

– "Travelling America." *Atlantic Monthly*, October 1942

– "Wartime Journey." *Atlantic Monthly*, February 1944

Taylor, John Russell. *Hitch: The Life and Work of Alfred Hitchcock*. London: Faber and Faber 1978

Taylor, Philip M. *The Projection of Britain: British Overseas Publicity and Propaganda 1919–1939*. London: Cambridge University Press 1981

Thomas, Ivor. *Warfare by Words*. New York: Penguin 1942

Thomas, Norman. "The Pacifist's Dilemma." *Nation*, 16 January 1937

Thorpe, Frances, and Nicholas Pronay. *British Official Films in the Second World War*. Oxford: Clio Press 1980

Tomlinson, H.M. *The Wind Is Rising*. Boston: Little, Brown 1941

Tree, Ronald. *When the Moon Was High*. London: Macmillan 1975

Treglown, Jeremy. *Roald Dahl: A Biography*. London: Faber and Faber 1994

Unwin, Stanley. "Books as Ambassadors." *London Calling*, 4 July 1940

Van Gelder, Robert. "An Interview with Ann Bridge, Novelist." *New York Times*, 27 July 1941

– "An Interview with Mr Cecil Roberts." *New York Times*, 30 March 1941

– "An Interview with Mr Charles Morgan." *New York Times*, 5 October 1941

– "Author of 'Captain Horatio Hornblower.'" *New York Times* 23 February 1941

– "H.G. Wells Discusses Himself and His Work." *New York Times*, 27 October 1940

– "Jan Struther, Who Created Mrs Miniver." *New York Times*, 25 August 1940

– "Miss MacInnes on the Pleasures of Writing." *New York Times*, 26 July 1942

Vidal, Gore. "The Eagle Is Grounded." *Times Literary Supplement*, 30 October 1998

Viereck, George Sylvester. *The Kaiser on Trial*. New York: Greystone 1937

Villard, Oswald Garrison. "Issues and Men: Neutrality and the House of Morgan." *Nation*, 13 November 1935
– *Our Military Chaos*. New York: Knopf 1939
Visson, Andre. "Suspicions Old and New." *Atlantic Monthly*, June 1943
Walpole, Hugh. "After the War – What?" *London Calling*, 8 August 1940
– "The Haven of the Arts." *London Calling*, 25 July 1940
– "We Cannot Expect a Paradise after the War Is Won." *London Calling*, 24 April 1941
Wedgwood, Josiah, and Allan Nevins, eds. *Forever Freedom*. New York: Penguin 1940
Weeks, Edward. "The Atlantic Bookshelf." *Atlantic Monthly*, October 1941
– "The Peripatetic Reviewer." *Atlantic Monthly*, March 1944
– "The Peripatetic Reviewer." *Atlantic Monthly*, December 1944
– *Writers and Friends*. Boston: Little, Brown 1981
Weidman, Jerome. *Praying for Rain*. New York: Harper and Row 1986
Wells, H.G. "Bringing the War Home to Germany." *Manchester Guardian*, 10 February 1940
– "The Honour and Dignity of the Free Mind." *New Statesman and Nation*, 28 October 1939
– *The War That Will End War*. London: Palmer 1914
West, Mark. *Roald Dahl*. New York: Twayne 1992
West, Rebecca. "The Hoover Frame of Mind." *Atlantic Monthly*, June 1943
– "The Man Who Came to Dinner." In *London Calling*, ed. Storm Jameson. New York: Harper 1942
Weymouth, Anthony. *Journal of the War Years*. 2 Vols. Worcester: Littlebury 1948
Wheeler-Bennett, John. *Special Relationships: America in Peace and War*. London: Macmillan 1975
Whitebait, William. "The Movies." *New Statesman*, 31 October 1942
Williams, Harry T., Richard N. Current, and Frank Freidel. *A History of the United States since 1865*. New York: Knopf 1961
Women of Britain: Letters from England. New York: Harcourt Brace 1941
Wood, Katharine. "An English Village Sees It Through." *New York Times Book Review*, 21 September 1941
Wright, Basil. *The Long View*. London: Secker and Warburg 1974
Writers' Congress. *Proceedings* of the Conference held in October 1943 under the Sponsorship of the Hollywood Writers' Mobilization and the University of California. Berkeley: University of California Press 1944
Writers in Freedom: A Symposium, ed. Herman Ould. London: Kennikat Press 1970
Young, Jessica Brett. *Francis Brett Young: A Biography*. London: Heinemann 1962

Index